MASCAGNI

AN AUTOBIOGRAPHY COMPILED, EDITED
AND
TRANSLATED FROM ORIGINAL SOURCES
BY

David Stivender

PRO/AM MUSIC RESOURCES, INC.
White Plains, New York

KAHN & AVERILL, LTD.
London

FIRST EDITION

PRINTED IN THE UNITED STATES OF AMERICA

ISBN 0-912483-06-7 (U.S.)

ISBN 1-871082-01-3 (U.K.)

For James Levine

Algernon. You think that in narratives, however wild and romantic, the poet should write as if he fully believed in the truth of his own story?

Morgana. I do; and I think so in reference to all narratives, not to poetry only.

— Thomas Love Peacock, *Gryll Grange*

CONTENTS

EDITOR'S INTRODUCTION

Of all composers whose reputations rest on a small amount of their music, none suffers more than Pietro Mascagni from a complex of misunderstandings, myths and plain ignorance of facts. When he died four months before his 82nd birthday in 1945, he was all but forgotten by the world at large, few people realizing he was still alive. Yet for many years he had occupied a prime place in the world of opera, at one time even being considered the "heir of Verdi." Throughout his long life he employed the many facets of his genius — as composer, conductor, teacher, essayist, lecturer and impresario — in fighting to uphold the highest ideals of Italian musical art, so that although the greater part of his music is today all but unperformed, his life makes absorbing reading. There is no better way to read it than in his own words.

The number of composers who have written their autobiographies is small. Verdi, when asked to write his, emphatically declined, saying that the world had had to suffer his musical notes long enough and should be spared his literary ones. It is obvious that he felt that what he had to say to the public was in his music, and anything else was his own affair. Indeed, it may be argued that the great majority of composers has felt the same way with the result that biographers all too often search for psychological information in their subject's music, a risky procedure at best. So it is not surprising to find Ernest Newman writing: "The assistance given to the student of musical psychology by the prose writings of musicians is so great, that one could almost wish that every composer of note had left the world a volume or two of criticism or of autobiography."[1]

Mascagni wrote no formal autobiography. This book, imagined to have been written in the winter of 1942-43, is made up of various articles, interviews and letters, arranged in chronological order.[2] At that time Mascagni was living with his wife in the Plaza Hotel on the Via del Corso in Rome. Salvatore De Carlo, an admirer, did in fact visit him for nine evenings during that winter, bringing a stenographer with him who transcribed everything the old man had to say. These reminiscences were to have covered his whole life, but unfortunately Mascagni left Rome for a short trip to Livorno and the meetings were never resumed.

---

1   In the essay, "Berlioz, Romantic and Classic".
2   For a list of sources, see Bibliography, pp.354-358.

De Carlo published his book, *Mascagni parla*, in 1945, immediately after the composer's death. In that volume Mascagni repeats, sometimes using the same wording, letters and conversations which had appeared years earlier. One can imagine the old man, alone in the Plaza Hotel, reading and re-reading the accounts of his great years, so that he had them memorized almost word for word. Because of the immediacy and greater wealth of detail of the original sources, I have used them whenever possible in compiling the *Autobiography* rather than choosing the shorter and more general ones in the De Carlo book. That volume, however, was very useful in providing the transitions from one episode to another. Because it was the last time that Mascagni was to consider much of his career in retrospect, I felt that it was logical to use the time of De Carlo's meetings as the point of view for the whole *Autobiography*; as a result, no material has been admitted which would not agree with Mascagni's own viewpoint at that time. The editing consists primarily in omissions of words and phrases, an occasional alteration of verb tenses (generally from present to past) and repositioning of paragraphs and sentences. The chapter titles are my own.

The book which has resulted is a picture of Mascagni as he saw himself. A number of dates and the spelling of some names (particularly in those passages drawn from *Mascagni parla*) have been silently corrected, but in no way does the book as a whole do violence to the spirit of the man. As the reader will quickly discover, Mascagni was a fighter, not one to resist any kind of challenge. As a matter of fact, it appears that he had a positive genius for involving himself in difficulties, but his optimism and enthusiasm never let him down. Gibbon, in his own autobiography, notes: "If an enthusiast be often absurd, he is never languid." That the situations in which Mascagni found himself were often absurd, there is no doubt; but neither is there any doubt that he himself found them absurd and, what is more, was willing to laugh at his own absurdity if he felt that it was justified.

Another quality which is evident is his wit. All who knew him testify to this aspect of his character, and anecdotes about him are still told. One of the most typical concerns a young soprano rehearsing the part of Matilde in *Silvano*. The lady had an inclination to sing flat; after endless repetitions she begged him. "Maestro, tell me what to do!" Mascagni calmly replied, "Get married as soon as possible." His wit often had an acerbic quality which did him little good, though he was well aware of it and continued on his way, always remaining what he was. It was no doubt this stubbornness in his personality which gave rise to the endless number of myths about him, myths which are still repeated as truth and which have found their way into nearly every standard reference book. One of the most often repeated is his supposed statement, "It is a pity that I wrote *Cavalleria* first. I was crowned before I was king." Unfortunately, no documentation is ever produced for this remark; as the reader of the *Autobiography* will realize, it is thoroughly atypical. Another myth is that it was Mugnone (the first conductor of *Cavalleria*) who convinced Mascagni to cut a supposed fugal finale on the words "*Hanno ammazzato compare Turiddu!*" and to have the words shouted. This is offered as proof that Mascagni, from the very beginning of his career, possessed no theatrical instinct, explaining the relative failure of his later operas to gain a permanent place in the repertory. Again, a reading of Chapter 6 reveals that not only was there no such finale, but that the idea of the shout was the first thing Mascagni conceived when composing the opera. It has to be admitted that his connections with Mussolini and Fascism were definitely not a myth, though the often repeated remark that *Nerone*, his last opera, was written to glorify the Duce and his regime may be argued. Certainly in his chapter in the *Autobiography* on the opera Mascagni is at pains to say that it was the figure of Nero the artist and his eventual downfall which had interested him ever since he first came across Cossa's play in 1891. If this Nero was intended to be an act of homage to the Fascist dictator, it may hardly be said to be a flattering one. Then, too, the fact that Mascagni, eleven days after the premiere of *Nerone*, could write a letter to Mussolini saying that his opera "was inspired by the grandiose work of the return to light of that Imperial Rome which was the Capital of the World and which by virtue of Your Excellency is on the point of repeating the miracle," is certainly tempered by the fact that he had been contemplating the subject for at least forty years and puts Mascagni's hyperbolic words to Mussolini in their proper perspective.[3]

Though the *Autobiography* is a compilation, it is not without a shape of its own. Certain "themes" appear and reappear: Maresca, *scopone*, watches and cigars are only a few of the most obvious. These "themes" are, of course, the result of Mascagni's wonderful eye for detail. His description of the contest Commission as he walked in the door to play *Cavalleria* is worthy of Trollope at his best and is as unforgettable. The conversations with Verdi, among the most memorable pages of the book, move at what must have been the leisurely tempo of the discus-

---

3   Further details will be found in the entry on Mussolini in the *Personalia* appendix, p.290, below.

sions themselves. The waiter interrupting is a small touch, but not only
is it right, its abruptness serves to set the established conversational
quality into higher relief. The heart of the book is the long chapter on
Parisina. This opera, surely the most unjustly neglected of the whole
canon, is fully worthy of the amount of space and detail which Mascagni lavishes on it. The picture of d'Annunzio is drawn with a perceptive,
if not always flattering, eye. It is also in this chapter and in the one on
Amica that the reader will find the most articulate expression of
Mascagni's artistic ideals.

In addition to the obvious "themes", a number of almost hidden ones
emerge, the most attractive of them being the "cashier theme":
Mascagni's reaction to the six professors' perusal of his music at his conservatory entrance examination turns up later in a delightful manner
in the person of Luigi Tozzi.[4] The basically dramatic approach of the
Autobiography is especially noteworthy in its extensive use of dialogue.
But in other ways he knows how to give point to an anecdote by a slight
elaboration of the original circumstances, for example combining two
men, Marinelli[4] and Palladino,[4] into his one "newspaper-barber."

Since it is drawn from many sources, the *Autobiography* cannot be
without a few drawbacks. Outside of a number of his early works, compositions other than his operas are almost never mentioned, and two
of the operas, *Silvano* and *Zanetto*, are only alluded to. Even more dis-
concerting is the first mention of his wife: we are never told how and
when he met her. He writes of the birth of his sons, but the first we hear
of his daughter is when he receives a telegram from her on his way to
America. Rather than overload the text with footnotes, I have included
a somewhat detailed appendix (*Personalia*) in the hope that reference to
it will clear up any confusion which may arise due to omissions or lack
of clarity in the original sources. These sources have been briefly outlined in the Bibliography by chapter only, since I felt that a sentence by
sentence description of them would add little to the book as it is conceived. The literature in Italian on Mascagni is voluminous, though the
curious reader should be warned that the great bulk of it is of the anec-
dotal and partisan variety. Those few items which form the cornerstone
of a future serious Mascagni scholarship are noted in the Bibliography.
Particularly to be mentioned are the two large volumes edited by Mario
Morini and published by Casa Sonzogno in 1964. Those readers who
are acquainted with these books will be aware how much I owe to them

---

4   See *Personalia*, p.290 below.

in my compilation of the *Personalia*. The Catalogue of Works, which is based on the Morini volumes, is as complete as I have been able to make it (since I feel that it is by his music, rather than his words, that Mascagni will ultimately be remembered). Because the present work is conceived as an introduction to the man's life rather than his music, I have left all discussion of the operas and their style to a separate volume.

When I first became interested in Mascagni, I planned on writing a critical book since nothing existed on him in English. Collecting the man's writings about his own life and art, I quickly found that there was enough material available to form a consecutive narrative in his own words. This has resulted in a volume which has far more immediacy and interest than any biography written by me could possibly have.

ACKNOWLEDGEMENTS

It is impossible for me to express adequately my deep gratitude to three great musicians who have been the spiritual fathers of this book. The first two, alas, are no longer alive. Luigi Ricci, with whom I studied in Rome in the early 1960s, was the man who encouraged my earliest interests in Mascagni. I have never forgotten the many hours under his guidance spent in playing over and discussing the operas. Maestro Ricci, who for many years worked at the Teatro Costanzi (today the Teatro dell'Opera), prepared all of the Mascagni operas which the composer conducted there, minutely recording Mascagni's tempi and interpretations, invaluable information which he generously shared with me.

No less deeply do I feel a debt of gratitude to the late Maestro Fausto Cleva, another great *mascagnano*. We had many discussions about Mascagni and I can still hear him playing on the piano, by memory, Act I of *Isabeau*, an opera he could not have worked on in the theater for many years and yet one which was as alive in his mind as if he were about to conduct it.

Finally I must make mention of James Levine, whose name stands at the front of this book. His interest in all kinds of music naturally embraces that of the early part of the twentieth century in Italy, the so-called *verismo* school. We have had many discussions about Mascagni over the years, particularly *Cavalleria rusticana*, *Parisina* and *Il piccolo Marat*. When he came to record *Cavalleria* I prepared a score for him of all Mascagni's markings from his great performing days of the twenties and thirties, as passed on to me by Maestro Ricci. Levine's uncanny ability to transform the authentic traditions of the past into an utterly convincing document for the present is attested to in his recording of Mascagni's best known opera.

In preparing this volume, I have had the generous help of a number of colleagues and friends. I am particularly indebted to:

Diana and Ruggiero Bondino, Carlo Simi, Daniele Carpi-Sertoni, Gabriel Cacho Millet, Dr. Salvatore Pancari and Bruno Cagnoli (the biographer of Zandonai), friends in Italy who helped locate elusive books and articles; Martha and Desiré Ligeti, who managed to track down several books which I thought I would never be able to locate; Adriano Petronio and Fabrizio Melano, who patiently helped with my questions regarding knotty translation problems; Thomas La Penna and Dr. Adrian Zorgnotti for books, information and advice; Norma Taubert, who typed the first stages of the translation; Mary Ellis Peltz and Robert Tuggle of the Metropolitan Opera Archives; Alberta Masiello of the Metropolitan Opera; Cecil Baker, Herman Marcus, Arthur Clark, Mark Verzatt, David Vando and Richard Bucci, who aided in the research; Maria Nunberg for the translation of the Goetz article; Janet and Don Smith, Elena Doria, Marshall Clements, and Kent Cottam, who read the finished manuscript and made important corrections and suggestions; Bismarck Reine and Mauro Fuggette of MRF Records, Inc., and Robert Jacobson of *Opera News*, in whose publications portions of this book have previously appeared. And finally Alfred Lorn and J.D. McClatchy whose interest in and enthusiasm for the book gave me the all-important impetus to put it in its final publishable shape.

David Stivender
New York, April 1988

PUBLISHER'S FOREWORD

David Stivender does both Mascagni and the world of opera service with this very special "labor of love" — an *autobiography* which he conceived, brought together from an impressive lode of source materials, put together in a fair and sensible way, and translated with consistency and fidelity to an idiom that is both colorful and, in its own characteristic way, extremely literate.

Opera lovers who know only the composer's *Cavalleria* ought to have their sights (and appetites) broadened by this book which frequently does indeed read "like a novel".

Should the editor/translator have omitted some of the self-congratulatory applause in which, at various times in his career, Mascagni liked to indulge himself? But that is part of the man! Indeed he cheerfully admits that "After all, no one has ever praised my modesty. Not even I" (p.113). Besides, the celebrations he enjoyed in his own country, and in other parts of Europe and the Americas, were indeed overwhelming, belonging to an age somewhat foreign to our own.

Should David Stivender have said more — or less — about the association with, attraction to Mussolini? I think he has said just enough in the present context. He neither excuses, nor exaggerates, either, Mascagni's role, and makes it clear that his attitude was of a piece with his having been flattered by the attentions of persons of "celebrity" at other times in his life (including Verdi, whom he revered so).

To conclude on a personal note: surely, just as musicians do, every lay opera-goer has his or her own favorites. The question is, how long should such a list be! I am sure I would be hard put to exclude *Les Troyens*, *Aida*, *Il Barbiere di Siviglia*, *Madama Butterfly*, *Die Meistersinger*, *Katerina Ismailova* etc. from such an inventory; but, perhaps one's "favorite" is the piece one happens to be closest to, at a particular time. The question is easier to answer if you set out certain qualifications. If I were asked, what are your favorite operas, scenes, or opera acts that combine all of the following: incredible richness of melodic invention... extraordinary dramatic effect... a variety of moods and techniques, all within the one scene or act or other unit... a seemingly effortless symphonic propulsion (the piece really *moves*)... *and all of this put together with incredible concision, or sense of wholeness or integrity*... a few select titles would come to my mind. There would be the forest scene of *Boris Goudonov*, Act I of *Rigoletto*, Act I of *Bohème*, *Lohengrin*'s Act III, the banquet scene in *Don Giovanni*, the whole of *Hansel and Gretel* (at least it works for me), the whole of *Pagliacci*, and... the whole of *Cavalleria rusticana*, especially in the great Scotto/Domingo recording conducted by James Levine.

LIST OF ILLUSTRATIONS

MASCAGNI

1. EARLY YEARS IN LIVORNO
(1863-1881)

With that experience which I have of life, I have always imagined that the tribulations of others must be far more diverting than any pleasant adventure. And not for any meanness of soul, let it be well understood, but for this other reason: that happiness, fame and perhaps even good luck always have something antipathetic in them which puts people's noses out of joint.

And there is something else, too: the man that the world knows in me is not the real, the true one. Everyone believes that I'm only a man of spirit and cheerfulness, but this is not the case: rather I'm somewhat melancholy and have always made an enormous effort not to display that which I really am. I think I've succeeded. During my life, I can say to have been very observant of two things: honesty and health. I have always thought of my health; I have never suffered from envy, I have never suffered from a bad heart. I have never had liver trouble. For pity's sake! Envy is the worst sickness that musicians, who often hate one another, can have. I have always been of a good humor, as a result of which I have never needed to go to the waters of Montecatini to cure an attack of bile. There is no danger: I am always well and have always been in good health, at the greatest distance possible from doctors. I have arrived at the age of eighty and still don't know what a headache is; I have not yet known a fever; a thermometer doesn't exist in my house.

Also in my work I have never gotten angry; rages are bad for one. And yet it is said that Mascagni treats everyone badly! It is not true; it is a lie. A saying spread around by the usual pernicious crowd. In the theater, everyone loves me, from the orchestra to the chorus.

For the rest, I can say that in my life I have also had some satisfactions. No one knows the good I've done for many people, above all for my colleagues. I don't care if they haven't been grateful, nor have I ever asked them to be. After all, I am content to have been made like this. It is a consolation to be able to say that I've always lived like a gentleman.

I was born in Livorno on 7 December 1863. I was born, grew up, and was educated as so many children, for many years past, are born, grow up and are educated in workers' families (we can even say *petit bourgeois*) whose father has his mind fixed on giving his children a position.

My father was a baker, he made *filoncini* and *brioches*. But he also had a hard head; even harder than mine: "My father made bread, I make bread, Pietro must make bread."

I wanted to study music but my father was against it and kept me tied to classical studies. I went to the *ginnasio* when I was eleven; I didn't take the second year; from the first I passed to the third; at age twelve I was in third, at thirteen in fourth and at fourteen in fifth. I was educated by the Fathers of St. Barnabas. Those were miraculous schools! Places, years and people which I cannot forget. The Fathers formed character by working on the will, developing a sense of responsibility and dignity. In intellect they belonged without doubt to the classic tradition, with gentlemanly taste and acute penetration. I particularly remember two Fathers: Fr. Danovaro, who put Latin before everything

Livorno — House where Mascagni was born

and Fr. Pannasilico, a first-rate Greek scholar, a man of great distinction, born an aristocrat, but possessing that refinement which comes from faith.

But since childhood I had also gone to the Schola Cantorum. I sang in church, with the voice of a mezzo-soprano, and I had a very good teacher, a certain Emilio Bianchi, a very congenial and aristocratic man. Later I began to study the piano with Maestro Biagini, another musician in the provinces.

But I wanted to become a composer and had already composed, without having studied. At age thirteen I had found a libretto: a libretto that has a long history in my life and one that I have never been able to find again. I came across this libretto in a street vendor's cart, a stall. It was by Felice Romani: a poetic marvel, as were all the libretti by Felice Romani, beginning with *La Sonnambula*, which is a masterpiece. It was entitled *Zilia*, a woman's name, but the subject, however, concerned Christopher Columbus. It was an episode in his life: Christopher Columbus, during his return voyage after having discovered America, encountered a storm; he was cast up on an island of barbaric savages and was captured along with his son.

There is a big scene in which these savages, happy to have caught the two whites, father and son, decide to kill them. Naturally the two prisoners cannot rebel and while they await their sad end, Columbus studies, writes and with great amazement takes notes on these barbarians who do not understand what he is doing. At a certain moment Columbus, resigned, asks to be killed himself, on the condition, however, that his son be saved so he may return to his own country in Europe. But the chief of the savages does not accept this at all. Unfortunately for this poor *caique*, his daughter falls in love with the son of Christopher Columbus (all this, naturally, invented by Felice Romani, but beautiful, very well done); the girl decides to save him, but is unable to do so. Meanwhile her father wishes at all costs that both be killed. Columbus, however, who has a secret, says, "If you decide to kill us, the sun will darken." (As a matter of fact he had found through his studies that a solar eclipse was to happen and he took advantage of this coincidence to frighten the savages.) While the tribe argues, he says, "Careful, do not argue about this any longer because if you decide to kill us the sun will darken." They decide to kill them and gradually see the sun darken. The fright of these primitive men, who cannot understand, is enormous. They all throw themselves on the ground, with

Emilia Reboa, Mascagni's mother (d.1873)

their heads in the dust, promising to save him and his son. Then he dictates a law and wishes to be free. The daughter of the chief weeps, etc. etc.

I don't remember how it ended, but I liked this episode very much. And I, at age thirteen, composed this opera.

I wanted to study music but there was no way. My father, hearing this son sing all day in the house, got annoyed and one day took the libretto and burned it for me. I did not find this libretto entitled *Zilia* again in any part of the world. I did find a book in which "Columbus in music"[5] was written about, and all the libretti written around Columbus and set to music were listed. There were a great many (not that of Franchetti, though; the book came out a year before he gave his opera in 1892 at Genoa) and there I found a mention of *Zilia*. It said that this was a libretto which was liked by many composers of the time, but no one wanted it. The idea of an eclipse on the stage was then an enormous difficulty; today it would be laughable, but for that time it was an insurmountable obstacle and no one wanted to tackle it.

The fact remains that I have never been able to find the libretto. I have found, however, some sketches that I made. I did not know how to compose music in notation; I just made some sketches, since I knew how to sing and always had music in front of me: that which I had to sing. This music written at age thirteen was of use to me later. I did not learn how to compose from anyone. We studied music by singing it: they gave us a part for soprano or mezzo-soprano and we had to decipher it; but this means one learned something. Naturally I didn't know how to put note against note, so-called counterpoint, but I put the theme together, since I sang and knew how to write as I sang. The music of these sketches I later put into *Guglielmo Ratcliff*. In fact, in this,

5   See *Personalia: Romani, Felice.*

my first opera, which is perhaps the most important I've written, there are pieces which belonged to *Zilia*. It's one of the most curious things in my life.

In 1876 I became the student of a certain Maestro Soffredini. My father gave in only to satisfy my whim: "Perhaps there's nothing wrong in a young man learning the piano," he must have thought, but God help us if he had imagined the rest! After three or four lessons I presented Maestro Soffredini with a small sheet of paper: "Look, Maestro, I've composed a *Kyrie.*" He looked at me as if I were talking

Domenico Mascagni, Mascagni's father

foolishness: "Are you crazy? A *Kyrie?*" "Really, and I want to perform it in church." In short, Soffredini didn't find that piece of paper to be too bad because he decided immediately to give me lessons in harmony and later in counterpoint; we changed courses, as a result, and I seemed to touch heaven with my finger. Good God. I was only a child, but I threw myself into studying with such patience and with such steadiness that soon I was able to digest for myself the entire method of Cherubini: and I even copied it out, in order to understand it better.

All those who have amused themselves by writing nonsense about me have never said how I became a musician. My father, as I have said, was against it. It was my Uncle Stefano, poor man, who did it all, and later Count Larderel from Livorno. My uncle died of an apoplectic stroke the first year that he sent me to Milan. It is because of him that I began to study in Livorno, with good teachers.

My uncle was a bachelor. Of the four Mascagni brothers he was the oldest and my father was the youngest, therefore, my uncle had a certain ascendancy over my father. One day in 1876 he came to our house and said to him: "Listen, Domenico; your son, my nephew Pietro, wants to study music. I have spoken with those *maestri* who teach him. They all tell me he has talent, that he would do well. His friends have also come to tell me the same thing. Now, I am alone. I'll take him with me. Naturally you'll see him everyday; we are both in Livorno; you live on one street, I on another, but we can see each other every day. It's useless: I shall let him study music, because if he has these tendencies, this stubbornness, one must not go against them. They have told me that you follow him from room to room to switch him when he plays the piano and you want him to study..." (My father, in fact had bought me an old piano at my teacher's insistence, who in this way had hoped to settle things.)

My uncle then said to me, "You come with me, don't worry, we'll go to my house right away." (He had prepared a bedroom, a sitting-room-study and a good piano for me.) "You stay with me and do your studies. And then I'll give you something else: I'll give you the house key and a subscription to all the theaters, the Lirico, Avvalorati, Goldoni and Politeama: you can go to the theater and come home when you please."

Oh, my uncle, how I bless your memory now more than ever! Who will be able to take from me the joy that I experienced in that lovely little room, clean and comfortable? How many dreams within those walls! How many times, seated there, did I believe to see my future road, straight, spacious, strewn with roses: and at night, asleep in that little white room, I saw again those dreams I had while awake! For me, this was the realization of a dream. While still a child to be free to live such a life! I played piano from morning til night; my piano teacher came to give me lessons, then I went to Soffredini, who ran the public music school, called the "Istituto Musicale Luigi Cherubini".

During those years I composed a Symphony in F; a song, "La tua stella", which was later "seasoned in all kinds of sauces," as Soffredini said; a Leggenda for tenor, and various other kinds of nonsense of which I quickly had a drawerful.

For a religious festival I dared to compose a Mass, a sung Mass according to the rules, which was performed in a large church. The crowd fought to enter and the public guard had to intervene be-

Bakery of Mascagni's father
on Via San Francesco, Livorno

cause at a certain point the people began to clap their hands and applaud as in a theater, to the great indignation of the clergy and the personalities present.

The success went to my head; remember that I was seventeen years
old and already all of Livorno knew me! I then decided to tackle a kind
of cantata. Soffredini wrote the text and I set it to music for soli, chorus
and orchestra. The title was *In filanda* ["In the silk spinnery"]. The success was enormous and I, that evening of 9 February 1881, when the
work was performed under the direction of my teacher, had honors
galore and a pile of gifts: gold watches, chains, rings, even laurel
crowns. "What a racket!" I said to myself. "Is my music really worth
something?" But meanwhile I was content to see that they sold my picture in the street for two *soldi* a copy.

My uncle was very pleased and it was at that time that he did a really grandiose thing for me. He said: "I've an idea. Let's perform this work
at the Teatro Avvalorati in Livorno. It's still a beautiful theater." "But
uncle, that takes money..." "Don't you worry about it, I'll take care of
it."

And so this poor man, who really wasn't interested in anything, who
didn't understand such things, did everything: he engaged the maestri,
he hired the orchestra and singers and this work in two acts was performed, under the direction of Maestro Soffredini, with a hundred and
ten singers. I said to my uncle, "You'll come?" "No, no; I won't come.
You think I should go into a theater?" When I came out of the theater
at midnight, however, at the end of the performance on 30 March, outside on the sidewalk I found my uncle who was waiting for me. "I've
heard from everyone that it went very well. I'm very pleased... I've gladly spent these few thousand lire. It was something I enjoyed doing..."
This is very important in my life: I would not have become a musician
if I hadn't found this encouragement on the part of my uncle.

The work was dedicated to Ponchielli who knew my teacher; it was
Ponchielli who decided to have me compete in the Exposition at Milan
that same year. I entered with an *Ave Maria*, a composition of little
worth; nevertheless I won an honorable mention; the reason for it was
very pleasant. Perhaps it may have been Ponchielli who caused me to
get it... who knows? I had this piece published by the Ditta Venturini
in Florence. At Milan, with Soffredini, I had the joy of meeting Boito
and Ponchielli.

Finally Soffredini decided to speak to my father. But he was not
about to give in. Soffredini, who was determined on insisting, could
not have done worse. But my uncle told me: "Now they say that you

need to go to Milan to study, there is a big conservatory there." "I know," I said. "I even know the professor who gives lessons: he is called Michele Saladino and he is the greatest teacher there is today in Italy for teaching counterpoint and fugue; I want to attend those classes. Therefore, I shall leave for Milan when you send me."

And he, in fact, sent me there. But my object was to study with Ponchielli. Now, by a very strange chance, my father had met Ponchielli at Livorno. Ponchielli had come to Livorno when they gave his opera *I promessi sposi* and at that time both my father and my uncle had spoken to him about me.

I did, in fact, study with Ponchielli who, however, was only able to give me private lessons, since I was not yet entered in the Conservatory of Milan.

Poor Ponchielli, he was fond of me! That first summer he did not want me to return to Livorno for vacation and he took me to his villa, a small one that he had at Maggianico, which his wife's uncle had built for him. (Ponchielli's wife was Teresina Brambilla, the famous singer.) They invited me and I went to their house. I spent the summer at Maggianico on "that branch of lake Como" made famous by Manzoni. And there began my artistic life: I found a gathering of people which filled me with enthusiasm. "In the evening we play *tresette*," said Ponchielli; "You will see what good friends they are." These were his friends: one was Gomez, the composer of *Guarany*, a Brazilian who lived in Italy and had a beautiful daughter called Bianca; there was Ferdinando Fontana, the librettist, who wrote the libretto for Giacomo Puccini's first opera, *Le Villi*; and Antonio Ghislanzoni, the librettist of Verdi's *Aida*. The four card players were two librettists and two composers. I watched. As I was a child, a young man — I am speaking of 1881 — I was bewildered. One evening Ponchielli said to me: "How do we play? Well?" "Go on, you are four donkeys, if you don't mind my saying so. This is my speciality: I am only good at this game. I don't know anything else but *scopone* and *tresette*." (I was a good *scopone* player; it was I who developed *scopone* in Italy, since no one wanted to play it.) I was so enchanted with this kind of life that I couldn't even think of Milan.

I spent the whole summer there and then returned to Livorno. One day in October I was with my brother playing billiards and while we were playing they came to tell me to run home: "Your uncle is dying, he's had a stroke." My father had run quickly, but there was nothing to be done. My poor uncle died. I was heartbroken. My career can hardly have been considered begun; it was broken off before it started. For me this was such a tragic fact that I can no longer think about it. Perhaps it has never been recounted by anyone because I have never wished to tell it.

After *In filanda* I wrote a composition beyond my powers: the *Hymn to Joy* of Schiller, translated by Andrea Maffei. Think that a great musician, the greatest musician in the world, had composed the *Hymn to Joy* of Schiller: Beethoven (the words of the Ninth Symphony are exactly those of Schiller's *Hymn to Joy*, in the original German text, you understand). Then there was another very illustrious composer, and one very dear to me, the Russian Tchaikovsky. When he was thirty-five years old he realized he

Alfredo Soffredini, Mascagni's teacher, director of the Istituto Musicale "Cherubini", Livorno

was born to write music — before that he did not know it — and he also composed the Schiller *Hymn to Joy*. This, however, I learned afterwards. On my part the Hymn cost me more than a scolding from Soffredini; I was not able to finish it, but then in two hours I conceived and orchestrated the fifty pages which Ponchielli, in a letter to Soffredini, called "a masterpiece." It was performed in Livorno 27 March 1882.

Then one day I was sent to call on the Count Florestano de Larderel, a nobleman and proprietor of borax blowpipes in seven towns, the largest of which was called Lardarello. He said: "Listen, Pietrino, I have learned of the misfortune that has befallen you; don't worry: I will do as your uncle did. Go to Milan. I'll send my administrator to you; get together with him about your stipend." (After the death of my uncle came that of my dear brother Carlo, who died in September 1882; and after this came that of my poor little sister, at only 14, dying on 8 January 1883. And that wasn't all: a few days after this misfortune, my oldest brother, Francesco, left for Cesena, a cavalry soldier, leaving my poor father alone with the smallest of my brothers, Paolo.) I remember that the administrator asked me how much my uncle had given me. "A hundred and fifty lire a month." He gave me a hundred and fifty lire a month. My father wanted absolutely no part of it; there was never any possibility of persuading him. After my success, he changed a little through the intervention of friends, but when *Cavalleria* was given he didn't want to come to Rome. I telegraphed, I sent friends to him: "Come, it has gone well; come and hear a performance..." Nothing. He was always stubborn. He never yielded. "Yes," he said, "all right, he was lucky, but if he had become a lawyer it would have been better." I have never understood why I should have become a lawyer. I never knew. The fact is that after the encouragement of the Count Larderel, I returned to Milan.

2   CONSERVATORY YEARS
(1882-1885)

I entered the Conservatory in 1882, that is, the year after I came to Milan. And it was the very greatest fortune, because it was the Count who enabled me to enter the Conservatory. Ponchielli accepted me willingly, also Saladino. But to enter the Conservatory I had to pass the examinations. Well, I studied day and night and managed it, but I remember that day – 12 October 1882 – as if it were today!

When I went to the Conservatory I was as white as a piece of paper and stood alone at one side with my little bundle of music under my arm.

As the height of misfortune I was the last to take the examination and so the agony lasted even longer. And when I saw my companions enter the cells to take the examination, from one viewpoint I was envious of them since they were going to suffer their fate, while from another I would never have gone at that moment.

If you could have seen the number of examinees! There were even three girls to take the composition examination and five or six for the violin.

Among my companions there were some who walked up and down the corridors with their hats pushed back and their arms crossed on their chests as if they were sure of their business, while I was only sure of having been born in Livorno. And I envied them, because in reality I was not very sure of even that, for all my having assiduously studied day and night.

And to think that when they went to take the examination those young men, who earlier had been outspoken and cheerful forgot themselves, stammered and were not capable of doing anything: and I saw some of them cry – young men twenty-two and twenty-three years old.

Instead, I was just the opposite; before the examination I remained in a continuous and tremendous state of agitation which increased out of proportion and was at its height when the porter called, "*Mascagni!*"

From that time on, as if an internal force compelled me to do so, I had no more fear, and with a firm step I entered the room where the Commission, made up of Bazzini, Ponchielli, Dominiceti, Galli, Panzini and one other, was. As soon as I entered I took off my hat and in a strong and secure voice said:

"Good day, gentlemen!"

"Oh, dear Mascagni," Ponchielli said to me. And he introduced me to the Commission, telling them all that I had written: two cantatas, etc.

I expected some word of praise or encouragement from those gentlemen, but instead, when Ponchielli had finished, they looked me over from head to foot and bombarded me with many questions unrelated to the examination; questions which, I believe, would have taken away all courage and hope from anyone else.

Bazzini and Dominiceti were very considerate to me, the former saying that he knew the Cherubini Institute by reputation, and the latter praising highly my *Filanda*, which he knew perfectly.

I underwent all those glances with my usual calm, almost smiling, and answered the questions in a very firm voice, and always coldly.

I well understood that if by accident I lost my self-possession I was in for it. So I explained my music and gave it to the professors, all of whom set about looking at it with scrupulous attention. Bazzini had me sit down, and I, from where I was sitting, attentively watched those six professors, the best in Italy, who held my music in their hands and perused it as might a ministry delegate sent to peruse the receipts of some cashier who would love to... flee.

I was so absorbed in watching those six men that I did not even remember that I was supposed to take an examination. All of a sudden I saw that they were conferring among themselves and then they gave me a piece of paper on which there was a musical phrase and told me to go and write some "imitations." I, without even thinking about it, took the sheet almost mechanically and went out. The porter then shut me up in a cell, alone. As soon as I entered I saw a piano: I, without bothering myself about the examination at all, sat down to play. It had been a long time since I had played and it seemed as if I touched heaven with one finger as I touched the keys of the piano with my ten. But all of a sudden I remembered the examination and took up that little sheet which they had given me and read: *Imitations*.

"I can do it, but I'm not going to get upset over it," I said to myself; "but all the same, courage and to work." And I immediately set about writing on the white half-sheet which the Commission had given me. In less than five minutes I finished it. So a few more slaps at the piano and then I went back into the room of the professors, who were still perusing my poor music.

As soon as I entered, they all fell on my paper and spied out every bar and every note. They told me it was all right and I gave thanks to God and hoped it would soon be over.

Instead they gave me a bass line, over which I had to improvise the chords at the piano.

"If you want to try it over first, please do," Bazzini said to me.

But as soon as I sat down at the piano, the members of the Commission rose and all surrounded me. Then I began to improvise and my head started spinning... All of a sudden, however, my eyes misted, my ears stopped up, I felt a noise in my head and didn't know how to continue.

"Go on," the members of the Commission told me, "the second and fourth above fa." To make it short, I didn't know how to find the note next to fa. I realized that I had lost my self-possession and immediately got up, saying that I absolutely couldn't continue.

The members of the Commission declared themselves satisfied and let me go after having returned my music to me. I learned afterward that they had forgotten to give me an examination in theory, and this displeased me greatly since in that branch I would have done well for myself.

But Ponchielli told me that what I had done was enough and that without doubt I would be accepted. In short I had some very good marks, which no one else managed to have.

So I entered the Conservatory, studying counterpoint with Professor Saladino. There was only one opening at the Conservatory in counterpoint and we were fourteen contestants. I won that competition also. It was a great stroke of luck. I, however, was not very learned technically, but I managed. I had prepared myself very well for that occasion. On the other hand I was not very well fixed for money. One time I wrote my father:

Milan, 5 November 1883

Dear Father,

My health is always excellent and I am even eating with a large appetite. The weather is rather good up here, but cold.

Listen, Father, if you would send me two bolts of cloth, I would have a pair of trousers made, since I have found a tailor who does good work cheaply.

I am also giving him my overcoat to remake. But you can wait another eight or ten days since there is no hurry.

I would like the cloth to be rather heavy and brown in color. Then, you see, I must have in Livorno a winter jacket of dark green, double breasted. If you would send it to me I will worry about having it redone. Think too, about having

that pair of shoes from Cosimi resoled. Low heels and
without an arch! Then you can easily send everything all at
once to me.

I have good news for you. Just now they came to tell me
that they have hired me as a double-bass player at the Dal
Verme, at three lire an evening. I'm wild with joy! I want to
send lots of money to Cecco too!

I am always studying. This year I shall do myself proud.
And you will see that even you will be pleased with me.
When I come to Livorno for Easter, how I would like to
bring you hundreds of lire!

Enough, let us hope so. I leave off writing you because I
have a friend waiting for me. Greet everyone, kiss Paolo and
Zaira, and many embraces for you from

Your very affectionate
Pietro

I was very sick—severe pneumonia—during my years in Milan, so
that they said I would die young. However, those who formulated the
prophecy have preceded me by a good many years.

Since I had no serious intention of dying, I went to find a good friend
of mine, a Sicilian pharmacist, and told him to caulk my lungs. He advised oil of essence of turpentine for me. I began to use it and actually
had good results from it. I later came to know that a noted faster was
able to perform the most admirable experiments... in fasting, thanks to
certain drops of walnut extract. He told me so himself: if he could stay
alive... fasting, thanks to walnut extract, those drops must really be
miraculous. During those years I was really a bit bizarre. Meanwhile,
however, walnut extract gave me back my health. And since that time
I have always been as healthy as a fish. And this is even more extraordinary, since my poor mother died of hemoptysis and one of my
brothers was taken, still young, by the same disease.

The fact is that an insurance company did not want to insure me;
with this background, it is understandable! However, the walnut extract—no one worried his head about me—saved me: I attribute the
miracle of my lucid old age precisely to it.

I was at the Milan Conservatory from October 1882 to March 1885,
and I had nothing to complain about, neither regarding the professors
who encouraged me with loving persuasion to study, nor regarding my
friends, almost all of whom wished me well.

I was in Milan about a year when I happened to read in a small pamphlet the translation of *Guglielmo Ratcliff* by Heine. I had heard that *Ratcliff* had been performed at the Teatro Manzoni by Andrea Maggi's company and that it had had a colossal success. A friend of mine said to me, "You see, that is a really beautiful subject for an opera!" "But to find it, how can one find it?" He took me to the Galleria, where there was a bookseller, Galli. We went in and asked, "Do you have, perhaps, the book of the drama *Ratcliff?*" "Yes, yes, it's here." It was luck to find it.

I paid one lira for it and I still have that small volume: I have never wanted to destroy it. I fell in love with it and immediately became fixed on the plan of setting *Ratcliff* to music. The verses of Maffei, the translator, seemed beautiful to me, and, judging by what I could remember of my school studies, I deemed them very musical. I declaimed them at night, walking up and down my room, and they inflamed me so much and caused me to love them like a madman that I dreamt of nothing else but the tavern of Tom, the fantastic passion of Guglielmo and the adventurous life of those highwaymen, in that drama by Heine. While dropping off to sleep I distinctly heard, in a dream, the words and music of the great love duet of Guglielmo and Maria. I nonetheless found no peace until I had written three pieces of what should have been my first opera. Later, on vacation during the summer of 1883 at Livorno, I jotted down a great part of the duet and completed it the following year in Milan. Thus *Ratcliff* was really my first opera, my first child, truly a love child.

Mascagni c.1885, approx. age 22

All this did not stop me from being an idler, and at the same time from feeling an agitation for independence and a longing to roam the world. Such living at close quarters with an art, only a glimpse of which I had seen, caused me to conceive projects, one crazier than another; also the spectacle of other people's vanity and its extreme worthlessness alongside my own led me to be expelled from the Conservatory without getting a diploma. Then too, I have always been a rebel: I have never liked school — and have attended all kinds of them. Naturally I didn't let anyone see me anymore. I let the Count Larderel know that I had to leave because of... incompatibility of character. Ponchielli wept over this. Poor Maestro Saladino was humiliated. When I later had the good luck of *Cavalleria* I was able to restore peace with these men. But Ponchielli was already dead at age fifty-one.

I owe a great deal to him. Unfortunately, not all of us always know when to say that which we would like to say: sometimes we are like slaves incapable of freeing ourselves.

Amilcare Ponchielli is one of the most authentic glories of Italian musical art. In general, authenticity of glory has fewer friends and fewer acknowledgements than forgeries have. For this reason, perhaps, the gowned critics have found it difficult and—incredible to say—still find it difficult to grant Amilcare Ponchielli the passport to immortality. But luckily the heart of the people, which is the most honest and disinterested judge, has placed this great musician in the aureole of the centuries. For me this is a great comfort, since I feel this compensates him for his life, which was miserly to him. Ponchielli worked hard in order to live his artistic career. He was gentle and good, he disturbed no one; yet he did not have success. When it seemed that destiny would smile on him, sudden and cruel death arrived to say: it is finished.

It is a cruelty to finish at age fifty-one when one still has many things to say, when the source gushes more plentifully. For this reason we must love him even more, if such is possible. And there is a way to love him even more: know that which he has given us. Which is a great deal, and all beautiful. Years ago, when consulted, I proposed a program of Ponchielli performances in his city of Cremona, a program which I consider to be the best adapted to re-establish, we shall say it thusly, a bit of "distributive" justice for his *oeuvre*. Today the great mass of the public knows and admires his *Gioconda*. But there is still more; perhaps a great deal more. I also proposed to perform, besides *I promessi sposi* and other operas, that admirable *Cantata* in honor of Donizetti, which is the greatest tribute one great man can make to another.

This is not the place to recount the life of Amilcare Ponchielli. It was above all the life of a great gentleman, of a simple, honest man, of an artist who obeyed his heart and did not know speculations. He lived at a time in which music had an architecture, style, manner and a redundant and pompous plumage of its own. But this was form; and while many musicians had only form, Ponchielli had a soul within this form. Even more; he knew how to be independent in an epoch in which independence was difficult, especially under the powerful and overwhelming influence of Verdi. It was said that he had little culture, but culture in a musician need not imply subtlety of knowledge, since even this, perhaps, fades. One must not extol the ignorance of certain old musicians, for whom everything was worthy to be set to music, and inspiration was, so to say, illiterate. No. But Ponchielli's period was certainly not one of great musical symbolism. It was a period in which one wrote music, in which melody had value, content, faith and joy for the composer and listener. Thus, because of such a language, he was a formidable orator. Look at the fourth act of *I promessi sposi*, or the first of *La Gioconda* or the finale of the first act of *Il figliuol prodigo*, or the overture to *I lituani*. These are pages which will always teach everything: inspiration, dramatic power, mighty breadth, a secure and stalwart theatrical sense. When Franco Faccio, in 1878, took the orchestra of La Scala to Paris and performed the explosive overture to *I lituani*, the Parisians seemed to go crazy. Few musicians knew how to "construct" as he did. He spread music like light over the words, and the words exhaled the feeling, they quickened, they became breath. For over thirty years he discharged his artistic life obscurely and painfully, in the humble drudgery of the country musician, organist and "Kapellmeister". Genius, in a bandmaster's uniform, with bandoleer and saber, seems a mockery. Ponchielli suffered all this in silence. And yet at age twenty-two he had already written *I promessi sposi* which was given at Cremona in 1856 and which moved none of the great scholars of the theatrical industry, who considered it a provincial success. The Maestro had to wait another twenty years to see his opera given at the Dal Verme in Milan. Then they realized his genius. But the suffering had already been lived through, the pain had already humiliated his heart. Yet the goodness in him always conquered over all: resentment against men, the meanness of little and great men, speculations and envy. He loved art because art loved him; he gave everything to it with the spontaneity of a boy and the melancholy of a veteran.

Honors came after *Gioconda*, without the bitterness ceasing, however, since those never cease in the life of an artist. But he continued. He wanted to say many things, for he felt them sprout in his heart for many years. In *Marion Delorme*, of which the public is wrongly left ignorant, he had begun to follow his own path. It was as yet a path, but already it was independence. That path could have become a highroad; it certainly should have become one. But, though he did not arrive at full independence, he did arrive where few, very few, arrive, i.e., he arrived at the power to move, to give an immediately comprehensible language to his music, a language for the heart, without obligating the mind to tortuous distillations to understand the sense of a phrase. Music needs this, and he knew how to be a musician. True, authentic, effectual, clear, powerful.

As a teacher he was admirable. I feel all the pride of having been his student. He loved me with a paternal tenderness. Since he was a good man, it was his way of life to love. He loved his family, children, home, music, poetry and heaven, all with a touching simplicity. In a letter to Maestro Soffredini he once wrote some lines about me which completely pledged his judgment on my future. Then his lines made my heart tremble with hope; today they make it tremble with emotion and gratitude. I owe much to this very great maestro of mine. His prediliction for me seemed prophetic and filled my spirit with high resolutions. He invited me to Maggianico, in his very modest home, sole indication of his hard won prosperity, and kept me there for whole periods of time to give me lessons. He taught in the same way he composed, with the joy of giving. He was patient and good, persuasive, enlightening and honest, even as a professor. At the Conservatory the students contended for the joy of being taught by him. It is untrue that he was not very companionable. He was a thoughtful man, tormented of his own accord. His famous distractions were not blanks in his mind, indeed, they were riches. They came from thoughts which overlapped, from inspirations which clashed, they were absences from this world so as to be presences in another higher one. The absent-mindedness of Ponchielli was phenomenal. One day, when I was a student at the Conservatory, I was invited to dinner at his home. At that time I no longer studied with him, I studied with Saladino, but since I knew him I went to greet his wife and stayed for breakfast with them. After breakfast, since it was Sunday, he left right away; he had to conduct the band in the Scala piazza. He was the bandmaster of Milan. I lingered on a little while and, when I was about to leave, looked for my hat but couldn't find it. "Could my husband have taken it by chance?" said the Signora. "It's possible." And yet Ponchielli's head was much larger than mine! I had to stay until he returned home. He returned, in fact, with my little hat perched on the top of his head; it was very comic.

The same kind of thing happened to him with his umbrella, when, as a guest of Ricordi at Cadenabbia, he was thoroughly drenched by a downpour, with his umbrella under his arm, carefully rolled up and absolutely... dry.

Another example: one day in the theater he was standing on the iron bar under the door of the steel curtain. "Maestro! Maestro!" The curtain went up and he went with it, astride the iron bar. It was a good thing that they brought it down immediately, otherwise a disaster might have occurred. Another time he fell from the ramparts of Milan, luckily without hurting himself too badly. He wasn't capable of saying who he

was when they found him there. They carried him to the police head-
quarters and he slept there until the following day when they could let
him go.

Another time, in '82, I went to the Conservatory at nine in the morning. I found Ponchielli in the piazza, rubbing his hands together and
blowing on them on account of the extreme cold. "Holy God, they're
not opening today!" "Maestro, it's not even nine yet, there are ten
minutes to go." "Really? Then I got here before eight. I've been here
more than an hour."

He was a man of such goodness, such simplicity! He was truly worthy of his wife, who was the sweetest woman in the world. Every now
and then he cracked jokes, often rather acerbic ones. I remember a day,
the famous day in February 1883 when Wagner died. I heard about it
in the morning and ran immediately to Ponchielli's house. "Maestro,
bad news!" "What's happened?" "Wagner is dead." "I should have
known it." "Why?" "Because every day there have been clouds and rain
but today the sun is out..." But he didn't say it out of meanness at all;
he said it to crack a joke. Imagine, he was a relentless Wagnerian! In
fact, he was the only musician of the Verdian epoch who did not imitate him.

On his wedding day they found him at home, engrossed in thought.
A friend said to him, "But people are waiting for you!" "Why? What is
there to do?" "You are to get married! Your bride is waiting for you..."
"Ah! You see? Since this morning I have been thinking what I had to
do today and I couldn't remember." But many other stories are told
about him and they would make one laugh if one were not to realize
that we owe his untimely end to one of his distractions. One January
evening he left the theater, in Piacenza, forgetting his fur coat. Without
realizing it, he exposed himself to the cold and caught pneumonia.
Eight days later he was dead.

The news of his death, on 17 January 1886, was terribly saddening
for me. I was conducting the orchestra in Scognamiglio's operetta company in Genoa and I remember that I could not even obtain permission
to be present at the funeral services, since I was without a substitute. I
had not yet repaid my maestro. I had only dedicated my *In filanda* to
him (which later generated *Pinotta*) but I swore that day to be worthy
of him. And, to be worthy of him, I have always tried to have my art inspired by his; and I have always felt a secret comfort when I have heard
it said that my music derives directly from that of Ponchielli. I have always loved, love and shall love the music of Ponchielli because I understand and feel it. And the soul of the people understands and feels

it with me. I find myself in good company. There is little harm to Art if his music does not reach the brains of the critics.

And I remain in my faith, in that faith which he knew how to instill in his students. Ponchielli, great as a musician and as a man, was a virtuous man. Since, if for a man to be an artist is a reward, for an artist to be a man is a virtue.

4   OPERETTA CONDUCTOR
(1885-1887)

After my misfortune of being expelled from the Conservatory in March 1885, since I had no more stipend and could not return to my father, from whom there was not to be had even a penny, I accepted the post of assistant conductor in an operetta company in Cremona to conduct my composition *"Il Re a Napoli"*.[6] As soon as I arrived, they attached a strip to the company's posters which announced my arrival and that evening I had applause and curtain calls. *"Il Re a Napoli"* was repeated the following evening and was encored both times.

It was the company of a certain Forlì, a good old devil, who had contracted to give me five lire a day. He gave them to me with a rather capricious irregularity, but sooner or later always honored his obligations. I have never wished evil on anyone, but I confess the truth when I say that wherever we traveled with the company I hoped that a cold would force the conductor of the orchestra to stay in bed for a few days and let me conduct, at least once. But that rogue was as healthy as a roach and he never would allow me the honor of the baton, not even one evening. This ambitious honor was conferred on me finally at Parma where I conducted *Cuore e mano* of Lecocq. During that period we went to Piacenza, Reggio Emilia and, after Parma, the Teatro Brunetti in Bologna.

I was not badly off in that company; I was young and I was satisfied with many things: a little satisfaction every now and then was enough for me. When one is young one lives on high hopes... But unfortunately things went rather badly for poor Forlì, so that one fine day – or bad day – he had to disband the company and send us all on our ways. I packed my bags and, as crestfallen as a whipped dog, had to return to Livorno. Only with great effort was I able to scrape up the money for the journey.

Summer passed, then autumn, when an invitation from Forlì called me to Naples. The company had been reformed and I was offered the post of conductor, nothing less, of the orchestra of the Teatro del Fondo;

---

6   For tenor and orchestra (1884).

rejoicing, I hurried to Naples, accepted the conditions offered me and was transported by the thought of continually feeling myself a "maestro".

I remember that one Sunday we gave an afternoon performance of the operetta *Satanello*; the theater was as full as an egg and noisy as only a Neapolitan theater can be. I was asked to repeat a number, and I, who did not want to tire the company since they had to perform that evening also, stayed firm and went on with the performance. Shouts and whistles, but I kept going ahead, when all at once a large object was seen to fly from the gallery and, making a graceful curve, precipitously crashed against the back of the conductor's stool. It was a cushion aimed in my direction. Naturally I gave the encore asked of me with such persuasive means.

After a little while the company left there and I signed with Scognamiglio, who pitched his tents at the Fondo. I was conductor and coach with a repertory of some twenty operettas and with the pay of seven lire a day. Those were my most tranquil days and the company did excellent business, so much so that the proprietor of the Politama in Genoa, coming expressly to Naples, contracted us for ninety performances, including the Carnival of 1886. This man was the good Daniele Chiarella, a true artist in his difficult work, one of those impresario-magicians who today are somewhat scarce.

I can say that beginning with Genoa my quiet manner of living disappeared, since then began the *via crucis* of the few-and-far-between performances, from one piazza to another. From Genoa to Alessandria, from Alessandria to Modena, from Modena to Ancona, from Ancona to Ascoli Piceno for the inauguration of a railroad; it was a breathless and continuous running around, but with few profits. That which I feared happened: the company was disbanded and I was left without a bit of money.

But there is a Providence for musicians as well as for alcoholics. I was a good friend of some excellent people who showed me great sympathy and one of whom, after hearing the parts of my opera which were already written, immediately became crazy about the music and, since I was working, helped me out with some money. I had written the Prelude to *Ratcliff* in Ancona and now in Ascoli, lacking anything better, I continued to be immersed in the opera and wrote the Intermezzo and then the entire fourth act, which I orchestrated in a few days.

My hunger was still very strong and I tried to divert it by contemplating those mysterious spectres that seemed to come out of the opera, those two phantoms that the hero of the drama always saw. But with all this the musical notes gave me nothing to eat and I resolved to return to Ancona, meanwhile writing letter after letter in order to obtain any kind of engagement. My entire riches consisted of a watch, a silver chain and a gold ring. I sold them one day when I didn't even have two lire with which to dine and I ate slowly, even giving up my cigar.

Finally one morning I received an invitation from Naples to leave for the Teatro del Fondo, and with the invitation came a check for a hundred lire. I had been engaged by the company of the Duke Cirella.[7] But after a month the company was once again disbanded for *force majeure* and I was left without work for a good month and a half. I did not waste my time: my entire lunch was a plate of macaroni; but meanwhile I worked full strength at composing and orchestrating the opera which rapidly grew under my eyes to a lovely quantity of music sheets which I religiously placed in a suitcase. It was the treasure of my future; at least I so imagined during my long walks to Villa, Posillipo and Portici, when it seemed to me I dreamed with open eyes, and in the luminous phosphorescence of the sea who knows how many crazy deviltries of fortune and destiny I saw.

Then I signed with Maresca, always at the Teatro del Fondo, and then began again the usual peregrinations. From Naples to Benevento for a few performances; from Benevento to Foggia; until at last, on 29 December 1886, we arrived at Cerignola, in the Puglie. And I didn't move from there.

I stayed for the entire Carnival of 1887 with Maresca; the pay was ten lire a day, sufficient for my needs and my wife's.[8] But that uprooted life, finding myself in the atmosphere of vendettas, jealousies and gossiping cured me of the desire to continue. I played the piano rather well and felt myself inclined, through a natural communicative ability, to teach others.

In Cerignola I met with great kindness from all the citizens; several gentlemen asked me if I would stay on there and give piano lessons, because there was no music teacher. I accepted with all the joy imaginable since for a long time I had waited for the moment to rid myself once and for all of that wandering life of a mountebank. Among the lessons which I found, one was the daughter of the mayor, Guiseppe Cannone, who,

---

7   See *Personalia: Scognamiglio*.
8   Lina's (abrupt) first appearance in the *Autobiography*. She was born Argenide Marcellina Carbognani, in Parma. They were married 7 February 1888, in the Cerignola Cathedral. See *Personalia: Mascagni, Lina*.

following the advice of several gentlemen, proposed to the City Council to make me the conductor of a local Filarmonica (which I was supposed to organize) with the salary of 1500 lire a year. This was great luck for me because in addition to the monthly salary from the City Council I would also have private lessons; I also would be able to finish quickly my *Ratcliff*, which was well along. My whole life depended on this chance. Only one thing was lacking; I had to present some documents which would declare my capability of teaching music and the piano. These documents were more a formality than anything else, but it was necessary to present them and the sooner the better.

I took a chance on asking how they felt about me in Milan. I wrote to the Director of the Conservatory, Bazzini; I wrote to Ponchielli's widow, Teresina Ponchielli; and wrote to Saladino, my professor.

I received documents which no one else was able to procure.

Imagine that Bazzini went to the trouble of altering the truth in my favor since he wrote: "The young Pietro Mascagni has been a student at our Conservatory and demonstrated some very superior qualities. Unfortunately, for family reasons he was called home and had to suspend his studies. He has not acquired a diploma, but what he has studied and what he knows are worth any conservatory diploma."

Ponchielli's widow was also very generous on my behalf and wrote: "My husband, Maestro Amilcare Ponchielli, adored this young man and said that he had much talent..." Saladino wrote: "Mascagni was my best student and I am an old teacher."

To be doubly sure, I then wrote my father, begging him to procure a document from Maestro Soffredini, which would state that I had studied at his Institute and that I was competent to give any kind of lessons. This was something that I greatly desired. I also endeavored to obtain for myself a declaration from Maestro Luigi Pratesi and others. I wrote:

Cerignola, 16 February 1887
My dear Father,
    I have delayed for a long time in writing you because I wanted to give you a good piece of news, a piece of news which will give you immense pleasure. I am finally abandoning this art of the nomad, of the acrobat, and I am remaining here in Cerignola, as a music teacher.
    Tomorrow the City Council is gathering to name me municipal musician; for now I will give piano and voice les-

sons, later on I will conduct my opera at the Municipal
Theater and expand the orchestra school.

Meanwhile I am content with this. Five lire like this are
better than twenty in the Company. Besides, I shall have at
least ten or so private lessons. Cerignola is a somewhat backward town, but they love me very much.

Here I shall put my own home together. I have already
started to buy curtains, etc. It will be easy for me to borrow
some money to make a good impression. Indeed, I beg you to
write to the Messrs. V*** that I shall send them the amount
of my debt as soon as possible, because I want to have my
safety deposit box back for some papers which I need, since I
must give a few documents to the mayor. And in this matter
it is necessary for you to do all I tell you. You must beg
Maestro Soffredini to draw up a paper stating that I have
studied at his Institute and that I can give lessons of any
kind, that I have studied, etc., in short, that which he will
think to write. Since the more documents there are the better, find out if, through Maestro Soffredini, one could have a
certificate from Maestro Menichetti in Pisa and one from
Cav. Magroni as Inspector of the Institute.

Then you must also beg Maestro Luigi Pratesi to write me
a declaration, saying I am qualified to teach music and piano,
etc. In addition to this, I ask all of them to write also at the
bottom of the certificate, besides their own names, all their
titles, qualifications, civil orders, etc. These are things which
make an effect and command more respect. I am very happy
about all this. Meanwhile I am assiduously working on my
opera, which will soon be completed. And you shall see that
I shall know how to do myself proud!

I beg you to do all I have asked you as quickly as possible.
My life may depend on this chance.

A million kisses from your
Pietro

One had to push oneself in that manner, especially in Cerignola.

Maresca learned about these innocent intrigues and on 17 February
called me to the stage and told me that I was wrong to leave him; that
in a few days we would have gone to Sicily and I would have done
badly to listen to the advice of false friends.

I no longer know now how it happened, but the fact remains that Maresca answered very excitedly to my replies; he got angrier, became infuriated and ended by hitting me. I wanted to hit back, but the artists of the company separated us and took me to the pharmacist to patch me up.

I was not very impressed by his method of persuading people to renew a contract, and reasonably considered myself excused from any obligation. I had the most authoritative citizens of Cerignola for my friends, and in accord with them I resolved to slip away. I was not afraid of causing difficulties for the company since I knew that Maresca had already engaged another, Balsimelli, and that he was soon to join them in Sicily. Nonetheless, I was supposed to go there with them for a few weeks, and I didn't feel at all inclined to continue that life.

Here then is the plan that I evolved.

We had come to the evening of the season's last performance and in the early hours of the afternoon I had sent my luggage and the famous suitcase which held the manuscript of *Ratcliff* to the house of a friend's family. My wife was to wait for me there. I went to the theater to conduct; Maresca, now sweet as candy, told me that business was booming in Sicily and I would not be sorry to have followed him — just the opposite. I neither answered yes or no, but I was firmly resolved to put the agreed-upon plan into action.

The performance barely over, I ran to where I was to meet my wife, who was waiting for me; I took off my tails (I could never conduct without tails on account of the respect that I have always had for the public) and, when I thought I could cross the city without danger of meeting someone from the company, we left. Our hosts were to accompany us to one of the vineyards. A coach waited for us there and, without a hitch, we set out.

What a night! It was February; the bitter cold whipped our faces, and I suffered doubly, since my pregnant wife felt every jerk of the bouncing carriage. I tried to distract her with jokes, since I rarely lose my good humor, but my words froze as if they were sherbet. We rattled on like this for five or six kilometers; when we alighted at the lonely cottage in the middle of the pitch-black countryside, we really were pieces of ice. My wife's hands were so paralyzed that she could only open them with effort.

Two Albanians lived in the cottage, but the notice of our arrival had gotten somewhat mixed up, and at that hour (it must have been three o'clock in the morning) they no longer expected us. They turned on all the lights and we put together a little supper as best we could; I was

The house at Stornarella where Mascagni and Lina hid from Maresca

more than just cold, I was also dying of hunger. There were no beds, and it was necessary to improvise some with *tufa* and sacks of vegetables. I remembered some lines from *Lombardi*, "*Sarà talamo l'arena/Del deserto interminato.*"[9] Wrapped up as best we could, we waited until it would be day, and I well remember that the hours seemed never to pass.

At dawn we went to a place not far from there called Stornarella, which was supposed to be the general quarters where we would await the news from the enemy camp. Since we were new there, my wife and I were taken for two lovers who had made an escape from the nest, i.e., a flight and abduction according to all the rules. The people that we met smiled discreetly and winked. We bore this, but the trouble was that at Stornarella it wasn't possible to have a bit of bread and meat for our lunch, and my dear Lina needed this after the difficult night spent on the ground. Only after a long search did I finally run a poor emaciated chicken to earth, which pained us to look at it: it seemed to have been fed on ration coupons!

We waited there a few days and no one showed up. I was very rest-less. At last the son-in-law of the mayor of Cerignola came and told us

---

9   "The nupital bed shall be the sand/Of the interminable desert." This celebrated
     verse is from the Giselda/Oronte duet in Act III of Verdi's opera.

what happened after my departure. It happened like this. The morning after the last performance, when the company was supposed to leave for Sicily, Maresca, not seeing me, went to knock on the door of my house. No one answered, naturally. He looked for me in the countryside, he asked, made inquiries in all the usual places, and made them give him the key to the house I occupied, and even went so far as to look under the bed.

Then all of a sudden, hitting his forehead, he shouted, "The suitcase, there must be the suitcase!"

It was the suitcase with my *Ratcliff*; with this in his hands as security, he felt certain of being able to catch me quickly. But the precious capsule was hidden in a safe place. The company left and Maresca stayed behind for another day, always hoping from one moment to the next to see me reappear.

Finally he left, swearing he would obtain justice; and my wife and I came back tranquilly to Cerignola.

There now was a serious problem to face: how I would be able to live. There were few lessons to be given as yet; my wife, as I've already said, was pregnant and this fact worried me greatly. It was necessary to set up housekeeping, and figuring up our bills we calculated that we needed at least five hundred lire. I obtained the amount from the bank in Cerignola, obligating myself to pay something every three months. I remember that the cashier, each time that I went to pay on the bills, bringing my renewed and reduced loan, said, looking at me: "You, however, do not have the signature of a borrower: you are not destined to take out loans."

The fact remains that on the day in which we were able to have our own bed and table, and my wife and I sat facing one another for that first family dinner, eaten by the two of us without the troublesome to-do of hotel customers and waiters, we were seized by a sense of tenderness, and looking at each other and squeezing hands we saw no more clouds in our future, which was unfortunately uncertain. I was young, I was healthy. I had a great desire to work, and in that friendly city which extended hospitality to me I did not feel abandoned in the least. But the piano lessons in those first months were few, and every miracle of the scrupulous and experienced economy was needed on the part of my wife to put a pan on the fire every day. I couldn't swear that there was always that!

On 25 March I got the famous post at the orchestra school in Cerignola. I received a hundred lire a month. At that time they were worth more than today but were still a hundred lire a month. I did have, however, those few piano lessons. And what a short time those piano lessons lasted in that town! The young girls, waiting to get married, forced themselves to study the piano in order to increase their own attractiveness, but once they were married, goodbye piano!

When the mayor called on me to share the good news, he said that before putting the nomination into effect he wanted to know if I were capable of managing the instruction of all the instruments which made up an orchestra. I boldly answered yes, and the post was conferred on me.

How did I manage this? In a very simple way. During the first six months I taught theory, which I knew very well. Since the instruments were at my disposal in the school, I learned to play them all in a fury of hard work, from contrabass to harp. After six months I went on to practical teaching and I don't believe, in all conscience, that I stole the monthly hundred lire assigned to me in the Council budget.

I was twenty-three years old — at that age I already had a wife and soon a child, a son who died in Cerignola after four months. I had given him the name of my father, Domenico, and he was called by the nickname "Mimì". I was crazy about

Giuseppe Cannone, Mayor of Cerignola

my son, who was truly a little angel; I spent all day with him, covering him with kisses, giving him a thousand caresses; and in those moments I was truly happy. I was a real man, full of cares; I was the father of a family!

In the fall of 1887 I was given the task of buying instruments for the Filarmonica, which was to be done through Pigna in Milan. At the last moment, however, Pigna no longer wished to deal with me.

I got the instruments just the same from a firm in Caserta. Pigna had made very good prices for me, and the money would have served to buy the instruments and in addition I would have had a little left over which, as I saw it, would have served to buy me a used piano. Oh, if I only had a piano! Instead I went to Caserta. The prices were not those of Pigna, but I could not return to Cerignola without the instruments. I had to procure them at any cost, and in fact I did get them. I naturally lost the extra money; and not only that: out of my own pocket I used 140 lire which I had kept in reserve, together with that which I spent for the journey. But that wasn't all. At Caserta there came a telegram for me to leave immediately. I arrived in Cerignola and found my wife in bed with typhus. The child, naturally, suffered through the mother's illness; a nurse couldn't be found, he was given milk artificially and to top it all off he was teething; and all this happened to me just when two loans were due, one for 500, the other for 200 lire and the rent was also due.

During my wife's illness the doctor advised her not to nurse the baby; but as hard as we searched, it was not possible to find a nurse; we found two of them, but they wanted to take the boy to their homes. I was absolutely unable to accept that condition, finding the baby very unwell as a result of administering him artificial milk from a bottle instead of my wife's milk. I finally found a woman, our neighbor, who came to nurse him during the day only; at night he was nourished with asses milk. All this according to the advice of the doctor, or better, of the doctors; since, our doctor being sick one day, I was forced to call another one because of a bad case of dysentery which the baby had; this doctor cured him and after two days the dysentery was over. My poor little son did not lack for care; and my wife, as soon as she was able to get out of bed, held him with that loving affection which only mothers know. But the baby got steadily worse in the sense that he visibly got thinner, his dear little eyes became sunken, he was morose and restless; in other words he was no longer the beloved Mimì which all loved and were partial to for his intelligence and really winning manners. Beyond all this, he began to teethe and at four months one tooth was already out and three more were beginning to show. I then called our own doctor and as soon as he saw the boy he told me there was nothing more he could do, since the warm milk of my wife, the artificial, the goat's and asses milk, in other words the multiple change of nourishment had produced a great upset in his intestines; add to this the strong case of dysentery (which was over) and a creature of that age was not able to resist such a strong disease. In spite of this he ordered me to give him a prepared potion and a few enemas of water and bran. Depressed by the doctor's words, on the advice of other gentlemen I called the other doctor again, who had the reputation in Cerignola of being the best and most frank.

This doctor, after a careful examination, said that there was no disease at all; only that the baby was so weak and listless that a paralysis of the heart was to be feared; it was necessary for the child to regain its strength and there would be no more danger. He ordered me to give him at night goat's or asses milk thinned with water (whereas the other doctor had forbidden this), to give him every two hours an enema with water, starch and tannic acid (as a substitute for the enemas ordered by the other doctor) and absolutely forbade that potion which the other had ordered. Thus I found myself faced with two opposing and contrary remedies and I didn't know what to do. I talked with several friends and decided to follow the treatment of the second doctor, in view of certain circumstances, i.e., that our regular doctor was very ab-sent-minded while the other was very assiduous; that our own was young while the other was very old, etc. With a heavy heart I decided on that treatment, deciding to ignore our own doctor who had cured us many times: who had cured my foot, who had saved, by a miraculous cure, the eyes of my child, who had cured my wife of typhus, etc. (never having asked me for a cent beyond the expenses).

But unfortunately this young doctor did not have a diploma. And here was the usual story of those who must be good because they have a diploma and of the others who must be donkeys due to the lack of same. I did not have a diploma, yet I would not change with many others who did have one, especially those who studied with me at the Royal Conservatory. Just as I would not exchange Dr. Nardò (this was his name) for many others who practice the art of medicine because they have a scrap of paper. However, Dr. Nardò had letters from the first professors of Italy and abroad who declared him extremely competent in matters, able in any cure whether it be medicine or surgery. What's more, the following year he was to receive his diploma after having taken the final examination, which he did not have time to take earlier due to his own negligence.

Meanwhile I had both doctors come twice a day at different times. The second doctor always found improvement in the child, whereas Nardò found a worsening and dashed our hopes, so much so that my wife called him "the bird of evil omen". He told me frankly that he washed his hands of us and no longer wished to treat the baby. I remained mortified to see this doctor, always loving and affectionate with us, so changed in this situation, and what was even worse was that in my eyes my son was always getting better, exactly as the other doc-tor said. In fact, the other one came one morning, looked at the child, found no more dysentery, was satisfied as to how the baby was being fed milk, and declared him out of danger. I thanked him profusely and paid him. Around noon Nardò arrived, so happy and carefree that it was a pleasure to see him. He barely glanced at the child's face and, cut-ting off my words as I was telling him my joy at seeing him return, said to me: "My lips do not lie; the symptoms which I have observed lead me to believe that the child will not last until evening." He struck sor-row in my heart.

That evening I went to the Filarmonica and left the child smiling and lively; I had played the violin for him as I did every day and he was really all right. They called me before I had finished the lesson. I arrived home and the child, my dear son, died in my arms without making a sound... he lay there and seemed to be alive. It was 10:45 at night. My desperation may be imagined. My wife, barely recovered from sickness, seemed out of her mind; I forced myself to encourage her, but my heart was breaking and I wept. This child, when he was born and while he was alive was the greatest consolation that I had ever had; now that he was dead, the greatest sorrow. He was so dear, so beautiful, so good, so intelligent; if he heard a violin play he was all ears and laughed and looked at me if I was playing; with his little hands he touched the violin, always looking into my eyes with his big eyes out of paradise. If he wept, it was enough to play and sing and he calmed down and listened, laughing; he even had his favorite pieces, and openly made them known. Poor little boy! He was four months and ten days old.

I found myself weakened, dejected, powerless to fight any longer against a fate which was gradually annihilating me, destroying me. So many doctor's visits, so much love, so many nights lost, so many sacrifices! And what in return... These disasters ruined me morally and materially. Think of the expenses: doctors, medicines, nurses, etc. I was in the depths. And then on 4 October 1887, I made the last expense for my son: the transportation to the cemetery. He went in the same carriage as that of his baptism; the mayor's carriage. I purchased a special grave for him and put a tombstone there to remember him. And the expenses still were not over; there was my wife, poor thing, beaten down by sorrow. As a result of all that had happened she could not bear to see the cradle, the little clothes and other things of the poor child in the house: even worse, as a result of her illness she needed a change of climate and I found myself in financial straits easy to imagine.

When I was a child, in Livorno, I went to the public garden every day, passing through Via De Larderel. There were two old shops below the street, where they pulverized chalk; there was a kind of mill and a horse always plodded around it, moving the stone cylinder which ground the chalk. It was my strongest desire to see that blindfolded horse plodding and it was almost philosophically that I watched him. Many times it came to my mind during those days to compare myself with that horse.

All the time I stayed in Cerignola I worked seriously. I had created a real orchestra and I gave symphonic concerts; I also wrote a Mass which was performed in the Cerignola Cathedral under my direction. It was later said that I was the band leader in Cerignola, but that is not true; it is necessary to clear up this confusion which has always offended me, although by this I don't mean to scorn band leaders in any way. They too, poor men, do their duty and perform a useful function. The band leader in Cerignola, however, was my worst enemy. Unfortunately his name was a famous one: he was called Prisciano Martucci, but he was no relation to Giuseppe Martucci.

He earned much more than I and I confess that I envied him. Besides the salary he had all the duties of the church, the processions, etc. If only I *had* had the band! Instead I was with the orchestra. I had to give lessons on all the instruments. I had an enormous hall, filled with wooden benches, and gave lessons every day. However, it was just this which helped me, since it allowed me to compose *Cavalleria* with a preparation that no other composer could have.

There was, however, a rival party which was violently against me; that is, not exactly against me: it was a political faction against the Commune, against the mayor. I couldn't have a fixed salary; every year I had to be reappointed. The law (this I don't understand) did not allow me to be hired permanently. And so every year this rival party, to oppose the mayor, attempted to forestall with every means the renewal of my appointment by the Prefect. They treated me like a scoundrel, said all kinds of things about me, asserting that those who were in power were in cahoots with this poor devil, who moreover was profiting from the Commune. But I had nothing to do with it.

This party had a newspaper; it seems to me it was called the *Risveglio* or something similar. The things they said in that paper against me, who had the sole fault of being supported by the Communal Administration, cannot be imagined. Now thinking about it again after so long a time I laugh, but then I had a lot of bad blood over it. I remember that one time they almost insulted me because I permitted myself the luxury of having a small dog. She was called Titania, poor little thing, and I later left her in a *pensione* with some friends. They found it laughable that I ordered several artistic publications from out of town through the local barber. I wasn't even permitted to spend those two or three lire in peace! They even criticized me—in the paper, with many articles—because two or three times I had ordered a small box of strawberries from Foggia! Things like that. On the other hand it was on account of that particular paper that an enormous blunder was made, as will be seen later.

In 1888 I was asked to try out a new organ in the Cathedral. I went in the evening; the sanctuary was closed to the faithful, and was barely illuminated by a few leftover candles, set on old candelabra no longer used, and placed on the floor at barely sufficient intervals so I wouldn't accidentally break my shins. I went up to the choir accompanied by the bellows men and the builder of the organ who had with him the contract and guarantee for all the materials which were used in the instrument that I was to try out.

The builder was somewhat agitated. He made a fuss of showing me that he had added one register more than was called for and that in the facing he had put four more pipes than were stated in the contract. He explained all of this to me with much gesturing and with such waving of the candle he had in his hand that I brought home with me the most unpleasant impression of it, represented by many wax stains on my poor jacket. And the tone of his voice also surprised me: he shouted like one possessed when he told me that he had made many sacrifices out of deference and devotion to his very reverend clients. Then later, as I was examining the bellows, all of a sudden he said to me under his breath that he would not forget me if the test resulted in complete satisfaction.

I began to understand. But meanwhile my mind was somewhat distracted by such material and mechanical things. Perhaps it was the effect of my surroundings, which were new to me in that peculiar light; perhaps by the same shadows which fantastically enlarged the arches of the church and revealed golden and shining objects in the dark; perhaps by the perpetual holy lamp which feebly burned in front of the Madonna at the high altar; perhaps by the whole scene, seen from the height of the choir; the fact remains that my heart was suffused with a sweet and devotional sense of meditation.

Almost unaware of what I was doing, I sat down on the bench in front of the organ; I pulled the principal stops and began to prelude with my head still wrapped in the veil of this new vision.

I do not know, and didn't even know then, what I played. Perhaps my mind followed, without reaching it, an idea which never before had appeared on the unlimited horizon of thought; and perhaps my fingers followed my mind in its endless course. I improvised... I dreamed.

I was roused by the noise of a sonorous baritone voice; it was a handsome padre, fat and jolly, who had come up to tell me that what I was playing was damned boring and put people to sleep, and that they wanted to hear something happy from me, something from an opera or an operetta. What a devil! The good Fathers had sent out invitations; down below there was a crowd of intelligent people, and one must not annoy them...

My dream, my vision, all vanished by magic. Reality returned limpid to my mind. The fat and jolly padre had even been too polite, since he did not add that, after all, I was paid to test the organ but above all to amuse the priests and invited listeners.

I mechanically looked at the builder who had stiffly remained on my right, with the candle still in his hand in the anxious expectation of pulling all the stops, at my signal, which was the *sine qua non* of his construction; he had the expression of one condemned to death in his eyes and in the trembling of his beseeching lips, his hand dripping with wax and his forehead with sweat. I took pity on the poor old devil who, as soon as the good padre disappeared on the steps to the organ, said to me in a lachrymose voice, "You are ruining me!"

And he was right. Away with dreams! Away with visions! Pull out the stops: the clarinet, piccolo, cornet, bombardon, bells — all the joy of happy, shrill and noisy voices, all their force! "There are also cymbals and big drum!" the builder said to me. Good! Very good! Long live the uproar of sound!

The test came out splendidly for the organ and... for me too. But how ashamed I was of myself when I descended the organ stairs, followed by the enthusiastic builder and when the good reverends complimented me on my playing and, moved, thanked me. With the excuse of sweating gained while playing, I exaggeratedly raised the collar of my jacket and blessed the darkness which surrounded me and which prevented them from seeing the blush of shame on my face.

One last uncomfortable glance at the great arches of the church, the golden and shining objects, the perpetual holy lamp of the Madonna and I contritely — and convulsively — went away.

Regarding my friends in Cerignola during these years, a special group of both finished and budding artists had been formed. But more than Cerignola it was Bari which represented the principal seat of his pleasant society, and my very dear friend Giannini, a dealer in music and instruments, was of necessity its fulcrum, since we often gathered in his shop to have a chat. Giannini was practically my first publisher, in the sense that I had my first musical dealings with him. He was so fond of me (and I returned his friendship with equal intensity) that, dying, he willed to his children the entire collection of notes that I sent him, among which, naturally, were several requests for loans.

In his shop, as I have said, we all gathered to exchange our impressions and to agree upon what we would do during the day.

One evening Sonzogno's representative, a certain Daspuro, came among us and said to me, "When you go to Bari I shall recommend you to my half-brother, who will deliver a letter to you from Sonzogno which will be very useful to you." That letter was, in fact, delivered to me and represented the beginning of my musical career.

That same evening at Bari there was a certain Tullia, a man full of spirit and a pleasant conversation. He was speaking off and on with Magno, another one of the crowd, also a wit though rather scatterbrained.

Tullia had not met Magno before that time so Magno thought it would be opportune and convenient to introduce himself to his new friend, and extending his hand said in a natural manner:

"Alessandro Magno!"[10] (he was really called Alessandro).

"Frederic Barbarossa," responded Tullia undaunted; and Magno in his turn, somewhat angry:

"You are making fun of me, sir!"

And Tullia, serene and impassive:

"You think, perhaps, that in answer to your high sounding name I should simply say my obscure and insignificant one?"

Everyone laughed at the good *mot* and went to dinner, invited by the good Giannini.

Happy times, then, those in Cerignola, when one had less fame and more hunger, but also lightheartedness and mirth!

Art was represented in this society in every aspect: from music to painting, from sculpture to architecture. One of my painter friends, since that time, created pictures of great artistic interest, which constituted an anticipation of what would one day be called futuristic art.

A certain Pattina, another of our unforgettable friends, was also a painter of great gifts and his pictures at that time won great approbation from the public and critics.

Another friend who was dear to me in that Cerignola society was Giacomino de Zerbi, of which I shall write later regarding the *Siciliana* which caused such a furor. The public immediately took possession of that piece and even Queen Margherita, who was present at the first performance of *Cavalleria*, deigned to compliment me especially on the music of that very fortunate piece.

Another friend from Cerignola comes to mind: Van Westerhout, a good musician whom many, if not all, have believed and still believe to be Dutch. He was from Mola, near Foggia, however, and his talent was as Italian as could be imagined. At his death I had the task of pronouncing the funeral oration.

---

10   Literally, Alexander the Great.

But there was also Michetti, the painter, another of our unforgettable friends. I have no work of his except a pen and ink sketch representing *Iris,* and in fact entitled "How I see *Iris".* It represents the figure of a woman, superbly and masterfully drawn.

The head of this Puglian brigade was Scarfoglio, the wizard of journalism, our very dear, unforgettable and lamented friend.

One might think that among us — potential artists — we spoke only of art, but this is not true. We created art, true art, but didn't speak about it through a tacit and very happy agreement. The critics then, as always, thought of speaking about it but perhaps more honestly than they do now.

Another very dear friend was the painter Plinio Nomellini, who, along with a few others, is still active. I have many pictures of his, among which is the one, considered his masterpiece, called *Piazza del Caricamento in Genova.* I have been asked repeatedly by many collectors for this very beautiful canvas — even 600.000 lire were offered me for it. Nomellini made a gift of it to me on the occasion of the Second Venice Biennale. As a matter of fact, he is seventy-eight years old now, two years younger than I.

Another beautiful picture which I have is one by Fattori. I knew Fattori in Livorno during my youth. Giovanni Fattori was a great painter, but this wasn't known at that time; now they are preparing the centenary celebration of his birth. This very skillful artist always lived in the most squalid indigence, in spite of his great talent. I remember that one day a mutual friend of ours went to visit him in his studio and Fattori showed him a very successful painting, a really beautiful picture. Our friend was struck with admiration for the work and asked the painter if he could acquire it and how much he would ask for it. Fattori, confused, gave the canvas to his friend and, since the other insisted on buying it, timidly asked the sum of 10 lire. The friend, moved, took the little picture, left two bills of a hundred lire each on Fattori's small table while the painter insisted on not wanting to accept such a sum, which then had some importance. Even many days after that visit the two bank notes were to be found on the table, in the same position they had been left by his friend.

Another day, as I was leaving to go to breakfast with several friends, I met Fattori on the doorstep of my house. He had come purposely to show me a small picture of his, in which were represented several Maremmian horses. This admirable canvas, which I still have, pleased me very much and I asked my dear friend for its acquisition. He was delighted to please me, and at my request of the price that he wanted for my acquisition of it, resolutely dodged, telling me that he wanted to offer it to me as a gift. But I, knowing in what financial condition he was, courteously insisted in my offer of acquiring it normally, and he then, somewhat confused, asked me to offer him breakfast. My emotion was so great that I almost wept, but since I was engaged with friends, I begged the good Fattori to accept a certain sum which I was able to offer him and made haste to thank him for the very precious gift of the little picture. I had to use all my glibness to convince him, however, and only by insistently begging him and excusing myself for the impudence I used with him was I finally able to make him accept the money.

More than once have admirers and collectors asked me for that very beautiful canvas — 300.000 lire were even offered!

Happy days of my youth, when all of Italy was seized by the sacred passion for art!

Then groups of young and old sprang up everywhere, all priests of a faith which enflamed the spirit and gave the grace to create in and for beauty.

How many are there among us who have not suffered from that sweet pain which opens to us the doors of hope and enthusiasm, and which binds us all, musicians, poets, painters, in a single host of believers?

Beautiful times, truly beautiful times... *Belli tiempi 'e na vota!*

THE COMPOSITION OF
CAVALLERIA RUSTICANA **(1889)**

My *Cavalleria* is fifty-three years old. I am somewhat older, agreed, but the enduring youth which my opera has retained may be said to have accompanied me all my life and been transfused into me; as a result it is understandable that I write of it, after more than half a century, with the same emotion with which I saw it born on the evening of 17 May 1890 at the Costanzi in Rome.

To tell how I came to compose this opera is to repeat what has been written about me for years now, and hasn't always been told with an accuracy of detail. I propose to relate things which perhaps no one knows, setting in order—as one would say today—certain old inaccuracies.

For too many people *Cavalleria* passes for an opera jotted down, like a flicker of lightning, written in a hurry, gushing forth in me like a gift from Heaven. I have always thanked Heaven for having given me this inspiration, but *Cavalleria* cost me much labor, or better, I enlisted all my study and all the knowledge that my illustrious teacher, Saladino, had given me. Also, I purposely wanted to write an opera which would convince the contest judges of the seriousness of my contrapuntal studies. And I shall always remember with intimate pride what one of the judges, Platania, said to me at the rehearsals: "How is that you, so young, can have such a deep knowledge of counterpoint?" I answered by telling him the name of my teacher and of the long vigils over the methods and works of the Masters.

One July evening in 1888 I stayed at the Filarmonica longer than usual. Leaving the house for my accustomed walk, I went to my barber, who sold newspapers. The paper I preferred was the *Corriere della Sera*, but for some reason which I don't recall, it hadn't come in that evening.

My newspaper-barber said, "This evening you'll have to be content with the *Secolo*."

"Very well," I replied, and with that paper in my pocket I returned home.

All of a sudden, opening it, I let out an exclamation: "Good heavens," I said, "here is something that shouldn't be passed up."

My wife, surprised, looked at me. "What is it?" she said.

"Maybe destiny is helping us, and it would be about time!"

"But can you tell me what has happened to you? What have you read?" Lina answered.

"Look," showing her the paper, "the *Teatro Illustrato* has announced a contest for an opera in one act, and I want to enter! I have the subject. *Cavalleria rusticana...* I even have Verga's permission to set it to music."

As a matter of fact this was true. Everyone has believed—and they almost made me believe it—that I had a problem with Verga, or rather that he had sued me because I set *Cavalleria* to music. It is not true. He never thought of suing me; Verga and I have always been good friends. I already had his permission before the contest. The problem, instead, was with Sonzogno. They were not in agreement on the sum offered, so Verga sued, costing Sonzogno many hundreds of thousands of lire.

When I was a student I saw *Cavalleria rusticana* for the first time, in Milan at the Teatro Manzoni. Many believe that I saw *Cavalleria rusticana* at that time with Duse; it's not true. I saw it done by Duse much later. The first time I saw it, it was done by the Pasta Company with Campi (Santuzza), Colonnello (Turiddu) and Pasta himself (Alfio). I became enthusiastic. With me was Giovanni Salvestri, a Livornese who lived in Milan.

"Holy God," I said, "what a magnificent subject this is for music! I would like to do it!" But I was too much of a boy then. And too, I already had *Ratcliff* on my mind. But *Cavalleria* impressed me greatly, so much so that Salvestri said to me, "Listen, Verga is a good friend of mine; if you want me to, I will ask him to grant the musical rights to *Cavalleria* to you. You have no obligation, but meanwhile, in any eventuality, you have this permission on the part of Verga.: "If God wills!"

And so he got me the permission which authorized Maestro Mascagni (I was not a maestro, but they called me such) to set to music, etc.[11]

I was very pleased. I put the permission aside and thought no more about it at that time. But when I read the announcement in Cerignola, that there was a contest for an opera in one act, it immediately came back to mind. And I sent Salvestri a letter asking him to get a new statement from Verga which would authorize me to set the work to music.

It is very true that at Cerignola, where I was Director of the Filarmonica, I longed for a better future. However well loved I may have been at Cerignola (and I remember how much esteemed I was at that time by the mayor, Cav. Giuseppe Cannone), it is natural that I sought

---

11   See *Personalia: Verga, Giovanni.*

to better my position. The idea of winning the three thousand lire prize had a very relative importance. Not that I couldn't say I didn't need it — I have already told with what difficulty I was able to put together two miserable pieces of furniture — but for me the principal question was something else. I wanted to get away from Cerignola. Although I had set myself up as well as I could, although I was really fond of my friends there, I was nevertheless fully conscious that for my artistic aspirations, for the desire I had of raising myself in my profession, a small port in the provinces like Cerignola was equal to death. In reality, there I was just another provincial; I had to go into the countryside with my friends and the most interesting diversions consisted in going to see the vineyards, the sheep and the cows. At Cerignola the position I had attained represented the apex of a musician's career. I would never have been able to do any more, and God knows how much energy it cost me to hold on to that!

Now, since I wanted to get out of Cerignola, it was necessary for me to start the ball rolling in one way or another. My winning of the contest could be the trampoline for the jump: one mistake meant giving up for good all my hopes, shutting them up in my baggage, perhaps forever, and returning humiliated to Cerignola, where the disdain of those dear editors of the *Risveglio* awaited me for sure.

The Sonzogno contest kindled the hope in me of being able to open a new path, and even though I already had an opera ready which was very close to my heart, *Ratcliff*, I thought of entering with an entirely new work, a necessity imposed by the contest which demanded an opera in only one act. In Cerignola I had found time to work on my *Ratcliff*, so much so that in nearly two and a half years I had almost brought it into port. In 1888 there were only a few scenes to go, but I had put the score aside and from then on had done no more work on it.

In January of 1888 I had gone to Naples to see Puccini, who was giving *Le Villi* at the San Carlo. He said to me: "You still have the idea of *Ratcliff*? Listen to me: *Guglielmo* can never be your first opera; first think of making a bit of a name, sacrificing a part of your ideals, and then later you can assert yourself." Thus the idea to try another opera had gradually taken root in me; but I waited for a propitious occasion. Now there was just that: the Sonzogno contest for an opera in one act.

I set about looking for a good librettist, but didn't find one: that is, I found as many as I wanted, but they all asked for money. That I didn't have, however, and couldn't come up with any. I turned to Ferdinando Fontana; to all those whom I had known in those early days when

I was in Milan; to those whom I knew in Naples. But I didn't find anyone. All asked me for the same thing in advance: money. Then I had an idea. The representative from Livorno, the Hon. Novilena, had died and new political elections were to take place. I, by chance, was not enrolled in the lists as a voter (which did not displease me since I have always been somewhat reluctant to vote) but for that occasion I wrote asking my father if he could get the voting certificate for me, which would enable me to take advantage of the 75 per cent reduction on the trains. The ticket from Cerignola to Livorno, with a 75 per cent reduction, permitted me to go to speak about the famous libretto, which was very dear to my heart, with my friend Giovanni Targioni-Tozzetti, a former colleague from school. So my father procured this certificate for me and I, with my 75 per cent, went third class to Livorno—a minimal expense.

At that time there was a musical exposition at Bologna and Martucci conducted *Tristan und Isolde* at the Teatro Comunale. I therefore stopped off at Bologna to attend the performance, which made a great impression on me, and a few hours later left for Livorno.

As soon as I arrived I went to find Targioni. "Can you write me a libretto?" "But I have never written one!" "What does that matter? You are a poet; I will give you the subject." "Well, we'll see; we'll try, we'll attempt it..." "But I need it right away, you understand! I have come expressly from Cerignola to speak to you about it." "Yes, I will give it to you right away, have no fear. What is the subject?" "*Cavalleria rusticana.*" "Ah! They've performed it here in Livorno. A great success. Beautiful idea!" "I tell you right off that I would like to stay very close to the original... except that I would add a few lyrical pieces, so as to be able to compose a bit of music, since with the drama alone one can't take music; I know what, an introductory chorus, a *brindisi* for the Easter Day occasion, etc. And then the other lyrical pieces come by themselves; when the tenor goes off to die, for example, the same words used by Verga can be expanded a little..." "All right; I'll see and let you know something."

And I left, after having done my duty as a voter for the first time in my life. After all, I was still very young.

But in the end the good Targioni answered negatively to my request; he had too much to do then and could not write me a libretto; he wasn't interested.

After returning to Cerignola, Professor Siniscalchi suggested his friend Rocco Pagliara to me as a librettist.[12] Pagliara answered that he would accept the undertaking only from the publisher who was to acquire my opera and naturally with the positive assurance of being paid. This contest was a means open to me by Sonzogno and I considered the hope of winning it a way of improving my state. But the hundred lire as a director and the few piano lessons, added to which two lessons a week at the Filarmonica in Canosa—a town several miles distant from Cerignola—did not permit me the luxury of paying for a libretto. I broke off dealings with Pagliara, wrote to Cave and other friends in Livorno to press Targioni to write me the libretto, and finally I had the solemn promise of a *Cavalleria rusticana*.

I waited vainly for a while for the libretto and many times wrote Targioni asking him to keep his promise. White waiting, I thought about the finale more than anything else. I heard that *"Hanno ammazzato compare Turiddu"* ringing in my ears, but didn't see the possibility of it coming off if I couldn't find the phrase and concluding orchestral harmonies which would make a strong effect. I don't know how it happened, but the finale dropped all of a sudden into my mind, in a flash, one morning on the main street of Canosa while I was going to give a lesson. And they were those same seventh chords which I have scrupulously kept in the manuscript. Thus I began my opera at the end.

And then, on postcards, a part of the solicited verses arrived for me. I had barely fifty days ahead of me! So!

When I received the opening chorus of the libretto in the mail (I thought of the *Siciliana* in the Prelude later), I very contentedly said to my wife:

"Today we must make a big expense."

"What is that?"

"An alarm clock."

"And what for?"

"To wake me up tomorrow at dawn to begin writing *Cavalleria rusticana*."

That expense meant a great alteration in our monthly budget, but I managed it without difficulty. We went out together for the great purchase, and by bargaining spent nine lire. I think that if I were to return

---

12   See *Personalia: Siniscalchi, Michele.*

to Cerignola today I would still find that alarm clock in good working order.

I set it before going to bed, but that time it wasn't needed, since during the night (it was 3 February 1889), precisely at three o'clock the second Mimì was born, my dear little angel, the first of my children. Nonetheless, I kept the promise I made myself and in the morning began to write the opening chorus of *Cavalleria*.

I received the verses a bit at a time, but I already had the situations in my mind. I had identified myself with the drama to such an extent that I musically felt it inside me. I liked the verses and immediately began to compose the music; without a piano, however, since I didn't have one in Cerignola![13] When I went to give lessons to my students I tried over what I had conceived and written as I was waiting on the young ladies.

I tried it over and was completely content, really content. As soon as I returned home I made corrections on those pieces already completed and went ahead; meanwhile Targioni continued writing the libretto.

But one day he said to me, "Listen. I have too much to do; I must go to Bagni di Lucca and am writing no more. There is a little lacking at the end but all the same I have had to be replaced by a friend." And he chose Guido Menasci, whom I did not know, whom I had never seen in Livorno. The libretto, therefore, was not written by the two authors together; it was done first by one and then by the other. Targioni wrote most of it, Menasci finished it.

There was however something in the libretto which I didn't like: there was a *stornello*.[14] "But *stornelli* are Tuscan, not Sicilian!" I said. "It's not right, this Tuscan *stornello*..." But I later found the reason even for the *stornello*. Turiddu was a soldier on the continent, not on the island. Coming back to Sicily, he swaggered before all the girls, smoked a Virginia cigar and gave himself airs because he had been in Milan. (All this, after all, is also in Verga's drama, which is truly a masterpiece.) And so it was plausible that he had also taught his mistress, Lola, this Tuscan *stornello*, and that she would sing it as a jest. This is the ready answer.

Someone has said that this *stornello* is "not very original." I say more: this *stornello* is not original at all, so much so that even in the scores for voice and piano there is a note which says just this: "imitation of an old *stornello*." Certain farfetched critics could do less than spit out their

---

13   But see *Personalia: Giannini Brothers*.
14   An improvised song.

Mascagni and his librettists, Giovanni Targioni-Tozzetti and Guido Menasci (l. to r.)

words, when these words make one laugh, if not weep, with compassion. I always walk straight ahead on my road, and I never turn to see who is throwing stones at me. If on the way I find someone who is going my way, I take his arm. Doing this will prevent me, I am sure, from finding myself face to face with those critics!

It's been fifty-three years since I've written *Cavalleria* and there still hasn't been one critic, one journalist, one friend who has asked me: "Tell me something—who wrote the *Siciliana*, sung in Sicilian dialect, for you?" It's strange, no one has yet asked me about it. *Ergo*: Rocco de Zerbi, who was a great politician and an excellent journalist, had a brother. This brother was a ne'er-do-well; he played and spent much of the good Rocco's money. Rocco, however, was not inclined to spend like his brother. One day Rocco became annoyed and came to Cerignola to speak with Beppe Pavoncelli, who was the greatest farmer in all of Europe, such a great farmer that the Italian government wanted to name him a minister. (They named him Minister of Public Works, though he hadn't even built a cottage.)

In agreement with Pavoncelli, Rocco, to get rid of this brother who was always in his office asking for money, sent him to Cerignola. Pavoncelli said, "I'll accept him with pleasure; Giacomino is such a clever boy..." He was a tiny little man, elegant.

So this young man came to Cerignola, to our town circle, and he immediately became my friend. In the evening he accompanied me to my house; I went with him, then he came with me... it was always like this. Once he said to me, "I, too, have written books of poetry; tomorrow I'll bring you some." In fact, the next day he brought me two of them. In one of these I read some verses in Sicilian dialect which ran:

> "Brunetta chi hai di latti la cummisa.
> Sì! bianca e rossa come una cerasa..."

"Holy God!" I said. "How wonderful it would be to set this to music! I'll omit 'Brunetta', change the line like this, 'O Lola ch'hai di latti la cammisa...' and make it the tenor's song to put in the Prelude of the opera!" Then I said to Giacomino, "You know, that little book of yours gave me great pleasure; I found verses there which I like so much that I set them to music right away." "Let's go to the Circolo and let me hear them." We closed ourselves in a room and I let him hear the song. "However, you must give me your permission, otherwise I cannot send it to the contest." "What do you think! Anyway, it's not mine; it's a popular thing... And where will you put it!" I wanted to put it in the Prelude of the opera, but how can I put a song in a symphonic prelude! There has only been Rossini, the musician with the best initiative, the profoundest of all, the most powerful creator who put a chorus in a prelude. In Meyerbeer's *Dinorah* there is also something similar, but a sole tenor voice in a prelude seems a bit hazardous to me... I'm afraid... nevertheless I'll think about it." Thus I wrote the Prelude with the *Siciliana*.

Here, then, is the man who really created that song; the good Giacomino de Zerbi. No one ever knew this. Giacomino has never had any recognition, any honor, but it really was he who inspired that song in me, which thousands of listeners have applauded, and which constituted for me such a daring thing then that I didn't have the courage to send it to the contest commission.

And so I composed *Cavalleria*.

The first draft of the opera finished, I wrote out the complete orchestral score which cost me enormous effort, since time was short; the orchestral score done, I had to make, in fair copy, the reduction for voice and piano. I who from the beginning was afraid of not being in time to submit the work, was terrified at the thought of arranging the entire opera for voice and piano and I was so disheartened that I was ready to abandon everything and lose my hard labors and those of my librettists! Fortunately, there is a *bête* for everyone: my Titania, my dear and intelligent little dog, jumped up on my thighs (I should say on my hams) and began to kiss me and tell me many things in her infantile jargon (she was a little older than two years), including the fact that I had been neglecting her. I must confess, however, that in that first moment I could have taken her by the collar and thrown her out the window. Nevertheless her yelping calmed me and I tried to translate those tears and entreaties of hers. At first I thought that she was singing, "*Carulì*" by Mo. Costa, but then I realized that "*Carulì*" is a happy song... I listened carefully and it seemed to me that she was singing the aria of Santuzza.... Poor beast! I said to myself, she has already learned my opera; and I was moved... but after short reflection I dried the tears that had not yet appeared in my eyes and I completed my thought out loud; indeed, it will surely be a dog who will sing my music! But I again set about translating that dirge, with the tenacity of Andrea Maffei translating German poetry, and finally I came to understand that which my Titania wanted to tell me. She who had seen my discomfort and humiliation put me back on the road to reason, and in her look, in her kisses, in her yelping I read a reproof, a hope, an encouragement. In that moment I took heart; now that I think about it in cold blood I am frightened by that resolution which could have cost me so dearly. I closed myself in my study and for seven consecutive days I worked from 16 to 18 hours a day. I did the impossible. Thus on 26 May 1889, at exactly midnight, the opera was entirely completed. On the 27th I took the two scores to the binder and didn't budge from there until they were given back to me bound and dry. Meanwhile, during those six hours in the binder's shop, I copied the libretto so neatly that I did not recognize myself, so I worked in front of a mirror. I was radiant. I was happy, I did not think of the outcome of the contest. It seemed to me that the only difficulty to overcome was having the score arrive in time. All appeared rosy to me, including the wife of the binder who was prune-colored; all seemed merry to me, even the face of that poor devil who cursed all the saints while binding those two poor volumes. It seemed to me that the sun sweetly caressed my curly blond hair (when I was five it was that color) while the rain and hail poured down combined with thunder and lightning and other edibles. All was joy for me; the barking of my little dog (Titania always came with me, even to the binder's) sounded joyfully in my ears and seemed to say:

"Tempo è si mormori da ognuno il tenero
canto che i palpiti raddoppia al cor."[15]

In short, my heart opened itself to hope. I was transfigured. I looked in the mirror and even it answered me: hope!

At three I returned home and gave the last touches to *Cavalleria*. I had had a small string put in the reduction for voice and piano and put the libretto there so that it could easily be extracted. (The rules of the contest said that the libretto was to be together with the vocal score.) Then I prepared the sealed envelopes, affixed the motto—PAX—and added below, "With the consent of Verga."

But now a battle arose within me. Looking at this, my opera, I had the impression of having committed a crime against myself, against my ideas. In fact, I was working at that time on *Ratcliff*, and in *Ratcliff* there is an elevation of concept which has nothing to do with *Cavalleria*. So I resolved to send an act of *Ratcliff*, writing to the Commission. At that time, however, I didn't realize that in *Cavalleria* there is much humanity and that the passion is expressed with an impetus and fire which are the Sicilian temperament exactly; the secret of the opera's success consists precisely in this. There was still the delusion of the student in me; of the student with good will who believes in the efficiency of technique, in the importance of nobility of concept, who disdains to consider the sentiments common to all, and denies the popular passions as the inspiration of a true and just expression of art. A great error. It is not superior concepts, more or less elevated sentiments, which make art; but rather it is art, true art, which is capable of lifting and ennobling even the most instinctive passions.

So because I tormented myself with that problem, whether the music of *Cavalleria* was musical art or not, I began to think, "I won't send the opera to the contest at all." And I wrote a letter to Giacomo Puccini saying to him: "I am in a moment of great uncertainty. I have composed an opera for the Sonzogno contest, but no longer have the courage to send it. It is not that the opera is not satisfactory; indeed, I tell you the truth when I say that it came so spontaneously, all of a sudden, that I wrote the entire work in a month. However, dear Giacomo, to me it seems so inferior to *Guglielmo Ratcliff*, on which I have been working for some time now and of which, indeed, I have completed the final act, that I feel quite undecided as to what to do. It seems to me that *Caval-*

---

15   "It is the time when the tender song which redoubles the heart beats is murmured
      by everyone." (From the opening chorus of *Cavalleria*.)

leria is not on a plane with *Ratcliff,* neither in conception nor in expression. But I cannot send a four-act opera. I had the idea of sending only the fourth act, but then I would lose the contest... I do not have much faith in contests, but then one never knows...."

Puccini answered me: "You are certainly right, especially after the fiasco I had in a contest with *Le Villi,* an opera which later had a great success. Which shows that the commission was wrong and that, therefore, you are right to doubt contests...."

As the termination date drew nearer, the discussions with my wife increased; I became discouraged, she excited; I was pessimistic, she shone with faith. "In a word," I said, "I don't feel like making myself a laughing stock with my enemies!" And she: "That's all right; he laughs best who laughs last." By now there were only three more days. It was the last discussion. "There's no more of anything because I've lost everything." My wife didn't bother to answer and went in another room. Only later did I know the rest. Without my knowing it she had gone to wrap hurriedly the package with *Cavalleria.* It was shortly before the mail was due to go. That day it poured rain. For fear of not arriving in time, my wife had not even taken an umbrella. She put a scarf over her head and ran through that torrent of rain. Near the post office she encountered Maestro Reale: "But where are you going in this weather?" "To the post office; I want to send off my husband's opera even if he doesn't want to." "Let me worry about it; give it here and stand in that doorway; can't you see that you're soaked from head to foot?" He took the package and ran off. My wife didn't move from the middle of the street. She was too anxious to see him return to think about herself. She followed him with her eyes. She saw him go in the post office; she waited, undaunted by the downpour, for a few minutes which seemed interminable to her, until Maestro Reale came back. "What, you stayed here? But don't you feel the rain?" My wife smiled, "Oh yes, but I didn't think about it. Thank you, Maestro." In conclusion: he had been sheltered and she was soaked. It was a fortunate encounter.... She took the receipt for the package and ran off. When she came back home she was wringing wet. "Now I'm content. Here's your receipt."

I was more than humiliated. "Ah good! Are you happy? Now you'll see a real fiasco!" "Nonsense, I'm sure that it won't be a fiasco." "I too! It will be a double fiasco!"[16] Instead it was a victory.

All the same, *Cavalleria* arrived late. The final day had passed and Sonzogno would have had the right to reject it, but partly because the package was sent anonymously, as the terms of the contest demanded and they wouldn't have known to whom to return it, and partly because of that Providence which I have mentioned, the fact is that the opera came to be added to the list of the other seventy-two contestants.

And note this: while it is true that in everything there is a destiny, often people's good sense and intelligence are also able to modify it. This shows how much importance in the world the choice of people has, to whom is confided the task of judging or making a decision in regard to others. The luck of my opera in that contest was to be examined by a Commission composed of men truly competent, just, and of pure conscience. My opera arrived three days after the contest was closed. The Commission could have refused it; instead it was accepted, because those gentlemen reasoned in a manner which, after all, was logical: "Why must a precise hour be set: until noon of a certain Thursday... And if one hasn't finished copying the opera?... And if one is waiting for the copyist to bring him the last four pages?... Or if the mail is slow? It is not right to be so intransigent!" And I was accepted like the others.

So after a few days I had to write Puccini again: "You know, by now *Cavalleria* has gone to the contest. My wife sent it for me without my knowing anything about it..."

Puccini, before receiving my second letter, wrote me: "Listen, do this: I have spoken to my publisher, Giulio Ricordi; send me the opera before sending it to the contest; we'll look it over." And I: "My Giacomo, I have already sent it. Pity!" "Well, send me something, if you can write it out from memory; if it comes back to your mind." "Yes, I can send you Santuzza's whole scene with Mamma Lucia. If you tell me that Ricordi will take my opera I'll withdraw it from the contest." In fact, I sent him Santuzza's scene with Mamma Lucia. He answered: "You know? Ricordi has seen it, the stuff you sent me; he is not convinced; therefore I cannot advise you. Perhaps the opera as a whole will go all right, but from that which you sent he did not remain convinced because he finds your

---

16   A traditional play on the Italian word for wine-bottle, *fiasco*, which is also made
     with two bottles (*fiasci*) joined together.

music somewhat daring in its harmonies." "Well, patience. By now it's gone. We'll speak about it no more. It's up to the contest."

And it was up to the contest!

From that moment I began to have the strongest apprehensions. The history of *Cavalleria* is one of glory, but for me it is also the memory of a period of anxiety and anguish much greater than any other I ever felt during my career as a musician. During the long wait, in the silence of not knowing, my courage and hope dwindled day by day. No period in my life seems as long as those months which passed between sending off my work and the first results of the contest. It seems to me, thinking about it again, that my whole life is summed up in the spasms, the dreams, the illusions, the fears and the mistrust of those distant days, still so vivid and close to my heart.

It was on 22 February 1890 (the opera had been sent off on 3 June 1889) that I received from the secretary of the Commission a telegram which summoned me to Rome.[17] I ran there quickly with a heart torn by hope and agitated by the most foolish illusions. I arrived in Rome on Monday, 24 February, at three in the afternoon. I wanted a hotel with a name which would provide a good omen for me, so I chose the Albergo del Sole[18] in the Piazza del Pantheon. I didn't tell anyone that I paid one lira a night, but the name was fine and I liked it. I imagined that it would bring me luck. In the event it did prove a good omen for me.

So I went to the Albergo del Sole, then to the Royal Academy of Santa Cecilia. I found no one. I decided to present myself at eleven on Tuesday as the telegram stated. In fact, on the morning of that day, at eleven, I went again to the Academy and was very courteously received by Comm. Marchetti and by the secretary, Parisotti. But here the surprises began.

Since the first part of February it had been known through the newspapers that the Commission had held back its verdict concerning the operas submitted to the contest, due to the great number of them (73) and due also to so few of them being discarded, since most of these

---

17　The 10th article of the contest rules as stated in the *Teatro Illustrato* read: "The operas must be anonymous, but they will carry an epigraph which will be repeated on the outside of an envelope enclosing the name and address of the contestant." Mascagni's motto was PAX (see p.52, above).

18　Literally, Hotel of the Sun.

works were recognized as being very good and thus the work and responsibility of the Commission was increased. It later declared that in order to judge better the three works to be selected for performance it would summon the composers to Rome so as to perceive the effect of their operas and better understand their intentions. When I came to Rome I did not know how many of us had been summoned; I quickly learned, however, that there were five in the first batch, I among them; immediately afterwards six more were called. Thus the real battle was fought in Rome.

Among those eleven there figured many known names, such as Bossi, professor at the Royal Conservatory in Naples; Ferroni, first professor of serious composition at the Royal Conservatory at Milan; and Pizzi, the fortunate winner of many contests, the most recent of which had been the one in Bologna with his opera *Ratcliff*, given in October of 1899 at the Comunale in that city.

I was desolate and discouraged. Then, too, for me, who had set *Cavalleria* to music, there was an omen which could be termed tragic, or so it seemed to me at the time: Maestro Gastaldon had set the same subject to music; after having diluted it into three acts and with the support of a group of gentlemen from the Roman aristocracy he had been able to present a magisterial performance at the Costanzi which was a clamorous success. Time later determined, even in this instance, how short a time the artificial flicker of fame and the ephemeral flash of friendly theaters last, but for me, in those days, that *contretemps* was enough to throw me into a deep prostration. I also felt myself to be in a state of absolute inferiority, the reason being that as long as the contest remained anonymous I could be the equal of the others, but, summoning eleven people whose names had been revealed, then other influences began to work. I had no protection in Rome, no acquaintances: I was alone, abandoned, without knowing to whom to turn for assistance. The one hope which I had was in my playing of the opera, of thus being able to communicate to the Commission all my soul, heart and ability which I had put into it.

My first reaction to these facts was profound discouragement. But I rallied immediately. The devil! Was I not sure of myself and of my music?

I saw Bossi, Pizzi and Seppilli again with pleasure, old (in a manner of speaking) companions from the Conservatory. We were always together and this pleased me a great deal. It was very beautiful to live communally with clever and studious lads such as these. I was the butt of our conversations; they found me greatly changed, especially in morale, and they said I no longer was the Mascagni of before. Poor lads! They did not know what this contest meant to me. To them it mattered little: Bossi was professor at the Conservatory of San Pietro a Maiella, a month earlier Pizzi had sold an opera to Ricordi for twenty thousand lire, and Seppilli ate, drank and slept *chez* Sonzogno!

They had good reason to find me changed! When the readings began, I gave up the first place (which was mine by right) to Bossi who was older and to Giordano because he had a sick stomach. The next night — Wednesday — at nine it was my turn. It is useless to describe my condition. I shall only say that I was unable to eat any food the whole day.

I went before the Commission in a deplorable state of distrust, so that my performance of my opera on the piano came out very badly; my hands trembled and I lost my voice. I nonetheless thought that the proof of the technical ability in my music would at least be obvious to the judges, all eminent musicians: Filippo Marchetti, Director of the Liceo Musicale of Santa Cecilia, composer of *Ruy Blas*; Pietro Platania, the great contrapuntist, Director of the Conservatory of Naples; Giovanni Sgambati, professor at Santa Cecilia; Amintore Galli, professor at the Conservatory of Milan; and the Marquis D'Arcais, exquisite musician and great critic on the paper *L'Opinione*. Even the secretary, the excellent teacher Parisotti, was an honored musician.

And how did they run the contest? This is something that pleased me a great deal when I learned of it. They had divided up the operas (no less than seventy-three) in five boxes, about fifteen per box, and sent one box to each of the men on the Commission, who held them a fixed number of days, sufficient to examine all fifteen operas. After the examination, each one was supposed to send back his box, containing also the examiner's opinion of every opera. The men on the Commission then exchanged these boxes in such a way that in the end all the operas bore the opinion of the five examiners.

When this work was finished, the Commission assembled to discuss each individual opinion and to issue the total one. Such opinions result almost always in an extraordinary equanimity and exactitude. A curious and appealing system, that. They had allotted two years to the examination of the operas, not just a day.[19] (Two years to examine seventy-three

---

19   Mascagni's two years are from July 1888, when the contest was announced in the *Teatro Illustrato*, to 17 May 1890, the first performance. The actual time of examination must have been about eight months.

operas! Today they examine two hundred of them in a week. It's because today they run a contest knowing in advance who will win it; at that time they couldn't know.) It was because of this, because no injustices were committed, that I won the contest. On this subject there comes to mind something that occurred when I presented myself at the contest. It was something extraordinary. At a certain point Sgambati asked me, "You are Mascagni?" "Yes." He said, "Will you explain why you have been recommended by so many people? You know that in a contest it really isn't good to have yourself recommended." "I?! Maestro, there is certainly a misunderstanding. I don't know anyone here. It is the first time I've come to Rome; who could recommend me? Perhaps you are confusing me with someone else." "I was joking when I said it. Of the seventy-three contestants there was only one who did not have recommendations and it is that one who will win."

I presented myself at nine. I entered a rather large low hall of the Santa Cecilia Academy. At last I was before my judges. I could not express the feeling which completely overcame me in that supreme hour. I was seized by a great timidity, or rather by a feeling of dismay. I was playing my trump card. I well knew what the decision of those five professors represented for me. The prize and performance of the opera mattered little; what mattered was to know at least if I could realize the dreams of my mind, yearning for the countless intoxications of art and fame, or if I must remain forever the humble little provincial maestro, with his sublime hopes folded up and put back in the suitcase.

Yet, in spite of my natural emotion, in spite of my dismay of feeling alone and without help or advice, in spite of my uneasiness, almost fear, of finding myself before so many illustrious men, nevertheless, in that moment, which was without doubt the most important of my life, I had the spirit, perhaps I should say the curiosity, to attentively inspect the new scene which was present to my somewhat stunned, but always eager and inquisitive eyes.

I knew that the Commission was made up of five musicians, and in those days I had learned to know them all by sight. But there were six of them in the room because the secretary also was present at the judging of the operas. When I entered the room all watched me with what seemed to me a suspicious air, but I didn't get ruffled and I thought it was I who should be suspicious of them. Altogether, my first impression was of an excessively severe atmosphere. Sgambati was seated in an armchair behind the table and sat as if he were in a bishop's chair, surrounded by D'Arcais and Galli. All three stared at me in a characteristic manner: Sgambati half shut his eyes to wrinkle his forehead, or wrinkled his forehead to half shut his eyes; D'Arcais had a look which he wanted to be gruff, but was a sweet smile; it seemed that Galli looked at me more with his mind than with his eyes; Platania was on the divan, wrapped up in an improbable fur coat and looking at me obliquely without moving; Marchetti was on his feet, with his hands thrust in his trouser pockets and staring at me tranquilly; while the secretary, Parisotti, completed the scene with the background of his small blond beard.

A few moments of perfect silence ensued. I must have been very pale, for Marchetti came up to me and said a few words of encouragement.

His mild voice had an immediate effect on my heart which suddenly roused itself. And I saw the scene transformed: Sgambati's frown was some sort of borrowed pose, perhaps to correspond to the importance of the magnificent armchair which seemed like a bishop's. D'Arcais' gruff look was conquered by the sweetness of his smile; and Gatti's mind cheered up, because he remembered that I had been his student at the Milan Conservatory. Platania now had a straightforward and almost grateful look because I had set a subject from his Sicily to music; and Marchetti openly smiled at me and patted me on the shoulder, as if I were an old friend of his. The first impression had totally vanished.

They put me through an interrogation on general lines, which raised my spirits all the more for its intimate and good-natured manner.

Suddenly one of them realized that I had a small bundle of music under my arm. He said to me, "What do you have there under your arm?" "I have the Prelude to the opera." "What? You didn't send it?" "Yes, I sent a bit of a prelude, but I have the real one here." "Why?" "Because I was afraid. Since there is a *siciliana* sung by the tenor behind the curtain, I thought, 'They will take it for too hazardous a thing; there is the chance that it will do me harm instead of good,' and so I didn't send it." "Well then, why did you bring it?" "If the gentlemen of the Commission want to hear it.... There is no obligation on their part, that is understood." "Let's hear it, let's hear it."

Thus the Prelude was to be accorded a hearing and the reading began at 9:30. I sat at the grand piano with the piano-vocal score; on either side were Marchetti and Parisotti who turned the pages; Platania sat on the divan; on a large table had been placed a music rack with the orchestra score and in front of the music rack sat Sgambati with D'Arcais on his left and Galli with the libretto in hand on his right. It was the decisive moment. My fright was such that I was unable to shake off the coolness of the judges. I began with assurance but inside I trembled all over. I played the Prelude, then launched into the *Siciliana*, singing it

as best I could. At the end of the song the Commission was enthusiastic. I was blushing with emotion. "But this is a wonderful piece!" they
said, "why didn't you send it?" "I repeat, it seemed a dangerous thing
to.... You know, I have lead feet...." "Let us hear it again." Then Sgambati exclaimed, "There are some very original things here! But why
don't you repeat it at the end of the opera?" "I can't; I thought about
it...." "And why not?" "Because the tenor sings this serenade to his
beloved, to Lola, but when he goes off to die, at the end of the opera,
he goes to die for Santuzza and no longer for this woman. How could
he sing it again?" "You are right." Then Sgambati asked the others in a
low voice, "At the Costanzi... are there two harps?" I realized that the
ice was broken. They wanted me to repeat the *Siciliana* and the Prelude
ended as a real success.

Then they began to debate: "But will a tenor voice be heard behind
a curtain?" "Gentlemen," I said, "everything is heard behind the curtain, since the hubbub of the people in the theater can be heard on the
stage, therefore everything which is done on the stage can be heard also
in the theater... So, if you want to keep it...." "Yes, yes; all the more so
because you are not deceiving anybody since the themes which are in
it are already in the opera; this is really the Prelude to the opera." I was
very glad they accepted it because I liked it.

In the continuation of the playing, Marchetti was a great help to me:
he played and sang with me. In the Prayer, in the duets and in the
choruses he perfectly rendered the most important parts which I would
not have been capable of executing by myself. This touched me greatly; the good heart of this illustrious musician who held out a brotherly
hand to a yet unknown youth who perhaps would fall back again into
obscurity after a moment of luminous hope appears before me in all its
greatness. Oh, how I would have liked to kiss that good and generous
hand! But I blessed it while I played.

One of my most serious preoccupations in those days had been that
of performing my opera well before the Commission. While I knew that
the other young colleagues of mine had a singer, a violinist or someone
with them who would help in the performance, I was there alone,
without acquaintances, without anyone, and would have to go to the
final examination without the least help. My consolation, therefore,
was immense when Maestro Marchetti all of a sudden offered me that
which I lacked... and even more, I was unaware of what the fate of *Cavalleria* would be, but if it were among those chosen for public performance, I would have to give a good part of the credit to Maestro Mar-

chetti who had so efficaciously cooperated in making my music enjoyable to the examining Commission.

I continued my reading with great spirit. The opening chorus was one of the most relished pieces. The carter's song was judged strong, theatrical and popular. The Prayer pleased more than all the other pieces. Marchetti was enthusiastic; in his excitement he said that the first part of this piece was a block of classical music. Platania approved the inner voices and told me that my studies were complete. The rest went very well. Marchetti embraced me every moment and said under his breath, "Bravo! Good!" and with his finger pointed out to me on the page what it was that he liked. Another outburst of enthusiasm occurred at the entrance of Lola with her *stornello*. Marchetti was moved. All held pieces of paper and took notes every moment. The *brindisi* was much liked and Sgambati said, "Discussion is useless; this is music which pleases the public." I took advantage of this remark to say that I thought I was supposed to write music for the public, theatrical music, as prescribed by the rules of the contest. And I said this because the greater part of the libretti set in this contest were mythological, idealistic ones and in oratorio style.

Finally we arrived at the Finale, at the question mark. I would not have believed it but it produced an enormous impression. The reading over, I offered to write a new finale if the Commission thought it would be necessary. But they told me no, and indeed accepted that one completely.

Then Sgambati asked me a thousand questions, always in a friendly manner and I said that I wished to look over my work again. Sgambati said, "Oh! there will be time before it is performed at the Costanzi..." but realized he had gone too far and immediately recovered with a smile: "if it is to be performed." I understood and smiled with him. D'Arcais asked me about Verga's literary rights; I told him about Salvestri. D'Arcais concluded, "In any case we must think about it."

Not the smallest observation was made in the field of theory, instrumentation and part writing. The Commission did not find a single one to make to me. And I was proud of this. They liked the subject and the libretto was judged excellent.

The audition over, the five maestri began to discuss the merit of my work. I stood apart, but from time to time was obliged to answer various questions tossed at me. During the continuation of the discussion I again heard the possibility of a performance hinted at, at which point I imprudently chimed in and chattered on, radiant with hope and joy.

Then the maestri, as if by magic, suddenly stopped talking and told me the audition was over and that I could leave.

I remained greatly mortified and recognized all the consequences of my imprudence. But on the other hand my heart was bursting in my chest! I humbly left, red as a cherry. Yet, as I was leaving the room, I thought I saw good natured smiles on the faces of the maestri.

Maestro Marchetti accompanied me as far as the corridor; when he had energetically shaken my hand, he said some words to me which I did not understand, but his voice was very sweet and his eyes were misty....

Down below, at the door of Santa Cecilia, I found my young colleagues waiting for me, anxious to know the outcome of the audition and above all my personal impression. I answered with enthusiasm and naively told them of my great hopes. My friends derided me and noisily cheered my sublime ingenuousness.

We went to drink something at the Gambrinus and for the rest of the evening nothing was spoken of but my provinciality. They said that only one who came from a town like Cerignola could believe in winning a contest solely because the judges on the Commission had said some kind words to him. "Go on," they said, "you're a real simpleton if you delude yourself that they don't say the same things to the others. Those on the Commission are obliged to act kindly to all the contestants."

I went back to my little room at the Albergo del Sole, full of sadness. But as I was going off to sleep I again saw the frank and good face of Maestro Marchetti, I again heard his sweet voice and I went to sleep with great hopes in my heart.

I got up around nine, having decided to leave for Cerignola in the afternoon; but since Galli, the preceding evening, had expressed a desire to talk with me, I went immediately from the Piazza della Rotonda to the Via dei Greci near the Academy library. A thousand ideas whirled through my head, and I had no idea what streets I travelled.

In the hall of the Academy I found Galli and Platania who welcomed me with the most genial deference. "I have a happy bit of news to give you," Galli said to me. "You are the candidate for the first prize. The Commission was unanimous in its verdict."

I felt a pang in my heart and had to lean against a table so as not to fall, so strong was the emotion of that moment. So my expectations had come to pass! And in that moment there passed through my mind the long labors undergone, my wife's loving comfortings and counsels to persevere and hope, the exhortations of my good friends in Cerignola.

I don't know what I answered Galli; I only know that he insisted at great length that I stay a few days longer in Rome to await the official verdict of the Commission. And because I remarked to him, with a contrite air, that reasons extraneous to my desire, but absolutely unavoidable, hindered my staying (in fact I only had enough money for the return trip), he insisted anew and ended by letting me read the Commission's report which proposed the awarding of the first prize to me.

"What will be a source of pride to you," added Platania, "is that in this contest the names of the most accredited musicians figure and you

Prof. Amintore Galli

have outdistanced them all." The good Platania then dwelled at length with me on the originality and technical worth of the opera, giving me some suggestions for performance.

What greatly amazed me was that all my judges already knew *Cavalleria* by memory. Platania, in a friendly way, advised a few cuts in the Prayer, adding that according to him the most beautiful piece in the opera was Lola's *stornello*, which constituted a magnificent contrast in the drama's development. "It is a piece which will have a great success in the theater, it's a real *trovata*. There is no doubt the whole opera will be given a very happy reception by the public, because the music is fundamentally honest and above all clear and the language of the characters is expressed in an admirable manner." Maestro Platania also exhorted me to stay a few more days and await the Commission's decision.

I left the Academy with my heart swelling with joy and returned to the hotel to write my wife a long letter telling her everything and saying that I was forced to remain in Rome a few days longer.

Later I went to the Corso and there met Galli. "Bravo," he said to me, "I am glad to run into you. I saw Edoardo Sonzogno a short while ago. He has taken lodgings in the Hôtel del Quirinale and wants to meet you." When, in thanking him for the news, I observed that I would no doubt be uneasy in the presence of the publisher and that I would like to be introduced to him by someone, Galli remarked, "No, no, go alone. Sonzogno is a very likeable man and very plain. You will see that he will receive you immediately and will treat you with the greatest deference."

I departed from the Maestro, thanking him once again for his valuable co-operation and assuring him that I would go immediately to the Hôtel del Quirinale. "The time is ripe," Galli himself had told me. Sonzogno was at the hotel to settle his affairs and his correspondence. There was no time to be lost. Therefore I turned my steps towards Piazza Venezia and Via Nazionale, not without having given a keen look at my clothes which were neither in the latest style nor perfectly new... just the opposite. But I took courage. By now, after the favorable verdict of the Commission, clothes took a back seat.

I arrived at the Quirinale and announced myself. The hotel porters looked me over from head to toe, hesitating at first whether or not they should announce my visit to the publisher. "Wait," one of them said to me, "I shall go and see if Signor Sonzogno is in the hotel."

A few minutes which seemed centuries to me went by. How many ideas passed through my brain in those moments! By now I unconsciously felt that my whole future rested in the hands of this man before whom I would shortly find myself. What impression would he have of me, what would he say to me, what hopes or doubts would he awaken in my heart?

The porter who had taken on the job of announcing my visit to the publisher tore me from my meditations. I understood from his changed demeanor that Sonzogno's welcome would be very favorable. With a quantity of bows and with a solicitude which contrasted profoundly with his previous behavior, he said to me, "This way, please. I shall accompany you myself to Signor Sonzogno's rooms."

I went up the stairs, crossed one of the corridors and found myself in the presence of the publisher. He was seated behind a table on which were piles of correspondence. The man's good natured appearance reassured me. He smiled at me, extending his hand in a friendly manner.

"You are the one who has won the contest? Good, a pleasure to see you. Galli has spoken very highly of you to me. We shall perform your *Cavalleria* immediately and you shall have first-rate singers! You live in a small city in the provinces... Cerignola, right? I must confess that I've never heard of it before, it's a small city in the Puglie, no? And tell me, what is needed to put your opera on the stage?"

I saw that he was afraid of being hit in the pocketbook and thought, "I'm more clever than you," and answered, "Signor Sonzogno, nothing." "What do you mean, nothing?" "Nothing. A small house over here,

the tavern of Mamma Lucia; a small church on the other side . . . everything made out of canvas, painted scenery; two small tables, ten tin
cups, some stools . . . that's all." "Well then, it costs very little." "Nothing, it costs nothing."

I never mentioned that there was also a procession, and there lay my
cleverness. As a matter of fact, the procession was never done during
Sonzogno's lifetime. The Prayer was heard behind the church, but the
monstrance[20] was not seen coming in under a canopy.

"This contest has not been a bad thing." remarked Sonzogno, "and I
have even more reason to be happy since the results seem satisfactory.
I have heard your *Cavalleria* on the piano. Do you want to know my impressions?" "I will be very happy to." "You are a good musician, but I
fear that the opera is not theatrical."

I thanked him for the opinion which he expressed on my worth as a
composer. I could not help, however, pointing out that his doubts of
the opera's theatricality did not seem justified to me. "I composed the
opera in a little more than fifty days, but the choice of subject is something much more long standing. I was present some years ago at a performance of Verga's drama and carried away from it a strong and unforgettable emotion. There was such strong passion in those scenes that
I remained deeply struck by it. From that time on I felt that if a composer knew his business he would create a really theatrical work."

"This is also the opinion of Maestro Galli, for whom I have a high
regard. After all, it is the public which must judge and I shall neglect
nothing so that the opera may be performed under the most favorable
conditions. And if, as is the unanimous hope, you emerge from this trial
the victor, I shall try to facilitate your future position as much as possible."

And so saying he rose from his chair, dismissing me. "We shall see
each other soon in Milan," he said to me. "It will be necessary for you,
in a few days, to come to my office to sort out and transcribe the parts.
If you need some advance on the prize, go to the office." He gave me
his hand, which I gladly took, and left the room.

I rapidly descended the stairs, went through the entrance hall of the
hotel and found myself in the street. At last! I needed air. My heart beat
violently. That interview with Sonzogno, the manner in which it was
carried out, the things which I had heard, all had strongly impressed

20   Receptacle in which the Host is held, carried by the priest and shown to the
     kneeling public.

me. Everything was going according to my desires. By now there was no more doubt. The Commission's verdict of the awarding of the first prize to my opera would soon be officially announced: Sonzogno had assured me of a performance of the work with celebrated artists: I was confident that the favor of the public — the supreme judge — would not be denied me.

Only one thing disturbed me: the opinion expressed by Sonzogno as to the scant theatricality of my work. Could I have been deceived in my choice? Yet Verga's drama had always aroused the liveliest response. And if I had mitigated the violence of those scenes with my music? Sonzogno must surely be well versed in theatrical effects! And why had the Commission not seen this defect?

But here I must make a revelation. Something never said to anyone, and which I had sworn to keep a secret.

No one knew, before the performances at the Costanzi, of the Commission's report. Now I must say that it was I who objected to having that same report made public. Why? Because during my playing of *Cavalleria* the judges had indeed voiced expressions of praise for

my opera, for its technical aspect, for the handling of the voices, for the homogeneity of the orchestration, and this praise had been repeated and even expanded in the report which explicitly affirmed that *Cavalleria* was the best of the seventy-three operas. However, the report concluded with a sentence that made poor Sonzogno's heart jump, and the sentence was nothing less than this: "A pity, however, that this opera is not theatrical." Sonzogno saw the shipwreck of his contest's purpose, I saw

Edoardo Sonzogno

myself diminished in advance in the public's estimation.

On the other hand, it was not right for the judges to put themselves before the public. They were only to choose the operas worthy of performance and it was up to the public to say whether those same operas were theatrical or not. It was the public I had thought of when I composed my opera, or better, I also had the public in mind. It was not to my advantage to predispose them in this way. Thus I arranged it so that the report would be published after the judgment of the public itself. And I must add that I guessed correctly. From the first orchestra rehearsals the judges themselves realized that *Cavalleria* was very theatrical. Indeed, I remember that one of them said to me, "But why did you play it so badly for us?" And he was not wrong.

Several months later, when *Cavalleria rusticana* was performed and had the success known to all, Edoardo Sonzogno, when I reminded him of that first interview and his doubts, also loyally answered me that he had been mistaken.

8

CERIGNOLA. MILAN. RETURN
TO ROME (March-May 1890)

I stayed in Rome for several more days. As soon as the Commission
officially announced the results of the contest, i.e., that my *Cavalleria*
had been chosen for performance along with two other operas, *Rudello* by Ferroni and *Labilia* by Spinelli, I left for Cerignola, anxious to see
and embrace again my wife and my delight, Mimì.

Without offending any city, it is without doubt that Cerignola loves
me. Who was there at that time who would have given me something
to eat and believed in me as that city did? There is even a book written
by a man from Cerignola, *Pietro Mascagni and "Cavalleria", Seen from
Cerignola.*[21] Much foolishness is said in that book, but the author only
repeats how much the people of Cerignola loved Mascagni, and it is the
truth. One has to admit that it is the truth.

I was starting to become known in Cerignola. I didn't have a penny,
but in the meantime I had won the contest with *Cavalleria*. The mayor
of Cerignola had helped me, giving me the money to go to Rome, since
I didn't have even that. "Don't worry, I'll give you the money." He was
very rich.

When the news came to Cerignola, however — the *Tribuna* reported
it — that I was among the eleven young contestants chosen by the Commission in Rome to play their operas, those in the rival party said, "All
right, his name is there too. But who knows?" When later, in a second
selection, those eleven names were reduced to three, published in al-
phabetical order (Ferroni, number one; Mascagni, number two; Spinelli, number three), then they said, "But he's not the first!" In short, at
Cerignola they didn't believe anything, so much so that when I
returned to Rome, summoned by the Commission for *Cavalleria* to be
staged at last at the Teatro Costanzi (and that was the worst period, the
most difficult hurdle), they said. "Now we'll see."

Nevertheless, the report that I had turned out the winner of the first
prize in the Sonzogno contest had made a great impression in Cerignola. I had a very warm welcome from the innumerable friends who

---

21   Daniele Cellamare, *Mascagni e la "Cavalleria" visti da Cerignola.* Rome: Fratelli
      Palombi Editori, 1941. (See *Personalia.*)

had always shown faith in me and they warmly defended me against the attacks of the rival party.

Giving in to their insistence, I prepared a concert in which I performed, two days after my arrival, the Prelude and Intermezzo from *Cavalleria* with my students from the Filarmonica. In spite of the small number of rehearsals—having been invited to go to Milan—my dear students played with extraordinary care and the whole program, especially the two pieces from *Cavalleria*, was received with enthusiastic and interminable applause by the public which crowded the theater.

This overwhelming reception, however, did not prevent the *Risveglio* from printing these words a few days later: "If all the pieces from *Cavalleria* are like those performed by the Filarmonica, the good Romans will really be bored."

The concert in Cerignola took place the evening of 8 March 1890. Two days later I left for Milan, where I arrived the morning of the twelfth, taking lodging at the Albergo dell'Agnellino.

On the Corso Vittorio Emanuele I met Giacomo Puccini. We embraced each other with great emotion and tears glistened in my eyes. Giacomo was radiant with joy over my success. Hardly had the news been spread around Milan than he had hurried to telegraph his congratulations to me in Rome, but his telegram had not reached me.

"I'm crazy to hear your opera. Galli here in Milan has praised it to the skies. In the Galleria nothing is spoken of but you and your opera."

"Listen," I replied, "I must present myself at the Sonzogno office and at one I shall be free. Let's set an appointment. I have a great desire to get together with you, to talk over our Conservatory days, our life together. If you knew how many things I have to tell you!" "Well then, we'll see one another at one o'clock at Biffi's, you must have lunch with me without fail. And during the days you are here in Milan we must not lose sight of one another. I too have many things to tell you."

We parted and I went straight to Via Pasquirolo where I was received with great deference. I was allotted an excellent room with a piano, carpet on the floor, a stove, an electric bell and three or four writing desks, so I could work either seated or standing, near the piano.

How different that room was from my poor little rooms in Cerignola! I lost no time and immediately began working on the parts of the opera. At one I ran to Biffi's. Puccini was waiting for me, and at the table where I sat down I also found Pigna, the publisher of several of my songs which had been well received. Pigna, who had lost no time after the result of the contest and had hurried to run off new editions of these songs, was there to ask me for other small pieces of the same kind and to hear what I thought of my *In filanda*. Along with him I saw Frugatta, Buzzi-Peccia, Mosca, Boscherini and Tedeschi again. All welcomed me and all asked for news of my work.

Many things were discussed. I learned that in Milan the victory had been given to Pizzi and Bossi for sure and that their defeat had given rise to a lot of tiresome talk. No one had even considered me and the news of the prize being conferred on me by the Commission had produced an excellent impression. And for a start postcards had been printed with my picture and the legend, "Pietro Mascagni, Winner of the Sonzogno Contest."

Lunch over, Puccini took me to his house and played several pieces from his *Edgar* on the piano. It was marvelous music, full of inspiration and melodically rich. Giacomo wanted to hear a few pieces from *Cavalleria* and was enthusiastic over them. He found the music very strong and dramatic and above all original. He assured me I would sell the opera under the best of conditions.

Leaving the house after the audition, Giacomo wanted to present me to Giulio Ricordi, who welcomed me with great affability and as an old friend. Ricordi was fully informed of the outcome of the contest and praised me highly, expressing a desire to hear my *Cavalleria*.

I shall always warmly remember the sympathetic and very cordial reception by Ricordi. During the days I remained in Milan I had occasion to see him several times and he always gave me sage advice as to the performance of the opera. He too showed enthusiasm over *Cavalleria*, foreseeing a sure success for it.

Meanwhile, I continued my work on the parts with alacrity at the Sonzogno office and in a few days everything was ready.

I learned that the principal interpreters would be Stagno and Bellincioni, that the Teatro Costanzi would open on 15 April, and that *Cavalleria* would be performed in May.

One morning, leaving the office to see Puccini and finding myself in the Galleria, I met Orsini and with him his friend Maresca. As soon as he saw me, Orsini embraced me and kissed me very effusively, but Maresca withdrew immediately. He still could not pardon me the flight from his company in Cerignola.

I learned much news from Orsini. Above all that the company, after my departure, had travelled and met with various vicissitudes, that it had been disbanded and reformed with new members, that things from the beginning had gone worse rather than better, then changed, and that Maresca had ended up rather well.

In fact, his company had assumed the stature of "primary" and was sought by the most important towns.

Maresca, however, had not forgotten my flight and for a time had not been able to convince himself that I had left him.

"All his anger," Orsini said to me, "stemmed from not being able to recover the suitcase with your *Ratcliff*. If he had been able to seize it for himself, I believe that you would still be in his company — he would never let you leave again."

"Many thanks," I said.

"However," added Orsini, "he has been very pleased over your victory. And when the papers printed the news he said, 'I am really glad. That devil of a Mascagni would have been my fortune if he had remained with the company.' "

I took leave of Orsini asking him to give my regards to Maresca, towards whom, after all, every trace of rancor had disappeared from my heart.

I could not leave Milan — and my departure was imminent, since my wife, who was somewhat jealous, was bombarding me with letters and telegrams — without first making a visit to the Conservatory.

So I took the occasion of the Romaniello Concert, which was given on 16 March 1890, to walk up again the stairs of the Institute, in which I had passed two years of alternate dreams and disillusions.

My entrance stirred up every one of the halls. I was recognized at first sight.

The superintendent (who would have imagined it!) gave me a festive reception. Bazzini, the Director, saw me again with great pleasure and jokingly called out to me. "Here's that dissolute Mascagni." Then he congratulated me on my victory, adding that I had brought honor to the Conservatory of Milan.

On seeing me, Professor Saladino was moved. He embraced me, wanted me to sit next to him, asked me many many questions, and was hurt that in my biography, published in Ricordi's *Gazetta musicale*, his name had not been mentioned. He had reason to be hurt, since during my stay at the Conservatory, he had taken especial pains with me and I had always felt the keenest gratitude to him. He made me promise that I would go to his home the next day for dinner and play a few pieces from *Cavalleria* for him.

I kept my promise. My old teacher heard me with religious attention, expressing his complete admiration for a fresh, original and inspired opera. I was moved by such a sincere manifestation of sentiment.

Professor Saladino told me he had learned that the Commission had been enthusiastic over the opera, the success of which would certainly be greater if it were not for the entrance of Alfio, "*Il cavallo scalpita*".

This blessed "carter's song" was found by all to be too strange, too barbaric. Lola's *stornello*, which breaks up the great dramatic duet between Santuzza and Turiddu, instead made a great impression on him. The old musician was exultant.

The work on the parts quickly terminated, I left for Livorno, where I remained only nine hours to see and embrace again my father, my brothers and my sister, then continued on to Cerignola, where I was anxiously awaited.

At the end of April I received the invitation from Sonzogno to go to Rome for the rehearsals of *Cavalleria*. It was then I realized that I didn't have a bit of money to make the trip. I realized that I could not resort to the bank, in spite of my friend the cashier's opinion, since unfortunately I had used my signature there once too often! Edoardo Sonzogno helped me out of this embarrassment with an advance of several hundred lire.

On the afternoon of 2 May I arrived in Rome. Near the Teatro Costanzi, where I went right away, I saw the big posters announcing the performance of my opera and of the other two winners. But while *Rudello* and *Labilia* were given no prominence, *Cavalleria* was announced in very visible letters. Presenting myself at the stage door on Via Torino, I asked the doorman for Maestro Mugnone. The doorman looked me over very carefully and answered me, "The Maestro is rehearsing and can receive no one." "But he and Sonzogno have invited me to witness the rehearsals!" "Chatter![22] If you will wait, when the rehearsal is over he will come out and then you may see him." "But I am Maestro Mascagni, the composer of *Cavalleria*." "A pleasure, but you cannot go in. These are the rules." I wasn't satisfied with not being able to go in and I grumbled. Then the doorman, relenting, said to me, "It is obvious that you do not know Maestro Mugnone. He is capable of causing a big scene on account of me. All that I can do is to give him your visiting card. Please oblige me with it." I pulled out my wallet and very carefully searched in it. It was difficult for me to find a visiting card for the simple reason that I knew very well I didn't have one. Then I exclaimed, "What a misfortune! It's no longer here. I'll run to the hotel and get one."

---

22   "Nonsense!"

I went out to the exit but turned instead toward Via Nazionale, with the firm resolution of buying a card from a stationer and writing my venerated name on it. But in Via Nazionale, a few steps from the theater, I met Maestro Sgambati. Because he was with his wife I limited myself to greeting him and continued on my way.

The Maestro stopped for a moment, uncertain, then called out to me. "Aren't you Maestro Mascagni?" "At your service." "I am very pleased to see you."

And, presenting me to his wife: "This is the composer of the opera *Cavalleria rusticana*, of which I have spoken to you many times, and which was a prize winner in the Sonzogno contest." Signora Sgambati gave me her hand, which I shook somewhat awkwardly but effusively.

"Everyone is enthusiastic about your opera," remarked Sgambati, "from the conductor to the soloists, from the orchestra men to the choristers. The orchestra men, especially, praise the opera, but because of the way in which the instruments are used! The work has a great efficacy in the orchestra, it has strength and extraordinary effect."

While Platania had advised me to make a few cuts, especially in the Prayer, Sgambati had insisted on not cutting anything. I didn't know whom to listen to anymore. I told the Maestro of the incident with the porter. He laughed heartily, then said to me, "Come with me, you will certainly get through."

So I returned to the stage door of the Costanzi where this time Cerberus, to whom the Maestro presented me, gave me much hat tipping. "You must excuse me," he said, "but I follow the orders which are given me."

So through a small low door I walked onto the stage of the Costanzi.

As soon as Mugnone was advised of my presence he put down his baton and ran on stage to embrace me. The entire orchestra, standing, gave me a great ovation. Maestro Mugnone dismissed the orchestra, saying to the men, "We shall continue tomorrow." Then, with all his Southern expansiveness, he praised me highly. He was very effusive. He spoke to me in Neapolitan dialect, but I understood all the same and his praise was very welcome to me. He had a very colorful way of speaking, with characteristic expressions. In those days they rehearsed from morning till evening. I was very pleased with the artists. Stagno and Bellincioni were as magnificent as ever. The baritone was Salassa; he too was truly a great artist. He had, however, one defect: he could not pronounce an "s" and, though not done on purpose, the baritone aria is full of "s"s!

Everyone thinks that Turiddu and Santuzza are the pro-tagonists of *Cavalleria*. It's not true. Two imbecile lovers can be found everywhere, but one does not always find a man who suffers for his honor, and is ready to lose his life for that honor, like *compar* Alfio. As a consequence they always have a dog do the part, and the public does not understand.

Leaving the Costanzi I went to see Spinelli and found him correcting the *Labilia* scores. He told me that he had heard *Cavalleria* and it had made a great impression on him. He remarked that his opera was much lighter and that he thanked God that it was being performed before mine.

I really didn't know if what I was witnessing, and of what I was the principal object, was reality. Instead I asked myself if it might not be a figment of my imagination. My previous successes disappeared before that which was happening to me now. I saw important people, celebrities, who bowed and who were enthusiastic over me and my music.

Next morning when I went out I went to get Spinelli at his house and then we went to the Costanzi. However, since Spinelli was to rehearse with Stagno and Bellincioni, I thought it better and more tactful not to attend and left him.

After breakfast I returned to the Costanzi and as I was going to the rehearsal rooms, I heard Stagno sing the finale of my opera, "*Sì, saprò in core il ferro mio piantar!*" I entered the room where there were Signor Sonzogno, Maestro Mugnone. Stagno and Signora Bellincioni. They were already at the finale, but they repeated the whole opera to let me hear it. What an impression! It no longer seemed my opera. They sang it with extraordinary passion, and were really enthusiastic over it. They gave me so many compliments and made such a fuss that I was very confused and unable to speak.

Bellincioni said that she felt she was singing the music of Verdi, and how she sang it! Sung like this, the two arias became really beautiful. I listened open mouthed.

There is no point in telling about Stagno. A single word is enough: he was sublime! He was immensely moving in the finale. One had to hear how he interpreted it! It was an absolute creation. But where the two of them really reached the height of effect was in the duet. In hearing this piece, I thought seriously to myself that the public cannot whistle, will not, absolutely will not.

The *Siciliana* also had taken on another aspect as sung by Stagno.

And then too he sang it in his own way, just like the Sicilians. Even he told me that I had really divined the Sicilian style.

The rehearsal over, Sonzogno called me and proposed that I add dances and divide the opera in two acts, but not then, after the Rome performance.

Then we left, Sonzogno, Mugnone and I. After having accompanied Sonzogno, Mugnone stayed with me and told me many things which moved me. He told me that *Cavalleria* would be given at La Scala the following year; he told me that Sonzogno would give me a commission for another opera; in other words he told me so many things that I no longer understood anything and really thought I was going crazy. Then I learned why my opera was being given second. Since mine was the one that was most effective, it should have been the third, but in rehearsing Ferroni's *Rudello* they found so many difficulties of performance that they were forced to give it last. It seems that *Rudello* had not pleased its performers, so they sang and played it with an ill will since it was difficult and of no effect. One could see the great master of counterpoint in it, but the complete lack of the composer's theatrical sense could also be observed. Ferroni had been asked to withdraw this opera of his, but he would not hear of it.

A few mornings later I went to the Academy of Santa Cecilia to visit Marchetti. He spoke to me of many things and assured me that Queen Margherita would be in the theater. While I was speaking with Marchetti, Maestro Tramontano, a professor at the Academy and first oboe at the Costanzi, arrived. Marchetti said to him, referring to me, "Here is one of them!" And Tramontano replied, "And he is really the best." Marchetti started laughing and added, "Let us not start to prejudice the public." But Tramontano immediately replied, "It is useless, sir; by now the whole orchestra has judged; there is no question about Mascagni's music." And Marchetti: "It's true, very true! Even the examining Commission thought the same thing. In fact Mascagni, with the unanimous consent of the five commissioners, was judged worthy of the first prize, while it took a month to decide on the other two."

They wanted to set the date of the first performance for Tuesday 13 May, but Bellincioni did not want to perform on the 13th, so they then set Saturday the 17th. The rehearsals by now were almost perfect and there was great enthusiasm in everyone. Bellincioni, dressed as a Sicilian peasant woman, was very beautiful, but above all very good, both as a dramatic interpreter and as a singer. She had studied the character in depth and her Santuzza was an intelligent and truly artis-

tic creation, so much so that she received an ovation and had a triumphant success. Stagno had original costumes sent from Sicily. One
morning during rehearsals he sang the finale for me in an astounding
manner. I was enchanted and told him so. He patted me on the
shoulder: "Dear Mascagni, if the music were not beautiful I couldn't
sing it like this."

Even Sonzogno, during those days, couldn't do enough for me. He
gave orders to his secretary to advance me whatever I should request
from the prize money. The performance, as I have said, was made up of
the three winning operas. The first in order of performance was *Labilia*,
by Nicola Spinelli of Rome who was very well known. It received a
succès d'estime, as did the third work, *Rudello* by Vincenzo Ferroni, who
taught at the Conservatory of Milan and enjoyed a great reputation. In
the middle place was *Cavalleria*, by a young and unknown musician. It
was therefore natural that I was very apprehensive in my heart. I realized that if I won this battle I would have no more to desire, and a great
way in Art would be open to me.

Thus I immerse myself in my sweetest memories and recall the days
of preparation for *Cavalleria*, up to the moment of the first performance
at the Teatro Costanzi. Days of continuous, inexpressible emotion: finding myself in Rome; being present at the piano rehearsals with Gemma
Bellincioni and Roberto Stagno; following the staging directed by Bazzani and recalling the scenery designed and executed by that same Bazzani, marvelous scenery, striking in its realistic locale and color, scenery
which for many years was used as a model for all the Italian theaters
and also those abroad; and then blissfully listening to the chorus, that
chorus made up of true artists, directed by the excellent Maestro
Molajoli; and lastly hearing my opera interpreted by Maestro Mugnone, conductor of the Orchestra Massima, which was called the artis-
tocratic orchestra and which always highly honored our lyric theater.
All this, to a poor, rough provincial youth who came from a small town
in the Puglie, represented something which could only bewilder him.

I had a good prophet, the illustrious Professor Eugenio Checchi, who
on the eve of the premiere said in print: "The name of Pietro Mascagni,
until this morning as unknown as that of Carneade for Don Abbondio,
will this evening receive the acclamation of a festive public and will obtain perhaps the most coveted among all baptisms, that of lasting fame.
His opera entered the competition without recommendations, without

notices, without the solicitations of influential friends." Checchi, who was the "Tom" of the *Fanfulla*,[23] was a fanatic over *Cavalleria*. A friend, apropos of that article which appeared before the performance, said to him, "But you're mad to write these lines! What if this success doesn't come off as you predict it? How will you look?" "It is faith," Checchi answered. "I have faith in Mascagni."

---

23 The newspaper *Fanfulla della Domenica*. See *Personalia: Checchi, Eugenio*.

9

FIRST PERFORMANCE OF
CAVALLERIA RUSTICANA
(17 MAY 1890)

A nd so the first performance, the evening of 17 May, arrived. Whoever was not at the Costanzi that evening cannot imagine what went on — an unforgettable evening in an artist's life!

Here my mind stops. Every memory becomes obliterated by the emotion which never left me during the entire performance. Gradually a few veiled visions: Queen Margherita, most elect of souls, in her proscenium box; Maestro Mugnone, the great propelling heart of that miraculous performance; the eminent musicians who had judged *Cavalleria*: Marchetti, Sgambati, Platania, Galli and D'Arcais affectionately surrounding me, with their secretary, the beloved Maestro Parissoti; the thunderous wave of applause at the entrance of the organ in the Intermezzo, that organ with its powerful sonority which was the real reason for that great success.

The Intermezzo is still applauded today, but this has to do with habitual applause, since the effect which I dreamed and which was accomplished in such an exemplary manner at the first appearance of *Cavalleria* no longer exists. Unfortunately our theaters, including almost all the largest and best subsidized ones, are without liturgical organs, something deplorable. Even the Teatro Costanzi (today the Reale) is without its own superb liturgical instrument, it having been given to the Cathedral of Nocera Interiore.

On the evening of the premiere I went to the theater, crossing the stage, naturally, and found all my friends in the hall: Gandolin, Vamba, Checchi. All great friends, great friends! I have lost them all, unfortunately....

Sgambati said to me, "I am going to my seat, since the Queen is supposed to come. The Prelude must be encored, since there must be an interruption when the Queen enters" (at that time they interrupted a performance whenever the King or Queen arrived). And so it turned out. Poor Stagno had to interrupt the *Siciliana* and Mugnone had to begin again from the beginning. Queen Margherita had come because Sgambati, Musician of the Court, had advised her not to miss it, and a large part of the better Roman nobility came also. In addition to the most important press, there were some of the most illustrious musicians of the time.

Prey to the liveliest emotion, I heard my music as I had heard it when the Divinity dictated it to me, without knowing whether I was really still alive, or if I was living in a dream which realized the dream I had had when the opera came forth from my soul, since the performance I was hearing was the exact expression of my feeling. I seem to remember that I heard the whole opera with my hands pressing my head and heart for fear that I would lose them, and on my lips I had a continuous prayer to the Omnipotence not to let me go mad.

Roberto Stagno (the first *Turiddu*) and
Gemma Bellincioni (the first *Santuzza*)

No one expected such a success. It was madness on the part of the public. My every hope, my every expectation was surpassed by the actuality. I had sixty curtain calls. When I showed myself at the footlights before that frenetic public I thought I was dreaming. I came and went like an automaton; all of a sudden the knot which I felt in my throat loosened and I started to cry like a baby. They told me later that I was seized by a nervous tic; I could do nothing but pull at the waist of my pants, as if I were afraid of losing them. Perhaps it was the habit of tightening my belt... In my head buzzed the memories of the hard struggles I had undergone, of the hostilities on the part of several friends in Cerignola, of the aversion of my father who hadn't believed in my vocation. And yet my father loved me, but from his point of view he feared that I might become a wanderer and dreamer. Now I had won! I was happy, very happy even for him. He could see at least that his son was worth something!

I felt all the joy of being able to offer a comfortable life to my wife, to my children and to my father... I saw everything in a new light... I thought of everything as the public applauded... applauded...

And to think that that evening the theater was not even filled! The public didn't much believe in it... Three one-act operas... a contest... the heat that began to make itself felt... But at the succeeding performances (there were fourteen in all) the theater was completely sold out before noon and there were awesome crowds. The management of the theater couldn't recall sold out houses of that sort.

The day after the premiere, I wrote to my father telling him of the enormous success, of my emotion, of my happiness. I wrote him that even the Queen had come and had clapped her hands in admiration. He certainly had read the newspapers, but there were many things he couldn't know. I told him that Sonzogno had assigned me three hundred lire a month and that I would surely arrange an excellent contract for *Cavalleria*. Above all that I was quite the big man and I felt as if I were going mad. I added that I had sent him all the Roman newspapers which praised me and that soon I would go to Livorno to embrace him. I wrote him (and it was true!) that even in the highest moments of my success I always had my thoughts turned to him and all my dear ones at home. Really a moving letter, feverish, full of the happiness and emotion which filled my heart.

But the people of Cerignola were still not convinced. Only when they read the enthusiastic press, then they decided to come to Rome, the people of Cerignola! As a matter of fact, there was one among those who were most fond of me who had already come on the sly. But then they all came, even those from the paper antagonistic to me, and these said, "Now what shall we do?" They printed an edition in white, red and green and suggested, "We'll bring a hundred copies to Mascagni and beg his pardon." But the director of the elementary school, Professor Nicola Pescatore, warned them, "Don't go. Mascagni is my neighbor; he's a mean character and he'll throw you down the stairs. I know him and I tell you this for your own good; *don't* go." But they wanted to come and that is just what happened—I threw them down the stairs.

At the second performance I wanted to have the pleasure of seeing the public instead of staying backstage. So I entered the theater by the main entrance on the street which was then called Via del Teatro Costanzi. I walked in and at the door they asked me, "Ticket?" "But what ticket," I said. "I'm the composer." "Composer or no composer, get out! Stop playing the fool!" That poor man was right—he didn't recognize me. It was a good thing that the Hon. Eugenio Maury, today a Senator of the Realm, was present on the scene. (At that time he was running

Livorno, August 1890: Mascagni with conductor and principals
(Leopoldo Mugnone, Roberto Stagno, Gemma Bellincioni,
Mario Ancona, Federica Casali, Ida Nobili)

for deputy from Cerignola and it was I who waged the campaign for him in the Puglie — he was elected.) Maury said to the ticket taker of the theater, "No, no, no! For pity's sake! Look, he really is the composer." I had the satisfaction of walking in and entering the theater. What a fantastic thing! I don't think I've ever seen a theater like it. Who knows how it happened? It was a miracle. Everyone said it is the merit of *verismo*. Well, I deny that *Cavalleria* is *verismo*. I've always denied it and I've found several critics who have agreed with me. All in all, the reason for such a success has always remained a mystery to me. In any case, the success — I may as well say it, otherwise no one will believe it — had already occurred beforehand. It had happened among the orchestra members and choristers who had taken part in the rehearsals and who, leaving the theater, said to everyone, "You're going to hear something really astounding!" This involuntary publicity had elec-trified the spectators in advance and prepared a ready made atmosphere for a success. I think this must have been the reason.

So the success took place which everyone knows about. I have never forgotten a thing of all that which came before it and no detail has ever escaped my mind — they are things too important in my life. I see those wonderful days of trepidation and hope, discomfort and trust as if they were yesterday. I see again, after the final excited bars of the orchestra,

Alessandro Bazzani sketch for the original *Cavalleria rusticana* scenery

all those arms of the public raised in the air and gesticulating as if they were threatening me, and I hear again in my soul the echo of those shouts which almost terrified me. The effect was such that at the second performance I had to ask, every time that they called me out, to lower the footlights since all that dazzling light seemed an inferno to me, and gave me the impression of a blazing abyss which would engulf me.

Thus in that sudden and noisy way I entered the field of art. Whoever was not around at the time has no idea what happened during those days in the field of music. They began to talk about Italian art and of the "youthful school". It may be said that there were only two of us in this new direction, Puccini and I, since Franchetti, though he could be numbered among the youthful school, was too sedate, too little Italian in his style, somewhat German. After the success of *Cavalleria* a good many of those who had participated in the Sonzogno contest wanted their operas performed also. Umberto Giordano was one of the first; then a Piedmontese, I remember, Armando Seppilli; then Emilio Pizzi. Many of the contestants moved on ahead with really good operas.

Leoncavallo appeared two years later, at the beginning of '92, with a very solid success.

A t Pisa there was a famous lawyer, a deputy to Parliament named Panattoni, an excellent person who was also the lawyer for Ricordi, the musical firm in Milan.

Two days after *Cavalleria* Panattoni came to find me. I already knew him because he was my father's lawyer; he had seen me often in Livorno. I was staying in a hotel in Rome which has a most pleasant memory for me, the Massimo d'Azeglio in Via Cavour run by the Bettoia brothers. It was the hotel which had the best cook in Rome. The cooks were all from Cotignola[24] and a cook from Cotignola is the best cook in Italy. I lived there.

They treated me well at Bettoia's. I was isolated and happy and had a little room on the second floor where I ate. When I saw Panattoni arrive I said, "Come have breakfast with me." "It would give me great pleasure."

"Listen," Panattoni continued, "I have carefully read all the terms of the Sonzogno contest. You have won with *Cavalleria* and I have observed that according to the terms of the contest you are the owner of the opera. I have come to offer you a certain sum..." "Don't tell me anything about it, since I cannot accept." "But it's Ricordi who is offering it to you." "I cannot." "But if the opera is yours, you can dispose of it as you wish." "I cannot." "But..." "I cannot play the ingrate, don't you see? If tomorrow it is learned that I have won Sonzogno's contest and then given the opera to his competitor, how will I look? No, no, Panattoni, you must not advise me to do this. It is not pleasant, it is not nice."

But meanwhile Sonzogno had never called me to sign a contract. I thought, "This means then that he doesn't want to buy *Cavalleria*..."

A week passed and then Panattoni returned. "Well?" To get rid of him I said, "I've already signed the contract." "Ah! A shame! You've done foolishly... Well, that's all right." (Luckily he didn't take it badly.) "When are you through with the performances here?" "Tomorrow." "Then another man will come with me tomorrow." "To go where?" "To Cerignola." "Really, you're coming to Cerignola? Why?" "Because there's an opera by Pietro Mascagni at Cerignola, and I know exactly

---

24   A town three miles southeast of Bologna.

where it is. This opera is called *Guglielmo Ratcliff*. Ricordi wants it; he does not have his heart set on *Cavalleria.*" "But how will I manage? Look, you're putting me in a bind... Well, listen, here's what we'll do. I can't come to Cerignola right away because I've already promised to go to Livorno. I want to see about making peace with my father. It would be ridiculous, even loathsome, after this success if I were still to clash with him. I adore my father. You know him..." "Yes, I met him at Livorno." "Listen, I give you my word of honor that *Guglielmo Ratcliff* will go to Ricordi. You can rest easy. I say it now and 'now' means forever."

Eventually he was satisfied and I left for Livorno. I stayed a short time, then had to go to San Miniato to see my relatives

At that time in Florence the monument for Umberto was unveiled and at the same time there was also to be the inauguration of the first electric streetcar in Italy. Since I wanted to be a part of this great novelty, I had left San Miniato and gone to Florence. As soon as I arrived I went to find Targioni-Tozzetti, my dear friend and author of the *Cavalleria rusticana* libretto. When he saw me he said, "I knew you would come, so I've bought a ticket on the streetcar for you too. The first run is being given on 20 September; we'll enjoy ourselves. Here are the two tickets, mine and yours. Come and get me tomorrow morning. Come early." "Well, I'll come around nine-thirty, ten o'clock; the streetcar doesn't leave until eleven."

In the morning, I was dressing when I heard a knock. "Come in!" Two people entered whom I knew. One was Canori, the famous impresario who brought *Otello* with Tamagno to Rome for the first time; the other was the Marquis Monaldi, Roman representative of the House of Ricordi.

"What's happened?" I said. "It's very good that we find you getting dressed, since at noon we have to go have breakfast at Colli's." "I can't. It's the first ride in the streetcar and Targioni is coming now to get me." "No, you have to come. Someone important is expecting you. We're having breakfast with Giulio Ricordi who has the contract for *Ratcliff* for you to sign."

In the meantime Targioni had come in. Canori and Monaldi said to him, "Listen, Targioni, this morning Mascagni has to do such and such... If you would excuse him from the business of the streetcar...." "Certainly, of course. It's right for Mascagni to come with you, it's important. I'll go alone and tell you later how the ride and the inauguration went."

It was an unfortunate inauguration. That first streetcar, at the Doccia turn, went right up in the air. The conductor didn't know how to drive. He lost his head and at the turn, instead of braking, turned on the current full force. The car went slamming on I don't know where and crashed. All dead — there was not even one person who remained alive. Poor Umberto himself went on the electric streetcar the following day, to show that there was no danger.

When I learned about the disaster I ran to the spot. Along the way I found Vamba. "Don't go there, for pity's sake. I went -- pieces of arms, of legs, half a head... all in bits! That wretch of a conductor wasn't experienced and made a mistake at the controls. The tragedy happened on the Doccia decline where the porcelain factory is." That day was a sorrowful one for Florence.

Poor Targioni was saved by a miracle and owed his life to his gluttony. He was already seated in the streetcar waiting to leave when he saw a confectioner carrying a tray of cakes. He jumped out of the car, went up to the man and said, "Sell me a cake." "I can't, they're for the Signora Biancolini." (She was a famous mezzo-soprano who lived in Florence.) "Well then, tell me where the pastry shop is and I'll go there." "But the streetcar's leaving." "It doesn't matter." he said. "I'll run and make it in time."

Targioni left and came back running with two cakes in his hand, but arrived only in time to witness the tremendous disaster at close hand. He had such a nervous shock that he almost died. I found him, dazed, sitting on the ground in front of his mother-in-law's house with his arms dangling and eyes staring. I called him, "Nanni! Nanni!" He couldn't even find the strength to answer me. I know that until his death he kept the famous ticket for that ride as a memento at the head of his bed. He had put it in a small frame and showed it to his friends, telling the tale.

But that morning I had gone to have breakfast at Colli's with Ricordi and my friends. Later we came back to Florence to sign the contract. Thus I gave *Ratcliff* to Ricordi. While we were still in discussion, my brother arrived, all out of breath. "Pietro! Pietro!" he shouted. And he threw his arms around my neck, weeping. "Then you didn't go?" "Be quiet. Thank God, it was only by chance I didn't go on that unfortunate streetcar. I'll tell you later. This is Signor Ricordi, the publisher, and these are my friends." My brother continued to stammer, "You're saved! You're saved, anyhow!"

All my relatives telegraphed immediately from San Miniato and from Livorno. They knew that I had expressly gone to Florence for the inauguration of the streetcar. I must admit that on that day Ricordi brought me luck. If it hadn't been for him! And to think that many say that Ricordi has brought me so much misfortune. It's obviously not true.

Meanwhile Sonzogno, who was at Torino, sent a telegram to Florence asking me to see him. "I'll expect you without fail tomorrow at Torino, etc...." I went. At the station I found him with a long face waiting for me. He took me to the Hôtel d'Europe and said to me, "This is your room, but for now let's go to mine."

It can be believed that at the time of my first contract with Sonzogno I was not perfectly *au courant* with the law which governs the author's rights. In fact, it cannot even remotely be supposed that in 1890 I came from Cerignola to Rome for the first performances of *Cavalleria rusticana* with the Civil Code in my suitcase.

On the other hand, what help would even the best knowledge of my rights have been at that time? Can one imagine that I would have had a *tête à tête* with the publisher to discuss the conditions of the contract?

One must think of my state of mind in those days: the outcome of *Cavalleria*, the triumph bestowed on me by the immense Roman public, the plaudits showered on my name and on my opera by the press, the whole whirlwind of unexpected and undreamed-of demonstrations which were even able to upset my brain; all these were not capable of allowing me to forget that I owed my success to Sonzogno and his contest.

As I have already said, Sonzogno had never spoken to me about a contract during the entire run of performances, but by now, in my heart and mind, *Cavalleria* belonged to him. Thus it will be easy for anyone to imagine with what emotion my heart was filled at the moment I entered his apartment. I said, "Has something serious happened?" He walked up and down. All of a sudden he stopped. "They call publishers sharks... but what are you?" "Oh God, I wish I were a whale to swallow all of you in one gulp. But I can't... It's obvious you all are stronger than I." "And you are the most ungrateful man that exists. I announce a contest, I make you a winner..." "Ah, no! I won the contest with my opera. In any case, it might be the judges who had made me the winner because they were satisfied with me, but the publisher has nothing to do with it!" "And are you giving the opera to Ricordi?" "I beg your pardon, Signor Sonzogno; I gave *an* opera to Ricordi. On 31 May the contract with you for *Cavalleria* had not been drawn up yet. Therefore I sold my *Ratcliff* to Ricordi before *Cavalleria*. I could have sold *Cavalleria* to him also. This is where my gratitude lies, in resisting that. No, *Cavalleria*, as I've said, belongs to Sonzogno." "But why?" "That's how it is. I have never played dirty tricks. Never in my life have I done so and I never will."

He presented me with the prize for the contest, consisting of three thousand francs, less, however, the one thousand four hundred which he had advanced me so that I could be present at the performances and bring my wife and child to Rome at the last moment.

Then he placed a piece of paper covered with stamps before me and told me to sign it, simply adding with a smile, "It's the contract for *Cavalleria*."

Now I ask: would it have been possible, at that moment and under those circumstances, for me to launch a discussion about conditions? Was it not Sonzogno, the generous patron recognized by public opinion, who offered me that contract? Did he not know that the other publisher had previously offered me a contract? I thought in all conscience that Sonzogno, too, wished to test my faith and goodwill with special conditions.

So I answered, "Signor Sonzogno, I won't even look at it. I'll take it with me as it stands, then sign it and give it back to you."

Certainly, when I was alone at the hotel and read that paper which earlier had appeared to my mind as an act of generosity, my sight was dimmed, my heart contracted and I wept bitterly. With that fatal paper I found myself deprived of all my legitimate rights: my opera, my *Cavalleria*, was lost forever; nothing more belonged to me of that first work which for long months had fed the sacred fire of my hopes; for me, for my little family, for my entire future. In just one moment all had been taken from me, all had been destroyed for me. I had worked, fought and won, but not for myself; nothing for me. I had been stripped, stripped of everything.

As a result of that contract the publisher would become sole owner of the opera and absolute possessor of all author's rights laid down and protected by the laws pertaining to Italy and all countries of the world.

To the wretched composer, as compensation for the sale of ownership and total cessation of all and sundry rights, would be given a miserable fee dependent on only one of the many profits; the rental of the opera. The fee established was 30 per cent and its duration limited to 20 years from the first performance. But at least if that 30 per cent on the rental would be payed me in one lump sum! Not only that: on the price of that rental the composer must almost always pay a brokerage fee of five and sometimes even ten per cent.

Nevertheless one may believe that with the act of the opera's consignment, the publisher would pay me a sum in ready cash. Not at all. I would have only the miserable prize money to look forward to and that was already half gone.

As a matter of fact, that contest was not as lucrative as a later one announced by Sonzogno. But that is understandable; the earlier one was a modest national one and did not carry a prize with it larger than three thousand francs. The other one, instead, was solemnly international and the prize rose to fifty thousand francs, won, almost as a justification of its internationality, by a foreign composer.

And that is not all. In that same contract for *Cavalleria* the publisher wanted to bind me to the promise of writing him a new opera *under the same conditions*, except for a small sum in cash to be paid me monthly.

Now even admitting that all this was the fruit of my ignorance in legal matters, it is permissible for me to ask why a law never existed directed at the exploiters of ignorance.

Today, by new laws, the authors have twenty-five years more of rights. For *Cavalleria* the rights last for fifty years after my death.

In the old days poor Ponchielli and Catalani had 15 per cent for ten years, then the ownership passed to the publisher. Verdi was an isolated case. He did things for himself, in his way. If they wanted his operas, they had to accept his conditions.

So after having read it, I took it back to him immediately and ripped it in two. I said, "Not even someone who is dying of hunger in Cerignola would sign this kind of contract. It's a scandal to offer it! What?! You hope to be able to take advantage of a poor musician barely started in his profession by offering me thirty per cent on the rental of the opera for twenty years! Surely you're joking!"

Then the anger of God ensued. Sonzogno checked with other people and at the end presented me with a somewhat better contract, but still bad, which I signed with an ill humor. I honored the conditions placed on me by that first contract but when later it became necessary to think of new business negotiations, I did not neglect to arm myself against any surprise whatsoever.

Afterwards we went to Milan and at a dinner in his home, with his friends, all faithful sycophants, present, Sonzogno said, "Do you know that Mascagni, as soon as he had finished *Cavalleria*, gave *Ratcliff* to Ricordi?" I hurried to correct him. "Don't listen to what Signor Sonzogno says; I gave *Ratcliff* to Ricordi before Sonzogno asked me for *Cavalleria*. *Cavalleria* was my property, as Sonzogno had established in the terms of the contest and it seems to me I've shown enough gratitude by not asserting my rights and arranging a good contract elsewhere. And if you want to know, my dear friends, there is something more: only at the end of all the performances did Sonzogno call me and say, 'Here is the contract.'"

"And if I myself had asked for *Ratcliff*?" said Sonzogno. "I was as ready to give it to you as it was possible." "And if I were to ask you for it today?" "Tomorrow I'll bring you Ricordi's contract, since he is hardly a man like Sonzogno. He is a gentleman, a man with a heart...I am sure that he will return the contract to me." "The usual chatter..." "All right, put me to the test, gentlemen. All here are witnesses."

The morning of the following day I went to Ricordi and said with my usual frankness, "Signor Giulio, I am coming to you on account of something annoying. Sonzogno wants *Ratcliff*. Would you be good enough to return the contract to me." "There is no problem. I did not ask for *Ratcliff*, I asked for an opera by Mascagni. Mascagni will give me another opera and all will be well. Here is your contract." And he gave it back to me.

At dinner time I returned to Sonzogno. "Well, well, how did your trip go?" "Very well. How was it supposed to go?" "But...the contract?" "Here it is." I brought out the contract. "Gentlemen, I have brought it to you." "But what did you do to get it?" "I repeat, Ricordi is a gentleman. He is not at all a man who only thinks of making war on a rival publisher."

Thus it happened that I also gave *Ratcliff* to Sonzogno. The following day I contracted with Ricordi for another opera and I wanted the libretto to be by Illica. He was contacted and so it was decided that *Iris* would be written.

Later I had an even more curious contract with Ricordi. He contracted with me to accept a second opera without, however, my being obligated to let him have it. This opera was never given to him though because he died and I didn't want to have anything to do with the relatives and heirs. Occasionally I do things contrary to my own interest, but in my life I have above all never wished to fail in my duty. This stems from the manners I learned in my family. We were poor people, but we didn't think about wealth. Each one of us has always been preoccupied only with carrying himself well. I have always been faithful to all of my friends and I have never forgotten those who have treated me well. I have always blessed them.

The success of *Cavalleria* made a great noise in Cerignola. I want to add several details to what I've already said, because the enthusiasm of Cerignola was something really powerful, all the more so since the *Risveglio*, that little local newspaper which had always made war on me, changed its opinion overnight and came out with articles in which I was straightaway called "glory of Italy," "genius," and other little things which make a great effect in the provinces. As soon as it was known in Cerignola that I would return from Rome (indeed, there was a delay as I arrived the day after I thought I would), even the band was sent around to let everyone know that I was arriving on the following day. When I arrived, the walls of the little city were covered with colored posters, on which were written "Long live *Cavalleria rusticana*," "Long Live the Genius," "Honor to the Italian Genius," "Livorno and Cerignola," "Mascagni is Our Brother," and so on. Tapestries of every color, blankets, garlands, ribbons and crowns hung down from the balconies. They even wrote a hymn for me, a hymn which began, "Blessed be the mother who bore you"; indeed, there were two hymns, one for the women and one for the men. The men sang, "The women in long pilgrimage greet the young conqueror." Pandemonium, I assure you. When I arrived my carriage was assaulted on every side. The parade which the authorities had decided to have was no longer a parade, it became a tide. When I finally made it home I was in a pitiful state. It seemed as if I had come from a hand to hand battle, full of knocks and bruises.

I couldn't even enter my house. I was pulled up to my own balcony with knotted sheets; hanging on I made it up. I was forced, however, to show myself on the balcony and greet those three thousand good people who seemed crazed by enthusiasm. In the evening there was a display of lights with Venetian torches and fireworks. Indeed, there was a torchlight parade under my balcony and then a mandolin serenade of my compositions. I shall never forget it.

During the following days it was impossible for me to walk around the streets. I was surrounded by a double row of friends, staying close to me to save me from the crowd; they jounced us from one side of the street to the other.

Thanks to the success of *Cavalleria*, my house became rather elegant and during those happy days in which I at last began to feel myself master of my life, I would not have exchanged my modest and comfortable apartment for a kingdom. My wife had even thought of a drawing room and every evening I met with my Cerignola friends.

After *Cavalleria* I had asked Targioni for another libretto. He had been impressed by the fact that the drama *I Rantzau*, by Erckmann and Chatrian, had been very favorably received by the public in the Emanuel Company's performances and talked with me about it. I went to see the work and liked it immensely. Thus it was decided that I would set *I Rantzau* to music.

But I had not neglected *Ratcliff*, my favorite *Ratcliff*, in the meantime. Since the day I had settled in that corner of the Puglie and thought of giving form and substance to my *Guglielmo*, I had become aware that I was capable only of realizing a very pale idea of that which I imagined. I saw where the deficiency lay and had attempted to remedy it. Since that day I had studied, studied courageously and passionately; I sealed off my existence, forgetting everything in study. Perhaps I grew old in study.

In March of 1891 I went to Naples for the performances of *Cavalleria*, inviting Sonzogno to come to Cerignola for the baptism of my second son Edoardo, who was born there on 3 January 1891. Sonzogno had said, "I am coming to Cerignola; I want to know this Cerignola." As a result, I had written to my wife immediately that we were coming. She was still in childbed at that time so my friends saw to the preparation of the festivities.

The Naples success was general, colossal, complete. There was, however, an opposing party and it was stronger than I could have imagined. After the enthusiasm for the Prelude, which was repeated to incessant applause, there followed an atmosphere of glacial cold which fortunately vanished with Santuzza's narrative, which was also repeated. The Santuzza-Turiddu duet made a profound impression and provoked such an outburst of clapping that it seemed the theater would collapse. Even this duet was repeated amidst indescribable applause.

At the Intermezzo the enthusiasm was absolutely...awesome; when I came to the footlights and saw that public on its feet, deliriously shouting, I was afraid. It was a moment which I shall never forget. From the Intermezzo to the end of the opera the enthusiasm of the crowd did not lessen for an instant. After the curtain fell I had ten curtain calls, everyone applauding: in the boxes, in the pit, in the orchestra seats, in the galleries.

The Prince of Naples was at the performance and applauded the whole evening. He had very-kind words for me. "I am not enthusiastic about theater and music in general," he said to me, "but *Cavalleria rusticana* has made a great impression on me. I shall return to hear it." He asked me if I had considered writing other operas. I told him about *Ratcliff*, the beloved opera of my youth, and added that soon I would have another opera completed.

"You are already into your work?" the Prince asked me. "I hope to perform my opera in November." "And where?" "In Rome. My gratitude for that historical city is that keen and strong." The Prince shook my hand firmly. "I wish you much luck," he said to me. "I have much faith in your talent." I bowed, moved.

Returning from Naples on the train with Sonzogno and Nicola Daspuro. Sonzogno suddenly said to me, "Now you must think seriously about another work, because you, dear Mascagni, have a great debt of gratitude to the public. Then too you mustn't lean too much on your laurels, especially at the beginning of your career. So a new opera is necessary."

He was right. "But where will I find a libretto like *Cavalleria*?" I said to him. "And then, if I do find it, it would be wrong to set it to music. No, I want to go a different route, also because too many newspapers, praising *Cavalleria*, have attributed its success to the libretto. Precisely because of this I would like a simple libretto, with an almost flimsy plot, so the opera could be judged on the music alone and not for the libretto."

Sonzogno, who was an intelligent man, said to me, "Perhaps I have the libretto for you." And he opened his bag and brought out a small volume. It was *Friend Fritz*, a comedy in three acts by Erckmann-Chatrian. I wanted to read it right away, so while the other two continued to talk to each other, I devoured it. Then I said, "Let's discuss it no further; I have found what I needed. I shall set *Friend Fritz* to music." I even convinced Nicola Daspuro to write the libretto and, my son's baptismal ceremony over, perfect accord was reached. Daspuro promised me to return to Cerignola at the end of March and not leave until the libretto was completed.

In the house there was a small room which barely held an upright piano, a chair and an inexpensive little table. There, at night (because even then I had the habit of getting up late and working almost all night), Daspuro and I created *L'amico Fritz*. I in pajamas and slippers, he with his beard and mustache. He wrote, I sought melodies and harmonies at the keyboard.

But the opera was really finished in Milan, at Sonzogno's home. I said to Sonzogno, "I am not obligated to give you this opera. I am obligated to give you *I Rantzau*, but I make you this gift: I give you *L'amico Fritz* as a present. But the verses must be corrected; parts of them are not beautiful and a few things need to be changed." The one who then thought of changing them was Daspuro, but the interesting thing is that he didn't know how to do it. From the beginning Targioni, of *Cavalleria*, had to be called in and he adjusted the verses but did not want his name used; it is not on the libretto. Instead there is an anagram of Daspuro's name there, since not even he wanted his name used. In short, no one wanted anything to do with this poor libretto — everyone repudiated it!

I was somewhat worried about its reception. This time, too, I asked myself. "Will the public understand my intentions? All my friends like the 'Cherry Duet' because they have heard it many times and know it by memory, but the public which will hear it for the first time in a large theater, will they have the same impression?"

Luckily, this second opera also went well. On 31 October 1891, again at the Costanzi, I had an enormous success: 34 curtain calls and no less than seven requests for repeats.

I liked this libretto in itself very much, in addition to wanting to write an opera very different from *Cavalleria*. Otherwise it would have

Three Italian composers: Mascagni, Franchetti, Puccini

seemed that I was always writing dramatic and tragic theater. And in fact I am very pleased with *L'amico Fritz* which in certain places, perhaps, surpasses even *Cavalleria*.

VIENNA EXPOSITION.
I RANTZAU (1892)

One day Sonzogno sent for me and said, "You know, there is a great musical Exposition in Vienna; they have expressly built a theater in the Vienna Prater. I have written that I want this theater for sixteen days. I want to perform the operas of our young musicians. You must engage a company for me, choose the artists, choose the conductors, everything. Let us be sure to have a good success." "The company, the conductors! But Signor Sonzogno, a great deal of money is needed!" "Don't worry about it; I am willing to throw away several million. This must be the affirmation of Italian art." "Even this seems a little hazardous to me. One doesn't know if this music...."

He speculated against the Casa Ricordi, which was not given to this sort of risk. Unfortunately, I couldn't bring Puccini because he belonged to Ricordi; yet for me he represented the biggest catch. I took with me, therefore, Leoncavallo, Giordano, Cilèa and Mugnone. For conductors I chose Mugnone and Ferrari — Rodolfo Ferrari, one of the greatest conductors Italy has ever had, if not the greatest of all. Three of us were conductors, since I also conducted. Giordano gave *Il voto*,[25] Leoncavallo *Pagliacci*. I was represented by *Cavalleria* and *L'amico Fritz*, which had already been given in Vienna.[26]

Since I had chosen Mugnone as conductor, he said to me, "Take my opera *Il birichino*[27] too." To be obliging I included it, but it was a disaster. A famous Viennese critic wrote in regard to this opera, "There is a mistake; the title should be in the plural since there are two scamps. There is also the composer." Outside of this fiasco, the undertaking was a great success.

The success was great, but the theater was small; therefore one could not make money. It's true that the theater was sold out every night, but the artists lost too much. All of the greatest Italian artists were there: Stagno, Bellincioni, Garulli; there was even Cotogni, the famous Roman baritone, the greatest baritone in the world. Thus Italian art was mag-

---

25 See *Personalia: Giordano, Umberto*.
26 On 30 March 1892, conducted by Hans Richter.
27 *The Scamp*.

nificently represented and greatly honored. We had wonderful reviews. Naturally everyone who was interested in music and musical enterprises, beginning with Ricordi, did not miss the occasion and they came too.

I arrived in Vienna with Sonzogno and, as a sign of the hotel proprietor's personal homage, had a princely apartment. That same day I had barely gone out when an ugly accident happened to me. While sitting in a cafe I was recognized and people mobbed me. There was a great smashing of glasses and bottles, an indescribable din.

I had barely arrived in Vienna before the crowds thronged in front of the hotel to see me. I couldn't take a step without people jumping on me asking for autographs. Every day three or four hundred letters addressed to me arrived at the hotel, mostly from females. All of them wanted a picture and an autograph. Certainly with all those photographs (and there were some beautiful girls among them!) I was able to put together quite a gallery of feminine masterpieces, but later, for intimate and family reasons let us say, I had to destroy that collection of Viennese photographs.

L'amico Fritz inaugurated the Italian season with De Lucia in the title role. One newspaper wrote that it was the most splendid premiere Vienna had ever seen. I had to present myself seventeen times before the footlights; the public seemed crazy and the shouts of "Hoch Mascagni!" made a tempestuous noise. And there were also thunder and lightning in the form of bunches of flowers with tricolored ribbons which rained down on me on the stage as if it were hailing. Unbelievable things.

Immediately afterwards Cavalleria was given and here the enthusiasm became fanaticism and I can hardly describe what the public did.

EXCERPTS FROM A VIENNESE DIARY

20 September 1892. Last evening the first performance of Cavalleria. What can I say? How describe the enormous success? How explain the fanaticism of this immense city for me? It is impossible. A triumph, a real triumph!

I had barely stepped down from the carriage to enter the theater, when I was assaulted and surrounded by an enormous crowd of women and girls who had sheets of paper, visiting cards and large cards in their hands. I had to write more than a hundred or so signatures in pencil in the middle of the street. The crowd kept getting tighter around me. I saw I was lost. My friends immediately encircled me. Padoa held me by the arm. I thought I was suffocating. All came to kiss my hand. I had some excellent Tuscan cigars in my pocket, my passion, and they robbed me of all of them, breaking them in pieces, dividing them up among themselves, perhaps to smoke them all their lives.

We had to resort to the police, and by gradually pushing and elbowing I was able to enter the theater.

Fortunately an opera in one act by Maestro Mugnone, *Il birichino*, was being performed before *Cavalleria*.

When I entered the pit there was a general shout. All rose to their feet without applauding, shouting only, "*Hoch Mascagni!* Hail Mascagni!"

What an audience! The crowd was such that it was frightening. The Imperial boxes were overflowing. The Court was all there, except the Emperor, who is away from Vienna. Even Princess Maria Teresa, who never goes to the theater, was there. They told me that she had come to see me. The entire Court remained in the theater to the end. I won't speak of the applause and curtain calls. Two pieces encored, the Prayer and the Intermezzo. After the Intermezzo they presented me with two enormous laurel crowns with white, red and green ribbons.

At the end of the opera the enthusiasm took on incredible proportions. I don't know how many calls I had. The audience wanted me to come out alone at least a dozen or so times. They seemed crazed, on their feet waving hats and handkerchiefs and applauding and shouting. Even the Princes, the Archdukes, the Princesses and all the members of the Imperial Court did not tire of applauding. I was compelled to speak and limited myself to thanking the Viennese public for such moving and cordial demonstrations for Italian art.

When leaving the theater it took more than a little effort to get in the carriage and depart.

The hereditary Imperial Prince Karl Ludovic, the Emperor's brother, asked me to come to his palace this morning. In fact I went there today at noon. Large servants, large doormen, large aides, large uniforms, large liveries. And immense luxuriousness. I was in white tie and tails. I was immediately received without waiting in the anteroom.

The Prince was in his general's uniform, with decorations on his chest and at the neck. I thought the interview would take place in French, but the Prince Karl Ludovic wished me to speak in Italian. He speaks splendidly. He received me in an enormous room. We talked only about art. The Prince is very likeable and informal. He knows all of Italy and is enamored of Florence. He told me he is enthusiastic about my music and that he will never be able to forget last evening. He spoke to me about Sonzogno, about other Italian musicians and about my operas. This very pleasant conversation lasted more than an hour. It was a pleasure to meet such a likeable prince.

As I was taking my leave, he said, laughing, "You were not at all bored by my conversation?"

I assured him that I would preserve an unforgettable memory of that interview, characterized by such high artistic awareness.

Many people awaited my exit, I had to walk a part of the way bareheaded because all saluted me.

At one point my carriage was taken by storm by journalists who wanted to hear a report of my interview with the Imperial Prince.

23 *September*. I have decided to give a reading at the piano of my new opera *I Rantzau*. It will take place tomorrow at noon in the large hall of the hotel. Present will be Leoncavallo, Mugnone, Cilèa, Giordano, Ferrari, Cave, Padoa, Jahn, Hanslick and his wife; Herr Šubert, the director of the Prague theater; Neumann, director of the Czech Opera; Ascherberg, the London Publisher; Bock, the Berlin publisher, Zichy, Intendant of the Budapest Imperial Opera; Pierson of Berlin, with his wife, a soprano, and Sylva, the tenor. The editors of the principal Viennese papers and all the Berlin artists will also be present. No artists from the Vienna Opera, because Jahn does not wish it. There will be about fifty of us. Sonzogno is offering lunch to everyone in his rooms. A pity that I'm in poor voice. But I shall get along.

24 *September*. The reading has been over for an hour; I had a great success. Jahn embraced me. All were enthusiastic, and all the publishers, impresarios and managers have asked me for the opera for their theaters.

I am not quick to delude myself, and though I am convinced that an opera as harmonically complex as *I Rantzau* may not make a sufficient effect on the piano, I noted a happy expression on the faces of the listeners, resulting from

those pages which to me seemed characterized by a
profound lyricism.

Edoardo Sonzogno, who also knew a good many pieces
from the opera, was strongly impressed too.

Šubert of Prague, Bock of Berlin and Zichy of Budapest
have declared their intentions of remaining in Vienna to
hear *I Rantzau* again and learn the tempi well. The theaters of
Austria, Germany and England have secured the new opera
for next season!

The run of Italian performances closed with a final performance of
L'amico Fritz, preceded by *Pagliacci*. I had to present myself seven times
at the footlights with Leoncavallo, Giordano, Cilèa and Mugnone. It is
useless for me to repeat what happened that evening. It may be imagined.

In short, this young Italian school aroused unanimous approval and
triumph. Sonzogno made a great name for himself, even surpassing
Ricordi. On the other hand, Ricordi did not take the chance; he did not
have the musicians. He had only Puccini. A pity that we lacked Puccini!
We should have had him along, then we would really have been complete!

Naturally after our success Sonzogno continued to maintain the important position he had acquired in Germany. From Vienna he immediately went to Berlin, Frankfort, Dresden, Leipzig and Munich, and
the Italian school garnered much honor, asserting itself everywhere,
even in Russia. *Cavalleria* was given in Paris, but Sonzogno, whose sentiments were basically French, had no luck in Paris with music. It was
in Germany that he became very popular.

I was the first Italian orchestral conductor to conduct in Vienna. In
a short time I conducted a good seventy concerts in Austria and Germany. I became very popular, in the twinkling of an eye, in all the German countries, and was wanted in every city, in Austria as well as in
Germany.

I Rantzau was finished at the time of the Vienna trip, on the occasion
of the International Exposition. The first performance was given at the
Pergola in Florence on 10 November 1892 with De Lucia, Battistini and
other very great artists. I had thirty-five curtain calls and six requests
for encores, but the Florence success was surpassed by that at the Costanzi in Rome where I gave *I Rantzau* later in November of that year.
The expectation in Rome was enormous. It seemed as if one were dealing with a first performance. I was very nervous. I had to confront the

Roman public, whose opinion I have always considered decisive. The Roman public, at least at that time, being somewhat outside publishers' competitions, found itself in the favorable position of judging with complete equanimity. Thus I counted a great deal on the judgement of the Romans, and it was for this that I was very nervous. In addition, *I Rantzau* was—how to say it?—somewhat outside the norm; I had attempted to avoid the old traditions as much as possible. I thought: after all, seeing that all things evolve, why should music remain motionless, compelled by the old rules? With *I Rantzau* I felt myself to be something of an innovator, but I was afraid, because the public was not prepared for modern music.

My friends gave me some comfort. I recall that several evenings before the first performance there was an enormous dinner at the "Orthography League." This League was a sort of society. There were Vamba, Gandolin, Pascarella, Sgambati and a great many others, representatives, senators, journalists; in short, a crowd of people. I was a new member in this society which did not have a president, but which now and then gathered at the Le Venete restaurant. We had barely seated ourselves at the table when Gandolin proposed to nominate the "dictator" for the meal. Once the dictator was named, who for that evening was Monteverde, Gandolin asked him if he could begin eating. Monteverde said yes and then pandemonium began. Between one course and the next, the "lictors", with sword and mantle (knife and tablecloth), called on the neophytes, among whom I was, to rise and speak. Now every neophyte, in other words all the new members, had to speak standing and must not say more than sixteen words; if these sixteen words had any common sense to them the member was sonorously whistled. I said four words and received a chorus of shouts and whistles. A new member began to speak: "I..." and the others: "Enough, enough; 'I' is personal and we want no personality here."

During the fruit course the naming of the "high priest" began. Sonzogno was named high priest, but he, however, was not there. He was lucky, since the high priests were obligated to pay for the champagne and that evening we had consumed a good many bottles of it. So we contented ourselves with "lesser priests" who sang the Sacred Hymn which concluded the banquet. Afterwards I had to seat myself at the piano and play a few pieces from *I Rantzau*, but without noise this time. Indeed, I was highly complimented. Then Sgambati played a few of his new compositions and Pascarella recited some verses for us. We left at one o'clock, without saying goodbye to one another, as was obligatory among the members of the League. Ah, that was an unforgettable evening. Those were really good times!

So *I Rantzau* had a great success and that success was repeated in Berlin the following year. I was at Cerignola, and since I was working on *Ratcliff*, it did not suit me too well to leave. Sonzogno insisted, however, and so I gave in. Kaiser Wilhelm himself, after the great success obtained by the Italian operas at the Viennese Exposition, wanted to have a run of performances too.

I arrived in Berlin in February of 1893 after a magnificent journey. We began with *I Rantzau*. What a mess! It is true that they gave me great celebrations, but frankly opera sung in German does not appeal to me. Then I conducted *Cavalleria* at the Imperial Opera. It was the Kaiser who wanted it. Indeed, it was decided that I should have an interview in French, with Wilhelm after the performance. I was told that he wished to offer me a decoration and I became annoyed, first because I dislike decorations and second, since I had not accepted even one decoration in Vienna, I did not want to accept any in Berlin. It did not seem right to me. Finally everything was worked out and they gave me the decoration as thanks for having helped with charity work.

The first time I saw Wilhelm he was on horseback accompanied by four aides on the Unter den Linden. Though there were a great many trees, there was not one linden. The performance of *Cavalleria* was a great success. An enthusiasm beyond description and a marvelous audience. After the performance the Kaiser received me in his box and gave me his hand. According to ceremony, however, he was not supposed to do this. He said, "I shall not forget this evening. I knew your opera but it has never seemed as beautiful to me as it did this evening. Then, too, your conducting has impressed me, even more than the opera." I thanked him in Italian and he gave me a cross with a blue ribbon, then shook my hand again as a sign of dismissal. A little more and he would have dislocated my arm!

When I gave *I Rantzau* (by hammering away I was able to get a great deal from the orchestra, but all the same I was not content) Wilhelm wished to be present this time also, with the Empress; indeed, it was he who gave the signal for the applause. I was given a beautiful reception in my honor. There were more than three hundred guests, among them the Italian ambassador, Count Lanza. The room was gorgeously decorated with huge Italian flags and colored lights in white, red and green.

When I entered, the orchestra played the Italian royal march and all shouted, "*Hoch Mascagni!*" Sonzogno was also with me and the meal

I Rantzau: "Cicaleccio" (Act II)

was very sumptuous, with an endless number of toasts. A German professor rose to give an analysis of my last name, saying that each letter was the initial of a facet of my talent. I didn't understand a word, but those on the floor never stopped applauding and shouting *"Hoch Mascagni!"* At the end they came to embrace and kiss me and I didn't know how to defend myself from that explosion of affection. It ended with me having to sign the fans of the ladies, the handkerchiefs of many girls and even the white ties and shirts of a large number of gentlemen. That was real comradeship, a true and spontaneous comradeship which came through art. Art can easily create ties more profound and sincere, even more touching, than any piece of paper, even if that piece of paper be a treaty. When I went to Berlin there was an enormous crowd at the station and my compartment was a greenhouse of flowers. Not only that. Since my route was known, there was an applauding crowd in all of the stations where the train stopped. But no one sent those people there. They were spontaneous demonstrations.

In July of 1893 I went to London. The crossing, contrary to expectations, was magnificent. There were numerous friends at the station to meet us: Paolo Tosti, Luigi Mancinelli, De Lucia, Mario Ancona and Sir Augustus Harris, director of Covent Garden. We took lodgings at the Hotel Metropole. The first morning I went to Covent Garden, which is a very beautiful theater. Maestro Bevignani presented me to the orchestra and all the players rose to their feet applauding warmly. I was on the stage and thanked them, then descended to the pit and began to rehearse *I Rantzau*. Applause was repeated at the end of the most important pieces. I rehearsed the whole opera this way. The rehearsals went on at length because Ancona and other artists did not know their parts.

England is called the land of liberty and I suppose it must be true, yet in no part of the world is there so much slavery. After midnight, for example, all the restaurants are closed and if one is hungry he must wait for the next day or die quietly.

That night at Covent Garden *Carmen* was performed in French. The part of the protagonist was played by Calvé who made a great impression on me, though her interpretation of the character did not seem to me to be the most proper. But what an intelligent artist! The tenor, Alvarez, was also an excellent singer and actor. The performance ended after midnight. I had not had dinner and had a hunger worthy of Count Ugolino, but all the restaurants were hermetically sealed. A gentleman of the company suggested taking me to his club. About time! I accepted the invitation and climbed the stairs of the club, which was truly splendid. I was told it had seven thousand members. I sat down happily with the enchanting prospect of eating quietly. But alas! I was told to eat in a hurry since even in the clubs the kitchens must close no later than one. I had to be satisfied with a bit of something cold, and when I asked for coffee I found myself hearing that at that hour it was not possible. They told me, however, that I could retire to other rooms to smoke and play a game of something. I thought of a good game of billiards with my friend Riccardo Sonzogno but quickly had to renounce it since, after ten, one could no longer play billiards!

The next morning I went to be shaved by the hotel barber. In vain did I attempt to convince him that I do not continue a duel after the first blood — he imperturbably went on nicking my skin. Since this barber spoke only his own language, I begged my friends to tell him that I would come every other day to be shaved. Astonished, they all began to shout, and since I did not understand, they told me it was impossible to be shaved every two days: it had to be done every day, otherwise one loses every consideration. So hail to liberty!

And I shall not speak of the interviews and of the thousand annoyances, nor the invitations which rained down on me during the day.

That evening I went again to Covent Garden to hear the first act of *Pagliacci*. De Lucia sang very well, but that music was not for him. Melba had a beautiful voice, but it seemed to me that not even she was really right for Leoncavallo's opera. I liked Mario Ancona immensely. He was an artist who had a splendid career.

After the first act we went to a *soirée* given by the Calvé in her home. There was good company. The young Ladies De Grey and Rochefort, the tenor Alvarez, Maestro De Lara and Tosti with his kind wife. A little music was performed and I played the mad woman's narration from *Ratcliff*, which was much admired.

The following day, after having received a good many calls and given six or seven interviews, I went with Riccardo to see Ascherberg, the great English music publisher. Tosti also came with us and we had lunch together at Pagani's, the Italian restaurant. I met Denza and many other Italians.

During lunch I committed an unpardonable *gaffe*. I was sure that Ascherberg did not understand Italian and I said under my breath to Riccardo, "Look what an indecent tie our friend has on." Ascherberg looked in a mirror, then went to the proprietor of the restaurant and was given another tie. I almost fell under the table for shame.

One evening I conducted *Fritz*. As soon as I appeared in the hall, I received a triple salvo of applause. All of the royal family was in the theater and applauded at length. *Fritz* could have been performed better, but nonetheless the success was enthusiastic. And how many pieces repeated! After the "Cherry Duet", superbly sung by Calvé and De Lucia, the enthusiasm turned into delirium. The duet was repeated with the same success.

Another evening I went to dine at Mr. Adolph Von Andre's, one of the most noted personages in London. His house was one of the most sumptuous. Ancona and De Lucia had also been invited to dinner but the latter did not come because he was indisposed. Among the guests were also Lady De Grey with her husband; the Duchess of Manchester; Mr. Schuster; and Tosti with his wife. After dinner we made some music.

Pietro Mascagni (oil by Malesci)

Tosti sang one of his very beautiful serenades and the little Neapolitan song "E levate 'a cammesella". Mario Ancona sang two Tosti songs splendidly and I let them hear the description of London from Ratcliff. The piece aroused great enthusiasm and I had to repeat it.

By then it was my fate to pass from one party to another, from one dinner to another.

The rehearsals for *I Rantzau* were proceeding with alacrity, but it was not yet possible to set the day of the performance. The artists were still not in full possession of their parts and I would not consent to the opening until I was fully satisfied with the performance. I wore myself out with the rehearsals. One morning I stayed more than four hours in the theater—never have I worked so hard in my life. I showed all the gestures to the artists and obtained a great success... as a dramatic actor.

Meanwhile it had been settled that the following Monday evening I would conduct *Cavalleria*. The theater had already been sold out at fabulous prices.

I shall not try to describe the splendor of one evening at Sir Augustus' residence: a real palace in the center of an immense garden in the suburb of St. John's Wood. Dinner took place at eight and it was an intimate dinner, only men participating. There were fourteen guests in all: Jules Claretie of the Comédie Française, Maestro De Lara, Bevignani, Randegger, Professor Stanford of Cambridge University, the publisher Ascherberg, the representative Temple, the celebrated actor-manager Bancroft, Lord Onslow and other very high ranking people. I was on Sir Augustus Harris' right and my other neighbor was Jules Claretie, one of the most noted writers in France. On the cards which bore the names of the guests were some notes from *L'amico Fritz*.

The dinner took place amid cordiality and cheerfulness. After dinner we went into the garden.

I have never seen anything like it. An earthly paradise, the *Thousand and One Nights*, an enchanted garden all lit up in Venetian style with surprising lighting effects, lamps amid the trees, jets of water and kiosks.

There were more than a thousand guests; all of the artistic and aristocratic world of London was there. In one part of the garden there was a large awning which led to a buffet, an enormous improvised room made out of Japanese curtains. Under a large tree the band of the Scotch Guard played.

I stood at the entrance to the pavilion and all the guests came to shake my hand. It was a not indifferent exertion. I was later asked to conduct the Intermezzo from *Fritz* and I could not refuse. Everyone seemed to go crazy. The ladies and young girls were the most enthusiastic; they all wanted me to affix my signature to their fans and handkerchiefs.

It was really an exceptional party, superb, such as had never been given in London.

At that time in London there was a doctor who passed for a very great scientist. He occupied himself particularly with anthropometry:

from characteristic signs on the head, face and hands he claimed to guess the temperament, grade of intelligence and habits of those who consulted him.

I was curious to question him, and so one day, together with Riccardo Sonzogno, Valera and other friends, I went to his studio. Naturally I did not state my name. The doctor, who was a handsome man of serious and stern aspect, had me sit in an armchair and began to examine my head. With his fingers he measured the distance from forehead to ear and from ear to top of the cranial vault.

After a rapid examination he said to me, "I must congratulate myself on having examined you. You have one of the most perfect cranial conformations. The distance from forehead to ear is very long and this denotes a rare intelligence, an exceptional talent in you." Then he turned to examine my head and asked me if I had a wife.

I answered yes, and then the doctor said these exact words: "You will never be sued for adultery. A particular and infallible sign assures me that you will never betray your conjugal fidelity."

My surprise and that of my friends may be imagined. No one had asked any question of the doctor; it was he himself who postulated in that manner after the observations made on the conformations of my head.

Another evening I was at dinner at Alfred Rothschild's. It is impossible to describe the sumptuousness of that house and dinner. When you realize that he was the richest man in Europe you can imagine what a reception in his house was. All the dinnerware was of heavy gold; all the plates were of silver and the tables were adorned with the rarest flowers in the world. There were thirty-two of us for dinner. All that London could offer which was elegant and aristocratic was collected in his magnificent salon. I sat next to Rothschild and Adelina Patti who was very amiable to me.

She spoke to me about my operas and was enthusiastic over *L'amico Fritz*. The "Cherry Duet" gave her a profound sense of enjoyment. She claimed that that page was the best that I had written. Her conversation was very pleasant, full of spirit. She asked me to write a song for her, exclusively for her, which she could sing in her concerts, and I promised her that I would do so, happy to be able in this way to give her a sign of my admiration for her voice and art which were still, in spite of her years, prodigies of beauty.

During the champagne Alfred Rothschild rose, speaking enthusiastic words in my honor. Among other things he called me the "beacon of the musical future" and said that everyone was proud of the celebrations which England was giving to the composer of *Cavalleria*. He ended with the three traditional English shouts, "Hip, hip, hurrah!" All the guests rose to their feet repeating those three shouts.

I answered in Italian, saying the most polite things I could about London and especially about my illustrious host. I imagine I was effective in my improvisation since my speech was received with interminable applause. After dinner a large reception took place on the top floor of the house, a building which need not envy a palace. There was an infinite number of people, many artists from the Comédie Française, Lassale, De Reszke, Mario Ancona and others. Coquelin from the Comédie Française recited, as only he could, some exquisite and very witty monologues. Other French artists sang and recited. Ancona sang two songs stupendously, accompanied at the piano by me.

The success of *I Rantzau* exceeded my own hopes. It was a splendid evening and the opera was a colossal success, notwithstanding the fact that I was little content with the performance. It is true that there was De Lucia, but all in all the whole thing did not please me. It was, like Desdemona, ill-starr'd. All the same, however, I had imposing celebrations and the finest public of London applauded me frenetically. The following day I had breakfast with Paolo Tosti, who told me that the next morning we would leave for Windsor. I had been invited by Queen Victoria to Windsor Castle to give *Cavalleria* and *L'amico Fritz* with all the other performers from Covent Garden, including the orchestra and chorus. I conducted. I was somewhat excited by this venture, but by now I began to be accustomed to grand trips.

We arrived at Windsor Castle on 15 July and Tosti presented me to Queen Victoria. The Queen gave me her hand, saying in French that she was very happy to make my acquaintance and that for a long time she had desired to know me personally. "I am enamored of your music, especially *Cavalleria rusticana*. When you write other operas always try to think of your *Cavalleria*." I answered her, also in French, but I don't remember what I said because I was very moved. In dismissing me, the Queen said to me in Italian, "I understand your language well but do not know how to speak it." That evening, at nine-thirty, there was the performance of the second act of *L'amico Fritz* and *Cavalleria*.

And there one of the most curious episodes of my life occurred. I have never worn gloves in my life; I even stayed for two months in Russia without ever wearing gloves and yet my hands have always remained healthy, without experiencing chilblain. On the evening of that important performance I entered the pit to conduct *Cavalleria*.

Shortly after a gentleman came and said to me, "Gloves; you need gloves." "Gloves for what?" "One may not appear before the Queen without gloves." "I have never worn gloves." "That makes no difference; we'll find some here." A stage director gave me a pair of enormous gloves. "Now," I said, "we also need gloves for all the violins, the clarinets, the whole orchestra. Why should I be the only one to have to wear gloves? They must have them also." "But they cannot play with gloves." "So why do I, who must conduct, have to have them?"

Not only that. There was another condition: I had to conduct turned around with my face towards the Queen who was at the rear of the room. "But the artists are not used to singing, nor the men to playing when the conductor does not face them."

But it had to be done perforce, so I conducted the Prelude to *Cavalleria* in that manner. But after the Prelude a gentleman in a grand uniform came up to me and spoke for a long time in English. Naturally I understood nothing, so I asked the concertmaster, who spoke Italian. "But what did he say, this gentleman?!"

"He said that Her Majesty the Queen allows you to remove the gloves and to turn around and concentrate on your performance." "It seems then," I said, "that in this room there is another intelligent person besides Mascagni, and that is the Queen."

The Queen immediately summoned me to her drawing room when the performance was over. She said to me, "I am very enthusiastic about your music. I already was so earlier, but this evening I received an overwhelming impression. And just as on the first time that I had the pleasure of hearing the Intermezzo I wept, so did I also this evening."

I committed a tremendous *gaffe* and replied, "*C'est dommage, madame.*" Francesco Paolo Tosti was behind me and gave me a kick. "What! She gives you a compliment and you tell her it's a shame!" "I have never written music to make people cry." "But you are a scoundrel."

The Queen then called her lady-in-waiting and said something to her. The lady went away and returned with a very beautiful photograph, in a magnificent frame of worked silver. On the photograph the Queen put her signature, a handsome dedication, the date and gave it to me. I still have it.

For us composers it is difficult to say which of our operas we like the best. We may have particular affections for what happened in our lives with certain works but generally it is the first opera that one favors.

It is certain that the public has always had a predilection for *Cavalleria*. It is a popular opera, full of melodies which please. Madrid was the first city abroad to applaud *Cavalleria*, with Bellincioni and Roberto Stagno. It was later given at Budapest, Hamburg, Munich, St. Petersburg, Berlin and Constantinople. At Paris it was the most important theatrical event of '92.

However, I prefer *Ratcliff*. It has always been my great passion, the "great work", as I called it when I was at the Conservatory. I have always considered *Ratcliff* better than *Cavalleria* and it rather annoys me to be considered by many people as just the composer of *Cavalleria*. I have written things far more beautiful and unified than *Cavalleria* — I am not the only one who thinks so.

But *au fond* I love all my operas. And why shouldn't I? In each work there is a little of me, of my torment, of my passion. In each of them I made an effort to keep up with the progress of technique and to say something new in this business of music. I have composed much music, but have daringly followed the new ways that I observed or simply intuited. I have worked much for myself and for art — but above all for our adored Italy.

Ratcliff was not performed until 1895. Before I decided to give that opera I needed time! I was never satisfied. For the premiere, at La Scala on 16 February 1895, a special telegraph office had to be set up, from which, during those three hours, a good 480 dispatches went out to Paris, London, Berlin, Vienna, Munich, Madrid, Lisbon and even to America. These were telegrams from correspondents from all over the world who sent word of the opera's great success to their newspapers. I was more worried than usual since expectation was very high in Milan, and also because it was the first time that a premiere of a new opera of mine was being given in the Milanese theater.

Then too, so many polemics had erupted around my name that I was awaited at the stage door. Everyone wanted to see how I would manage in this new battle which I fought for Italian art. The theater's surrounding areas were thronged with crowds. Puccini and Gomez were in the theater.

Ratcliff was the greatest success that I ever had in the theater. At one point there was such enthusiasm on the part of the public that I had to interrupt the act. I was taken off the podium and carried in triumph. One cannot have an idea of the importance that a theatrical premiere had in those days, above all an operatic premiere.

And to think that at the first performance it was performed in the strangest manner possible! An almost incredible thing. I was all ready and the opera was about to be given. The house was sold out. Suddenly the mezzo-soprano, Vidal, became ill. Sonzogno, desperate, said to me, "Look here, the performance will have to be postponed." "No; it must be given." "But are you crazy?" he said to me; "what about the artist?" "Without the artist?" "But how?" "I'll worry about that."

I took an American girl, Della Rogers, taught her to gesticulate according to the action that the character was supposed to perform and thus she substituted for the mezzo, silently, without singing.[28] It was one of those things which happens once in a lifetime. It needed courage on my part to present a completely new opera, never before performed in any city in the world, in a theater like La Scala, with a very difficult public, under those conditions. It was foolhardy audacity. I was asked, "Excuse me, Maestro, but why did you do without the mezzo-soprano?" "I cannot say." To tell the truth, I would have preferred to perform all of *Ratcliff* without the artists, with just the orchestra. I am sure that it would have pleased more than with the artists.

Anyway, with all this, the success was phenomenal and very gratifying to me who for months had lived only for my *Ratcliff* in a way which, at a distance of many years, I can say I did not live for any of my other operas.

Sixteen performances were given and Sonzogno was very content, since he had just taken over the management of the Scala that year on his own account.

Why then is *Ratcliff* no longer given? It will never be popular with the public because the subject is too gloomy and the plot too obscure, but if any parts of my music will live, those will be a few scenes from *Ratcliff*. The form of the music is somewhat special; there are almost no set pieces; the general character is the continuation of the musical idea which follows the drama. The artists must put their lungs to a hard test,

---

28   But see *Personalia: Vidal, Renée.*

Scene from *Guglielmo Ratcliff* (Act III)

not only on account of the vocal tessitura, but also because of the prolonged length of singing, owing to the verses taken from Maffei's translation, or better, from Heine's original, since the translation is almost literal. In the entire work I cut only about a hundred lines.

Still, in Rome *Ratcliff* was the most popular opera of all, even more so that *Cavalleria*. It was given innumerable times at the Teatro Adriano.

Another reason why it is performed less often is that the libretto was written by a Jew who had the courage to say many nasty things about the Germans: Heinrich Heine. Among other things he asserted, "The vilest people are the German people." I am still able to perform the opera every now and then because I never set a word of Heinrich Heine to music, only a translation by Andrea Maffei. It is strange, however; the subject does not seem to be written by a Jew, but rather by a Catholic religious man. There is even a child who sings the Lord's Prayer, conducted by his father who teaches him.

So it is understandable why the Germans hate Heine, but the Italians have no reason at all to hate him. They still give the opera, but stealthily. I recently gave it in December in Florence, a beautiful performance. The critics, to praise me, said nasty things about Heine, asserting that he had had the luck to find a Mascagni who, with his music, was able to make the public like a drama which in reality was worth nothing. The journalists spoke in this manner to go along with the political moment, but they knew they were lying and saying an unjust thing. In fact, before I had set it to music, *Ratcliff* had been performed by Andrea Maggi at the Teatro Manzoni in Milan with great success. The dedication which Andrea Maffei wrote for his translation suffices as testimony of this. It is a dedication to Achille Torelli which speaks of the enthusiasm of the public at the performance and in which it is explained how the concept of the work had been perfectly understood and shared by the spectators.

Thus there is no question but that the drama, even without my music, has a great value of its own. There are those who say that Heine may have written it to parody the excessive romanticism of the time, but not even this is true. Heine wrote it in total good faith, and in fact there exist two of his dedications for this work, one of which says, "I shall die, my name shall die with me, but oblivion shall not fall on this work." Therefore no doubts exist. The man who signs himself Heinrich Heine and writes these words means it in good faith.

But in regard to *Ratcliff* something really interesting happened to me in Germany with the Kaiser. It had been decided to give *Ratcliff*, and Kaiser Wilhelm wanted to be present at the rehearsals. I had permission to sit next to him. The rehearsal began. All at once Wilhelm (who until then had not opened his mouth) sprang up, shut with a bang the libretto that he had in his hands and grumbled something which seemed to be an oath. I was astonished. The rehearsal was stopped. Naturally I tried to learn what could have made the Kaiser so irritated (he had said "pig" or something like that). He was angry over Heine. Who knows, perhaps he hadn't known that Heine was Jewish and only realized it at that moment? The fact is he said "pig" only on account of the libretto. And no more performances could be given. Yet I must say that Kaiser Wilhelm was an enthusiast of my music; but he wasn't angry with my music, only with Heine. The Germans have always had a fixation over the matter of the Jews.

When I was young, after *Cavalleria*, I had a secret ambition which I considered a kind of good luck charm for my artistic future; during the days when I stopped in Milan, I wanted to stay where Verdi was accustomed to stay. It was an ingenuous ambition of mine which comforted my spirit. And so I habitually occupied his apartment in the old Albergo Milano, escaping to a small room as soon as the proprietor, Comm. Spatz, solicitously came to tell me, "The Maestro is coming." Verdi knew of this and pardoned me.

But meanwhile for several days I was blissful there in those rooms where Verdi lived so many days of the year. I seated myself at the desk where he wrote, and I played the piano which he played; and I slept in the bed where he slept... I believe that in those periods of my Milanese residence I learned to dream, with open eyes, the dearest and happiest dreams of my life, dreams which I have always dreamed and dream again in the devoted and loving memory of the great Maestro.

I owe to this Immortal some of the keenest satisfactions of my life. I met him after *Cavalleria* and I am still grateful to Giulio Ricordi for having presented me to him.

After the first performances of *Cavalleria rusticana*, a legend went around that was repeated and believed in Italy and elsewhere which said that Verdi, after having read my opera, had exclaimed, "Now I can die content!" Verdi never spoke these words, which were believed unconditionally by the imaginations of a few pompous enthusiasts who imperfectly knew of a courteous and affectionate episode. And, to put things in order, I would like to recall just this episode, even at the cost of appearing immodest. After all, no one has ever praised my modesty. Not even I.

Actually, after the success of *Cavalleria*, the rumor had been spread by my adversaries that the opinion of the great Maestro was anything but flattering. Indeed, they related that on an evening in 1890, in Verdi's apartments in Genoa, that great man, in company with Tebaldini, Giulio Ricordi and Boito, had seated himself at the piano and had played a part of *Cavalleria*, shaking his head sometimes as a sign of disapproval and that, arriving at the end of the duet between Alfio and Santuzza, had closed the score with a distressed gesture, grumbling, "Enough of this stuff!" By these words—which neither Tebaldini nor

Ricordi, and much less Boito, all of whom knew the Maestro's moods well, dared to refute — my enemies naturally profited. Those people had defined *Cavalleria* as a heap of stupid vulgarities, a shameless plagiarism of fragments and tunes drawn here and there from the operas of Verdi, Donizetti, Bellini and even from Wagner. These denigrators, who vented all their poison of irony and sarcasm on *Cavalleria*, painted me as a naughty boy without ideas and culture, a harlequin suddenly appearing on the lyric stage to make fun of the dolts, or at most a lucky man who had known enough to choose a libretto which in itself was enough to assure the success of *Cavalleria*. (According to these people any mediocre student from a conservatory could have obtained this success with such a libretto; but they forget that precisely in those years other operas on that subject by the same Verga, such as Gastaldon's *Mala Pasqua*, had miserably failed.) All these people, then, threw themselves on those words of Giuseppe Verdi like a band of starving men: "Enough of this stuff"; and these words, naturally, served as a formidable weapon against me. As it happened, even if those words had really been spoken by Verdi, the episode went somewhat differently. It was related to me by Giulio Ricordi, *el Giuli*, as he was called by Verdi.

One evening at Sant'Agata Verdi had guests: Boito, Ricordi, Gallignani and Tebaldini. At a certain hour (which was always the same, since Verdi was orderly and precise in everything) he retired to his room and went to bed. The others still remained in the living room to chat and play cards. At Sant'Agata the Maestro had a piano in his bedroom; indeed, that was *his* piano. Whoever has visited Sant'Agata will remember it well; against the wall, near the door which leads to that small alcove where, in the greatest simplicity, he wrote. *Fuge magna*, as Horace says.[29]

A short time had passed. Verdi should have been asleep already, when the echo of a few chords came to the guests. Was the Maestro composing? At that hour? What divine impulse had come to touch him at that moment? With easily understood trepidation Ricordi and Boito slowly approached the room and listened. A few measures were enough to understand that he was at the piano reading *Cavalleria rusticana*. Giulio Ricordi had brought the score to Verdi, according to his own wish.

---

29 "Beware grandeur" (Ep. Bk. 1,10,32). The quotation continues: "Though humble be your home, yet in life's race you may outstrip kings and the friends of kings" (transl. Loeb).

"The following morning" — it is Giulio Ricordi who is speaking — "I found the Maestro as usual in the park of his villa. We exchanged a few words, then, returning to his room and pointing to the score of *Cavalleria*, Verdi said, "So it is not true that the tradition of Italian melody is finished!"

This was the praise of Verdi for my opera, and no praise, no homage was ever dearer to me. I made the words of Verdi the religion of my art, and I made of them the banner of my battles which I have always waged with ever stronger faith, and which I shall wage to my last breath, for art and for Italy.

Giulio Ricordi (1895)

In relating this episode to me, Ricordi added, "When you come to Milan, Verdi wants to meet you." At the time of this episode about *Cavalleria*, then, I did not know Verdi yet. After a while I went to Milan to give some concerts at the Scala. Then Ricordi said to Verdi, "Mascagni is in Milan." "Bring him here to me." So Ricordi came into my room and said to me, "Come with me so I may present you to Verdi."

I followed him trembling. Verdi... It must be understood what it meant for a musician to be presented to Verdi. As soon as he saw me, he shook my hand with much cordiality. He was not, in general, expansive; indeed, rather dry and sparing of speech. His eyes penetrated deeply. They did not see immediately, so deep were they among his bushy eyebrows, but they felt immediately: piercing, keen, searching. That kind of eyes which read everything in us, even that which we would like to keep a secret. His words were slow, savoring, meditative. He never spoke at random, there was never the danger that he would pontificate or that he would abandon himself to verbal excitement. When he said something, however, it had the weight of gold.

What attracted one to him and caused all fear to vanish was his smile. He smiled only at those he chose, but *when* he smiled... it was to feel oneself seized and carried on high, near to him. The close proximity of my lodging brought me further meetings and even a certain confidence of an artistic nature. When he knew that I was in Milan, he had called, and he willingly lingered with me speaking of and discussing artistic matters.

He once confessed to me that the Parisian orchestras seemed to him more sonorous than the Italian ones, finding the reason for this in the quality of the stringed instruments, all made by the same establishment and for that reason perfectly homogeneous in sound. I was bold enough to observe that I was unable to share his opinion, since the instruments of the great Italian makers cannot be confused with those of modern ones, however more perfect. I immediately added, to lessen the conflict, that certainly it was not possible to make up on orchestra entirely of musicians who owned instruments of the same maker; the lesser sonority of the ensemble could be looked for in the inequality of the voices. The Maestro did not answer, but I had the impression that he remained of his own opinion.

One day, later, he seemed to me even more confidential and affectionate. He wanted to know on what subjects I had cast my attention for my future operas, and without giving me time to answer, told me that he had heard that I was thinking of *King Lear*. "If this is true," he continued, "I can tell you that I possess a vast amount of study material for that monumental subject, material which I would be happy to give you to facilitate a burdensome task."

I felt myself seized by a keen emotion in finding myself near that man who said these great things with sublime simplicity. I was unable to speak for the knot in my throat, but with a great effort I was able to make my voice, which was trembling, ask a question which was close to my heart: "Maestro, and why have you not set *King Lear* to music?"

Verdi closed his eyes for a few moments, perhaps to remember, perhaps to forget. Then softly and slowly he answered, "The scene in which King Lear finds himself on the heath terrified me!"

I jumped to my feet with eyes wide open, and certainly I was very pale. He, the giant of musical drama, was terrified... and I... and I...

Never again in my life have I spoken about *King Lear*.

I never heard a word from Verdi which referred to himself or to his art, but he spoke and discussed willingly about art in general. In his speaking there spontaneously flowered the vastness and profundity of his artistic culture. And he still studied, he always studied.

One day I stopped to look at a few pages of Bach, open on his piano rack. I said, "Maestro, what a comfort to find a score by Bach on your piano!" "Look, Mascagni, I owe this to you." "To me?" "I have read that in your concerts at Pesaro you performed some things by Bach and I wanted to reread that music. Bravo! It should be obligatory that in every conservatory the music of Bach is performed, the most modern of the polyphonic composers." The Maestro even kept up with my programs.

And he was actually my maestro in the repeated discussions which he loved to have with me in the later afternoon of every day. He liked to see me before dinner, during the period of the day when I remained alone. And they were discussions which for me indicated the road of my future. We sat down on the sofa and the subjects of our discussions were varied, ample and very interesting. Verdi spoke of everything and everyone, since the subjects always pertained to our art. He remembered singers, conductors and instrumentalists of epochs long gone; he spoke of new composers and even asked me my opinion. He was particularly interested in Grieg whom he liked for his delicate and original intervals. "The music of Grieg," he said, "does not speak a national language, but rather a dialect."

There is one memory of Verdi which is particularly dear to me, one which is one of the most important episodes in my artistic life. One morning in 1895 I was in my room in the Albergo Milano when, waking, I heard the unusual pawing of horses in the courtyard. I got up, opened the window, and saw a closed carriage drawn by two superb horses. Verdi got down from the carriage, dressed all in black, with a large tattered hat and in an overcoat. He was alone. He walked slowly, but firmly. He was really a handsome old man. That very day I felt the need to send him a note of affectionate greeting. But I received no answer. Indeed, four or five days passed without Verdi letting me hear from him. I would have liked to visit him, but didn't dare since Spatz, the proprietor of the hotel, had told me that Verdi was in a very bad humor and gruffer than usual. Meanwhile, the performances of *Ratcliff* being over, and because I was arranging to go into rehearsal with *Silvano*, I had to leave Milan for several days. I had decided to leave that night at eleven. Around seven Spatz came to find me as I was dining in the company of several friends. "Maestro, Verdi wants to see you and greet you before you leave."

A deep emotion took hold of me at that invitation. I left dinner and friends and went off straightaway to Verdi's apartment. I stopped before the door. My heart beat violently. But I took heart and announced myself. I entered the parlor. Verdi, seated in an armchair, was reading. As soon as he saw me, he resolutely arose, came over to me and, as I was beginning to bow, put out his hand and shook mine with great effusion.

"Bravo!" he said to me, "you would leave without greeting me!" I excused myself as best I could, mentioning my note and my desire to be received by him. "I am very pleased by the success of *Guglielmo Ratcliff*. It is an opera deeply felt, rich and vibrant in inspiration. A pity that the subject is somewhat gloomy, but the opera will go just the same."

I thanked him, moved by these words which were more welcome than any triumph. And we sat down, he in his armchair, I on a small sofa next to it. I spoke to him about many things and referring to *Ratcliff* I related the vicissitudes of that opera to him, the conditions under which it was written, the hopes I had placed in it since my years in the Conservatory.

As I was speaking (and Verdi listened to me with his eyes fixed always on my face) a waiter entered the room bringing a tray on which there was the Maestro's dinner. I made a movement to rise, but Verdi, quicker, turned to the waiter and asked him to put the tray down on a table and go. "Oh," he said, "there is no hurry. Please continue. Your story interests me greatly." I took courage and continued to speak about *Cavalleria, L'amico Fritz, I Rantzau,* and to unburden my soul, I referred to the harsh battles, and the unjust critics who had come to be my adversaries.

At this point the Maestro, who had always continued to follow me with great attention, interrupted me. "But you are young, you are strong and well hardened for these battles. So have faith in your strength and do not be disheartened. It is the fate of the man who works to be stubbornly fought against. If, as I hope, you do not stop at these operas, if you enrich our theater with other works, you will always be the target of the most violent critics. And then with your impetuous and exuberant temperament, you will have many problems in life. That which happened to me will also happen to you. They have done everything possible to me; they have whistled at my operas, they have covered me with insults, they have repeated *ad infinitum* that 'my star' had set forever.

"Well, I let them print, say and shout what they wanted. After all, how could I stop them? But I have not given thought to so many accusations and annoyances, I have instead continued on my way, playing the bear. Little by little I have tried to isolate myself from the world and I have been successful at it. But truthfully speaking I was not a bear, but was forced to play it to assure myself a certain tranquillity, and in my fury to play it I have really become one. But I am not sorry about it.

"Now that I am old all adore me, praise me to the skies. And you will see," he added in conclusion, "that the same fate will befall you. But it is necessary for your hair to become white; before then do not think to be left in peace! After all, it is right that it be so."

And it was not a judgment. It was the simple remembrance of his own story.

One morning in April of 1898 he called me, a strange thing because he never called me in the morning. "Mascagni, I am very upset with you." "What has happened, Maestro?" "But why? You have three youngsters, three such beautiful and dear children,[30] and I didn't know it! Every morning I saw these youngsters go by, all with long, curly hair, and I heard them talking. They didn't speak Italian, they spoke German, so I asked the proprietor, 'Whose children are they?' 'They are Mascagni's children.' 'But these are German!' 'No: they have a German governess, but they are Italian and speak Italian.' 'But really, are they Mascagni's children?' Therefore I am upset. I didn't know these were your youngsters; I want to meet them, as I want to meet your wife."

"This is a great honor." He had stopped my children in the hall various times, but never thought they were mine.

---

30   Domenico ("Mimì"), b.1889; Edoardo ("Dino"), b.1891; and Emilia ("Emi"), b.1892.

So I went and told the governess to bring them right away to Verdi. When I entered with my wife I saw a spectacle which moved me. Verdi was standing with all three of my children in his arms. I said, "My children, if you knew how many people would like to be as you are, on the breast of this great man!" Verdi even offered some toys to my children which I jealously preserve among my relics.

After his death, looking at the papers scattered on his desk, I found his letters answering the greetings my children had sent him for the New Year.[31]

Verdi was very robust. He had gone down somewhat in his last years, but earlier he was strong. He lived in the country. He always wore a large hat and carried a cane to support himself a bit, but after all he managed well. A wonderful constitution without doubt.

If one observes the monument that has been erected to him in Milan, that is Verdi; it is a very good resemblance. And the picture in oil by Boldoni is the best portrait resemblance — it is a striking thing, that famous picture. Verdi has a *cache-col* and top hat on his head. He was a handsome man, and as he got older he became more handsome. As a young man I had seen him when *Falstaff* was given at La Scala and earlier on the occasion of *Don Carlo*. I was at that performance. He had a frown...whereas as an old man he had such a sweetness...he was the most tender, affectionate man that one can imagine.

For me he is still the man whom I knew personally, who gave me the honor and opportunity of his confidence, and whose voice taught me so many things which formed the rules of my life and my art and have created in my soul the religion of love and goodness. And I have never forgotten a word of those discussions, true lessons for me who always has regarded Verdi as my maestro.

---

31   Letters not yet mailed. See p.152.

16   THE PESARO YEARS (1895-1902)

Pesaro, the city where Rossini was born, will always remain bound up in my memories as the city where I carried out my most noteworthy musical activity. But what a wretched city! In truth, my stay there was not happy.

Rossini, dying, had left a great part of his fortune to the city so that a theater and conservatory for singers could be built. There has always been a misunderstanding concerning this bequest, the municipal administration of Pesaro considering itself Rossini's heir, when actually it was only the executor of the will.

Now it happened that after Pedrotti it was I who was entrusted with the direction of the Conservatory, a burden I accepted, and I was determined to given the school the reputation which it lacked until then. News of the nomination came to me in October of 1895 while I was in Germany conducting a series of concerts and operas (in a very short length of time I conducted 180 of them).

Passing through Livorno I went to Pesaro, my father accompanying me, and immediately set to work with the ardor of my still youthful age[32] and with the enthusiasm of a neophyte. Thus my great work began, directed especially to giving the Conservatory the best teachers.

I had lived in Cerignola for many years and would still be there if it had not been for a very sad occurrence. My children's German governess, whom my wife had taken very much to her heart, died there at the beginning of 1896. I was in Pesaro and my wife was denied permission to bury this woman in the Cerignola cemetery because they had been unable to convert her to Catholicism. Lina said that she could not allow it that this woman, who had belonged to one religion until her forty-fifth year, be obliged to be converted against her will. I sent a telegram; the German consul general, who was in Barletta, was called and finally everything was arranged through the mayor of Cerignola who was a gentleman. But after this happened, I believed it to be duty to leave Cerignola forever. I was disgusted and saddened.

During the time of my directorship I gave the Pesaro Institute all the best activity and all the musical intelligence of which I was capable.

---

32   Mascagni was 31.

Among my students, many of which were successful, was Zandonai, who later became Director of the Institute. But I was succeeded by Zanella, a capable man, though somewhat unsophisticated. So deep was the obligation I felt towards the reputation of the Conservatory, and so fruitful were my labors, that one day the director of the Milan Conservatory came to Pesaro and told me he wished to apply my methods at his conservatory, so excellent did he find them.

I had formed an orchestra of first rate players and was proud of it. In 1899 I had the good fortune to be able to perform the *Pezzi sacri* of Verdi, the last work that he wrote. He had not been happy with its performance at La Scala. I wanted to perform this work at Pesaro and he wrote me a letter which dumbfounded me, for it said, "I shall summon the doctors and try to get permission to come to Pesaro. I want to hear this great performance."

This was something of an embarrassment for me since I had to install an elevator in the Conservatory. He was eighty-six, an old man, and couldn't walk up the stairs. But in the end he was not allowed to go. He wrote me:

> Milan, 20 May 1899
> Extremely gratified by your very courteous letter. I thank you from my heart. In spite of my good intentions, my years condemn me to quiet, rest and inertia. I praise, and am happy to be able to do so, these great musical performance, which, conducted by you, shall as a result have Italian spirit and further our art. I wish to present my respectful greetings to your wife and give a kiss to your charming children. I shake your hand and call myself.
> Your G. Verdi

Verdi sent me a telegram when he heard of the reception of his pieces.

> I have heard with the greatest pleasure of the outcome of the Pesaro concert and combined praises are due you, who promoted and conducted it, to the exceptional Venturi,[33] and to all the able players and students who performed. I

---

33 Aristide Venturi, who taught the chorus. He was chorus master at La Scala, 1894-1902.

repeat again that these great performances which you alone
are doing will continue to hold aloft the banner of our Music.
Verdi

I still have many letters from him. Verdi always wrote to me. But, and
this is curious, he wrote me without my giving him any reason to. When
later I returned to Pesaro from Germany where I had been for six or
seven months, Verdi wrote me, "Welcome back to the city of your work.
Regards with all my heart." These were letters which he wrote me.

My labors with the orchestra soon attained an unhoped for result at
the musical Exposition in Paris. Pesaro, together with the major capi-
tals of the entire world, took part in the contest fixed by that Exposition, and, something epoch making, won the contest by virtue of the
great number of symphonies which made up its program and for the
excellence of execution.

One day Ricordi came to Pesaro to hear my orchestra and for the occasion I performed the Sixth Symphony by Tchaikovsky. Ricordi and
the others in the audience much admired it and Sgambati, sent by the
government on inspection, said that the Conservatory of Pesaro would
be dead if it were to lose the directorship of Mascagni. In the event was
this what happened? I cannot be the judge of it.

To carry out my intentions I needed the assets of the Rossini fund
and I asked the city administration for the free use of them. But this request began a locked battle between me and the city council, which
opened the hostilities with a thousand intrigues, not the least of which
was a press campaign in the city newspaper, in articles of the most spite-
ful and treacherous criticism of my behavior. I remember that the most
active of the journalists en-trusted with waging war on me was a certain Lusignolo, to whose accusations I answered in the columns of the
Roman daily papers.

Later the Socialist Party also entered the fight, and one day sent their
emissaries to one of my evening performances, informing me that the
party would back me on the condition that I carry out an electoral
propaganda campaign for their victory.

I, who up to that time belonged to the party of honesty (the only
party which does not issue cards to its members), hurried to disabuse
them of every illusion in this respect. "I belong to the party of honesty," I said to the interested solicitors, "of honesty, which for the moment
does not exist in politics; therefore..." Because of this brusque and, if
you wish, somewhat arrogant response, I naturally lost their un-
solicited support.

At that time fantastic rumors circulated about me, among which was one that I had been a victim of attempts on my person. I found it necessary to declare that all this was nothing more than the result of an overheated atmosphere, devoid of clear thinking and sincerity.

The president of the Conservatory was the Hon. Carnevali, a perfect gentleman, who suffered greatly from the senseless war made on me by the city council. When he died I was in Mantua on account of certain of my obligations, and I immediately left for Pesaro to carry my heartbroken farewell to my departed friend. When I arrived in the city, the mayor energetically opposed my taking part in the funeral, but did not succeed in his intention. I did not consider myself beaten and I attacked that gentleman in my funeral discourse, stigmatizing his behavior. I was not content with this, however, and, seeing the mayor as he crossed the prefecture square together with Michetti, director of the mental hospital, I leaned out of the window of my carriage and vigorously addressed him: "Pig! Pig and coward!"

I was threatened with arrest but I wasn't worried and, to thwart the conspiracy, left for Fano and later continued on to Rome. The mayor, offended, lodged a complaint of defamation against me. But I wasn't intimidated and, assisted by two excellent lawyers from the Roman bar, I returned to Pesaro.

In the morning, at an early hour, I found myself in court ready for battle, which did not take place, however, since the mayor withdrew the complaint, fearing some serious complications on account of his not too clean administration. In fact, I was able to prove that at least 80.000 lire had been taken from Rossini's patrimony and used for... streetcleaning! Not satisfied, I then made recourse to the Court of Reckonings, citing the arbitrary and illegal tactics of my relentless enemy's behaviour. Many personalities of the time entered into the thorny matter as supporting actors, among whom was even Giolitti, who advised me to desist from my resolutions for love of tranquillity. "Dear Mascagni" (these are his words), "in spite of the saints, one does not live in Paradise! Why are you so insistent about staying in Pesaro? Come away!" But I have a hard head, I remained firm and won a victory.

In spite of these easy triumphs, the atmosphere did not clear for me. Because of this, one day, weary and disheartened, I decided to abandon Pesaro and the Institute. In the none too easy business of my departure I was ably assisted by my friend Michetti, director of the Provincial Mental Hospital, who was more valuable to me than I could have hoped for.

Later I had to return to Pesaro to withdraw my effects from the Banco d'Italia, and on that occasion I received very festive receptions from the good people of Pesaro. This was the true popular sentiment and the most coveted reward for which I had gone through so much.

That city saw me again a third time on the occasion of the fiftieth anniversary of Rossini's death; in fact, I was invited to preside over the celebrations. The Institute, in the meantime, had passed to State ownership. At that time I conducted *Barbiere* and *Iris*, obtaining triumphant successes, but what most satisfied my pride was finding my old adversaries penitent and confused.

In later years I had occasion to see Pesaro again, but only as conductor of the orchestra. I never stayed, however, at the hotel that is on the sea; it was full of mosquitoes and there was no peace there. I did find, though, a modest hotel, good enough and without mosquitoes. On its facade there was a plaque: "IN THIS HOUSE LIVED GIUSEPPE VERDI". Evidently the name of Verdi had been engraved in place of Rossini's and on account of this a few friends and I decided to remove it during the night, but we were deterred by the police. As compensation I have in my collection of watches (eighty-eight very rare ones, belonging to great men of all times) that of the Swan of Pesaro.

For me, Luigi Illica was more than a librettist or friend; very often he was also my advisor and inspiration, since he had, as few do, the vision of grand scenic lines. In short, he created the drama and was not a simple adapter like so many others. He was a tireless and marvelous worker. With all his libretti, many of which are linked with the names of Puccini, Catalani, Giordano and mine, one could make up an actual library.

Illica and I were great friends. He was the best of my librettists, but we fought often because I was never satisfied. Since my youth I too was a bit overbearing and nervous, especially when the verses gave me no inspiration. Well, one fine day Illica burst and handsomely blessed me out. I looked for another poet. But then I calmed him down.

Illica also worked for Puccini, but the temperaments of these two friends, both excellent artists, were not in harmony. Illica had his own particular creative strength and his style tended somewhat to the tragic, while Puccini leaned rather to nostalgic sweetness and light and vaporous emotion. Thus it was because of this difference in temperament that the Illica-Giocosa collaboration was born. The latter could sweeten harsh situations, smoothe corners and mitigate difficulties. To some extent this was useful to Puccini's inspiration, but many times the original beauty of the work suffered.

The first libretto which Illica wrote for me was *Iris*. I was at Pesaro and we were in agreement from the start; indeed, we decided that I would go to his Villa di Castellarquato, near Piacenza, to work on the composition of the opera. I went there in April of '97. Castellarquato is a sort of very steep knoll, a beautiful place, an hour by carriage from Fiorenzuola d'Arda, where I arrived at four in the morning of 15 April. To my great amazement, I did not find anyone at the station, not even a carriage. The lone railway clerk looked at me with a diffident air. I asked where one could find some coffee but was told that there had never been any at the station. I called the one porter and had him carry my bags to town.

It was a splendid night. In Fiorenzuola I found a very rundown cafe...but open. I went inside to wait for daylight. Around six, after a pleasant walk through the countryside, I had them hitch a horse to a carriage and I arrived at Castellarquato. The trip did not last an hour. But the carriages stopped at the edge of Castellarquato since horses cannot climb such improbably steep streets. So I went on foot and, arriving in the town, didn't need much to discover Illica's house.

He was already up and amazed to see me. "From your telegram," he said to me, "I had understood that you were going to Milan." And in fact he was not wrong. I had sent a very misleading telegram which told him, "Tonight at 3:57 I will be at Fiorenzuola d'Arda. On account of the impossible hour do not trouble yourself."

Illica had supposed that I passed through Fiorenzuola d'Arda without stopping, and that with that telegram I had only wished to send him a greeting.

I had a very affectionate welcome. The place was enchanting, made precisely for thinking and writing.

We spent the entire morning reading *Iris* and *Le Maschere*. The two libretti made an excellent impression on me.

Iris is the fragile *mousmè*, who "daydreaming, understands the warm language of the sun and translates it into goodness, caresses and promises"; who, almost brought to betrayal in the Yoshiwara, "the throbbing heart of the pleasure-loving city, where ever faster beats the life pulse of the diverse fevers which agitate the people," when she opens her eyes to the ugliness which surrounds her, transforms herself, becomes "energy and will" and throws herself into a gloomy and deep sewer where, though the body finds destruction, the spirit, from the dark visions of human egoism returns to the harmony and splendor of the light, "the language of the eternals." Iris is the symbol of immortal art, triumphing over all the filth of the base world, but what graceful contours, what delicacy, what sweetness surround this symbol!

Illica told me only a few things about *Le Maschere*, but enough to make me fall in love with it.

After lunch we had an idea; to go to Busseto to greet Verdi. Illica had two good horses hitched to an open carriage and we set out. As we went along we realized that very probably the great Maestro was not at Sant'-Agata, but in any event the prospect of the outing was very pleasant. From Castellarquato to Busseto is twenty-three kilometers. When we arrived in Busseto we went into a cafe. A musician, a certain Mastrucci from Parma, recognized me and introduced himself to us. From him we learned that Verdi was in Genoa.

We were prepared for the news but I was sorry nonetheless. I very much would like to have seen and greeted the glorious Maestro. In my

Luigi Illica

spiritual condition his presence and speech would have been very good for me.

Busseto is a pleasant town. I admired the large palace of Pallavicini, I saw the Castello and the Teatro Verdi, which is very grandiose. After a few hours, with the horses hitched up again, we left.

And now comes the good — or bad — part.

We were barely two hundred meters out of Busseto and the horses were going at a good trot, when one of the rear wheels of the carriage came loose from the axle, the vehicle tilted to one side and the horses bolted. It was a terrible moment because the carriage was about to capsize. With a quick movement Illica and I attempted to restore the equilibrium. The horses stopped and the danger was avoided.

We got down. The carriage was in a deplorable state, even the front wheel was broken. The danger over, we laughed over the adventure and stayed in the middle of the road, waiting for another vehicle to be brought. And thank heaven we were only a short distance from Busseto.

The vehicle finally arrived and we were able to set off with a very beautiful moon, arriving at Castellarquato at nine o'clock at night.

We ate, and at ten-thirty went to bed. I slept very pleasantly after a night spent on the train and fifty-four kilometers spent in a carriage.

Returning to Pesaro I set to work on *Iris*. I wanted to write a work of art serenely conceived, written according to my criteria; with ideas sprouting from my imagination; a very light thing, really delicate, and I believe I was successful since the critics were favorable.

Music must not be an arid comment on the drama: it must narrate the drama and develop it with its own inexhaustible powers. In *Iris* I wanted to reinvigorate the melodramatic opera, still maintaining the equilibrium between the voices and orchestra. In writing the opera I always had fixed in my mind the object of being judged not by the drama but by the music.

Let me explain with an example. A composer who had to deal with the horrifying dramatic situation of a father forced by the petty tyranny of a powerful man to expose his own son to the danger of death, today would rely heavily on the impression aroused in the public by this given situation, and I cannot say he would be wrong. And if the librettist had put in the mouth of that father a moving plea to his little son to think of his distant mother, the composer, sure of his *effect* would content himself in having those words declaimed with the stress of anxious trepidation, without giving a thought in the world to embellishing them with a long impassioned melody. But just think what Rossini did. William Tell must pierce an apple, placed on the head of his son, with an arrow; and as he stands there, with the bow in his left hand and the sharpened arrow in his right, he sings (note well, *sings*) the sublime phrase, *"Gemmy, pensa alla madre!"*[34] And so in the listener words and music are combined in a single impression, since the music expresses with sublime notes the maternal memory which is in the words. And so the composer triumphs over the librettist.

---

34   "Jemmy, think of your mother."

Iris (Act I)

I have sufficient knowledge of the public and believe I possess enough of that thing the critics call "theatricality" to be able, by exerting myself, to earn for myself with a scale, a cadence or a big orchestral effect thunderous applause, two or three curtain calls and an insistent demand for encores. I wished to abstain from vulgar evils in *Iris*. Rather than exaggerate a mood, where it would have been easy for the tenor, soprano and baritone to flaunt their virtuosity, I toned down, lessened. There are some moments in which the interruption produced by applause could offend the aesthetic continuity of the opera, and so I really exerted myself to render such applause impossible. But how much stronger, more beautiful, more noble is the artistic emotion which one gathers and concentrates in silence! For one who stands listening in the wings, the variety of the silences in a crowded theater is enormous, and we understand the significance of these silences very precisely, just as if we could see those intent faces, those movements of the heads, the increasing attention from moment to moment.

There is much music in my *Iris*. I did not content myself with two or three ideas which return (in all senses of the word) and are repeated, reproduced and concealed; so that one cannot see that they are always those same ideas, due to the flourishings and unfoldings of complicated harmonic combinations. Instead, I always searched for melody, and hoped I would be accused of even having found too much. "Searched for" in a manner of speaking, it is understood. If I did not feel the melody come all at once into my brain, my imagination, my soul (I don't know how to indicate the precise place), I left off writing and waited for it to arrive. The serenade that the tenor sings in the first act, and which gives the impression of a scholarly elaboration, came to me all at once, suddenly, and I wrote down that first impulse, without later changing even one note. I have wished to be sincere above all in my music.

The premiere of *Iris* was given at the Costanzi on 22 November 1898, with a splendid house, overcrowded with a most select audience. There were Puccini, Franchetti, Mugnone, Boito, Tebaldini, Sgambati and critics from the most important newspapers all over the world. When I went to the podium I was greeted by one of those ovations which have remained most unforgettable in my life.

I have said that the critics received the opera well, but it was not so at the beginning; indeed, many found that not only was the libretto empty and inconclusive but that I had put too many abstruse things and harmonic subtleties into the music. It was the public who decreed the true success of the opera, and was enraptured by the "Hymn of the Sun".

I then gave *Iris* the following March at the San Carlo in Naples, in the presence of the Prince and Princess of Naples. Applause which never ended. All, all, all applauded. Up to that moment I had never seen similar enthusiasm. A real delirium — more than *Cavalleria*!

18

A LIBRETTO BY GANDOLIN
(1899)

I must mention my great friendship with Luigi Arnaldo Vassallo, the famous "Gandolin", director of the Genoese daily newspaper *Secolo XIX*, a very subtle and droll humorist, a man of impeccable principles and generous heart. Gandolin was very interested in each of my works. I listened to him, considered his opinions—and so we loved one another!

Gandolin was a real character, as is well known; for a time he seriously applied himself to being a spiritualist. He caused tables to move, called the dead; in other words, a thousand deviltries. While I was at Pesaro—around '99 or thereabouts—Gandolin sent me a libretto. It was a clever piece of work which was entitled *Spiritualism*.

The piece opened in the sumptuous apartment of Count Valfreda, a convinced spiritualist, who surrounds himself with many practitioners of the spiritual sciences and the most celebrated mediums of the time.

The room in which the action takes place is of great elegance in its architectural lines and in its decorations, but at the same time simple in its furnishings: a large table in the center with many chairs around it. A crowd of adepts already occupies the room, people from all classes, of all ages. While waiting for Count Valfreda, whom everyone calls the Master, his secretary does the honors of the house and receives the guests. And now, for their first time, a husband and his wife enter. She (Maria) is very young and delicate; he, Giorgio, a mature (older) man, but with a strong constitution. He has just married for the second time, and Maria, his young wife, has been discovered to be an excellent medium due to her extraordinary nervous sensibility.

During the gathering she will have to give proof of her gifts and is rather disturbed, however sincere a believer in spiritualist doctrines she may be. Giorgio, instead, is a complete skeptic and in his heart derides the people around him.

Count Valfreda, the Master, enters. All rise to their feet and greet him deferentially. The experiments begin immediately. A medium sits in an armchair, the lights are extinguished and the scene remains barely illuminated by a pale and feeble light.

Meanwhile the adepts begin their entreaties and make their invocations. The scene is dappled with tiny lights which describe fantastic arabesques in the darkness of the room. All of a sudden the background of the scene is illuminated and various shadows are outlined. From their midst emerges the superb figure of a man.

The Master asks, "Who are you, spirit?" The shadow answers that it is Pier Luigi Palestrina, the great musician, and he presents himself to the adepts' gaze. He is accompanied by composers equally great as he was. The apparition of these spiritual beings was to be accompanied by fragile, almost impalpable music. Gradually the shadows disappear. And the celestial voices are lost in the vastness of space.

Light returns to the scene, and another medium, inspired this time by Beethoven, seats himself at an organ which is at the right side of the room. He plays and sings, accompanied by the chorus of those present. The last to undergo the experiment is the young wife. Pale and trembling, she goes to sit down in the armchair. The Master goes up to her, stares fixedly at her and hypnotizes her.

Giorgio, who until this moment, in spite of the prodigious results obtained in the preceding experiments, has remained almost indifferent, now experiences a sense of fear. He rises from his seat abruptly and would like to stop his wife from continuing the experiment. But the Master calms him. The lights are again extinguished and the semi-darkness returns.

Now the background of the scene is suddenly illuminated again, and the vague figure of a woman, as light as air, is gradually outlined and becomes more substantial.

The Master asks, "Who are you, spirit?" but before he has finished a fearful shout resounds in the room.

It is Giorgio who screams, "I alone know who you are! You are Cecilia, my victim, and you have come here to demand revenge for your murder!"

All rise and attempt to calm the maniac who, beside himself, continues to shout and attempt to flee.

But the shadow speaks and says that it has not come for revenge but rather to pardon. Its voice is an enchantment. It is Giorgio's first wife who was poisoned by him. But she does not bear him a grudge for his crime. Her love for him is greater than his offense. And she turns to Giorgio, exhorting him to be good, to do charitable and pious deeds and God's pardon will descend on him, as has already that of the poor innocent dead woman.

The emotion of the bystanders is inexpressible. The shadow slowly disappears and its enchanting voice is lost, fading in a final halo of divine light.

The room becomes light again. And now what a scene! Giorgio stares fixedly at the back of the scene and shouts that the shadow is still there, even more distinct and real.

Those present are silent and dismayed. Giorgio can stand it no longer and confesses his crime. Yes, he has poisoned his first wife to inherit her wealth and coldly watched her last moments. After a terrible fit of madness he falls dead to the ground, as the bystanders invoke peace on his spirit, which must wander for a long time in the infinite regions of nothingness.

All this happens in half an hour, drama and music; in short, a sort of detective story set to music.

At first, since I liked the libretto because it was new and also because I wanted to please Gandolin, I thought of setting it to music. It was above all a clever libretto, very well done. But then I reconsidered it; it was too unsuited to my temperament and I ended up doing nothing.

But Gandolin didn't bear a grudge against me; we continued to love one another. Indeed, every now and then he sends Lina and me a few postcards with little figures drawn by him. I still have a few of them.

19

CONDUCTING IN RUSSIA
(1900)

In March, 1900, as a result of three German impresarios' offers, I went to Russia. At that time I was still in Pesaro and was working on *Le Maschere*, but that disgusting Pesaro business had so worn me out that because of this and also to escape from the enervating work of the school, I accepted the offer.

Because of an enormous amount of snowfall, I arrived in Berlin three quarters of an hour late. The coach was without heat due to an accident, so I suffered greatly in spite of being wrapped up in my fur coat and travelling blanket. I was unable to sleep. At the Berlin station I found my three impresarios who accompanied me to the hotel, where I finally was able to sleep for a bit.

My companion, Seveso,[35] and I left Berlin, taking seats in a magnificent two-bed compartment. We dined cheerfully, but when we were about to go to bed the conductor advised us that at one-thirty in the morning the train would arrive at Aleksandrów[36] where the customs were. So we decided to wait, playing cards.

I really thought the customs would be nothing at all but we stayed in the office until three, something incredible. The officials collected our passports, and when these were in order, a noncommissioned officer loudly called out the names of the owners, who then had to open their baggage, which was scrupulously examined. The suitcases were emptied completely and every object was gone over minutely. If, however, a passport was not in order, its owner was immediately sent back in a special train which was waiting in the station. An amazing police force which one had no idea of at that time. The police were able to know how many people entered the Empire, what they were going for, what their professions were and what they carried! Forty years ago in the rest of Europe one could go and come as one pleased. Now everything is changed, but that is something else.

---

35   A German impresario.
36   A city in central Poland, between Berlin and Warsaw.

Lina Mascagni, 1899

It may be imagined that when they saw the tam-tam[37] for *Iris* they wanted me to pay the customs at any cost. So I identified myself and told the purpose of my trip to an official who spoke French and only in this way was I able to have the cases passed.

I got back on the train and went to bed, but at seven in the morning I had to interrupt my sleep. We had come to Warsaw and had to change trains. The tracks of the Russian trains are fifteen centimeters larger than all the other tracks in the world and as a result no foreign coach can enter Russia. Farewell fine coaches, farewell luxury, farewell convenience. The Russian compartments were something unique. Bare, empty, without taste, small windows with two immovable pieces of glass, no electric light, no gas, no oil, only tallow candles for illumination; all this, I was told, to avoid any possibility of fire, for if a fire should occur in the middle of that wasteland of snow, the poor travellers would be quite dead.

The beds were without sheets and blankets; one low and hard mattress. One slept dressed. The dining coach was worse than our third class coaches. Even there each table had its own candlestick. An inexpressible sadness!

We found a very kind Russian who spoke German rather well and he kept us good company. In the next compartment was Ysaÿe, the celebrated violinist, who was going to Moscow also.

When we went for dinner in the dining car (we had lunch at a small station where the stop was longer than half an hour), a curious scene ensued, because the waiter only understood Russian and we did not know how to explain ourselves. A Russian gentlemen, a lawyer who spoke good Italian, came to our aid. We ate and drank rather well, but what a bill at the end!

---

37   Large gong.

After dinner I went to bed dressed. Heat did not come from the heater, but was rather given off by some colossal cast-iron stoves, which were in each coach. Imagine, outside it was more than twenty degrees below zero!

All at once the train stopped. What had happened? I jumped from my berth and asked Seveso. Fortunately it was only an accident which, having been caught in time, was not very serious. The wheels of the dining car had overheated (in all that snow) and threatened to come loose from the axles. The personnel noticed it, the train was stopped and the dining car had to be abandoned. A delay of more than forty minutes. In the morning, however, we were left without breakfast!

We finally arrived in Moscow at four in the afternoon. More than forty-three hours on the train! And always in the snow. My agent, Glass, was waiting for me at the station. The weather was beautiful and it was a warm day, so the Russians said. In fact, it was barely twelves degrees below zero!

Next morning I went with Glass and Seveso to the Imperial Theater. The orchestra welcomed me with great applause and clapped at the end of every piece. This was the first program: Overture to *William Tell* by Rossini; *Rêverie*, Schumann;[38] *Gavotta delle bambole* (for strings alone), Mascagni; Symphonic Prelude to *Iris*, Dream and Intermezzo from *Ratcliff*, Mascagni; Scherzo from the *Quartet* in E minor, Cherubini; *Symphony* in C minor, Beethoven.

That morning, the rehearsal began at ten, which was our eight-thirty, and lasted until one. The orchestra wasn't much, but they played the Beethoven symphony very well.

Afterwards Glass offered us a magnificent lunch at our Hôtel du Bazar Slave. Then we took a short walk, it being a very beautiful day (fifteen degrees below zero).

I saw Mattia Battistini who gave me a princely welcome. No other Italian artist at the time was able to win such keen favor in Russia as Battistini. All were talking about him with great admiration. I reminded him of his performance in *I Rantzau*. How great he was in that opera! No one else was able to arouse such deep emotion in the public as he. Oh! those beautiful performances of *I Rantzau* in Rome with Battistini and De Lucia! It was not possible to attain greater perfection in singing, greater distinction and security of the stage. Battistini was as sovereign an actor as he was a master of Italian *bel canto*.

---

38 This was a favorite concert piece of Mascagni's, an orchestration of *Traümerei*.

We then left for St. Petersburg, since I was to give the first concert there, the second in Moscow. Moscow was a city which had some great and beautiful things, but one lived better in St. Petersburg. I gave a good many concerts in both cities, conducting one in Moscow, then one in St. Petersburg and so on; I shuttled back and forth like a commuter.

Out of six numbers at the first concert I had to repeat four, which were the *Rêverie* by Schumann, the *Gavotta delle bambole*, the Intermezzo from *Ratcliff* and the "Hymn of the Sun". The Beethoven symphony was admirably played. It was a real triumph. The whole audience was on its feet shouting "*Viva Mascagni! Viva l'Italia!*" The Slavic soul was profoundly moved by our music.

This was my second program: the *Pathétique* by Tchaikovsky, the Overture to *Tannhäuser*, *Le Rouet d'Omphale* by Saint-Saëns and the *Peer Gynt* Suite by Grieg. When I rehearsed the *Pathétique* they gave me an ovation. Many of the players, who had performed that marvelous symphony under the direction of Tchaikovsky himself,[39] told me that I conducted with the same vehemence and color with which the composer conducted it. This statement pleased me very much!

But I couldn't wait to get away from that country. It is a country so different from ours that I could not understand it. Tobacco was not to be found; no one understood me; at the hotel there were neither waiters nor maids, just cossacks who frightened me.

King Umberto I died during the summer of that year.[40] At the time I was in Pesaro and a telegram from the Hon. Panzacchi, then Under Secretary of Public Instruction, invited me to conduct the funeral mass which was to be performed on 9 August in the Pantheon on the occasion of the arrival of the corpse of the King. Gianturco proposed to have the Cherubini *Requiem* performed; I, naturally, would have preferred that of Verdi, but after a long discussion with Santa Cecilia and Filarmonica Romana officials, we agreed to perform only music for voices alone: Anerio, Victoria, Palestrina, Renzi and Terziani. We arrived at this decision primarily because the choir of the Pantheon is really too small to accommodate a large orchestral group, but there was also another reason. Since the occasion dealt with a national sorrow, we wanted the performance to have a mystical character. I was very pleased with this decision. I invited all the conservatories to collaborate, using their best voices, in the realization of this very Italian performance and thus had

---

39   Seven years earlier. See the Tchaikovsky entry in the *Personalia* appendix.
40   From an assassin's bullet. See *Personalia*.

at my command a choral complement of the very first order. It was a superhuman task, days of work and fever, but I managed an extraordinary performance.

It is impossible to give an idea of that day which for me was so memorable. I got up at five because I could not have slept. The Via Nazionale was thronged and the soldiers began to march at four in the morning. I was at the Albergo del Quirinale which is right on Via Nazionale, so I could see the whole cortege. When the gun-carriage with the coffin passed, covered by the tri-color flag, tears came to my eyes. In the front of the carriage was the King's horse, covered in black velvet. The new King, Vittorio, came immediately after, his face very pale. As soon as the delegations from the various ruling houses passed, I left the hotel in order to arrive on time at the Pantheon. What a spectacle that was! There were the two Queens dressed in black, surrounded by all the Princes; the public wept in silence and several times, referring to Margherita, repeated in subdued voices, "A saint, a saint!" Panzacchi said to me, "Queen Margherita spoke with no one, but I who was near her and attentively observed her, had the impression that in certain moments she felt a sense of comfort at the sound of that admirable music."

For me, my theater was the Costanzi. I gave *Le Maschere*, however, in seven theaters at the same time, on the same evening. I wanted to demonstrate abroad the potential of the lyric theater in Italy, which was able to give an opera in seven theaters[41] at the same time, which meant using thousands of orchestral players, thousands of choristers, seven conductors, sixty-three singers (since nine were needed for each theater) and all had to be ready the same evening. And it was done, let it be well noted. That evening of *Le Maschere* remained a memorable one. Italy did something which will remain in history forever. There was no other nation in the world which could do such a thing.

Naturally the event, which was without precedent, focused complete attention on *Le Maschere*, and it was precisely for this reason that the critics seized on the opera. *Le Maschere* was an enormous amount of work for me, the most important opera which I had written up to that time (which was '99). The principal difficulty consisted in the spirit which the music had to have, and I naturally tried to write music full of spirit.

I wanted to write a quintessentially Italian opera and used this subject. No one was prepared for these masks, no one knew what they were. At that time neither Illica nor I could find one book in Italy which discussed the *teatro dell'arte*. Only in France was such a book found; indeed, many of them were. The *teatro dell'arte* emigrated from Italy in the seventeenth century and went abroad, going to France with Italian comedians.

The *teatro dell'arte* was an improvisational theater. A subject invented and the parts distributed, the artists added the words. Then Goldoni came and gave the Italian language to the *teatro dell'arte* but still continued the same type of theater. In general, the contents of the Goldoni comedy are very lightweight. It sparkles, instead, on account of its freshness, vivacity and the glitter of its dialogue, but these qualities disappear, or are enormously reduced, by a musical adaptation. It was

---

41   In the event the premiere occurred in six theaters on 17 January 1901: owing to the indisposition of the tenor, the Naples performance occurred on 19 January; but this does not invalidate Mascagni's point about the extraordinary resources of the Italian lyric theater of that time.

necessary, therefore, to think of something different. Obviously I could not set a rough sketch to music.

I thought: Nowadays the public goes to the theater to be distressed, to ruin its digestion with violent emotions; we composers no longer know how to laugh on the stage. It could be said that the marvelous vein of Italian humor dried up with Rossini. I was seized by the nostalgia of that beautiful and immortal smile, and I attempted a re-evocation of it.

It seemed to me, and still does, a worthy task of a conscientious artist to make the *commedia dell'arte* rise again. Did not Rossini, our magnificent master, our theater's great optimist, draw on the purest sources of the *commedia dell'arte* for his *Barber of Seville*? And why, after him, should none of us open a chink in the gloomy environment of our contemporary theater to that smile, to that joyous and serene satire, to link again our activity to that glorious tradition, by now too distant from our time and souls.

My characters descend directly from the satirical comedy; after all, even in the *Barber of Seville*, if we think about it, we have Florindo, Rosaura, Colombina. The same artists, in short. Illica and I detached them from that world and transported them into ours, in the firm conviction that we were serving, however humbly, the highest motives of art.

The opera was given, as I've said, in seven theaters. In six theaters it failed, succeeded in one: the Costanzi in Rome.

I wrote a few words in the columns of the widely circulated *Messaggero*, not to defend my music, nor to discuss the various judgments of critics and the disparate and contradictory verdicts of the Italian audiences, but only to answer all at once the innumerable quantities of letters, postcards and telegrams which were sent to me the day after the first performance with the vehemence of a raging torrent:

> ...I divide this inundation of paper in three sections. In the first, I place friends and all those who, though not knowing me personally, have sent me words of sympathy and affection and show they have faith in my future.
>
> I, too have this faith, and I can proudly affirm that the storm of these recent days, rather than discouraging me has reinvigorated my energy, repurified my forces and sharpened my will; to that artistic ideal, which is not always reached but to which I have constantly looked, I shall continue to consecrate all my soul, all my youth, with the con-

science of not working in vain for this lyric theater which is so much a part of the glory of Italian art.

I pass to the second category, alas! the most numerous. In it I place those gentlemen who entrenching themselves behind anonymity, rejoice in my fiasco, exultantly sing hymns at every downfall of those who think and produce, and range from plebeian impertinence to refined injury.

In the infinite number of letters addressed to me, whether special delivery or not, I am mistreated (and how!) not only as a composer, which is a natural right of everyone, but even as a private individual: they spare neither my family nor my children, to whom were even sent postcards with drawings anything but complimentary to me, accompanied by comments and epithets, which are obvious proof of the noble sentiments and ferociously destructive joy of those who sent them.

All of these people are unanimous in expressing the hope that a vacuum be formed around me, that not one more note of music be written by me, that on my work, which is not entirely sterile and unfruitful as far as the Italian theater goes, may fall an inexorable oblivion.

I knew that I had a good many adversaries and some enemies, but really would never have imagined that they could have proliferated so quickly: and confronted by this phenomenon of prodigious fecundity—which is reminiscent of certain insects—I think with deep sadness of the sorrow which I would have involuntarily brought to all these good people if my poor *Maschere* had obtained the success in all the Italian theaters which I had hoped for and which it shall obtain in spite of the contrary opinion of my denigrators.

Several of these have accused me in the newspapers of having wished, with this *Maschere*, to make fun of the public. How is it possible to answer them?

But these 'blessed children of heaven,' do they know what the work of mind and heart costs; do they know the anxieties, the trepidations, the bitterness which inexorably accompany the life of an artist, in the bitter day-to-day battle with an ideal which seizes and which escapes us, and when grasped vanishes again; do they know what it means to one who has fought and hoped, what an artistic battle may be, lost reasonably or by fault?

I pass to the third category, which is the most important, indeed, the only one which has given me the desire to write these few lines; I allude to those who have both said and written that the fortunate outcome of *Le Maschere* in Rome is due exclusively to the love which the Roman public has for me.

I answer that no praise has been able to touch my heart more than this, which to those who gave it must have seemed an irony. If I were forced to spend my entire youth and whole life to earn and keep the spontaneous affection of the citizens of Rome, I would bless my fate and would feel myself the happiest of Italians.

And with a grateful heart I think of these citizens, who have such an exquisite feeling for art and who, through their unity and indifference to editorial passions, carry in their every verdict the sense of justice and proportion, and I express my strongest thanks.

At Rome, twenty-two performance were given without interruption. It seems incredible to me! And they were called fiascoes then! Now two performances of a new work are given and they can't give a third because the public doesn't come to the theaters, but today they are called triumphs. But those were different times, times when there was enthusiasm and even a spirit of sacrifice; and then, a true, a great love for art.

In November of 1905, *Le Maschere* was revived at the Teatro Adriano in Rome, and I took advantage of this occasion to retouch the opera.

The management of the Adriano, who had the idea of this revival, was enthusiastic before the event. I, naturally, was still the same: calm and full of faith, that faith which has always sustained me and which has left me the same man, whether it be 17 May 1890 after *Cavalleria* or 17 January 1901 after *Le Maschere*.

The reason for this revival was very simple: I could not accept the verdict, somewhat brutal, which the public and critics passed on my opera in 1901 and I believed my desire to be legitimate and human in appearing before this same public, in the hope that they would want to hear me. I believed firmly in the worth of the attempt and in the reasons which inspired it. I fell in love with this theme as with no other and I had studied so as to give to each character a particular form, to assimilate it with a *genre* of existing music. That's why I was accused of plagiarism. The accusation was unwarranted, since imitation of style is not theft of ideas, and I tried to clothe my ideas in the styles of the most celebrated and recognized masters. And frankly, the storm unleashed on the opera had taken me by complete surprise.

The success of *Le Maschere* in 1905 was immense, unanimous, magnificent and all in all the performance was superior to the famous and memorable seven of 1901.[42]

For after all, what are these masks of mine? What do they mean to represent in the contemporary theater if not to return to the healthy serenity of our great traditions and the smile of the *commedia dell'arte*?

And it cannot be said that the public cannot or does not want to accede to this form any longer, judging it *passé*. No, humor is eternal, eternal the happy satirical spirit of the Italian mask.

Only we no longer have, unfortunately, any link with it in our daily lives. Even less in music (one no longer finds an *allegro*). But Truth, impersonated by the masks, is more alive, vibrant and active than ever. Let us look around us; is Florindo not seen flitting everywhere, the fatuous, elegant and lightheaded Florindo, in the theater, the cafes, the salons, the streets, all worldly gatherings? And Pantalone? The harsh, pathetic figure of Pantalone, has he not appeared everywhere before now, on the trains, at meetings, in markets, in public squares, in the cities and in the country? And Tartaglia, the man of few words, breaking off, characteristic, but acutely satiric and profoundly human? And Arlecchino, a quick spirit, imaginative, testy, chattery, but as superficial as Tartaglia is deep? And Brighella the reconciler...

No, no; the masks, beyond being a respectable product of a great epoch, are symbols of types and truths which do not die. They are obvious representations of the truest life, indeed of ironic life. Therefore they are really alive.

---

42   Mascagni was to revise the opera yet another time, the definitive version
      appearing in 1931. See *Personalia: Illica, Luigi.*

27 January 1901.

No one who did not live through those days, through that time during which one wept and suffered, can understand what the death of Giuseppe Verdi meant for Italy and for the world. No grief was more unanimous, more profound, more solemn, more overwhelming. It truly seemed as if a material, physical darkness descended over the minds and hearts of everyone. One felt that Verdi had died in the material sense only and that his spirit would continue to live among us, that his immortal art would continue to enliven us. And yet the departure of this great soul from the world of the living was, in its human inexorability, something overwhelmingly tragic for everyone.

I remember that I received the announcement while I was in Rome conducting *Le Maschere*. I interrupted the performances to run to Milan. Emotion overwhelms me every time that I think of him lying on his deathbed. The death of Immortals has a cruelty even greater than that of the ordinary living: it seems that They pay a tribute from which They should be exempted. On the trip to Milan I found myself in Bologna with Giuseppe Martucci; he too, like every musician and every conservatory director, was making a pilgrimage to the great dead.

I arrived on a Tuesday evening and was immediately admitted to view the body. It is impossible to describe the feelings which, at that sight, agitated my heart, just as it is impossible to give a tangible form to all that passed through my mind in that solemn and sorrowful hour.

The room had been cleared of the usual furniture; only the piano and small writing desk remained, and there, between the two windows where the sofa had stood beneath the large portrait, rested the coffin which already held the body of Giuseppe Verdi.

Only two candles at the foot of the coffin illuminated that great glory. I remained immobile and breathless, with my eyes fixed on those eyes closed forever, on that face no longer animated by the divine ray of genius, on that mouth no longer open in its candid and sweet smile.

And my thoughts returned spontaneously to those unforgettable days when there, in that same room and in that same place, I had spoken with him about many things relating to our art and had heard much advice and was blessed by his words and glances, and my children had been moved by his smile and caresses.

And in mind I saw him again: handsome, noble and proud, while my eyes saw only his body without life.

But was it possible? Would there never come from his mind again any concept to maintain and enlarge the fame of our art, the glory of our country? Would there never come from his breast, from his heart again any song to move our people, to irradiate the entire world with civilization and enthusiasm? Was it possible?

Alas! Verdi was dead! His soul had abandoned the earth!

I knelt, prayed and wept for a long time. Then I rose and went to the desk, where an inexpressible sense of emotion awaited me: on the desk were three short letters, with their corresponding envelopes already addressed to my children; Verdi had answered my offspring, thanking them for their New Year's greetings. Until the last day of his life he lovingly remembered my children. This is how I knew the man who wanted to be known as gruff.

But there were those who denied that Verdi was a genius. This was the verdict of the scholars, who granted this high creator of expressive music an enormous talent but denied him the living gift of genius. It was then that I had the idea of writing a sort of essay on the subject *Genius*.

I outlined an original and somewhat daring conception which I wanted to bring to a positive conclusion. I wanted to begin my task with the advent of Christianity in the pagan world, taking my cue from Rapisardi's profound poem *Lucifero*, which presents the Demon as almost afraid when, roaming the world to preach his diabolical achievement, he meets the mild Man, who all alone is preaching the law of love, goodness and justice. The writer Ratti, in his strong drama *Giuda*, depicts the episode of the Hebrew elders who assemble in their school to choose the most intelligent and cultured man among them and send him to hear the new law preached to men by this mild Man and to report to the awestruck and anxious people from what unknown source he drew his theories and convictions.

We Christians know that the sweet and mild Man who, alone and isolated, preached goodness to humanity was Jesus, and we know that Jesus was divine: Father, Son and Holy Ghost; but He came on earth for His divine mission in the guise of a mortal man, and the men who heard his law of love fell prostrate, with a new feeling stirring in their hearts. So when the messenger sent to hear and study this law returned to relate his impressions, he was unable to speak, so tremendous was his emotion. "Speak!" the elders shouted at him, "what is His concept?

From whom or what does He draw His tenets? Speak!" He manages to say with difficulty, "His concept is divine; nothing and no one prompts His theories: He creates, creates divinely." And from this moment the crowd begins to feel in their hears a new voice, a new flame burning with a goodness and love. The people are divided, the incredulous remain unmoved, attached to their primitive law, the believers become preachers in their turn, always more and more stirred by Peter and Paul who gather the neophytes in the Roman cata-combs, braving the anger of the Imperial agents; and the proselytes of the new law of Jesus increase.

Meanwhile Lucifer, afraid and overwhelmed, has hidden himself in his house of fire.

Jesus was divine; this leads us to believe that Genius is a divine gift, since only divinity can create that which does not exist. Therefore Jesus, come to earth in the guise of man to tell His new law to men for the good of humanity, remains divine but can be considered as the first man of Genius for the creation and divulgation of His divinely human law.

All this formed the beginning of my essay on Genius. I then proceeded directly to men, through the score of Saints (first among all St. Francis of Assisi) and I stopped at the artists, beginning with Leonardo da Vinci.

Is it possible to imagine that the life of one man, even a life of long years completely and intensively dedicated to studies, is enough to acquire the science of all human knowledge and wisdom such as Leonardo acquired? Not even the lives of ten great men put together would be enough to manage the conquest of all his wisdom. It is true that the two hemispheres of his brain functioned contemporaneously, each one on its own account, as the illustrious anatomists have informed us; but this does not give sufficient reason for his immense knowledge. This leads us to conceive of the idea that Leonardo did not learn what he knew from any study. He created, invented. Therefore he was a man of Genius, who had the divine gift of creating new things not yet existent. And therefore I believed I could postulate that the Man of Genius is very close to Divinity.

Now art, truly to be art, has need of the divine gift in its creation. In intellectual circles they say that painters and sculptors create their works by studying human models, from nature and also from dead nature; while architects and musicians have no models and must draw their inspiration from the imaginations of the creative artists themselves. Such an assertion seems exaggerated to me, since architects can choose their models from Imperial Rome up to Bernini; and coming to musicians, I do not have the courage to say what models one can turn to from 1500 up to Giuseppe Verdi. It is true that in both cases one runs the risk of the accusation of plagiarism, but who worries about that? One could tranquilly go on and speculate on the ignorance of the public at large.

But after all, to create a work of art one must have received the divine gift of Genius. Study only serves to discipline spontaneous creation; he who does not have the divine gift cannot create a work of art, not even if he possesses a trunk full of studies and theories.

Giuseppe Verdi had this gift to an exceptional degree but it was not recognized by everyone; indeed it was precisely the scholars who denied it to him.

I read my essay on *Genius* to Enrico Ferri who listened to me in silence, but when I arrived at the list of celebrated musicians and read the name of Verdi, he burst out, "But you are crazy! Verdi was not a genius." I remained surprised and amazed, and wanted to know on what he based such an absolute judgment; and Ferri, with the assurance of the scholar, espoused his concept to me: Verdi was never the author of a new art, one which would have indicated a new road to young musicians, but was a magnificent and active producer of music which developed in the path of the majority of his contemporaries, therefore not an inventor, not a creator, but simply a follower, an imitator. I scornfully rebelled against this concept which, besides offending Verdi, offended a world of admirers of his art; and I was about to ask Enrico Ferri what profundity of culture, of the art of music he possessed... when the judgment on Verdi expressed by his great master, Lombroso, came to mind. Lombroso, too, laid down the law that Verdi was not a genius, but for a reason very different from that of Ferri: because Verdi occupied himself with his own rural interests.

Thus two illustrious Italian scholars handed down the same verdict on the art of Giuseppe Verdi... but for entirely different reasons. Yet the reason was only one for both: Lombroso and Ferri belonged to that part of humanity which does not have the faculty of comprehending the joy of singing. This part of humanity is very numerous and extremely cumbrous due to its intellectuality and general culture. And for precisely these reasons many voluntarily wished to dedicate themselves to the study of the art of music, deluding themselves into producing some music. Vain delusion: they simply produced musical notes, enormous masses of notes but without the minimum sense of melody. Nevertheless everyone, producers and listeners, was happy. Finally, even to them the moment came to listen to some sounds which answered their lack of melodic comprehension. And to let it be understood that they were not lacking in the comprehension of sounds, they invented the humbug that one must understand music through the calculations of the brain. Lucky they![43]

Giuseppe Verdi, with his divine output, held and holds his head high against theses barbarians of art. His genius is formidable. The gift which he received from the Divinity is without measure. His music expresses the word and feeling to such an extraordinary degree that no creator of melodies has been able to approach him. When one wishes to define music by calling it "the universal language" one thinks of Verdi, whose music speaks and converses with all humanity, which understands and feels it. Music is a speech: if it does not speak it is not music.

Verdi's adversaries shouted at his back that his music was vulgar and trivial; and they cited various pieces of a popular character from his operas, without understanding that the popular character was the exact expression, more than of words, of feeling and immediacy. Faced with the people's enthusiasm and emotion for Verdi during the fateful years of our Risorgimento, they attempted to assert that such feelings were generated in patriotic hearts by the patriotic subjects chosen by the Maestro. But the reports of the time inform us that it was not only at performances of *Battaglia di Legnano*, *I vespri siciliani*, *I Lombardi*, *Giovanna d'Arco* and *Nabucco* that the thunderous shouts of the public exploded. The height of the patriotic demonstrations by Italians was recorded at the first performance of *Un ballo in maschera*, at the Apollo in Rome, where there were even some cases of madness provoked by the emotional excess.[44]

And *Ballo in maschera* is not a patriotic subject; indeed, it is one hundred per cent *bourgeois*.

The reason for all this was found in those melodies which spoke by sounds alone to the hearts of the Italians, who, excited by feelings for

---

43   Like Verdi, Mascagni was preoccupied with and defended music of the "heart" in
      contrast to music of the "mind"; vocal music in contrast to "abstract" music; and,
      in particular, Italian opera (with its emphasis on singing) in contrast to opera in
      which the orchestra appears to play a more prominent role (i.e. as in German
      operas by Wagner). Ferri and Lombroso had emphasised orchestral elements, and,
      in that sense, would have appeared to be more "German" than "Italian" in their
      sympathies.

44   This was the first time, 17 February 1859, that the acrostic "Viva VERDI" was heard.

their country, interpreted that music as the most fervid hymn of national redemption.

It can be asserted that all of Verdi's operas have the power and virtue of exalting Italian spirits and propelling them to heroism through love of their country.

And how much good did Giuseppe Verdi bring to Italy with his immortal melodies! Let the Italians not forget it!

Without doubt the patriotic subjects helped the music to enflame the spirit in those moments. How could any heart, panting for the redress of its adored country, manage to resist the choruses in *Lombardi* and *Nabucco*? And how could it resist the *allegro* in the Overture to *I vespri siciliani*, when at the explosive roll of the drum the theme of liberating revolution bursts in? And then, at the arrival of the grandiose and serene theme of Liberty,[45] how could Italian hearts resist, hearts which felt all the joy and happiness of that theme, the interpreter of all spirits' aspiration?

Here we are dealing with symphonic music, without words; but the sounds of Verdi's melodies speak to the hearts as if they were singing of the solemn triumph of a country reborn. The creator of those melodies had the power of lifting Italian hearts, causing them to rise to the heroism of the elect. Verdi's patriotism will remain immortal among the glorious deeds of Italy.

Certain passages in the Verdi operas reach listeners' hearts and ears with an unexpected impetus, without passing through the brain, and cause the pulses to race. In *Trovatore*, for example, there is one of them which strikes one strongly and calls up heroic gestures. It is that of the Gypsies, in the den of Azucena in the second act, when with open throats they shout their song, marking the rhythm of it with hammer blows on the anvils: *"Chi del gitano i giorni abbella"*. My God! Does a more convincing melody than this exist? And to think that this piece was classified as something vulgar! Perhaps it fell too vigorously on the ears of those who were unable to grasp the melodic sense, perhaps it was music which spoke with too much voice, but it spoke directly to the heart: it was music!

Even in the *Messa da Requiem* a way was found of explaining away a criticism which has no reason to exist: Verdi was charged with having

---

45   In the opera, the theme occurs in the Monforte/Arrigo duet, where the former is
      thinking of his newly-found son, and the latter of his dead mother.

interpreted the Latin text of the Mass theatrically, rather than modestly accompanying it with the formulas of liturgical music. As I see it, the defenders of Verdi's art have exaggerated by taking the critics seriously and by broadening the field of their defense. It is enough to say Verdi has interpreted the text of the Mass with exactitude of feeling. Indeed, if in the *Recordare, Hostias* and *Agnus Dei* the music gives the precise and touching expression of the word, in the *Dies Irae* Verdi wishes to offer us a complete representation of the Universal Judgment, managing in sound the marvelous conceptions which Luca Signorelli and Michaelangelo obtained with brushes. Verdi attained divinity in his setting of the text of the *Messa da Requiem*. If the critics find that Verdi's *Messa* is dramatic and theatrical, let them attribute that drama and theatricality to the Latin text. But let them not add that it is profane and irreligious. After all, even Perosi had to endure the same accusation and replied by citing the liturgical fitness which needs must be alien in its smallness when faced with the monument of art accomplished by Verdi. It was not Verdi who was the first to freely interpret the Latin text according to the human sense of the word. Beethoven and Rossini had already done as much with the *Missa solemnis* and *Stabat Mater*, two powerful conceptions. If one likes, the *German Requiem* of Brahms may also be compared with the *Messa* of Verdi. In reality, too many words have already been wasted in this regard. It is enough to say that the musical setting of the Latin text, when it is right, takes nothing from the sense of the word, indeed, the expressiveness of it is augmented; the liturgical fitness, a stingy thing when compared with the creation of grandiose works, must be left aside; and one must not point out the irreligiousness of such works which bring all the emotion of religion to the spirit. To compare the two works of Brahms and Verdi, the first out of the Protestant religion, the second out of the Catholic, is something which I approve of, but I give a very simple musical judgment: the *Messa* of Verdi is interpreted by Italian music, the *Requiem* of Brahms by German; therefore Verdi's is the more beautiful. And be warned that I consider myself a rather sincere apostle of Brahms.

It is sad, however, to confess that modern performances of Verdi's *Messa* do not exactly correspond to the composition of those moving melodies. First of all, the singers do not arrive with a preparation fit for the profundity of sentiment of that music; in the second place, the overall performance itself is always distorted, even to a strange imbalance of sonority. Certainly we are lacking the tradition of a perfect performance, such as that which Franco Faccio conducted[46] at the first performance at the Church of San Marco in Milan under the vigilant guidance of Giuseppe Verdi. I could not attend that performance, which goes back too many years, but I had the good fortune to hear a masterly performance in 1883 at La Scala in Milan, that too conducted by Faccio.

I still have Faccio's interpretation in my heart, and beside it present-day performances cannot bear comparison. The fact is that one judges somewhat at random when dealing with interpretation which the critics and public have very little familiarity with.

All the operas of Verdi are in our hearts, in our blood; and we must realize with pride that we were born in the country which gave life to Giuseppe Verdi. We cannot forget that in the same century in which Verdi lived and created his divine art there lived the other three greatest Masters: Rossini, Bellini and Donizetti, three Geniuses who with Verdi formed the golden century of melody.

Verdi was dead! Following the coffin in the funeral procession I see again the dismay of everyone. Mussi, at the time mayor of Milan, followed the bier with me and I remember that he supported himself on my arm. Never did a funeral gather around itself such an atmosphere of sincere sorrow.

The immeasurable greatness of his simplicity may also be called modesty. Verdi was modest, not for any feeling of mortification of the ego, but in the sense that he did not love the exterior manifestations which seemed to him incompatible with his austere life and with his art, which for him was a sublime religion.

The man who had departed was known personally to only a few of the thousands of people who followed the coffin; and I say "personally" in the sense of having come near him. How he caused everyone's heart to flutter! His language was universal. His speeches occurred between him and the world.

No one more than he touched the depths of the human spirit and the heights of divine beauty. He sang everything because he felt everything: joy, sorrow, torment, love had in him the most vast and over-

---

46   See *Personalia: Faccio, Franco.*

whelming interpreter. *"Tutto nel mondo è burla!"*[47] sings Falstaff; and it seems that Verdi wished to synthesize the *nulla* of life with a mocking dejection.

Ah, no, Maestro! It is not true that everything in the world is a jest, for there is an immaculate Divinity, austere and eternal, before which you yourself bent your head and She kissed you: Art.

Verdi was dead! But he still lives in our minds and hearts; and he will still live in future generations, since we shall know how to educate our children and grandchildren in the religion of art and feeling; and he will live in eternity, as long as the sense of beauty and love or our country is stirred, until the last human breast feels the final emotion.

---

47   "Everything in the world is a jest!"

AUSTRIA. RUMANIA. SPAIN
(1901-1902)

A few months later I was given the honor of conducting the *Messa da Requiem* by Verdi in Vienna. It was on the occasion of the Master's death that the invitation came from the Austrian Government. I was already very popular in Vienna, but the reception I received on that occasion moved me in the particular manner, perhaps because it was associated with the memory of Verdi. The Minister of Public Instruction flattered me very much, telling me that no one could have been able to commemorate the great figure of Giuseppe Verdi on Viennese soil better than I. Even Costantino Nigra, the Italian ambassador to Vienna, was very kind to me on that occasion, and also Mahler, the great director of the Imperial Theater of Vienna.

The performance was given at the Musikverein on 25 April 1901, with Italian soloists and the Viennese chorus and orchestra. For soloists one could not ask more, and I may say that never again will there be a similar ensemble of voices, feeling and style to equal those four artists. The tenor was Francesco Marconi, the great Roman Checco; and the bass was another "Checco", Navarrini; the contralto was Virginia Guerini; the soprano was a phe-nomenon for the power and sweetness of her voice and for the expression of feelings. She was very young, a Sicilian *contessina* by the name of Giuseppina Uffredursi who had finished her studies at Santa Cecilia at the time. A total phenomenon, since she decided not to sing any more. She began and ended her artistic life in Vienna, with the *Messa* by Verdi.

It was a profoundly intense and emotional success; the enormous Viennese public was incapable of resisting the enthusiasm which seized it while hearing that music and those four voices which they will never hear again in the world. The most frenetic applause exploded at every phrase. It was the greatest triumph of Italian art abroad.

Several wreaths were offered me and the Prince and Princess von Fürstenberg gave me their autographed photographs, indeed, the Prince added an ornament of the first order, a magnificent diamond. But I received the most precious gift from Nigra, a truly priceless gift, the large cane which Rossini always carried on his walks in Paris and Passy, with a small golden apple and the letter *R*.

Mimì, Dino and Emillietta Mascagni, c.1899-1901

I went to Bucharest in 1902, in April; it was a dramatic and thrilling trip. My wife and I came from Warsaw, where I had given a series of concerts. Checco Marconi was also with us, along with his wife.

The whole trip, from Warsaw to the Rumanian capital, was a succession of... dramatic scenes. We had been told that, leaving Warsaw at eight in the morning, we could arrive the following night at eight in Bucharest, or that, leaving at eleven at night, we could instead arrive at ten in the morning, always on the following day, however. A railroad clerk had shown us the schedule, assuring us that it was followed exactly.

In Warsaw it was not possible to have our passports validated, so the St. Petersburg legation had to be telephoned. But since the answer could not arrive before Saturday, we decided to leave Saturday evening and arrive in Bucharest on Monday morning. The first concert was announced for Monday evening so we would also have time for a rehearsal.

We counted the hours and there was no time to waste. So we got in the compartment and slept in our four-bed coach, amazed at Checco Marconi's transformation, who by day sang as a tenor and by night snored as a bass.

But the following day even sadder notes began. We got off the train and took an excellent omnibus. I began to feel vaguely suspicious, but could not ask anyone for information since there was not one person who spoke any French, and in that immense Austrianized Poland they spoke a German which was incomprehensible, a sort of Genoese dialect of the German language.

Towards evening I was certain there had been a mistake; it was no longer possible for us to arrive in Bucharest the following morning (Monday), so farewell to the announced concert! Neither my sorrow nor even a portion of my rage can be imagined. In fact, that evening we had only reached Lemberg, while according to the schedule shown us by that clerk, we should have been there six or seven hours earlier!

We took another train, one without beds, and very annoyed on this account continued our *via crucis*. Even Checco's good humor had vanished. Then on Monday morning the worst happened.

When we arrived at the Rumanian frontier it was necessary to renew our tickets and send the heavy baggage on ahead. As usual, no one knew a word of French.

Meanwhile we learned that the express to Bucharest was supposed to come by and that we would have to board it to reach our destination by eight-twenty that night! But in the interim, in sending on the baggage, we lost an infinite amount of time and when we returned to the railway shed, the train had already left, leaving us there. The station master advised us to take a carriage to Burdujeni, which is on another part of the frontier. So we raced off with all of our small luggage and took three carriages, charging pell-mell.

There were four kilometers to cover and we ordered the driver to whip the horses. All this by gesturing without understanding a single word. The horses flew, but half way there, our carriages were stopped by Rumanian customs wanting to see our luggage and check our passports.

In the rush we had forgotten to have them validated. We had, however, received a telegram from the Rumanian legation in St. Petersburg which advised us to continue on and that the necessary information had been telegraphed to the Burdujeni station. Faced with this new obstacle, we could not continue. We were only two kilometers from the station where everything would have been put in order, but instead we had to remain where we were for who knew how long. And meanwhile our heavy baggage tranquilly travelled on ahead!

The anger, shouts and confusion may be imagined, with all our luggage on the ground and we unable to make ourselves understood. The customs clerk had taken possession of our passports and I realized there was nothing more that could be done. The drivers, the same the world over, watched the clock and sneered, by now certain that we could no longer arrive in time. I had an idea. From my wallet I took out the telegram from the legation in St. Petersburg and showed it, shouting like one obsessed at the clerk, who seemed impressed.

Finally our passports were returned to us and the order was given to free the luggage. We got everything together quickly, showed the drivers some money, and set off at breakneck speed. I found myself in a carriage with Lina and Signora Marconi, while Checco was on the driver's box of another carriage, with Lina's boa around his neck. The carriages lurched from side to side and I was sure we would be overturned from one moment to the next.

Finally we came to Burdujeni. A gentleman came up to me and said in Italian, "Are you Maestro Mascagni?" At my affirmative answer, many persons surrounded us, calmed us down and assured us that we still had five minutes. We heaved a sigh of relief.

Here there was no luggage check, no showing of passports. The station master accompanied us into the coach, offered to telegraph Bucharest and overwhelmed us with kindness. When the train left, all those who were in the station bared their heads to us and we responded to that salutation with a certain satisfaction.

When at length we came to Bucharest, an overwhelming spectacle presented itself to our eyes. The station had been invaded by many thousands of applauding people.

I realized that we would have a nice danger to run. The police, ten or so in all, were powerless to hold back the crowd. Lina and Signora Marconi were in front of me, surrounded by many men who made a chain: Checco and I, instead, were swept away by that flood. Those good policemen did what they could. They locked themselves together and pushed with all their might against that mass.

Powerless to resist, we were forced to take refuge, after a thousand hardships, in the station restaurant. Meanwhile, police reinforcements were requested. Somewhat to satisfy the curiosity of the public, they advised me to appear at the door of the restaurant, surrounded by policemen and standing on a chair, since everyone wanted to see me. With all my strength I tried to oppose this demonstration of my person, but there was no way to avoid it and I had to give in. At the moment the Italian band, dressed like our *bersaglieri*, played some marches amid enthusiastic applause, while a short distance away a group of Italians unfurled our tricolor flag.

Then a Rumanian student, who spoke Italian very well, gave a handsome speech, giving me his country's greeting. I answered from the height of the chair, thanking them for the unforgettable demonstration, but at my cry, "Long live Italy! Long live Rumania!" the crowd tried to lift me up. The policemen then stubbornly resisted, while those who were in the restaurant grabbed me and pulled me inside, closing the door.

A few minutes later there arrived a police inspector, who told me that we were free to leave and that there was no more danger, since his person was a guarantee of order. But as we were leaving, the inspector himself, who was holding Lina's arm, was swept away by a wave of people. Checco Marconi, with his burly figure, protected his wife Amalia, shouting, "Get back, get back!"

The crowd in the square was overwhelming. All of a sudden an open carriage, hitched to two magnificent horses and with a coachman in red, came plowing through the crowd, while a man inside shouted like one possessed. It was the carriage of Cav. Romeo, an Italian painter, who introduced himself to us and said that his carriage was the only way to save ourselves from the dangerous enthusiasm of the crowd.

But it was impossible to walk; the crowd thronged around the carriage and wanted to carry me on their shoulders to the hotel. Cav. Romeo ordered the coachman to race; the crowd clung to the carriage, got up on the footboards, grabbed the horses... Finally we reached an agreement: the carriage would move slowly. It took us fifty minutes to arrive at the hotel which was five hundred meters from the station, always accompanied by the crowd which shouted, *"Evviva Mascagni!"* They applauded from the balconies. I stood up without my hat on and thanked them, but was half dead.

In front of the hotel the demonstration reached its maximum intensity. Twice I had to show myself on the balcony and speak to the crowd. Meanwhile the band played the Royal March and Garibaldi Hymn.

Queen Elizabeth was not in the capitol, but she answered my telegram of greeting with words of profound sympathy which I shall not forget. Her telegram was truly kind and I still preserve it.

In May of that same year I went to Madrid. I was summoned for the coronation of Alfonso XIII to conduct several concerts for the festivities.

Arriving in Madrid, I found no one at the station, not even my theatrical agent Rajo: in compensation I found a room reserved for me at the hotel for the small sum of 330 pesetas (repeat, three hundred thirty) a day.

I was informed by a messenger from the theater that the rehearsal would take place at one, but shortly afterwards I saw Rajo arrive at last, who, with a wholly mysterious air, told me not to go to the rehearsals. A representative from the Spanish government was supposed to come and talk to me regarding the concert.

My agent's behavior made me suspicious. I asked him a number of questions, to which he replied evasively. I insisted on knowing the reason for this completely unexpected occurrence but was unable to find out anything.

I waited several hours, then went in search of Rajo to request other explanations, but was it impossible for me to find him. What had happened? I didn't know what to think.

Signor Fereal, an excellent friend of mine from Genoa, came to visit me at the hotel and tried to cheer me up, saying that probably some misunderstanding had occurred and that I must wait for the government representative, who meanwhile was nowhere to be seen. But what sort of misunderstanding? After having been invited by the Spanish Minister of Public Instruction, after having left Pesaro to come to Madrid, now I was no longer wanted. What sort of figure would I cut in Italy as soon as they learned of this strange and inexplicable refusal? I even forgot that I had not rested for three days and three nights and I waited, resigned, in the hotel for Rajo. I waited for him in vain until one in the morning.

Meanwhile the good Navarrini had come to the hotel to ask for news of me and Bonci had also done the same.[48] Both asked me why rehearsals for the performance had been suspended. Good men! They asked me that which I wanted to learn from them!

---

48   Alessandro Bonci (tenor) and Francesco Navarrini (bass), two of the artists
      scheduled to appear under Mascagni's direction.

The great mystery was finally revealed the next morning. The Spanish Society of Authors, jealous and offended by the fact that Italian artists had been engaged for a national festival, had made a thousand protests. They even had printed in the newspapers that the Minister of Public Instruction had invited a foreign musician to conduct *Don Giovanni*, a musician who had written a hymn glorifying Dewey, the American admiral who had destroyed the Spanish fleet! There were even threats of dismissals in the Ministry. The report was believed to be true, all shunned me as a traitor, and the government for fear that complications might arise, wanted to get me as far as possible from Madrid.

It was Lucchesi, the correspondent from the *Giornale d'Italia*, who told me all this.

I declared that the report was not only false, but that when I had been invited to write the American hymn I had hastened to refuse, so as not to cause grief to our sister nation, for which I had always felt the keenest liking. I wrote a letter saying this which was printed in all newspapers. There was a visible change. The ambassador sent for me, with Lucchesi, I went with him. The ambassador himself gave me a letter for the Minister of Public Instruction, who received me immediately.

But because of this unlucky business I was able to have only one rehearsal, orchestral and dress together, for *Don Giovanni*. The performance went very well, but the unusual nature of the occasion did not allow the audience to think too carefully about the execution. The gala performance was by invitation, offered by the King of Spain to the official representatives of all nations.

When the King entered his box at the center of the third tier, I began the Spanish Royal March, conducting standing up, and with my back turned to the state. The ovation which the King received was colossal.

The opera began amid such a racket that it was not possible to hear a note. Then one must add that interest in *Don Giovanni* was very equivocal for the audience of that time. Those interminable recitatives with cello and bass accompaniment, and the small orchestration could not draw the attention of that very special public, nevertheless, at certain times there was keen attention, especially for Bonci's aria, which he sang in a heavenly manner. Some applause and a few bravos broke out, but they were immediately hushed up, because applause was not permitted when the King was in the theater.

All in all, the vocal part went well. Pacini, D'Arneiro and Petri did well. Bonci seemed unsurpassable to me, and Navarrini was colossal in the part of Leporello. The chorus was all right and the orchestra magnificent but inattentive, perhaps because it was distracted, in its turn, by the unusual nature of the performance. The scenery was very modest, even too modest, for a theater with such high traditions.

One day with my wife I saw the royal limousine go by and saw at its door a man of herculean proportions, very down at the heels. I was very surprised, well knowing that around kings' carriages there are generally military men or civilians in livery or society dress.

That evening, re-entering the hotel where I stayed, I saw the same individual of the morning at a short distance from me, but this time dressed in tails, on which several decorations made a handsome show. I came near him, and recognizing him as an old acquaintance of mine from Livorno, murmured in his ear, "Pallino!" The man turned abruptly. It was actually Pallino.

We greeted one another and I asked him about the mystery of his presence near the royal limousine and the reason for his shabby dress. And he explained the secret to me. He was entrusted with guarding the King's person, having been summoned for this from Italy, because of his world fame as an international police agent. He told me that he had performed this, his most delicate duty, more than once at the courts of all the European countries. As a rule he worked privately, since he only trusted his own exceptional instinct and particular perspicacity. Occasionally he used several boys whom he himself instructed and who served him as informants. One day, however, the police of a state where Pallino had been called for his usual mission played him an ugly trick, because they arrested as suspects the two boys whom he had chosen to help him. Not much was needed to free the two arrested boys, thanks to the very high prestige which Pallino held; indeed, he always made it a condition that the local police should be placed unconditionally at his orders during the time of his difficult work.

I think I have already mentioned that we had known one another for a long time and for this reason our talk was very cordial. He had managed to accumulate a substantial fortune and would have liked to retire from service and enjoy a bit of well-earned rest in the bosom of his family whom he adored and by whom he was adored, but his fame was so great that he was always being called by the courts to protect personages of certain importance. No serious accidents had ever befallen him, and for this his value was recognized everywhere. Pallino died in Genoa several years ago, and his loss was deeply felt, not only by his friends who loved him, but also by those who felt safe under his protection.

Returning to my presence in Spain for the coronation celebrations, I must say that very cordial receptions were given me and that a very select audience of personalities of every kind and every rank rushed to the concerts which I conducted. The King of Spain honored me with his friendship and very often he summoned me to discuss music and our country.

I recall that during a gala evening at the principal theater of Madrid he was in a box with Victor Emanuel, and summoning me during an intermission, overwhelmed me with praises in the presence of the King of Italy. It is not easy to describe my great emotion as a result of such royal condescension, which was the most sought after prize for my labors. But not only that. One day Alfonso XIII summoned me and, after very cordial and kindly words, drew from his pockets a decoration. "I offer you a small remembrance," he said simply. This episode reminds me of good King Fuad of Egypt, another admirer of Italian music: "I do not hold with decorations as such, but as a remembrance of a friend!"

While in Spain I was frequently invited to witness the famous *corridas*, several of which occurred at all important solemnities, and I remember one of them in which officers from the Spanish army participated dressed in the picturesque costumes of *toreros*.

These spectacles, however, are not made for the Italian temperament, which, more than any other, shows traces of the ancient Latin people's tradition of kindliness. My wife had not the slightest desire to watch it, and at a bull fight, at which it was impossible for me to be absent, she fainted from agitation. During my stay in Spain a great personage of that country asked me my sincere opinion of Spanish music. I, who was at the time completely taken with enthusiasm for the glorious tradition of our music and that of Germany, answered, ungenerously perhaps, that I considered Spanish music a graceful *zarzuela*.[49] The opinion was perhaps somewhat harsh, but nonetheless corresponded more or less to the truth. And by then it was too late! I won't describe what a face the Spaniard made, but thinking it over again carefully, I was right. Spanish music is too faithful to local color and to the traditions of the Spanish people, who more than anything else are addicted to the dance and love song, to be able to elevate itself to the heights touched by ours in every age.

Later on, during his stay in Rome after the fall of the monarchy, Alfonso XIII always honored me with his friendship and almost always

---

49   That all Spanish music, in general, is nothing more than light operetta music.

attended my concerts, for which he never forgot to lavish on me his most agreeable compliments. He was a man of much spirit and uncommon intelligence, and he made himself particularly pleasant to those who approached him. Once, when he was still King, presenting his First Minister, De Rivera, to me, he said, "This is my Mussolini." And the smile that accompanied that statement was very significant for me. He was charming, in spite of my never being able to feel tenderness for the Spanish.

In Spain I met the famous Doctor Assuero. He experiences with reflex therapy interested me greatly. A sharp controversy was going on at that time among the scientists, who were divided into two camps. Some, favorable to Assuero's theories, attempted to study their application with a seriousness of intention; the others, against him, accused Assuero's theories of charlatanism and painted him as a vulgar imposter.

I, in spite of my absolute ignorance of medical matters, agreed with the former, since I had had occasion to ascertain how in Assuero's clinic patients of every sort entered and left there completely healed. These patients all showed peculiar disturbances, principally concerning the nervous system.

Nevertheless, I wished to try the effects of reflex therapy and, back in Italy, I went to Doctor Vincenzini, a student and follower of Assuero.

At that time a strange phenomenon had happened to me, in which I perceived any distant sound or noise but only weakly sensed those close by. This fact disturbed me greatly, since it would have impeded me in continuing my favorite work as orchestral conductor. I had already noticed that when in front of a full orchestra I did not hear the sound of the nearby violins with the necessary clarity, though I perceived very well that of the percussion and doublebasses which were more distant.

So I underwent reflex therapy, lovingly practiced on me by Vincenzini, and in a short time I could hear normally again.

Even Vincenzini was accused of fraud and worse, but I can affirm that he worked with perfect good faith and the most absolute honesty. Vincenzini was, besides a doctor of medicine, also a worthy and passionate musician, and frequently conducted small local orchestral groups around Pisa.

He earned a great deal but also spent a great deal. He died in my arms as a result of acute peritonitis, after having been operated on for appendicitis. His wife, assisted by worthy doctors, now carries on the work begun by her husband.

I was in Pesaro, going through all those troubles which I have written about, with even my liver gnawing me for a good while, when
the Mittenthal brothers, American impresarios, offered me the
proposal of a long tour with Italian soloists, orchestra and chorus, in
New York and the states of North America. So to forget the bitterness
of the Pesaro happenings for a while, I accepted.

And I left for Paris with my wife and the artists...

EXCERPTS FROM A DIARY

25 September 1902. We arrive in Paris, late as usual, at six
forty-five in the evening. We go to the Nouvel-Hôtel. We eat
immediately so as to see the great city in the evening hours.
Going out on the *boulevards*, from one of the many cafes the
sound of an orchestra reaches us, performing the Intermezzo
from *Cavalleria* very well.

This little episode strikes us as a good omen. We traverse
on foot all the *boulevards*, the Opéra, the Madeleine, to the
Place de la Concorde. We get in a carriage and gallop off to
the Champs Elysées. We drive around the Eiffel Tower and
back again to the hotel in Vie Lafayette near the hotel. I
enter a miserable little room with my friend Leonino Nunes
to have a vermouth. The proprietor is Italian, a certain Motti,
who, when giving me the vermouth, looks at me fixedly and
asks Nunes if I am Maestro Mascagni: at the affirmative
answer, he shakes my hand very hard, saying he is very fortunate to meet me. In spite of every attempt, he does not
want me to pay for the vermouth.

26 September. We slept well, also because of the joy of
receiving a nice telegram from our adored Mimì and Dino.
Many telegrams also arrived from our friends, which has
greatly consoled us.

Last evening at the hotel, before going to bed, I found a
letter addressed to me. The letter was from Mr. Cane of the
Tribune, who acting for Comm. Capon of the Paris *Tribune*
says that Capon would like to meet me personally and in-

vites me and my wife, in Capon's name, to lunch. He asks
that in the meantime I telephone him in the morning.

As soon as I got up I went down to telephone Cane that
previous commitments prohibited accepting the courteous invitation of Signor Capon, alias "Jacopo", alias "Folchetto".

But as soon as I entered the booth I was surprised to hear,
shouted in Italian, "I am waiting for Mascagni." It was a
gentleman on the telephone. So I said to him, "If you are
waiting for Mascagni, here he is!"

The gentleman then introduced himself to me. It was Mr.
Cane telephoning to Capon. He gave me his place at the
telephone and it was in this way that I spoke with "Folchetto" for the first time. When I had explained to him that I
could not accept his lunch, he became enraged and, on the
telephone, answered me that he would not listen to reason
and he wanted me to come see him, along with my friends.

And he hung up on me! After ten minutes I see a Gioacchino Rossini, born and grown up, arrive at the hotel. I almost had a hallucination, or at least a pleasant illusion. It
seemed to me, with my mind always cluttered with Pesaro affairs, that I was standing before the statue of Rossini which
stands in the courtyard of the Institute, and I thought for a
moment that the *Gran Papà* would rise from his armchair and
come shake my hand, right here in Paris, where the memory
of this Immortal still vibrates intensely. The giddiness of imagination even brought me to believe that Rossini had come
to thank me for the holy war that I was fighting for the greatness of the Institute. But it was only a moment!

That Gioacchino Rossini was none other than Giacomo
Capon. A good and likeable man! We all had lunch together
at Arrigoni's Italian restaurant on the Passage de l'Opéra, en-
livened by the lively and sparkling spirit of Capon.

27 September. At eight-forty the train for Cherbourg leaves
from Saint-Lazare station. Last evening I had told the personnel of the hotel to wake me up at six and everyone present
exploded in great laughter. But I had insisted, explaining
that I needed a lot of time to get up and dress and that I
desired to be awakened at six sharp. So they all answered me
that that was impossible. When in Rome do as the Romans.
Get up at seven and have black coffee.

We hurriedly pack the bags and go to the station. This
train, made up of first class coaches only, runs on behalf of

the International Navigation Company, which would be the
navigation trust, in which is also included the American
Line, and only carries passengers who have first class tickets
on the Company's steamships: on each coach is attached a
label with the names of the persons who must board there.
But the train is not at all attractive or comfortable. The
coaches are not interconnected and to go to the dining car
one must get down from one's own compartment, with
grave discomfort. The old oil lamps rule over even this train.
Its speed, however, is almost alarming. We arrive at Cherbourg at three-thirty in the afternoon. In a kind of large bar-
racks there is a post and telegraphic office. What joy! I find a
telegram from Mimì and Dino and another from Emilietta.
Then I find another five telegrams from friends, whose greetings move me to tears. I answer a few telegrams and with
Lina I send another kiss to our adored children. We are to
embark at four forty-five. Meanwhile the porters labor over
transporting the baggage. We do not embark directly on the
Philadelphia, however, because the large steamships take too
much room and cannot enter the small harbor of Cherbourg.

We get under way in the small ship, which is called the
Ariande, at four forty-five sharp, and enter the large military
harbor of Cherbourg, where seven battleships are anchored,
which we triumphantly pass through. After some twenty
minutes we stop near the breakwater of the military harbor,
awaiting the *Philadelphia*, which is not yet sighted.

The military harbor of Cherbourg is rather interesting: the
breakwater at which the ships are repaired is about two and
a half kilometers from the small harbor and is almost two
kilometers long, stretching out in a curve, just like the new
pier at Livorno. The whole breakwater is equipped with can-
non, in groups of five; at the eastern end is a blockhouse
equipped with much artillery. Then there is another fort,
separate, and then there are the land fortifications.

We still wait a long time without the *Philadelphia* appearing. Finally, beyond the breakwater, the masts and very tall
funnels of the superb ship are seen. I am one of the first to
see it, thanks to the powerful binoculars which I own.

Meanwhile we still stayed on the *Ariande*, behind the
breakwater. The *Philadelphia* nears with an admirable speed,
at a certain point it gives some signals and the *Ariande*

resumes motion to circle around, then returns to the earlier position, but nearer the breakwater.

The *Philadelphia* enters the military port from the east at five forty-five in the afternoon. It is a splendid sight: on the north side, the fortified breakwater, with the majestic and imposing *Philadelphia* arriving at full speed; on the east side, the land fortifications; to the south the seven battleships at anchor and the skyline of the small city; to the west, the immensity of the sea. The *Philadelphia* stops three hundred meters away from us, and we reach it immediately, coming up to its left. And so, without anchorage, the transfer of passengers and baggage is effected. At six-thirty this is completed and the steamship weighs anchor. The sea is enchanting, the sky very clear.

We take immediate possession of the cabin, which is for four but which we two occupy. At seven in the evening there is dinner; there is no time to be lost—a wash, a wipe and off we go. The trumpets sound. *"À table!"*

Lina is full of courage and spirit, but as soon as she sits down she begins to feel the rocking of the ship and turns pale. The rocking becomes ever more noticeable. After a few moments, Lina retires to her cabin and goes to bed. I dine with Smith and Cappelli, the husband of the *prima donna* Bianchini-Cappelli, who did not have the strength to move from her cabin.

After dinner we go up to the bridge to smoke a cigar; the evening is still beautiful and the sea rather quiet: the rocking of the ship is somewhat strong on account of its great speed.

Until now I do not suffer at all, except for a slight headache, no doubt brought on by the confusion of these days.

Meanwhile, in the magnificent night, my thoughts fly to my country and to my dear children whom I have left. It is for them, for them alone, that I venture these labors, these discomforts. I want their youth to be tranquil and happy, so that they will not experience the hardships that accompanied my youth!

In this nocturnal hour I feel a strange exaltation in my spirit. With the roll of the ship strange melodies buzz around my ear... I stayed on deck a good while. My friend Cappelli spoke of many things, sometimes making strenuous efforts

Aboard the *Philadelphia*, 1902

to overcome a certain stammer, which became more noticeable during the crossing; but I have heard nothing.

At midnight I retired to my cabin and sleep conquered me.

The *Philadelphia* was superb; there was everything, even a shop to print the menus for each meal. There was also a telegraph without wires (Marconi), and one morning I telegraphed the children. I would also have liked to telegraph all my friends, but... it would have taken a patrimony.

It was a pleasant satisfaction to find yourself in the middle of an ocean and still be able to telegraph your family, with a good Tuscan cigar in your mouth and a big plate of macaroni with tomatoes in your stomach! The head of the kitchen had them prepared for me everyday.

We amused ourselves greatly. I played every game, English and American, and especially distinguished myself at *scopone* with our Neopolitan cards. Even on board, as in Pesaro, Rome and Milan, I was invincible at *scopone*!

I also participated in a benefit concert, with lots of printed programs, and was treated like a sovereign.

The celebrated General Booth, of the Salvation Army, was travelling with us, together with his staff. He was an interesting figure.

On 4 October we arrived at our destination, New York. I had gone there with a handsome program; as always, I had the intention of fighting for the affirmation of Italian art throughout the entire world, as I had done in Germany. When I arrived, however, I found a real disaster and was forced to suffer a terrible battle.

First of all, the German element, which was very strong there and tried to overpower the Italian element, could not bear seeing me arrive in the United States, not so much because of the Italian company which I brought with me, as for me personally and my operas. Everyone knows how I have fought to support Italian art in the whole world: the tour in Germany with an Italian orchestra. Verdi's *Messa* and Rossini's *Stabat* had still not been forgotten by the Germans, who feared, however, that I wished to continue.

In New York they took advantage of an insignificant occurrence to create every obstacle for me. At the departure from Italy, eight orchestra players were missing and we decided to find substitutes for them in New York. But when I arrived there I found utter ruin. Imagine, the secretary of the orchestra, who had preceded my departure by several days, had had the exquisite notion of sending the music directly to New York, so that during the crossing the company found itself without music and could have no rehearsal, and Maestro Jacchia was to prepare all the operas during the fifteen days of our voyage!

I found that the orchestra had barely read *Iris*. Imagine! I had arrived on 4 October and on the evening of the 8th I was supposed to go into performance with all the operas ready.

But now came the real troubles. The orchestra was incomplete, because I was lacking those eight players who at the last moment had declared that they no longer wanted to go, and these eight should have made up the number sixty, as established for the tour; but since the orchestra in New York was to consist of seventy-five players, I was therefore lacking twenty-three in all.

The company was referred to the famous Union, an orchestral society, which had agreed to furnish the players which we needed, but the day after my arrival a large group of American players presented itself, rumbling.

I immediately understood that I would have to throw myself into the fray and so I met with the head of the orchestra, the celebrated violinist Franko (German). He reported to me that Mittenthal, my impresario, had told him that the Italian orchestra was not presentable and had asked for the entire orchestra from the Union. This orchestra punctually presented itself, but Mittenthal had declared that Maestro Mascagni "resolutely refused to conduct an American orchestra."

It may be imagined how I felt! I immediately called Mittenthal who denied categorically what Franko had said and protested with all his energy against such a calumny. Then three players from the Union arrived to support Franko and the thing started to take a bad turn. That episode was enough to make me understand that I would have to suffer a great battle so as not to compromise the company.

The same day, the large New York newspapers reported the incident with an unlikely squandering of fantastic details. There were those who said simply that I under no circumstances wanted to conduct an American orchestra; others invented my protestation of the Italian orchestra; others, instead, maintained that we could not go into performance and a few pernicious ones whispered that the great tour was organized on pure speculation.

In the first negotiations the Union refused to give the players required to complete our orchestra — either all or none. However, it not being the normal season for performance, I had my doubts that the Union could provide the entire regular complement, knowing through experience that such an orchestra is filled out every year with foreign elements.

I had a stroke of genius: I made a public declaration in the newspapers protesting against all the insidious and malevolent voices on our account; I added that I had never dreamed of objecting to the Italian orchestra and that I would conduct my operas with my orchestra, it seeming neither right nor honest to abandon the players whom I had expressly brought from Italy. I formally declared, however, that it had never passed through my mind to refuse to conduct an American orchestra and to prove my statement I offered to conduct, gratis, the Union orchestra in a grand concert at the Metropolitan for the exclusive benefit of the Union itself.

This declaration of mine made a great impression and cleared the way completely. The journalists no longer knew what to say, and Franko was forced to print a letter in which he declared that the insistence on the part of the Union wanting to perform my operas should be interpreted as a great desire to play under the direction of Maestro Mascagni.

But my offer was not accepted, because the Union did not have a complete orchestra; but meanwhile our own orchestral performances came to be damaged seriously by these unexpected incidents. Nor had a remedy been found, since it was impossible to hire any players, not only in New York, but also by applying to other states, the Union being a group spread over all of North America.

We sent telegrams all over, but we were answered negatively. The situation took a bad turn because I did not want to give in to anyone, and I meant to go into performance on the 8th with *Zanetto*[50] and *Caval-leria* as announced. But on the day of the 6th we were at the same point. Finally on the 7th an offer came to us from a number of Italian players living in Philadelphia; some other Italians belonging to the New York Union joined us, protesting Franko's behavior, and so on the 8th at noon I had a complete orchestra. Then I gathered all my strength and worked a veritable miracle: that evening, as I had promised, I opened at the Metropolitan with *Zanetto* and *Cavalleria*.

It was an immense success. Bianchini-Cappelli was much liked; Mantelli was the favorite of the American public. Bellatti and Bianchini-Cappelli made fanatics of the audience, something new for New York, in the duet between Alfio and Santuzza, so much so that it had to be repeated; Schiavazzi had a great success with his beautiful voice. The chorus was very good, excellent rather, on account of the quality of the fresh voices and the number of them (around ninety). The orchestra was perfect, but by now the damage had been done and the New York papers took it out on them, but rather casually, more to say something. If I had circulated optimistic opinions about the orchestra earlier, the papers would have spoken wonders of my orchestra! Except, however, the pro-German papers, who were constrained to acknowledge the great success. They all vaguely admitted that I was an exceptional worker and that I wrought miracles. The punctuality of going into performance surprised all of them.

Certainly the uproar made was somewhat detrimental to the undertaking, but only in the New York area. After we were away from there we had no more to fear. But meanwhile I had to think of the other operas, having only *Cavalleria* and *Zanetto* ready. (*Zanetto* was liked more than *Cavalleria* in America.)

In Philadelphia on the 14th I gave *Iris*, which I performed in New York on the 16th[51] and then we remained for another three performances. It was a triumph, also because *Iris* was the kind of opera which they like better in America than in Italy; indeed, it made me more popular than *Cavalleria*. But in Philadelphia I had more terrible trouble. I don't know if it is like this now, but at that time the Italian element in America had factions which said all kinds of things about each other. One of these factions had promised a large banquet in my honor. The end of the world occurred upon my arrival: the crowd was frightening and

---

50   First performance, Pesaro 1896.
51   *Iris* had already opened under Mascagni's direction on 11 October.

Lina and I were able to save ourselves from that wave of enthusiasm only with the help of the police.

The parade was very imposing: forty-two flags, bands, flowers. And up to this point everything went well; but when it came to the banquet, to my deep regret I had to refuse to attend because I did not want to turn myself into an instrument of battle between my fellow country men. I also added that I was dead tired.

I should say that it was the Mascagni Society which gave the banquet. In almost every city in the United States, beginning with New York, there was a Mascagni Society. I did not know that I enjoyed such extraordinary popularity. (In Toronto I was nothing less than honorary president of the "Bersaglieri La Marmora" Society. And all these groups amused themselves by offering me banquets which I refused.)

My refusal of the banquet in Philadelphia gave rise to a thousand incidents: the banquet took place just the same, but the Consul backed out. The pro-German newspapers took advantage of this incident to embroider many lies, and said that during the banquet insults were thrown at me and that my picture had been turned against the wall! Fortunately, all the lies were refuted by the American papers, which declared all the humbug spread around to be nonexistent. The St. Louis and Cincinnati papers, where the German element is prevalent, naturally echoed those of New York and Philadelphia. But seeing that I remained imperturbable and that I serenely continued on my way to the applause of the public at large, even my enemies found this attitude of unconcern likeable and began to say that a disposition for work such as mine should be appreciated in a country of strong workers.

We did wonderful things in America. We went to New York, Toronto, Philadelphia, Montreal, Boston; but I was exhausted. One can have no idea of my life. What work! Several entire days went by without my eating anything but a couple of sandwiches and drinking a bottle of beer, while standing in my room at the theater! I thought I would not be able to endure, but God helped me. As of 30 October I had conducted twenty-eight performances in twenty-three days!

But now comes the good part. With all the money we took in during the tour, the Mittenthals did not pay the artists' salaries punctually. On the eve of the first performance in Boston (the first week in November), a good many left. I didn't know what to do and so I turned to the Consul who advised me to hire a lawyer. The best part is that the Mittenthals owed me more than ten thousand dollars. The lawyer thought it over and then said, "We will have the Mittenthals arrested."

Well, I don't know what mess this lawyer, the secretary of the consulate and the Mittenthals got themselves into but the upshot of it was that it was I who was arrested. That is, they didn't really arrest me, but they held me in my hotel and I had to pay four thousand dollars in bail to be released.

This matter of arrests must have been pleasing to those people because there had already been an earlier attempt. One day at the station I heard a whistle and I saw an approaching *figure* which, without saying a word, accompanied me to the theater. (This incident also occurred in Boston.) I conducted a concert and took more than fifty calls, but since I trusted no one I conducted with a revolver in my pocket. Meanwhile, going out, that *figure* told me to be careful because they wanted to arrest me for having given the concert on a Sunday. So I got my wife, and still in my tails I left the theater. We arrived at the ferry boat, the *figure* still with us. During the trip I directed a good many improprieties at the unknown man, but he finally clarified everything. He was there to guard me and his name was Guiseppe Petrosino.

Returning to the Mittenthal business, the Boston Supreme Court later declared that I was right, but meanwhile the affair had prolonged my stay in America by several months and caused me to lose my post at the Pesaro Institute. In this legal business three famous American lawyers saved me. But with all this I had to turn over the bail which I have already mentioned. While they were waiting for those lawyers, the sheriff kept an eye on me. The best part was that at eight o'clock I had to give the sheriff permission to go home to eat!

My liberty regained, another Boston lawyer, a gentleman who spoke French correctly, proposed to continue the tour interrupted by the Mittenthals and volunteered to be the impresario. This lawyer offered me the opportunity of touring all the states of America.

I had to pay the debts left by the Mittenthals, but was then able to work quite easily. The box-office was excellent. But now it happened that my new impresario appropriated some of the earnings made in various cities. In short, I discovered that he had taken on the affair without even a dollar in his pocket, and to produce the money for the train trip had sold to a piano manufacturer the right to print that the piano manufactured by that firm would be used during the tour. And that's not all. It may be seen that my impresarios had acquired the taste of having me arrested and even this second impresario, in fact, had me arrested in a Chicago hotel. The first had had me arrested for nonfulfillment of contract, this second one for undue appropriation of five thousand dollars. Well, this time they asked me for ten thousand dollars bail to be released.

It was Christmas Eve and I had suggested to my wife that we invite to dinner the Italian Consul, who had married a Jewess from Livorno. They both were lovers of music. During the dinner my dear lawyer-impresario who spoke French so well arrived. All of a sudden the police entered with the sheriff at their head and declared me under arrest. I called the lawyers immediately and, God knows how, was able to save myself the bail. The following day the trial took place; there were more than a hundred people in a room four meters square. One couldn't breathe. The famous Frenchman spoke and asked for my conviction. The discussion lasted four hours. When I was to speak the judge excused me from doing so, saying he was aware of everything. The trial changed aspect and from accused I changed to accuser. Thus I was declared innocent and the affair closed with long, noisy and enthusiastic applause for me.

In regard to Chicago, a small but very clear detail comes to mind. I went to visit the Chinese Quarter. There were many curious things, colorful and exceptional. A few opium smokers offered me their drug. I in turn offered two cigars and they accepted them heartily. Even in Chicago the cigars did better than anything else!

From Chicago, where I had clamorous successes, I went to San Francisco in California. Whereas in Chicago I felt somewhat dejected by the cold, in California I really felt good. California is the most beautiful state in the Union. In San Francisco, at the Alhambra Theater, I aroused delirium and enthusiasm; indeed, I was told that a similar enthusiasm had never been seen in the city, and when I performed the famous *Pathétique* of Tchaikovsky, the theater seemed to be transformed into a room in a mental hospital. I stayed almost two months in San Francisco. I had arrived nineteen hours late (since at that time even lateness, like everything else, was on a large scale in America) and I stayed there a good while.

While in San Francisco I went to Los Angeles. I was supposed to go back to Chicago but I preferred instead to leave directly for New York, without stopping in Chicago. From San Francisco I wrote to a friend in Rome, Peppino Hirsch:

> I must write you a few words *in secrecy*, but *real, authentic secrecy*. I entrust myself to you and your friendship. Let no one know what is written in this letter.

We are leaving San Francisco in a few days on 27 March. We are going straight to New York, without even stopping in Chicago. I have given up all my engagements. I have lost many thousands of dollars, but it doesn't matter. Mexico alone offered me 5,000 dollars for six performances. We are arriving in New York on the evening of 31 March or 1 April.

On 2 April we are leaving New York on the steamship *Savoie*, one of the French Line. On the evening of the 8th we will be in Le Havre, the morning of the 9th in Paris, and on 11 April in Florence, where I will be able to embrace again my Emilietta. I want Mimì and Dino to be brought to Florence. I want to spend Easter with my children, all of us reunited in joy and happiness, forgetful of my troubles.

It is necessary, therefore, to find someone who can take them from Rome to Florence. I would like to ask you, but am afraid you will not be able to leave. In any case, think about it and in one way or another let me find my children in Florence.

I hope that this reaches you in time. To Florence, to Florence! In fifteen days I will be able to embrace my angels again. One day of well-earned peace and blessed happiness and then to Rome. But I beg you, not a word to anyone!

I couldn't stand any more. I wanted to return to Italy, above all because I felt nostalgic for my country; and then there was this fact: I loved my children too much and it seemed a thousand years since I had seen them.

America had seemed to me to be a country like all others and Americans, people like all others, excepting some who wanted to pose as Americans.[52] But they received me very well, and, after the early incidents which I have related, approval became almost unanimous. Of some performances, especially *Iris*, I could even speak of frenzy and delirium, but then the Americans have always gone crazy over Italian art.

---

52   That is, those who liked to overdo their posture of "being an American".

24

CONDUCTING IN PARIS.
AMICA. VISTILIA (1905-1909)

I was the first Italian who went to conduct symphonic concerts in Paris and there, too, I had great successes. But I have never had too great a liking for the French; perhaps a bit of Gioacchino Rossini is reflected in this — he inoculated this antipathy in my blood.

At that time Paris was the city which had taken the supremacy from Vienna. Earlier it was Vienna that commanded, and the famous artistic battles took place there. Meyerbeer, who elongated his surname, went to Paris in order to fight against Rossini. His uncle had many millions. Inheriting the millions, Meyerbeer said,"I am going to Paris to fight against Rossini." But he was not able to win — he died first.

We Italian musicians have had several misfortunes but have always pulled through all right. We had Piccinni from Bari who went to compete with Gluck. It was an epic battle, and in 1900 I gave a lecture in Bari demonstrating that in this competition Piccinni beat Gluck. Of course it was not true at all, but with lectures one can remedy many things...

Then we had Spontini who went to the Viennese court after having been at the Prussian one. He was a megalomaniac, a man who saw only riches and grandeur. And to think that he came from such a tiny town, Maiolati, in the Marches...

The one who lived longer than all of them was Rossini, who lived until 1868. Since I was born in 1863, in December, I was almost five years old when he died. Rossini lived 68 years. And at that age he said he was very young! He counted, however, only the number of times his birthday came. Since he was born on 29 February in a leap year, his birthday came every four years; less another four because, with the passing of the 1700s to the 1800s he lost another four years at the end of the century, so that when he was twenty years old he said he was only four.

In 1905 I had come to Paris to work on *Amica* but I wasn't able even to take my pen in hand. I was absolutely overwhelmed by visits, receptions, performances — by a thousand things which took up all my time.

One day the Prince of Monaco gave a "five o'clock" in my honor. I played five or six pieces from *Amica*, making a great impression on the exalted audience. The Prince was exquisitely courteous to Lina and me, and formally invited us to his palace at Monte Carlo.

My first concert at the Salle Lamoureux was an authentic and triumphant success. The hall was full and applause thundered at the end of
every piece. The *Pathétique* aroused the public's delirium; after the third
movement, all the spectators jumped to their feet, frenetically clapping
and asking for an encore, which was naturally not given. I had to take
three bows.

The pieces which pleased most were the *Meistersinger* Prelude, *Le
Rouet d'Omphale*, and most of all the *Coriolan Overture* by Beethoven.
After the *Pathétique* Symphony, and at the end of the concert, the whole
orchestra joined the public in applauding—a demonstration which
greatly moved me. The press, naturally, cut me to pieces in the most
cruel way; something which saddened all my friends, but not me, because I knew beforehand the fate which the critics had in reserve for
me.

In France at the time they were too respectful towards German composers. The French critics would not admit that an Italian not only knew
how to conduct a symphony but that he was able to do it. The success
awarded me by the public in such a clamorous fashion, and so out of
the ordinary, increased the hostilities of the critics who inveighed
against me to the point of becoming discourteous.

The *Gil Blas*, for example, said that it was useless to waste time on me,
and to say this filled three columns in the paper. It seemed a bit excessive to me: three lines are enough for someone who has no merit. The
Echo de Paris ended its article by asking itself, "But what is Mascagni
doing in Paris?" *Le Matin* concluded by invoking the quick return of
Chevillard, so that he could be pardoned for having confided his
celebrated orchestra to Mascagni. And *Le Figaro*, after many outbursts,
had the kindness to devote a handsome front page article to me!

Conversely, the public attended in such great numbers that many
were unable to find seats. They applauded and success was spontaneous. This was my strength. I say these things with my usual sincerity. There is no need to believe in a lack of modesty, since I have even
suppressed many details which could better demonstrate to what degree of enthusiasm the Parisian public abandoned itself during my concert.

Another newspaper thought to make me a gift of an insolence by
saying that it was not able to understand how the orchestra could submit to playing, under my direction, music which it had played under
other batons in a completely different manner. Well, that paper gave
me great comfort. I attained my purpose: I brought something of me, of
my heart, of my brain to that performance! That was what I wanted.

It was not important that the critics slashed me to pieces. They had also slashed me for *Cavalleria* and one evening I went to hear the 395th performance, which took place in an overflowing theater, to the warmest applause. What distress for me, however. They changed all the tempi, everything was done faster, more hurriedly, and since this had gone on for years, the habit of hearing the music with those tempi was so ingrained that any other interpretation, and I mean an exact one, was considered worthy of censure.

The second concert on 29 January gained me another great, affectionate and enthusiastic demonstration from the Parisian public. It was a difficult program, consisting of Berlioz, *Carnaval Romain* Overture; Brahms, *Second Symphony*; R. Caetani, two movements from the Suite in B minor; Saint-Saëns, Prelude to *Le Déluge*; Beethoven, *Leonore* (No. 3); Wagner, *Tannhäuser* Overture; Brahms, Two Dances. After the *Tannhäuser* there was an explosion of applause which went on for many minutes in the overcrowded hall.

It should be noted that all were lying in wait for me with the Overture to *Tannhäuser*; indeed, a few friends had advised me to drop it from the program, all the more so since three weeks previously the same piece had been conducted with great success by Weingartner. And so an overture, which I had conducted since I was ninety-five centimeters tall, was able to earn me even the respect of the Parisian critics.

But here is the interesting point: with the second concert they completely changed their opinion! And this in spite of the first concert being infinitely superior. But this is the way the world goes. Always the blessed posturing!

On 3 February I went with Re Riccardi to visit Sardou at his home (to which Sardou had invited me) and I stayed with him for two hours. He refused me *La Haine*, but formally promised me another libretto. Later a newspaper announced the thing; Sardou denied it in *Le Figaro* and swore that he did not know me. He was answered that he had asked me to his home and the day and the hour were specified, but Sardou replied in *Le Figaro* giving his word that he had never seen me. Then I sent a letter (Gandolin[53] wrote it for me) to Calmette, director of *Le Figaro* describing things as they happened. Calmette showed the letter to Sardou who sent a telegram to Re Riccardi asking him to have me withdraw the letter and declaring that it was all true, but that for the moment he could not let it be known that he was writing a libretto for

53   Luigi Arnaldo Vassallo. See p.138, above, and *Personalia*, below.

an Italian, and he concluded by promising me a libretto as soon as possible, but nothing ever came of it.

The first performance of *Amica* took place in Monte Carlo on 16 March. It is not a perfect opera, but in the inmost fusion of words and music it was, along with *Guglielmo Ratcliff*, the attempt which at that time I considered the most successful and which most corresponded to a high purpose of art.

Here too, as in *Ratcliff*, the characters appear delineated with an extraordinary precision of outline, and I shall never be able to describe the deep pleasure which I experienced in translating the formidable passion which these characters are a symbol of into musical language.

My loftiest artistic inspiration has always been to attain the highest level that is possible for me in the *melodramma*: the most profound unity of poetic and musical textures. The *melodramma* is the richest and most perfect form of the drama in general that we can imagine. In it music is joined to representative art and poetry, penetrating it with a new spirit and carrying it to the most elevated regions of feeling and thought. The problem of the unity of drama and music was always discussed, even before Wagner, by various composers who resolved it from their own points of view; some giving the most beautiful part to the drama, forcing themselves to model the music as exactly as possible on the poem which it was describing; others asserting to the contrary the right and necessity for music to follow its own laws, to remain always music, proclaiming with Mozart the principle that in an opera it is absolutely necessary for poetry to be the obedient daughter of music.

One of the most original parts of Wagner's reform was precisely that of blending together the double personality of poet and musician and he was the first to present a detailed and precise theory of what a drama conceived in spirit and in music must be. Wagner is the first and greatest of modern musicians to make his art serve the most daring poetic invention, and caused personages and characters totally new to the poetic domain to enter the midst of the musical drama. In this sense only have I ever felt myself to be a Wagnerian, whereas in spirit and form I have always remained frankly Italian.

Wagner, in the choice of his subjects and in his manner of treating them, truly demonstrated himself to be a creator and performed the deed of a great poet. He drew on common tales of sea-faring peoples, medieval German legends, Celtic traditions, and finally on the heroic epoch of German and Scandinavian mythology. So strong was his bent for the noble and perfect that he almost always transports us to a region superior to the terrible conflicts of the human drama.

The more dramatic, warmer and more passionate Italian musical temperament permits us to part from myths or legends and to create and shape human characters who may represent, however, a symbol and a meaning. Human figures, then, real personages; but an expression of the ideals, aspirations, feelings, passions and sorrows not of individuals but of all people should live and shine in the modern *melodramma*.

The most limpid, precise and felicitous delineation of these characters imagined by my fantasy is *Guglielmo Ratcliff*, the opera which I prefer above all and with which I began my career as a composer amid the hardships of life and with the difficulties of a libretto in hendecasyllabic verse.

But my artistic ideal, propounded in concrete form in *Ratcliff*, has never cooled, and even today I have reason to congratulate myself for

Amica (Act I)

having kept an unaltered and sincere faith in that which I maintain to be the most elevated artistic attitude to follow.

My artistic ideals are summarized in the concept of absolute alliance of words with music, in such a way that the music becomes the words, becomes the expression. And the music must remain unalterably and frankly Italian. To part from this would be a mistake and an unpardonable blow. I fought for these ideals with the sincere and deep faith of the artist, and consecrated all my energies to them. A part of the public, that which at any cost wanted me to be unchangeably faithful to *Cavalleria*, no doubt parted from me, but I have always renounced the easy and passing applause of the crowd to rise to a higher concept of art; this is a purpose for which not even my adversaries could reproach me.

At this time, wary and disheartened by the useless struggle with the Italian publishers, I collected my sorrows and emigrated, taking shelter under the wing of Choudens, a French publisher. I confess that I was as ashamed of that step as of a crime, but on the other hand I managed to soothe my conscience with the thought that the tyranny of the Italian publishers had forced me to that extreme measure.

There was no question of dealing with Italian publishers, especially after Ricordi had refused my *Vistilia*, set to a libretto by Targioni and Menasci. I had fallen in love with this subject in 1891 after reading the beautiful novel by Rocco de Zerbi. It seemed to me that his *Vistilia* would offer the material for a musical drama, equally beautiful, and I spoke about it with Targioni and Menasci. We came to an agreement, and they wrote a really beautiful libretto for me. Only, when I began to write the music, after having gone up to the third act, I realized that the drama was lost under a superabundance of detail. It was necessary to add something more robust to it. In short, the hand of a man of the theater was lacking in the poetry of that fine work. And then I thought of Illica who would be able, completing the work of the two poets, to make of *Vistilia* the drama I wanted. Targioni and Menasci consented to this collaboration and we came to an agreement with Illica on the modifications to make in it. Then Illica took all the papers and spoke no more about it...[54]

Ricordi, however, insisted that I set a *Marie Antoinette* libretto (by Illica) to music. He was in love with it; he seemed to see the an-

---

54   Mascagni would use the *Vistilia* music some forty years later in *Nerone* (see Ch. 31).

nouncements already posted, with the title *éclatant* in the streets. Such is the art of publishers!

So I discussed the conditions for *Amica* with the Parisian publisher Choudens (I at least had that satisfaction) and ultimately I arranged an extremely advantageous contract. Choudens, while reserving for himself the printing rights, gave me two different percentages of all rentals (including the small rights); for Italy 75 per cent, for all other countries 50 per cent; fixing the length of terms according to French law, i.e., for 50 years after my death. For my other operas Sonzogno had allotted me 30 per cent for twenty years and Ricordi 40 per cent for the legal term of 80 years.

What advantage did I reap from my new and better condition? Alas! My opera stumbled over the same obstacles and was not able to move easily; at every exit it found the road barred by the Italian publishers.

One may not wish to believe that I was so naïve, after what had happened to me earlier, not to have foreseen all the inconveniences which would accompany the entry into Italy of *Amica*, belonging as it did to a foreign publisher. But I had relied on the name and authority of Choudens, who had many interests with our publishers, to whom he had given for performance many of the operas in his catalogue which became extremely popular in Italy; and I expected, at least, a bit of a truce on the part of our publishers.

I confess that once more I was disillusioned. *Amica* took a few short steps in Italy, but always during the so-called "half seasons", when the terrible claws of the publishers have a weak grasp. In the important seasons, however, where the autocracy of these tyrants despotically prevails, my poor opera did not even make an appearance.

An example? Signor Re Riccardi, Italian representative of the publisher Choudens for the rentals of my opera, demanded a regular contract with the management of the Teatro Costanzi to give *Amica* during the 1905 Spring season (as was given) and to repeat it during the Lenten season of 1905-06.[55] According to the agreement reached by both parties, a single contract was made, also combining the total sum of the two rentals, determining however the prices of the two different seasons, since the price of the rental is paid beginning with the act of consigning the material for performance by the publisher. I was present at the discussion which was held in my home and I approved the contract.

---

55   That is, Carnival Season, 26 December–Mardi gras.

Well, in the Lenten season *Amica* was not given again at the Costanzi.

For what reasons? I will be asked.

It is superfluous to ask me the reasons after what I have shown. But if one had asked the management of the theater, one would never have been able to get to the bottom of it. Who knows what excuses and what fabrications would have been put forth, and how far all of them would have been from the truth.

The diplomatic art of the publishers will never admit them to be wrong, and the impressarios and management of the theaters are agents who marvelously lend themselves to their own interests.

There was an old idea of mine which I had in 1903 or 1904, when I found myself on the Roman Palatine for a big concert which was given on I don't know what occasion. The idea, nurtured for some time, was this: to perform *Vistilia*, an opera which dealt with ancient Rome, on the Palatine. But these were dreams from a time long gone, distant aspirations. *Vistilia* was composed in short score, sketched. I had worked at it from 1891 on at lengthy intervals, and since 1901 had begun to study the costumes with Michetti in order to reproduce the milieu faithfully. It was an endeavor which was alluring, fascinating, but... later I no longer worked on it. Up on the Palatine I saw again all at once the grandeur of that Imperial Rome in which the drama took place and it seemed to me that in that frame, still so alive in its ruins, it would find its ideal completion.

One of the things which struck me most was the magnificent sonority of that superb place. It is extraordinary. Why that may be I don't know and no one could say why. If there is something mysterious, it is the law of acoustics. Up there on the Palatine, chance has created one of the most harmonious surroundings that I know. I spoke about it, mere chatter, with a few friends. As an idea it found an enthusiastic welcome here and there; but later it was not mentioned nor did anyone come to me to ask me anything.

So in 1909 I was the first to be surprised by the proposal to give my opera in 1911. I met a friend who was part of the committee and I said to him, "But what are all of you doing? You give out news of something I spoke about five years ago, without first coming to me to learn if by any chance during those five years I may have changed my mind."

Do you know what he answered me? That I should not worry about it, that I not pay attention to what the newspapers said, that the committee was studying the idea and that when the time came they would talk to me about it. And he even said to me, "But would the idea please you?"

"Naturally," I answered him, "why shouldn't it please me? It's mine!"

25

THE COMPOSITION OF *ISABEAU* (1908-1910)

I am anything but slow in working, but I confess that I wrote no opera with more facility than *Isabeau*. I did not spend more than three months on the actual composition, but I thought about it and would almost say carried it inside me, elaborating it, for about two years. With this opera I found, or I deluded myself in thinking to find within me a new vein, perhaps a more spontaneous one than in my preceding operas.

I began composing *Isabeau* on 1 October 1908. I wrote the entrance of *Isabeau* and it seemed to me to be a very successful little piece. I then intended setting to music the first scene between Folco and Giglietta, which I liked very much, and as a matter of fact, I composed that entire scene in a few days, including Folco's dream, up to the entrance of Cornelius. It seemed to me that what I had written was beautiful, very beautiful; and new, very new; and above all mine, very much mine, all mine!

When it comes to music I can write as much as I want, by the yard, by the mile... but I wanted to write music which says something, which exists, which will live. For this reason I abandoned working, resisting the magnetic attraction which Illica's magnificent libretto had for me.

But there was something else, based on two serious and important points.

First of all, the difficulty of the libretto, accompanied by the necessity of writing an opera which might designate a new era in opera. I meant for *Isabeau* to be something entirely new and for it to represent the exact and complete concretization of the concept which I had of modern opera. For this reason a very long period of preparation was needed.

The other serious point was perhaps unforeseen by no one, certainly not by the publisher, who did not want *Isabeau* because it was a "short libretto" whereas it was precisely its extreme length which made me more perplexed every day. The kind of music in *Isabeau* enormously lengthened the libretto, based as it was on the commentative prolongation (expressed by the orchestra) of the sentiments and words of every single character.[56]

It is not true that the *melodramma* is finished in Italy. The problem is that there is a lack of enthusiasm. Certainly no one today would do all I did at the Costanzi in 1909-10; impresario, conductor and composer together. I had the courage to conduct all the operas in the season's repertory, and my bookkeeping was very simple. As a result, the box-office was as simple as possible.[57]

I gave up going to Naples where Illica was waiting for me with the *Isabeau* libretto since I wanted to get through that season without either changing an opera or skipping a concert.

For *Isabeau* I was Illica's guest at Castellarquato. In 1910, on the eve of his birthday, I found myself with him. We worked together like two brothers, the better to blend our ideas. Illica praised me very highly for the duet, telling me that it left him overwhelmed. "You are really very kind," I said to him, "but your verses are ugly." He did not answer one word.

The following morning, when I entered the living room, I found a packet of papers on the piano rack—it was the new duet for *Isabeau*. A handsome act of friendship which marvelously paints the heart of that man!

Illica was really very good to me and while I worked he was always nearby. So I sat down at the piano and set the new duet to music. At the breakfast table I found a small coral horn in my glass. "Look," he said to me, "you have not presented me with a gift, but since I wished to give you one, I have presented you with a horn."[58] It was his birthday and I had not thought to give him a gift. He was upset because friends and acquaintances had sent him many signs of affection. Moved, I responded, "I too have a gift for you, and here it is: I have set the new duet to music. I will let you hear it; I wrote it this morning."

But the staging of the love duet, as it is done today, was born on the stage, as all love duets are truly born. That's why I had two duets for *Isabeau* and went crazy choosing between them, as in the waltz for *Lodoletta*, for which I wrote at least ten pieces.

---

56   A few words of text "sprouted" (a favorite word of Mascagni's) a great many notes.
57   See *Chronology*, 1909, for list of operas Mascagni prepared and conducted during this one season. By keeping everything as simple as possible, he was able to make it a financial, as well as artistic, success.
58   Horn=*corno*. A play on the idiom *far le corna a*, to cuckold.

With *Isabeau* I attempted a return to that romanticism which inspired so much Italian opera. It seemed to me that in the lyric theater, *verismo*, of which I myself was a fervent follower, had had its day. I did not feel the classicism of Greek or Roman tragedy, and even less the symbolism of philosophical pretense; so I turned to romanticism, in the sense which was given to this word a hundred years ago; that romanticism which is explained by the fantastic and sentimental re-evocation of the

The 1909-10 Costanzi season: Mascagni as impresario, conductor, composer

Mascagni at the piano, composing *Isabeau*

proud and courtly, harsh and knightly, passionate and cruel medievalism of the

> Women, knights, weapons, loves,
> Kindnesses and bold undertakings.[59]

And yet I began with *verismo*. But *verismo* kills music. It is in poetry, in romanticism, that inspiration may spread its wings. To write music one needs to become drunk, otherwise one writes "free" music. It is true that there is not yet a law which condemns badly written operas, but that is not a good reason to abuse it. Certainly this opera is not linked to any other in my output up to that time. Perhaps it might have some kinship with *L'amico Fritz*, but it would be a very distant kinship. In that opera the tenuity of the atmospheric color attracted me; in *Isabeau*, on the other hand, I was seized by the enormous poetry of the legend.

It has been both said and written that the subject of this drama is taken from the legend of Lady Godiva. That is inexact and managed to give rise to an accusation which had no reason to exist—the accusation that Illica and I had distorted and spoiled the legend. But the fact is that in no way did we mean to develop that legend. The original idea for

---

59   The opening lines of Ariosto's *Orlando furioso*.

the *Isabeau* libretto may have come to us from it, indeed, I admit that it did come from it, but nothing more. It has nothing to do with either a remaking or an adaptation, rather it has to do with a new drama, which may have a few points of similarity to that from which we got the inspiration, but which may absolutely not be mistaken for it, and which constitutes, it seems to me, an original work.

In writing *Isabeau* I abandoned myself to a more elevated ideal of art: to make the innermost feelings vibrate with our music, frankly Italian in inspiration, in the development, in the form of orchestration rich in all the most learned harmonic combinations (including distortions or eccentricities); to evoke vanished dreams, living passions; to inspire a strange melancholy or strong joy to live and struggle. Music must not be a precious privilege of the few, but the voice of every soul; it must sing with the elusive harmonies which vibrate in and around us, it must be a consoler of our tortured and anxious life.

In *Isabeau* I think I have truly attained this very beautiful dream of mine, especially in the second act Intermezzo which begins after the close of a small hymn of glory sung by the two maidservants. I was inspired by two lines of the libretto:

Illica's villa at Castellarquato, where the poet read *Iris* and *Le Maschere* to Mascagni, and where parts of *Isabeau* (2nd duet) were composed

Il sol t'ha guardata e baciata col raggio:
Il suo sguardo, il suo bacio t'han forse ingiurata?[60]

I wanted to intone a hymn to the sun, to the sun in which the nude girl rides. After a festive peal of bells, the Intermezzo starts at the maximum level of sonority. From a single theme there issue, through the most complicated harmonic combinations, three distinct themes full of passion, color and violence, and from them blossom many other motives which blend and intertwine with the principal themes. There are three orchestras joined together and yet distinct which impress themselves on one's mind in an organic unity as the great and marvelous compositions of Bach are an insuperable example.

There is no description. Only at the return, when the girl comes nearer, is the ride hinted at. But it is a moment. The appearance of the nude girl on stage had even been discussed. But for what purpose? Anyway, it would have been useless since not all singers would consent to it. There would be, among other things, the danger of catching cold. *Isabeau* returns through the streets beyond the ramparts of the castle, and from those very ramparts Folco turns to look at her and scatters lilies and roses over her, so that on her beautiful nude body a rain of petals may be shed. He does not consider his homage an offense. No base desire has prodded him, only the irresistible need to salute that apparition of beauty which offers itself in the joy of the sun.

Thus, when *Isabeau* furiously asks him, "What have you done", he who knows the punishment answers, "Die!" That vision was well worth death. The act closes thus, by surprise. I could have written one of those big finales which move the public. No, nothing. Some friends asked me, "What, you are not going to develop this episode?" "No, gentlemen, I am not going to develop it."

In the autumn of 1910, while I was in Milan intent on completing the orchestral score of *Isabeau*, Puccini asked to see me. Puccini then had a large studio in Via Guiseppe Verdi in Milan and I was staying in a hotel a short distance from him.

I felt I was living far from the world in those months; I never went out. I knew nothing of what was happening. I didn't even read the newspapers—I was an almost happy man. No one yet knew anything

---

60   The sun has looked on you and kissed you with its ray:/have its glance, its kiss injured you perhaps? (Act III, vocal score page 212.)

precise about my *Isabeau*. After all, it can be explained; even I didn't know about it. A few people spoke to me about it, a few wrote about it, but they must have been mistaken about the person, another *Isabeau*. Her sister perhaps, if *Isabeau* were not an only child. Then, there is this mania for interviews about new works. It is always better to say nothing.

Perched at the piano, I racked my brains to resolve the problem of this score, which in certain moments gave me actual discomfort. In *Isabeau* there is the "Song of the Falcon" for which I had conceived certain effects, but to realize these it would have been necessary to have a hundred and twenty or thirty players, an impossible thing to obtain since it meant asking too much of the publishers and theaters. Which is why I was there in Milan, to try to reduce and adapt the score to a smaller orchestral mass. A misery for me, a misery which lasted a good many nights.

So Puccini sent a friend to me. This friend was sent to tell me that Puccini would gladly embrace again the companion of his artistic youth if he were sure to find me alone. It is necessary to know that Puccini was on the point of leaving for America and he wanted to see me, perhaps also because greeting a friend, who for him had been a brother, seemed to him a good omen. A mutual friend came to me and told me this. I said to him, "Tell Puccini to come, he won't find anyone."

It was truly a moving encounter. We threw our arms around each others' necks as if we hadn't seen one another for ten years and that embrace at once took us back twenty years when we lived during the day at the keyboard and in the halls of the Conservatory, existing in the few cubic meters of very modest little rooms. And to think that there were some who had insinuated that, on the point of leaving for America, Giacomo Puccini had a grudge against me or I against him; that we spied upon one another like two enemies!

We reminisced about the past and then I sat down at the piano. I played and sang parts of *Isabeau* for Puccini and to me he seemed content, really content; indeed, he gave me some advice and suggestions. In short, the encounter was beautiful for both of us and I remember it with great emotion. Naturally all those who wished to sow seeds of dissension between me and my great friend were much put out, but ultimately friendship always conquers, true friendship is always superior to insinuations.

At the door, shaking hands, we did not say a word, but in our eloquent silence there was a promise of always being close at hand and loyal in our artistic battles, both of us for the good name of our Italy. We were always two of the most intimate friends.

Puccini's music is the kind that has a perfume, and for this reason the music of Puccini can never be argued about. It is somewhat uniform, but it was the character of his music. I have always called it "Luccan music", since if you observe the other Master from Lucca, Catalani, you will find that he is Puccini; they both had that vehemence, that relish, that ardor. Beautiful music, music which cannot be argued about. It was said that these two were decadents, that they had no profundity. I never argue about this. One does not argue about these things. The public has never been wrong in the judging of works of art. Never, never; and thus they have never been wrong in applauding Puccini, even if he has some operas which are liked more, some which are liked less.

Enroute to South America, on board the *Tommaso di Savoia:*
Maria Farneti, Maria Poggi, Mascagni, Lina Mascagni (*left to right*)

In 1911 I went to South America. I arrived in Buenos Aires in May on the *Tommaso di Savoia*, a large and magnificent Italian steamship, with an opera company organized by Walter Mocchi. I was given a formidable welcome. At my arrival there was a crowd such as not even an Emperor could expect. There were two bands, one city and one police, and I disembarked to the sound of the "Hymn of the Sun". To receive me I found no one less than the Cav. Maresca, the same one who had made such a ruthless hunt for the *Ratcliff* suitcase so many years earlier in Cerignola. There must have been at least fifty thousand people. A terrible press of people. I don't know how I was able to get in the car, because the enthusiasm was such that it almost seemed they wanted to tear me in pieces. All wanted to shake my hand. There were, above all, many Italian laborers, the calloused hands of Italian laborers. I even had to speak and I said, "Gentlemen, I am moved by this reception and I am grateful to you, the people, for your enthusiasm." It was a colossal celebration such as has never been seen and I was forced to fight like a lion because they tore my clothes, they bruised my arms and chest. This time, too, it was the mounted police who were able to save me, but the car was smashed.

I opened in Buenos Aires with *Aida* and many said that this was a bad choice for my debut, since unforgettable performances by Marinuzzi, Mancinelli and Toscanini had preceded me. I then gave *Lohengrin* and later, on 2 June, the premiere of *Isabeau*, which was received with indescribable enthusiasm. That tour made an almost fantastic record in the field of the lyric theater in those countries.

It is true, though, that there were also the usual annoyances, oppositions, little wars and envies. My God! Annoyances and oppositions cannot be avoided in an operatic company which has to give seven performances a week. One knows what singers, orchestras and choruses are! But for me these are foolish things for which I, with my energy, always know how to find a remedy. Little wars and envies, however, find me helpless. What could I do with certain people who for years had preached my incompetence and always tried to prevent my going to those countries, and who strongly feared that I might return every year? One must let them do what they want, laughing at their fear. The

little wars were carried on in such a way that there could be no personal
intervention by me. Some people expect to force their own tastes on the
public by denigrating the Italian opera, and throwing vituperation on
the name and art of our great men in these young countries, which
therefore remain without any tradition.

Besides bringing together all the envy and systematic aversion of
certain anti-Italian elements to everything which comes from Italy, it
was more than natural that my presence would reawaken many dor-
mant poisons. But I was happy about this war, because I had a justified
reason to unfurl to the winds the full banner of Italian art and I had the
supreme comfort of feeling the whole heart of the public which followed me. And I held in the bottom of my Italian heart the wish that
my going to those distant lands may have caused some good seeds to
take root.

Thus it must not be thought that it was an easy battle in Buenos Aires,
or that my success was owed solely to the resident Italians in the Ar-
gentine capital. It was, instead, an extremely dangerous battle. As soon
as I arrived in Buenos Aires I was immediately aware of the danger and
I confess that for *Isabeau* I was afraid—perhaps I was afraid for the first
time in my life. But there was no time to remedy it and I faced the fight
with all my strength and all my faith.

No one will ever know the agitation of my soul in those fearsome
days, completely filled with doubt and anxiety, when my thoughts flew
to my distant country and recalled other similar moments, saw many
friends again, and was aware of faithful hearts... while there I was alone,
isolated, regarded as an invader, an intruder, a conqueror. But my heart
had the strength to resist. I coldly reasoned that the minimum disturbance of my spirit would be fatal for me, so I asked God for energy and
presented myself for the ordeal, calm and serene. And I won, and it was
a colossal victory. It was a triumph! A triumph decreed by an enormous
crowd from every country, in every language.

There were nine performances in eighteen days, with theaters overflowing with applauding audiences. And it must be noted that in spite
of all the goodwill, the opera was hardly given under the best conditions.

But if the critics were favorable, I must add that I still had a few quarrels and many adversaries. The German element there was even
stronger than the French; they were making great efforts to see that
Italian art did not burrow into the Republic. Among the music critics a
small group of young men had been formed which vaunted its anti-
Italianism.

From this group came certain sweet-and-sour criticism, certain allusions to imitation of Strauss and Debussy, and many other cheerful things, as if it were not true that I had already written the second act of *Amica* and that in 1897 I had already written *Iris* with that third act which was anything but useless to the very new and impressionistic school of young[61] (?) French; and that before *Cavalleria* I had already written *Ratcliff*. But on the other hand, how prevent the usual outbursts? The public, however, is always the public, and when it is seized by emotion and enthusiasm it no longer thinks and reasons but abandons itself completely to the spontaneous manifestation of its feelings.

The *villotta*, the "Song of the Mantle" and the "Song of the Falcon" made a profound impression. Then the Intermezzo had to be repeated amid frenetic acclamations. The production was very beautiful but troublesome on that improbably small stage. All in all I had fourteen calls after the first act, fifteen after the second, and twenty-two after the third. But they were not calls, they were really shouts. Moreover, the women, contrary to custom in these countries, were on their feet applauding and waving their handkerchiefs, something never seen before. I was truly moved and needed all my strength of spirit not to break down.

But there was worse. I had to speak and thank the whole audience, which greeted my words with an immense acclamation. Later, when I was able to leave the theater, an enormous crowd waited at the door and I was forced to climb up on the automobile and thank them again.

I received many telegrams, among which was one from Torre del Lago: "I share with a fraternal heart your glory for *Isabeau*'s triumph. I embrace you. Puccini." What was most comforting to me was that the first evening's success was very small compared to that obtained by later repetitions. Many pieces, missed at the premiere, had an enormous reception later on.

The box-office of the first evening of *Isabeau* came to the sum of 60.000 lire. And later, at regular prices, not less than 25.000 lire were taken in per performance. Every evening that *Isabeau* played, it was all sold out. In comparison, the 82.000 lire for *Nerone* in 1935 were nothing if one considers the 60.000 lire of 1911. For that time it was a preposterous sum!

---

61   Mascagni refers to the fact that while Debussy (b.1862) was the somehwat younger man, Mascagni was the first to use the whole-tone scale for an entire composition, namely, the Act III Prelude for *Iris*.

From Buenos Aires I went to Rosario and there a painful episode occurred. I had left Buenos Aires to join the company, which had preceded me by 24 hours, at Rosario. The train reached its goal at eleven at night. I went to the window and saw the station crowded. As I was getting ready to leave the train, several artists from the company informed me that the crowd was waiting for me. Among those present were the authorities, notables from the Italian colony and children from the public schools. In a moment I was surrounded and jostled. I had my wife with me and this worried me. I needed to look for an escape route. I was barely able to reach a door and slip through it, dragging my wife behind me. Thus I found myself in the kitchen of the station buffet. I crossed it in an instant. I emerged onto the square outside and jumped into a two-horse carriage, shouting at the driver the name of the hotel where I was to stay. The carriage, however, was slow in moving, so that soon it was surrounded by the crowd which recognized me. They unhitched the horses from the vehicle and replaced them with some people. So I jumped up on another carriage and flew away like the wind, followed by a few automobiles.

The next morning the visit of maestro Donizetti was announced. "But he is dead!" I laughingly said to the servant who didn't know what to say and shrugged his shoulders.

The visitor was sent in. He was an old friend of mine, a school companion, who had made his fortune in America. "You know that you will be terribly whistled at your first performance in the theater?" he said after greeting me. "Why?" I asked. "Because you escaped from the crowd which had come to the station to wait for you and carry you in triumph." "I didn't think they would honor people by killing them."

At first I didn't give much thought to the event, but the first evening that I presented myself in the theater, the crowd, which was squeezed into every corner, began to whistle, and the whistles were not about to stop. At a certain point, a gentleman stood up in the audience and said in bad Italian, "It is the members of the Italian colony who are whistling." After these words, the tempest was calmed and I could then begin the first notes of the "Hymn of the Sun", which were drowned in noisy applause.

We went on to Rio de Janeiro and here another pleasantry happened to me as I was disembarking. The previous night had been really terrible. The rolling of the ship was so strong that one fell out of bed; almost all the passengers suffered terribly. Lina went through some ugly hours and I even lost the desire for my eternal cigar, since I didn't feel well. I wanted to go up to the highest bridge to see the sea. What a marvelous sight! There was the moon which illumined a scene which no painter could ever reproduce. I stayed there attracted and enchanted by a hypnotic power and was totally unable to tear myself away from that vision of formidable strength.

As God willed, in the morning at seven-thirty we entered the bay of Rio; as soon as the ship stopped, several persons came on board. They were members of the Italian Commission of Rio de Janeiro, come to welcome me. I heartily thanked them and we conversed at length together. There were many journalists and a few photographers among them. Meanwhile we prepared to disembark.

In Rio the steamships do not touch the land, nor do they even come near, but remain in the bay, several kilometers from the city. Some very comfortable launches do the job of transporting the passengers; but that morning, with the sea so rough even in the bay, the transfer from the ship to the launches was very difficult.

The Italian Commission had a special launch for me and Lina, but a gentleman presented himself and told us that the Ministry of Justice had sent its launch, and we decided, on the advice of the Commission itself, to accept the offer of the Ministry, who had even put an automobile at our disposition on the pier.

The difficulty of going from the stairway of the ship to the launch was very grave. The waves were high and steady and did not permit the transfer; I was able to make the jump all right, though I got a small bruise, but it was much more difficult for Lina, so she was carried across bodily by several gentlemen. The sea in the bay was wild; many people suffered from sea-sickness even during the journey from the ship to land. But the most interesting thing happened at the moment of descent from the launch onto the dock. The waves inundated the dock, rising up very high, and the launch could not approach the pier. Mooring was impossible and one had to get off by jumping, taking advantage of that moment when the level of the launch was the same as that of the dock. This time also I was able to do it successfully, but as I was turning around to see if Lina's landing was possible, an enormous wave repelled the launch by a good many meters and literally covered me, compelling me to take a lovely sea-bath.

Finally Lina was able to land too, but she was terrified, and feared for me who was as soaked as a flea. We lost more than three-quarters of an hour managing the disembarkation.

On the dock waiting for me were a good many people, among whom were the Italian Consul and his wife; then there was an immense crowd who gave wing to our passage, greeting us and shouting, *"Viva Mascagni!"*

The automobile carried us to the hotel where I found the King of Italy's Minister to the Government of Brazil, who greeted me with great cordiality. Our hotel was very far from the theater and city, in a magnificent location, seeming to be in the country. It was almost four kilometers distant from the theater.

The Municipal Theater in Rio is splendid. It has all conveniences possible: a restaurant (a room in Egyptian style which is beautiful), bathrooms and rehearsal rooms. The artists' rooms are actual apartments with a parlor attached; the stage is a mechanical marvel; everything of iron and electrically powered, an unheard of complexity at that time. The hall of the theater, however, is relatively small, while the staircase, entrance and foyer are a marvel. All together it is a thing of exaggerated luxury, but did not seem practical to me. It cost 11.000 million *reis* or 25 million lire.

At Rio I gave *Aida*, *Isabeau* and *Iris* and we then went on to São Paolo, Santos, Montevideo, Valparaiso and Santiago, always with triumphant receptions and an astronomical box-office.

In Montevideo, where the students possess an enthusiasm which passes all limits and who are aflame with a marvelous energy, the most unheard of things happened. They gathered in the gallery to organize their own pleasant conspiracies. One evening, not knowing what more to do, they surprised me in my dressing room where, tired and perspiring after having conducted *Isabeau*, I was changing clothes to return to the hotel. Well, they took me as I was! And carried me around the theater! In my shorts! The delirium reached impossible forms. It was madness, but an unforgettable madness which stays in my mind as one of my most pleasant memories.

Returning from Valparaiso, at a certain point the director of the train came up to me and peacefully asked, *"El señor maestro Mascagni!"* "It is I." "Well then, I must tell you that a musician has fallen off the train." "A musician? Impossible!" In one moment I experienced the most varied thermic sensations—I felt faint. I thought, that poor man will be smashed. I ran to the back of the train with Padovani and Mocchi. "But is it really true? *Really* true?" Then a countryman of the vanished man, one hired to help out in the *Isabeau* trumpets, answered very coolly, "It may very well be, since he is no longer here. Which means that he was drunk." The blood ran to my head and I felt dizzy. I could already see the torn body of the unfortunate man, the tour interrupted and the phantom of ridicule. At the first station we telegraphed for news along the line. Nothing. Mocchi was very worried, since he should report the occurrence. We held a council of war. Padovani muttered between his teeth. "If he had been one of our men, I could understand your dismay? But they don't feel as we do."

"Wretch!"

But the grotesque side of the thing made us split our sides laughing a moment later when Mocchi reporting the incident, heard himself asked, "What, a musician fell from the train? All right. And the trumpet? Who took it?"

We looked at one another in dismay, preparing the big laugh which would come later, when the man who was questioning us, seeing the ecstasy of reprieved men on our faces, added, "We ask these elucidations because the Municipality loans each player a trumpet free. Now it happens that these rascals get drunk with a frightening facility and, once drunk, pawn their instrument."

In the evening, after an unspeakable series of agonies and doubts, the unfortunate man appeared before me as if nothing had happened. And he said to me, "I'm the one from the train, as you well know. I came on the next train. I would like to be reimbursed for the price of the train ticket."

I looked at him, horrified. The wretch had forgotten the pleasantry of thirteen coaches rolling over his fallen body and over his drunkenness...

And I reimbursed him the cost of his trip.

The tour lasted seven months. I performed *Aida, Bohème, Iris, Cavalleria, Isabeau, Pagliacci, Gioconda, Mefistofele, Lohengrin, Ratcliff, Trovatore, L'amico Fritz, Ernani* and *Amica* — a good hundred and fifty performances. But what cheered me most was not so much my personal success as the conviction that in Latin America I had left some kind of healthy sprout of the Italian spirit.

D'ANNUNZIO AND *PARISINA*
(1912-1913)

I hear news of a new opera. How was it born? How did that first thought flash forth which later in the working out gave life — and in some cases, death — to the work? An inquisitiveness which always seemed to me very easy to satisfy. But now if I ask myself how *Parisina* was born and if I want to be conscientious, I must answer myself, "A moment, while I put my ideas in order."

So, I really don't know what transpired earlier, i.e., the business of the publisher and poet getting together. At a given moment I knew that a libretto had secretly arrived for the publisher, and I later knew that this libretto was by d'Annunzio, and that Lorenzo Sonzogno, the publisher, wanted an interview with me. I went to him and he said to me, "What would you say if I offered you a libretto by Gabriele d'Annunzio to set to music?"

I immediately asked, "An adaptation?" "No, no, an original libretto." "What? d'Annunzio has written a libretto for an opera? And for whom did he write it?" "For some question marks." And he showed me the manuscript, on the frontispiece of which was written in magnificent calligraphy, in red and black ink, "*Parisina*, lyric tragedy by Gabriele d'Annunzio, set to music by ??????????"

"Do you want the letters of your first and last names to cover the question marks?" "But that is impossible," I said, "since there are ten question marks and my first and last names add up to fourteen letters." "We shall ask d'Annunzio to add another four question marks." The idea was so attractive that I could not resist; then too, the original libretto attracted me.

On other occasions, many years ago, I had already had some dealings with the poet. In an article which appeared in September 1892 in the Naples *Mattino* entitled "The Bandleader", a rather ferocious article against my person, it was said among other things that I was accustomed to treat my fellow man badly, and that I, perfect citizen of Livorno that I was, used the most vulgar blasphemy; in addition, it stated that in the intimacy of my home I always dressed in red. The article was by d'Annunzio. Naturally I responded, contesting all of his insinuations, among other things taking care to affirm that I still had not had the pleasure of knowing the poet, but that only now had he revealed himself to me for what he really was. "He," I wrote, "does not dress as I do in red, but in the most elegant clothes, à la mode, ever since he had the good luck to be dressed by a tailor from Cerignola (Petroni) whom he pays with IOU's." As for my habit of blasphemy, I answered, "One day in Livorno we saw five young men dressed like officials pass by on the street and I was told that one of them was d'Annunzio. I came out with the following: 'Just look at those fops; don't they look like homosexuals?' "

The disagreement between the poet and me lasted for some time, what with the reciprocal diffidence and the insinuations; but one day, due to the good offices of mutual friends, this changed into the most cordial friendship. It was at a dinner among friends that d'Annunzio let me know that he would be willing to be reconciled with me. I consented to the proposal and we embraced one another. Indeed, the peace was perfect even if during the meal there ran between us a number of darts dipped in the most glittering irony. D'Annunzio, dressed with a rather eccentric elegance, on that occasion flaunted his wealth of two watches; I, not to be outdone, drew from the pockets of my everyday jacket, one after the other, at least six of them. The business of watches was always one of my innocent manias.

I was also supposed to compose an Orlando innamorato with him. But there is always a danger in setting a tragedy by Gabriele d'Annunzio to music, and the thought of that danger came back to me even in that moment in which Lorenzo Sonzogno showed me this libretto: "If I say yes, and then am not capable of setting it to music? If the libretto is not suited to my temperament? If d'Annunzio is not able to compel his winged poetry into the straits of a work for the lyric stage? Everyone will take it out on me – d'Annunzians, anti-d'Annunzians, my friends, my enemies. It would be ruin."

So I said to Sonzogno, "I make one condition before accepting – I ask twenty days' time to give you an answer." Sonzogno was gentleman enough to accede.

Those singular question marks in the libretto had a quota which I shall call an evaluation. In the contract made up between the poet and the publisher, the poet calculated the question marks at various rates, putting different composers in different categories. If it was a question of a known composer, the figure asked by the poet had one value, let us say ten. If it was for an unknown composer, then the figure increased – fifty. Naturally I did not concern myself with learning in what category the poet had placed me.

So I took the libretto with me. Rather, I didn't want to take it at all. I simply said to Sonzogno that I was leaving for Rome and Sonzogno came to Rome and delivered the libretto to me. To him I delivered a letter in which I said that in twenty days I would give a definite answer. And in those twenty days I set myself to study.

To call *Parisina* a libretto would be a profanation. It was a perfect tragedy, perhaps the best d'Annunzio had written, and even without music it would have enormous success. Indeed, it was this thought which dismayed me. If the success did not respond to expectation, this time all the critics would be right in pouncing on me. I no longer would be able to entrench myself behind the libretto. Who says that the mediocrity of libretti is only a convenient excuse for musicians to save themselves? If the music is good, no one worries about the verses and the subject; if the music does not please, the composer, confronting the critics and even somewhat confronting himself, can always blame his collaborator. This time there would be no escape. If the success were not complete, it would be the composer who was involved, since the poet would have only to entrust this tragedy to a dramatic company to demonstrate that the fault was not his. It would be a counter-proof which would be un-necessary, since it would be enough to read the text of *Parisina* to be convinced.

I remember that I did not have the curiosity to read the tragedy all at once. Not only did I read the first act and then re-read it, but I stopped at each thing which made a strong impression on me. Every time I had the impression of finding myself in front of an obstacle, I went back to re-read. I wanted to enter into the spirit of the tragedy. In fact, it took me no less than five days to read it. And after these

D'Annunzio at Arcachon

five days I was still not decided, because in certain moments those marvelous verses, so sonorous and measured, swelled my veins and I felt my brain on fire, but in certain other moments, I found myself up against such difficulties as would disturb any musician who approached setting a similar libretto to music. And I was also disturbed by the fact that the publisher had told me that not one syllable, not one comma of the libretto could be changed; only a few cuts, if necessary, and these to be discussed with the poet.

Sonzogno, impatient to give an immediate answer to the poet, decided to send a telegram to d'Annunzio saying it would be I who would set *Parisina* to music. Naturally that telegram perplexed me somewhat, since who knew if d'Annunzio would be pleased by the choice? But on 24 April I telegraphed to d'Annunzio in the following manner: "Received letter/tragedy which has made deep impression on me. Shall be very happy to meet you Paris before setting to work. Renzo Sonzogno will communicate date to you. Cordially, Mascagni."

I had decided in the affirmative because I felt myself seized by the beauty of the verse and the vehemence of the tragedy. What I found in *Parisina* was the transparent simplicity of the word. I seemed to find myself confronted by a poet who had not altered his style and his mood in writing the libretto, but confronted by the inspiration of a new form, had been free of every burden. From here on, immediate enthusiasm, even when confronted by the difficulties which I thought I had come across.

The following day d'Annunzio answered me with this polite and affectionate telegram: "Thank you. I expect great things. I shall come to meet with you when you like. I shake your hand. Gabriele." At that time we still used the polite (*Lei*) form of address. I said to the publisher, "I need to hear this whole tragedy declaimed by the poet."

On the first of May, 1912—the worker's holiday, which I always celebrate working, like a good proletarian—I went to Paris, found d'Annunzio full of enthusiasm and I told him my reason for coming: to hear him declaim the tragedy because I wanted to absorb into my spirit all the inflections of his voice, to see if they could be reproduced in music.

D'Annunzio was somewhat surprised by this. He said to me, "What? You intend to make music in the voice parts?" I did not understand that question very well. "So you don't follow the modern school, which has the voice declaim and the orchestra comment on what it says?"

I confess the truth that in that moment I felt disheartened, since all my life my constant thought has been to reproduce the verses in music.

Not to comment on them, to fuse them. In music one can express the word and the sentiment of the poet without resorting to that system much in vogue today which is to have recitative above with orchestral comment below. This is *melologos*, cinematic music. [62] Substitute mime for the recitative and immediately the cinema appears, with the soundtrack sighing away in the dark. I think that recitation, even with a musical accompaniment, does not make lyric theater.

I highly appreciate the attempts of various foreign composers, or even Italian, who in order to render particular homage to a poetic text limit themselves to "barely coloring it" by sounds, imposing an eternal recitative on the singers, while all of the musical interest is concentrated in the symphonic discourse which the orchestra unfolds on its own account. But this attempt, however noble and theoretically defensible, seems ineffectual in a practical way to me and destined to lasting failure. Then, too, the composer has the duty not of avoiding but, through his ability, of resolving the greatest problem of the musico-dramatic art, which is precisely this: to give to the voice part a beautiful musical line, one as melodic as possible, still conserving the character of the words of the text and their greatest expressive power.

In truth, it is too easy to leave the predominance to the words in an opera when true song is abolished, even if a melodic form is given to the *declamato*. On the other hand, to place every element of the poetic discourse in relief and yet have the human voice (the most delicious instrument a thousand times over) expand in waves of melody, this is a fearful problem, one to frighten the most experienced and expert composers. Wagner alone, perhaps, has solved it with his marvelous *Meistersinger*.

I want to defend the Italian system, seeing that that is what it is called. I am told, "But aren't you aware of this gust of modernity which agitates and overturns, which stirs up new systems, new ideas?" Yes indeed! Even we Italians are very well aware of it. And we study and investigate this modernity in which one substitutes melodic design for melody. But I have never followed it. Does one imagine the public feels and follows it? If they did, composers would then have little to do. I could set up a shop: "Music Factory — Current Styles".

"But then," continued d'Annunzio, "perhaps it is I who do not understand what you mean. Is it not made more difficult for you than you want it to be, is it not an enormous effort, this taking upon yourself a

---

62   Mascagni is referring, of course, to the silent cinema.

work of this kind, even more so since today you have a poet near you who could say, 'Throw out this or that piece which is not right?' "

"Naturally, it is precisely because of this that I want to hear all of your poetry declaimed by you. I already have all the music within me." "Well then, why don't you let me hear it?" "When you have read me the tragedy, I will let you hear something on the piano."

D'Annunzio was kind enough to read me Parisina without interruption, magnificently. I let him read it without speaking. I felt flow through me not only the sound of the verses which the poet declaimed, but all the music. When d'Annunzio finished I said to him, "I thank you. You must be exhausted." "Reading doesn't exhaust me. Indeed, I find it a pleasure. I know all of my works by memory. When will you let me hear the music?" "When I return." "When shall we see one another? Come every day. I shall await you."

This occurred in Paris, at the Hôtel de Jena, a little-known hotel. I had noticed with pleasure that there was no piano in the apartment.

The following day, as soon as I entered the poet's room, I saw that there was a piano. And d'Annunzio said to me with great simplicity, "Look, I have been able to find a piano for you." "But just like this, right away, you want to hear the music?" "Didn't I read you my verses right away?" "But it's not the same thing, since you had already written them. Anyway, I'll let you hear something." I went to the piano and improvised. I hadn't written a note, but I had absorbed that poetry in such a way that it seemed to me I had already written the music.

For me, the conceiving of music is one of the most inexplicable things. We musicians continue to live our everyday lives, we are with friends, we play, we lose, sometimes we get angry, but we always have this thing in our minds. The idea works and works; it is a delicious torment, a function which seems almost unrelated to us, so much does it continue by itself. And it is always working, never stopping. It is very curious. This work is never absent-minded, no matter what one does. I could even say that when one is sleeping one only thinks of that. How is it that when one awakens it seems that one has followed one's thought the entire night? Well, who knows! I could have lost the entire manuscript of Parisina and would have been capable of rewriting it just as it stands. I think, and perhaps I repeat an old saying but I don't mind, that music is a way of feeling, a way of thinking. To us musicians every sight, every impression — a color, a shout, a picture, a sunset, a river — gives a musical sensation. Merit of the musician? Merit of the fact which originates the idea. And thus if the power of a beautiful poem arouses musical sensations I say that the music was aroused and caused by the poetry. I see, for example, my work as a satellite which receives light, color and force from that sun which is the poem.

After I had played something on the piano, d'Annunzio said to me, "Do not touch this music anymore. You have expressed that which I felt. Indeed, I tell you that in this music there is something more than is in my verses."

And so I set to work. The musician must penetrate the poet's thought intimately and profoundly, and exalt the form and impress upon every emotion of a note, an accent, an ideal mark. And d'Annunzio was convinced, and had faith in me.

D'Annunzio did not know music. He had, however, one of the most refined musical spirits, even in the sense which I shall call mechanical. One day I played him a phrase. He said to me, "Very beautiful." Naturally, when we write down music we have the misfortune of a technique which is a science, and which therefore always spoils that first spontaneity. I wrote the phrase down and played it for him again. Right away he said to me, "You've surely changed it on me. The other day I heard my poetry and now I no longer hear it." And in fact it was true. So I re-read the libretto and recomposed the phrase at the piano. And he, immediately, "Now it's all right." This was not only memory. It was an exquisite musical sense. Once, however, I heard d'Annunzio sing and play the piano... And how did he sing and play? Come, let us not be too indiscreet....

When I was studying books of sacred music to find songs which would be most suitable for d'Annunzio's Latin words, I am sure that no one could have given me the help which he gave me. And at one time I said, "You know music." And he replied, "I had a great bent, but I have never studied."

Yet it is certain that music set to words had an extraordinary hold on him. And one understands this because there was no man who was more a poet than he when he said, "I have written this poetry and do not admit that it can be done in another manner."

After that early preparatory work I returned to Italy with the idea of working. Without even beginning, however, I realized that it would not be possible for me. When I took up d'Annunzio's tragedy I seemed to be alone, everything was missing. It seemed that the libretto had escaped from my mind. "I think," I said, "that the poet's collaboration is necessary for me. But perhaps it is not so." And one fine day I took the train and went to Switzerland. It was the 10th of July.

I went all over Switzerland but I couldn't work. It was impossible. So much so that I wrote d'Annunzio about it. And d'Annunzio answered by inviting me to Arcachon.[63] While I was still in Switzerland (where I travelled incognito as a nobleman under the name of Armand Basevi, engineer) d'Annunzio, who was a marvelous stimulation and knew how to find the direct route for spurring me on to work, even sent me some illustrated postcards to keep my interest up. I remember one of them. It said, "Here is the climax of the second act. The statue rises." And the postcard showed an enormous wave. And another postcard which represented a larger wave bore the legend, "See what a wave! That of inspiration was even larger!" And another on which was represented an overwhelming sunset, "The sunset over the Adriatic on the evening of the battle should resemble this."

Then afterwards the telegram inviting me, which said, "I await you. The country is more musical than ever. Until we see each other. Gabriele." D'Annunzio sent me some others. "I have just come back from the hermitage. I long for news. I hope you are working and that you will come. Until we see each other." "I shall return to the country next Wednesday to wait for you." But I could never decide to go and continued to play the false Basevi in Switzerland. And I did not work. But perhaps in that abstinent nervousness of mine there was instead a continuous work of conception and completion.

Meanwhile d'Annunzio continued to invite me to Arcachon. When I found out that there were no electric lights or heaters there, I was frankly frightened. It was winter and I was worried about the heat, asking my friend about it. He, in his stupefied and ingenuous manner, answered me, "There are pine cones," and I shot back, "You've got pine cones in your head." I decided not to go.

But as soon as I learned that he went to Paris every month, I resolved to go there. My first problem was that of reminding the poet that I was somewhat demanding by nature and that, like Spontini, I could not do without clear and fresh water. Paris, like other cities of the world, was short of water, but d'Annunzio thought of referring me to Potin, who furnished me with as much as I needed.

Unfortunately, Paris is not a city adapted for work. So I looked for a villa in the outlying districts. One day I was taken to Bellevue, very

---

63   A city in the French Landes, on the Atlantic Ocean (Bay of Biscay), where
     d'Annunzio made his home: the Chalet Saint-Dominique. It was here that he
     wrote the libretto of *Parisina*.

close to the capital; there there was a villa which had formerly belonged to the mistress of a famous painter who had frescoed the walls in an admirable manner. This house was connected by a secret passage with another villa, of a more modest appearance, almost a cottage, but charming enough, where I thought to install my daughter, Emi. The fact that my daughter was not to live with me was due to the necessity of my working at night, something which would have caused her the greatest annoyance.

I, as the engineer Basevi (I was also in Bellevue incognito), occupied a building nearby; in one room there was a wonderful library and a comfortable stove. The curtains were of red linen but characteristic, and on the majestic furniture, graceful little objects of pewter in seventeenth-century style, Sèvres majolica and Baccarat crystals, were placed.

The little villa my daughter lived in had belonged to a young American millionaire who had died on a return voyage to America. The furnishings were luxurious and the living room felt very comfortable.

In my room there were two beds, one of which served for my sleeping, the other for the poet when he couldn't go back to the hotel where he had taken provisional lodging. The villa had two attractive parks, with shady trees, little lakes, tennis courts and other pleasant things; all this constituted the most felicitous environment for a poet's and musician's inspiration.

Though d'Annunzio had already written his *Parisina* some time before, he needed to perfect and finish it. He had written the poem with a vertiginous rapidity, truly possessed by a frenzy of inspiration. It is enough to see the manuscript to realize the impetuosity with which he caught his images and animated the characters of the tragedy. He had wished, however, that it be called, "Libretto in 4 acts".

It must not be forgotten that *Parisina*, unlike *Fedra*, *Figlia di Jorio* and *Francesca*, was not a previously written tragedy adapted for the purpose of being set to music. *Parisina* is a *lyric tragedy*, in other words a *libretto for music*, expressly written as such by the poet.

We started to work with a good will, both of us inspired to some extent by the attractive countryside and by the tranquil atmosphere which surrounded us. D'Annunzio was content with me and I with him. He had to confess one day how well I was able to set his verses to music in the same rhythm with which he declaimed them. This is the best proof of his innate poetic spirit and of the musicality of his soul.

Regarding the character of d'Annunzio, I remember a fact which brings to light the great esteem he had for himself. One day a friend came to visit him and he was made to wait many hours, without there being any need for it. To my just observations he candidly replied, "I must act like this to conserve my personality!" D'Annunzio was extraordinarily attached to money and was ferocious in the contractual stipulations which pertained to him. He was accustomed to compute the value of his writings by taking the word as the unit of measure, and because of this I was in the habit of asking him frequently, alluding to his daily expenses, "How many words have you spent today?" However, he was also extravagant and generous; he often brought us sweets, especially *mont blanc*, little cakes made of chestnuts and whipped cream.

D'Annunzio did not speak French at all correctly, but wrote it very well; to tell the truth, I have never worked as well with other librettists as I did with him. He had a disposition, however! He did not want to make cuts because he said that an author must never cut. But I made cuts all the same.

These cuts were made with extreme circumspection, not touching anything which was essential to the presentation of the whole work of d'Annunzio. But to do this, I had to edit the form of the verse, so that no cut left a single mutilated line;[64] thus with d'Annunzio's words themselves I had to reconstruct the verses. Of one thousand, seven hundred thirty lines I omitted three hundred thirty; the remaining ones, then, were set to music by me without the smallest alteration. I wanted the d'Annunzian drama, rather than suffering injury, to appear in its poetically eloquent entirety. And I had the greatest satisfaction in seeing all that I did approved by the poet, in addition to his genuine approbation for my "poetic and literary effort."

I hope that in *Parisina* the fusion of words and music was accomplished in a perfect manner. To obtain my purpose, before beginning to set a single line to music, I committed the entire poem to memory and mentally repeated it hundreds of times to the point of being steeped in it, so to say, and having made blood of my blood of it. But he nonetheless understood – because he had a very refined intuition – that I interpreted his creations to perfection. We had, moreover, decided to call my music, "essay in the musical expression of Italian poetry".

D'Annunzio stayed fifteen days on his first stop at Bellevue. He arrived on 2 September 1912, and from that day I was able to begin the work with such serenity, such rapidity, that if later I had had to recopy

---

64   That is, so that the hendecasyllabic verse (composed of eleven-syllabic lines)
      would always be preserved.

my manuscript, I am sure it would have taken me twice the time it took me to compose it.

I have some delicious memories from that period. During the day I walked and played with my daughter Emi. D'Annunzio arrived and we played *bocce*. In order to play he put on white gloves, set his monocle in his eye, played, and always made mistakes. One day I invited some mutual friends to play this classic game. The poet had the honor of playing the *boccino* himself. He placed the *boccino* and then hurled his ball near—"near" in a manner of speaking, since between the *boccino* and the ball there was a distance of at least eight meters, all that was allowed by the size of the ground. There was general laughter. And d'Annunzio turned around very seriously, "Why are you laughing? Isn't the point mine?" I had then a little dog, Tonina, and she brought the ball back to us, carrying it with her teeth. (I really loved her; when she was sick I had her operated on at the University of Pisa clinic).

One day at Sèvres we happened to meet a gentleman who went out of his way to greet us. We wanted to know who he was and followed him. He was the country doctor and offered us some wine. But all three of us—I, my daughter and d'Annunzio—were teetotalers and told him so; he showed great astonishment, since he imagined that all Italians were strong drinkers.

D'Annunzio's visits were frequent and short, he would then go back to Arcachon, but always asked for news of the work. In October he was absent for a while. And then he wrote me a letter with his motto *"Per non dormire"*[65] garlanded with laurel: "My dear Pietro. I receive marvelous notices from all quarters about your work. A publisher's letter tells me, in the unusually lyric tone of a circumspect servant, about the duet in the second act. But the third act! The fourth! I cannot tell you my impatience. I am well. The rest and good ocean wind have comforted me again. Until we see each other. I embrace you with a full heart."

During that first fifteen day period I had worked a great deal with the continual assistance of the poet. Then d'Annunzio left and I felt myself slipping, all the more so as I had lost courage before a difficulty which for me was insurmountable—the song of the nightingale which had to be depicted in musical notes. And I confess that never in my life have I heard a nightingale sing, something which I believe has also occurred to those who have described it so magnificently. It only remained to be seen if that which they described is the song of the

---

65   "So as not to sleep."

nightingale. I hoped that d'Annunzio could tell me how they sang.

"We must go together to Versailles," he told me. "Let's go." "Nightingales don't sing now." "What? You cannot tell me how they sing, you who have described their song so well?" "I have described it, but I couldn't recreate it for you."

In Paris there are men in the variety shows who imitate the songs of birds. And so I went around there looking for a nightingale-man, which I couldn't find. One day d'Annunzio confided to me, "There is a marvelous book, whose title doesn't come to mind, which describes the song of the nightingale." In fact, he found it and sent it to me. It was a book by a Professor Hoffman on bird songs, very beautiful, but gave Beethoven's, Wagner's and other musicians' interpretations of the song. Alas, I continued to hear the song of the nightingale as others had hear it! Desolate I wrote to my publisher, and one day he came to Paris from Milan with a marvelous cage and a magnificent nightingale. Mechanical! But which sang to perfection. One only needed to wind it up. Was that the real song of the nightingale? I had several experts come: hunters, dilettantes. They gave evidence of perfect accord. One said to me, "That's it exactly." Another said, "That has nothing to do with the song of the nightingale." Thus was I well illuminated! But the mechanical bird served me to play a joke on d'Annunzio. He arrived at Bellevue from Arcachon on a rainy November evening. I said to him, "You have deceived me. You told me that nightingales don't sing in the winter, while I have found one that really does." "It cannot be." "I'll let you hear it now."

I sent my daughter into the living room to wind up the automaton. And there in the silence was the song of the nightingale. D'Annunzio lit

Mascagni at Bellevue,
as "Ing. Armand Basevi"

up with surprise. "This is an illusion! It's miraculous!" "Do you want to see it?" And taking advantage of the shadows I led him to see the nightingale. He looked and admired ecstatically, then all of a sudden he heard the noise of the spring and exclaimed, "But this is mechanical!"

It is understood that as soon as he realized it was mechanical he declared that the song of a real nightingale was completely different. But then one day I told d'Annunzio that I had written the music for the nightingale. And I let him hear it. He remained perplexed and in silence. Then he advised me, "You know? If this isn't exactly the song of nightingales which are heard in spring you can always say, 'From now on nightingales will sing as I have written!' "

And I left the song of the nightingale as I wrote it. But in the spring I didn't go to hear them. I was afraid they would disprove me!

I worked so hard at Bellevue that on 11 December 1912, the opera was finished. During that period, as a pastime, I had found a little game, a little tin billiard set. When the spring was set off there was a small ball that jumped out and indicated the points. But we had hardly begun to play when d'Annunzio won two *louis* from me. So I said, "Let's stop." And I wanted no more to do with it, although every time d'Annunzio arrived he said, "Do you want to play the billiard game?"

D'Annunzio arrived at Bellevue for lunch. He came in a cab, but did not send this cab back to Paris. He left it there at the foot of the steps which led to the villa, in spite of the taximeter. The cab stopped, but the meter went on. After dinner we went to work and it became two or three past midnight. We worked and so did the taximeter.

I asked him, "Is there no danger that the meter will break down?" "They are perfect machines," he answered. "And what does the driver do?" "I have told him to eat first and then get in the cab and sleep."

D'Annunzio was always impassive. I once observed to him, "For forty *centimes* you can comfortably come on the train." "But to pay forty *centimes* you need to have them, and you know that my monetary unit begins with five *francs*."

One day he advised me that the following day he could not come; he had to write some articles for English and American newspapers which paid him five *francs* a word. "And how many words do you write?" "Oh, two thousand." "Your health!" The next day d'Annunzio arrived. "The article?" "Already written." He left again at two-thirty in the morning. As soon as he reached the cab which was waiting for him, I saw him lost in thought. "I want to see," he said, "how many words of my article are used up on the taximeter!"

To go to Bellevue from the villa we had to traverse a long stretch of country road, since the villa was hidden. And there was not one street lamp. I had a tin lantern, which I carried on an iron wire, and with this lantern I accompanied d'Annunzio to the center of Bellevue. One evening d'Annunzio said, "Just imagine if some Italian journalist were to discover that the three of us" — sometimes my daughter was also with us— "after midnight, with a four *centime* lantern, with an air of evildoers, wandered the countryside... what ruin!"

I continued my incognito at Bellevue. And once I even ran a fair danger of passing for a spy. Oh, it was nothing! My villa was near Issy-les-Moulineaux where there was a large airfield. Profoundly disturbed by my mysterious behavior, the agents of the local police had come to the conclusion that I was a German spy, charged with furnishing information on the military airfield.

And one morning my two maids, one Spanish, the other French, told me that they had been summoned by the police to say who we were, my daughter and I. It seemed strange, the police said, that a foreign engineer and a young lady did not go out during the day and that sometimes they only went out at night with a lantern and with a third unknown who allowed the taximeter to climb to fabulous amounts. Ah, that cab! And that meter! The feeling of dismay is indescribable which the mysterious presence of that cab aroused in all the good citizens of Bellevue, that cab which stopped and stayed there waiting, waiting. At times there were groups of people around it. There were not many amusements in Bellevue; watching d'Annunzio's meter go up had become the pastime most in vogue.

We were in agreement in everything, d'Annunzio and I, but one thing divided us; the problem of smoke. I have a notable passion for cigars. I smoke thirty-six — thirty-six cigars, mind you! — a day. D'Annunzio, however, could not bear the odor. I knew this and never smoked around him. Friendship does not count the sacrifices.

In intimate surroundings, d'Annunzio was the dearest person. He was a man full of delicacies. What consideration he had for me when I was working! And the reverence with which he listened to what I had composed! Extraordinary! He had an armchair in my small studio. He sat there and did not move. I later had to find out from my daughter what the poet did. I could not see, because I was at the piano and I read my music wearing glasses with tortoise-shell rims. My daughter said to me, "D'Annunzio pays surprisingly close attention. You were at the piano an hour and a half, and it seemed to me he didn't bat an eye. Only in the salient moments did he imperceptibly move." It was where the music pleased him the most.

Oh lovely days at Bellevue! Oh childish pastimes! Besides *bocce*, we also played *tamburello*. D'Annunzio was not a great *bocce* player, but at *tamburello* he was even more original. When the ball came to him on the rebound he dodged it. "What do you expect? It frightens me!" But the memory of that period was delicious for him also. In one of his later letters he wrote me, "Correcting the proofs, now and then I am struck by some parts of the music. Entire phrases, whole sections, especially in the second act, rise up again from the depths of my soul with a marvelous vigor. Oh beautiful days, fervid nights of creation and expectation! Do you remember?"

The birth of a few phrases in *Parisina* is rather curious. One day in Rome a friend to whom I had read some of the tragedy told me of the strong impression Ugo's lines to *Parisina* in the second act had made on him, where Ugo, wounded and out of breath, says:

> *Or voi*
> *composto m'avereste nella bara,*
> *poi, legata la cassa in sul giumento,*
> *ricondotto laggiù per la via lunga,*
> *accompagnato fra le dolci cose*
> *di primavera...*[66]

These were lines which had strongly impressed me also—I had them totally in my mind. We returned home, I sat down at the piano, and those lines stand composed today as they came forth from me.

Another day I went to Florence to conduct a performance of *Isabeau*. I found my friend Franchetti who invited me to lunch, and naturally the whole lunch was taken up with *Parisina*, all the more so since Franchetti had set another d'Annunzio tragedy to music. "Have you found any serious difficulties?" Franchetti asked me. "I shall certainly find them, since I have written nothing yet. The work of conception is the most demanding. Look. In the first act there are a number of popular *stornelli* which I would like to compose well. You know, a few have come to my mind, and I shall leave them like that, since even if I am told, 'This

---

66   "Now you would have arranged me on the bier, then, the coffin lashed on the
      beast of burden, brought back down by the long road, accompanied amid the
      sweet things of spring..." (Vocal score, page 170.)

resembles such and such a thing,' I shall answer, 'Thank you, that's what I want. If it is to be popular it must be born in the soul of the crowd.' "

"So sit down at the piano!"

I sat down at the piano and improvised the chorus of servingmaids in the first act:

> *Che foco è questo ch'arde e non consuma?*
> *Che piaga è questa che sangue non getta?*[67]

During the first scene, eleven *stornelli* are sung at various times, all in hendecasyllabic verses! I shall not mention what that cost me, to give to each one of these *stornelli* a special characteristic.

It may have been the presence of d'Annunzio, it may have been the great fervor aroused in me by this poem, marvelous in its poetry and tragedy, but the fact remains that I wrote this opera of mine — more vast in size than all my others — in a hundred and thirty-four days. I sacrificed pages and pages of music written by me with emotion and sincerity, symphonic pages which, taken by themselves, would have been, I am sure, of the greatest effect. But the theater has its laws. A work of mordant passion, such as *Parisina* actually is, must not be too long. It must run rapidly, without interruptions, without useless pauses; if not, it would end up being tiresome. Among the most saddening suppressions, however necessary, is to be noted that of the prelude to the last act. I later found myself a bit embarrassed, since during that act there are two recallings of that prelude which I had pitilessly amputated.

I had passed several sleepless months because of *Parisina*, working as many as twelve hours a day. And this artistic undertaking of mine was burdened by a continuous preoccupation, that of not betraying in any way the poet's thought and of conserving the value of special punctuation of the poetic speech and giving an exceptional relief to the accentuation, often new and daring, of the d'Annunzian verse. For the first time in my career as an operatic composer I found myself confronted by a tragedy palpitating with poetry, rich to the point of improbability in its very precious verbal details. I was not able to conceive, even remotely, of having d'Annunzio change the rhythm of one of his

---

67   "What fire is this which burns and does not consume? What wound is this which does not spurt blood?" (Vocal score, page 73.)

strophes, not even by a hendecasyllable. I had decided on the task of respecting, even in its details, the exquisite work of the poet. Before d'Annunzio's *Parisina* I conducted myself with an absolutely Franciscan humility.

I am not exaggerating at all. Is proof needed? One day Gabriele came looking for me and found me while I was composing. "Are you working?" he said to me. "Yes, I am doing shoemaker's work." "Namely?" "Namely; you have given me the measurements for a pair of shoes and I am carefully cutting the soles, the upper portions, etc. So much the worse for me if I mistake one of the measurements!"

When I came to the end I felt sad, and looking at the pile of manuscript I said, "You have given me back a prodigious youth. Now that I have completed you, *Parisina*, it seems to me that you abandon me, and with you your prodigious youth abandons me! But it gives me a sense of infinite sweetness, oh *Parisina* of ours, flower of passion and of poetry, to remember the dear and agonizing time of creation, when you were born in the excited silence of our hearts and were ours alone!"

But there was the orchestration to do. This opera had welled up in me not only in the voice parts, but also in its vast complexity, and in various parts the orchestration was already indicated. So true is this that my first draft contained everything, since instead of the two staves for solo piano, it was written on four and five. I now saw the entire bulk of this work, and had need of rest: because I didn't feel the effort which I had made while I worked, but after. I completed the opera, as I have mentioned, on 11 December. I began to orchestrate on the first of May, 1913, on the usual workers' holiday. And I spent all those months in between without working, divorced from *Parisina*.

Rather than work in Rome, I took a villa in Milan, and found that Milan is an excellent place for climate, especially in summer. But the orchestration, the writing down of it, cost me much more time than the composition of the opera. I began on the first of May and finished at the beginning of November. I used a very large orchestra for *Parisina*, 110 players. I wrote for a contrabass clarinet which is an octave lower than the bass clarinet, a novelty for Italy. Saint-Saëns used it once in France. Then bass flutes which give a strange, mysterious sound. Albisi, first flutist at La Scala, invented them. And also a small flute in G for the song of the nightingale. Three bassoons, plus the contrabassoon and six horns. A phalanx absolutely necessary to render the effects of sonority which I imagined. But then, I believe that in reality the modern orchestra is too weak in the woodwinds, considering the exuberant sonority of the brass.

Re-examining *Parisina*, I believed in all conscience that if nothing else it represented a rare example of fidelity to the interpretation of the word. The opera is strong in its musical content, very daring in the expression of the word, extremely strong and violent in its tragic situations. In form it is very free (excepting a few pieces), irregular in rhythm, cadence and tonality. The opera is thematic to a degree, with continuous recallings, reproductions and repercussions of odeas; however, these recallings and repercussions are inspired by a profound conception, at times philosophic, which reflects the souls of the characters more than their figures and words. All the recurrences of the themes are always veiled, a few times actually hidden, except in certain special cases, in which their recalling must impose itself upon the listener's understanding. I saw all this later, from the examination of my finished work which I made. When I worked I did not even know if I had reproduced some already expressed musical ideas. The work of conception and of composition came to me with a spontaneity which I would call miraculous; and the proof of this is in the length of time which I needed to write the opera: 134 days.

I let myself be carried away by the poem, with the idea of following it, never of exceeding it. When critics say that Mascagni tied himself to d'Annunzio, I answer, "Perfectly." An example. When the poet evokes the vision of the Church of Loreto in Act II, I should have let myself go. Do they not say I am a *mascagnano*, thank God? Put the music down, then. Instead, nothing. A few indications, and go on. This act concludes with the first kiss between Parisina and Ugo after the tumult of the battle, the songs of victory and the psalms of the prayers. The words are lost, disappearing in the night, then the music also becomes faint and is silent. It is ecstasy in the silence. Thus the act closes. And with the fourth act the opera concludes by having almost no action. It is the shortest, and there are two souls who sing—ecstasy in the face of eternity. The poet here rises to the purest heights. And I let myself by borne by the lyricism of the verses. I felt the harmony, the warmth, the poetry in them, and it is this that I wished to recreate, to reproduce. I clothed the poet's feelings and mine in notes.

In *Parisina* I sang d'Annunzio's tragedy with emphasis. Nothing else. But I sang it, I did not recite it. And here is the whole difference. But I could only make an attempt of this sort for a great poem. And the poem was there. But I do not hide the difficulty of the attempt, which even filled the poet with fervor, this poet who was my greatest collaborator not only on account of the tragedy which he prepared for me, but also because of the enthusiasm to continue which he infused in me. And for him, at least, I attained my goal, since he later wrote to a friend of his, "Mascagni has expressed all that I felt." It was that which I hoped to attain.

But there were some people who said to me, "Are you setting d'Annunzio's verses to music, verses which are already so full of music?" Very true. But poetry has its own inexpressible harmony which is precisely its intimate and hidden perfume; the sensation we experience in hearing it. And this is what I wanted to express. I did not write a musical work; I wanted to absorb myself in the thought of a poet, to penetrate his spirit. I believe that a re-semblance can be found between my very first opera, *Ratcliff*, and *Parisina*. This resemblance is a result of the loftiness of the tragedy.

So the work was finally finished? Not at all! The choosing of the soloists, the scenery, the rehearsals....

Parisina saw the light at La Scala, where, among other things, there was the advantage of having at one's disposition a large and very good chorus, which earlier in *Feuersnot*[68] had given proof of an admirable discipline. Actually, the choruses in *Parisina* formed one of my most insistent preoccupations. There were 160 choristers, all on stage in the first act, all in the galleries of the castle. This first act opens with a lament by La Verde, Parisina's nurse. Then, from four sides, rise the voices of the laboring workers, divided into four choruses — each complete in itself — which alternate, almost as in a contest, and at length combine in a powerful mass.

This is a characteristic of choruses of the fourteenth and fifteenth centuries and I believe it transports one immediately into the milieu and spirit of the tragedy. I wrote them in imitation of the old traditional songs which flowered in Tuscany and later spread everywhere. I did the same thing with a small chorus of hunters which is also a literal reproduction of a fourteenth century song.

Parisina is a tragedy which needs a grand performance. The singers must sing as if they were reciting, with clarity and infinite expression. *In fine*, the music is only an extended harmonious discourse. d'Annunzio's beautiful, sonorous and hammered verses are constructed according to a superb rhythm and the public should not lose one word of them. It seems to me that *Parisina* is one of the most beauti-

---

68   The Strauss opera, which had its Italian premiere on 16 November 1912, under
      Tullio Serafin.

ful and most human of d'Annunzio's tragedies, full of ardor and poetry. It is necessary for the public to feel this, to be immediately transported so as to experience the spirit of the poem.

Thus the greatest difficulty was that of having the right performers; we not only needed the voices, we also needed the figures. In this d'Annunzio was very demanding, and he was right. I was in perfect accord with him. D'Annunzio counted greatly on having two youthful figures for Parisina and Ugo. Parisina is a young wife, small and fragile. And yet, because of a trait which may have its reasons but which for the moment escape me, all sopranos display a tendency towards the monumental. Parisina is a young girl twenty years old, delicate, witty, bewitching; she absolutely cannot be impersonated by a physically abundant singer, not even if that singer were to sing like an angel. Twenty-year old *prime donne* are easily found — almost all *prime donne* are inclined to be twenty years old. But it is indispensable that they also have the other qualities that Parisina must posses. We found Tina Poli Randaccio, excellent and small.

But who could impersonate Ugo well? Who would know how to give him the formidable and passionate impetus, the outbursts of anger and love, so frequent in the second and third acts; and then, finally, to sing with an unruffled diction those lines where the melody is "uncovered", as in certain Bellinian pages? The Ugo d'Este conceived by Gabriele d'Annunzio is a superb creature in whose soul the gloomiest ardor and most tender passion strangely alternate. He must also be graceful, tall and slender, enflamed with love and a believable nineteen years old. Oh, how much did I have to study to express musically that pulsating tragic figure! The speeches of the young man are at times panting, painful, bordering on madness. To translate them with correct expression into music I had spent assiduous effort, entire months.

The first Ugo was the tenor Hipolito Lazaro, a young Catalan with a very beautiful voice. The other two singers were well known; Luisa Garibaldi as Stella dell'Assassino and the baritone Carlo Galeffi as Nicolò d'Este.

I also took upon myself the burden of the stage direction of this newest tragedy, in addition to that of conducting the music. A double obligation. And the poet, who continued to help me from afar, did not want to be present. I felt myself weighted by a great responsibility since d'Annunzio's poem would be judged with my music, and the poem was not a revision or adaptation but completely new. Thus it was necessary that the scenic production be worthy of the nobility of the tragedy and of the poet's standing. Not an easy thing.

What need is there to say again that Rovescialli designed some scenes — and they were delicious — after sketches taken from the originals and framed in arches as d'Annunzio advised? Or that Caramba designed some wonderful costumes, he too drawing his inspiration from the Schifanoia frescoes indicated by the poet? Or that Previati painted five pictures for the score, or that Nomellini prepared an enchanting shadowy poster with Parisina reclining in the anxiety of expectation, her hope illuminated by a tiny flame?

I was annoyed about the noise that went on in the newspapers over *Parisina*. We were at least a month away from the first performance, and there were articles and more articles!

The public reads, arms itself with expectation, gets annoyed, and says, "Ah, that Mascagni, what an advertiser!" And I pay the price of my over-zealous friends. When an opera has been given, then it is worthwhile speaking about it. Beforehand it is irritating. I believe I am an intelligent man, despite my writing operas. An artist should be left in peace with his work. The opera is finished? Very good, let it be performed. It was liked? Cheers! It wasn't liked? Good-bye! But at least let it be born quietly.

These friends continued to say that for *Parisina* a very jealous discretion had been observed, but they had been writing this for two years. I am very much in favor of discretion. The newspapers vent themselves on their own account. Can I not vent myself on my account? Indiscretions here, indiscretions there, columns everywhere. Even pieces of the music were published, which Sonzogno had given out to please me but which also annoyed me.

I entered the pit on 15 December 1913. There are people who ask about the feeling of discomfort which I must have felt as composer in personally conducting the first performance of an opera of mine. But I would have felt a much greater discomfort if I were not there! Because the idea of my being responsible for the performance holds me as strongly as my shoulders hold my head. And then I always wanted to pay in person. It is a duel with the public, it seems to me, and I wanted to be there too. However, I assure you that the very beginning, when I didn't yet feel whether the public was with me or not, was something tremendous. I had not always conducted my operas. I began, I remember, with *Ratcliff* at La Scala, and I experienced a great impression as a result of it. But I always felt better than if I were not there. However, the *toilette* of that first evening, of presenting oneself in the pit before the crowded and impatient theater, and the terrible silence before the first attack... It was to feel a sensation of bewilderment, that same chill that the novelists call a cold sweat. I did not sweat, but I felt the cold.

D'Annunzio and I fought our battle and the public was kind enough to offer the tokens of victory to *Parisina*. This was what we wanted and this we obtained. But we wanted to give them the entire fruit of our labor. The opera had to be judged by the public exactly as it was born. And the judgement of the public was precisely that which I had foreseen — in everything, even the impression of its length. After all, I too have a few watches which run rather well. Why didn't I look at them? Just the opposite! They told me, "How long this *Parisina* is!" And I answered, "It is undeniable!" It is very long. But I left it as it was. Because d'Annunzio and I both felt and thought thus. Was it a somewhat long thought? So much the worse for us.

It was said that already at the rehearsals cuts had been advised, and this was quite true, just as it was also true that advice had already been preceded by my own impressions. Arnaldo Fraccaroli wrote an article for the *Corriere della Sera* accusing d'Annunzio's text of excessive prolixity, but I had already told d'Annunzio that his tragedy was too long and this had not turned out well for me. So I took my cue from

Mascagni in France at the time of *Parisina*

Fraccaroli's observations and returned to the attack. But d'Annunzio was inflexible; one day he even invited me to a meal at the *Ristorante degli Italiani* to tell me again, "Don't forget that you have given me your word of honor not to cut anything from my libretto."

And then, too, I understood the necessity of not disturbing the massive structure of the opera, also because, as I have said, I wanted the judgement of the public on our entire work. After the first performance I knew I was in accord with the public, that public in which I have always trusted from the time of *Cavalleria rusticana*. During the rehearsals of *Cavalleria* in Rome in 1890, all those who were present were scandalized by the scream, "*Hanno ammazzato compare Turiddu.*" They found it really ridiculous to base the finale of the opera on a spoken phrase and proclaimed a disaster. And instead the public was electrified by that scream and the finale was hailed as a very fortunate novelty. And one can see that *Cavalleria* has travelled!

Now the theater has some exigencies and customs before which one must bow when one creates a work for it. And no one in good faith had been able to accuse us of weakly feeling the dignity of art — the fact of our having met the first judgement of the public with all the dangers which we knew about saved us. After the premiere Fraccaroli came to me. In reality he had been sent by Albertini[69] to see how to make *Parisina* more agile.[70] I showed him a pack of telegrams from d'Annunzio in which he prohibited me from cutting. But now I was able to win out and I made some cuts in Acts II and III, making them immediately. I could almost say that I had them ready. But even with these the opera's dimensions still remained enormous.

It had even been said by a few critics that I had slowed down the tempi. Note it well, the tempi marked by me and then changed by me! Mascagni against Mascagni, the orchestra conductor who tries to ruin the composer, when both are one person. A thing somewhat... somewhat fratricidal, no? But I had no intention of criticizing the critics, for pity's sake! I only said "From the moment that I wrote the music for *Parisina* the tempi were continually marked with care, and the critics

---

69   Luigi Albertini, director of the *Corriere della Sera*. See *Personalia: Fraccaroli, Arnaldo*.

70   That is, on the assumption that additional cuts in the text would make the opera lighter, more "supple". With respect to this delicate issue Mascagni had, of course, already removed more than 300 lines from the 1,730 lines of the original (see p.215, above).

may check my conductor's tempi with those marked with a metronome in my composer's score."

But to return to the massive structure of the opera. Even with the cuts I had made, the length was still overwhelming. So, in accord with d'Annunzio, a radical resolution was thought of. The tragedy virtually finished with the third act, when Nicolò d'Este confides the two lovers to the executioner:

> *Abbian l'istesso ceppo*
> *sotto l'istessa scure*
> *i due capi, e i due sangui*
> *faccian l'istessa pozza.*

The fourth act is a "fixed" act: the exaltation of love and of death, of love above everything, of love in the face of death. The duet of two souls in the face of the reality of Stella the mother who is on the other bank—in life—and whose call to her son does not cross the river already traversed by those two. The public had received and greeted this final act with applause. Thus it was not a question of an act which did not please. But it lengthened the opera immeasurably. So we omitted it entirely. D'Annunzio and I had presented it on the first evening of the battle even while knowing the danger of the attempt, and the public accepted it. But as I have said, the stage has its exigencies and we bowed before them. We wanted a full battle and we fought it. Thereafter the tragedy of *Parisina* was given in three acts. Naturally Fraccaroli afterwards prided himself on having been the one to convince d'Annunzio and me to suppress this fourth act.

Later d'Annunzio again reproved me for having cut the fourth act— perhaps he no longer remembered having finally authorized the cut himself!

---

71   "Let their two heads have the same block/under the same axe/and their blood/form the same pool." (Vocal score, pages 293-294).

28 THE GREAT WAR. *LODOLETTA. SI* (1914-1919)

After *Parisina* I had a few subjects in hand, but I was afraid, at that time, of a work of large dimension. I feared that my mind, preoccupied with heavy and sorrowful thoughts, was not able to bear the weight of study for a deeply conceived opera. And for that reason I preferred a work of pure sentiment.

War puts us back centuries. It forces us to travel the road of the human race in an opposite direction. Also politically. The most daring social concepts, the conquests of internationalism and socialism — where do they go? Everything is destroyed, disappears. I believe no other war generated so much hate as World War I.

War should return us to music which has feeling, to the founts of melody. Because in days of strife, little or no thought is given to the scientific evolution of the art. As long as such a state of affairs continues, the creators of art cannot think this way, neither can those who recreate art. At most, the evolution, or — better — the revolution of art has always been conceived and carried out in cold blood, in times of calmness and serenity. The opposite is true when the public spirit is most fervent and stirred-up.

I had observed what an evolution the years of universal calm previous to the war had produced in music and thus had hopes that the war would bring us back to the simplicity and purity of melody. Our soul is so constituted that after a storm of sorrow has disturbed and upset it, it feels irresistibly drawn to thoughts of gentleness and goodness, towards the sweetest and purest memories. I felt that art must return to drink at the most ancient emotional founts.

In creating *Lodoletta* I especially wanted the music to call forth a sweet sense of comfort, a restorative quality, for the spiritual life of humanity which had passed through the great drama of the war.

As soon as I decided to set to work, I telegraphed to Giovacchino Forzano, who quickly joined me at Antignano. So that the collaboration might progress as rapidly as possible, the librettist agreed to stay at my home. On 29 October 1916, we both set to work.

By 9 December I had already completed the first two acts. I wrote with such fluency that I sometimes got ahead of the poet and then had to stop and wait for him. Thus between the second and third acts there

Giovacchino Forzano

was a hiatus. Then on 2 January 1917, we took up the work again. Until 15 January I wrote continually without tiring and without rest.

The premiere took place at the Costanzi on 30 April 1917, with Rosina Storchio and Guiseppe Campioni. A later interpreter of Flammen was a dog of a tenor. One of the audience said, "Poor little bird (referring to Lodoletta[72]). This dog will eat her in one bite."

But regarding tenors, another one comes to mind. He was Schiavazzi, a light tenor but able, and it was he whom I wanted for *Iris*, which really demands a light tenor. So I went into production in Livorno with *Iris*, at the opening of the season, and with Schiavazzi as the protagonist.

Now there is a small fact which complicates things. I have never been able to stand the claque in the theater. I endured it because it was forced on me, but I have never been able to stand it. I am the enemy of all that is not clear, sincere and spontaneous. So I didn't want the claque, but at Livorno the claque decided the good and bad weather.

Well, on account of this business of the claque, hardly had Schiavazzi come on when whistles sounded from the gallery. I stopped the performance and said very seriously, "Mascagni does not conduct in a theater where there are scoundrels who do not respect the artist which he has chosen." Then I laid down the baton and went out. The end of the world happened. But I did not want to return to the podium and there was nothing anyone could do about it. The performance had to be postponed and the management reimbursed the price of the tickets.

I began to compose *Si* on the first of August, 1918. At last in an Italian operetta, frankly Italian music. And it was about time, too, if Italianate

---

72 Lodoletta: little lark.

quality in music was not to be a meaningless expression. The operetta in Italy at this time was undoubtedly in an evident and humiliating decadence. Whose fault was it? More than anything else, the performances. And it is useless to dwell upon the... out of tune singing. Italian musicians had the fault of blindly following the Viennese style and it became worse the more they were forced to steal fluent and assertive waltzes from prohibited pastures. But Italian composers in this art form had, according to me, another fault, and it was that of writing emotional music such as would find a place in an opera.

Now in an operetta, there is nothing to be taken seriously — not even love. Everything in it is or has the quality of satire, wit, levity, caricature. And yet look at all the love duets in the numerous and unvaried operettas of those years, and try to eradicate the impression that those cadenzas, those short motives, those trends would be more worthy of a serious opera than of one of the many small pathetic scenes in the lamp-lit shadow of the elegant rooms in... Maxim's.

Certainly it is more difficult and a much more arduous task to write an operetta than an opera, since in the former everything is based, or should be based on melody; and in the latter the composer takes advantage of completely different resources.

I wrote the music of *Si* with all my artistic probity, without any artifice, without any deviation, without any pose. I forced myself to rescue it from the meddlesome and prevailing Viennese style. I certainly would have wished that the libretto, too, had been an equally Italianate brand of satire, but I did not have that opportunity. The novellas of the fourteenth century are an inexhaustible mine for anyone who wishes to investigate them.

I was also determined, so as not to remain a slave of the... Aristotelian dogmas of the operettas then in vogue, to destroy, to pass over the so-called *ritornello* which, because style may not suffer a slap in the face, had taken on the exotic name of *refrain*. And so I determined to be somewhat anarchic and rebel against the outmoded systems of style.

Since the operetta, if it is to be national, cannot repudiate that which at one time was our comic opera, I used the so-called "separate numbers" in which I wrote only simple and ear-catching melodies which flow, sparkle and glitter like water from a pure, fresh fountain. If I had been able to affix a motto to the head of the score, I would not have hesitated to choose the testament of Rossini: "Variety in rhythm, simplicity in melody." And in *Si* I abandoned myself to my imagination, in the Italian style, according to the precept of our *Gran Papà*.

I wanted, I repeat, in *Si* to destroy the belief that an operetta may only be Viennese, i.e, with its stereotyped and easy waltzes, with its love duets in a pathetically langorous style.

But in 1919 it was performed against my will in Rome. My music was not performed as I wrote it. I had tried something new, and perhaps I was successful. I had written waltzes and marches... without rhythm. It was really so. Count the bars in the periods of the *Trionfo del rosso*. The first, seven; then five, then... an extra one! But everything was "corrected" in Rome; perhaps they thought that I had made a mistake and

Mascagni at the time of *Lodoletta*

had forgotten that dances must have periods of eight bars! I was greatly pained by that massacre which Carlo Lombardo produced for me in
Rome.

It is a pity, however, that they continue to give the operetta *Si* in Italy
with the earlier text and in the earlier edition. The new version which
I made in 1925 for Vienna is much better.

For a long time I had been attracted by the idea of setting a subject on the French Revolution to music. But I wanted a libretto with a revolutionary background which excluded the great historical figures of that period. To bring the heroes of history onto the stage is highly ridiculous. Can one imagine Robespierre or Napoleon, Julius Caesar or Garibaldi singing from the stage?[73]

In 1919 Giovacchino Forzano presented me with *Il piccolo Marat*, a libretto which suited my nature and my sensibility exactly, and those aesthetic principles which have always guided me and advised me in my work. F. Martini, to whom Forzano had turned, gave much advice, suggested the episode from *Les Noyades de Nantes* and provided many books, as Forzano himself told me, among others the volume of Lenôtre and that by Victor Martin, *Sous le terreur*. From the latter the librettist took the substance of the play, reproducing other episodes from it also. The idea of the *noyades* refers to those numerous shipwrecks caused at Nantes using large boats on which the ferocious Governor Carrier had prisoners loaded and which, set afloat at the mercy of the Loire, were sunk by the exploding of a prearranged box of powder. It was a quick and sure method of emptying the prisons. The second part of the first act is developed around this episode.

The libretto, as I wished, had no real personages; no Robespierre, no Carrier, no Sénéchal. There is the president of the Committee, the Ogre (bass); Mariella, his niece (soprano); the Little Marat (tenor); his mother (mezzo soprano); the Soldier (baritone); the Carpenter (baritone); and then the Thief, the Spy, the Tiger, the chorus of prisoners, the crowd, the Marats, and the American hussars, called "the Black Devils".

I fell in love with the subject on the spot as soon as Forzano presented me with the verses of the libretto, but not all of them, as I immediately protested. The librettist was so convinced of the necessity of finishing some parts and correcting many others that, for this purpose he was my

---

73   It might be argued that Mascagni's own Nerone sings from the stage... or, that Nero is not a "hero"...

guest at Ardenza[74] for a good six months. He corrected the scenic parts according to my indications.

I began the composition of the opera in 1919, on 1 May as I have always begun writing my operas. Others celebrate that day by resting, I with work. But Forzano confessed and proved himself powerless to finish the poetic portions according to my criteria. Sonzogno, more than I perhaps, was convinced of this and worried about it.

So naturally Sonzogno, faced with the impotence of Forzano, advised me to have *Marat* completed by another poet. And, with the approval of Sonzogno himself, I turned to my friend Targioni-Tozzetti who for me wrote the verses which were still needed and new pieces to substitute those of Forzano which were not acceptable. Indeed, for the love duet in the second act Targioni even received a specific payment from the publisher. This duet was the last part of the opera which I wrote, because I didn't have the verses.

Giovacchino Forzano, unknown to me, had already given the libretto to Renzo Sonzogno. But since the music was my property it was therefore logical that the new parts and the corrected ones not be included in the contract made by Sonzogno and Forzano. Then on 26 November 1919 Renzo Sonzogno, in spite of my protests, signed a contract with the Costanzi including my opera in it, though he had not yet made a contract with me. Sonzogno, to do the theater a favor, had included that opera knowing he could not give it. And the management of the Costanzi announced it on their posters, being certain that it would not be performed in that season.he purpose of this may have been to publicize the Costanzi season, merely by including Mascagni's name in this fashion.

So it was that a year later I found myself with a completed opera without knowing exactly where to give it. I thought of La Scala, but it did not open that year; I had extremely attractive offers from Catania, Palermo and from the San Carlo in Naples, but the premiere was ultimately given at the Costanzi on 2 May 1921. This was something I strongly desired, since I am tied to Rome by great affection. It is to Rome that I owe my artistic baptism, it is in Rome that I have made a home where my dearest memories are kept. And precisely in Rome I have old and dear friends.

---

74   A sea resort about two miles from Livorno where Mascagni made his home away
      from Rome.

Ferroni was the Ogre; in 1920 I had already played the part over for De Angelis and he was enthusiastic about it; for Mariella I had Della Rizza, a complete artist; for the Piccolo Marat I needed a tenor who had dash and knew the opportune moment to shout and yell, yet in the scenes with his mother and Mariella would know how to sing with exquisite sweetness and great sentiment. Thus is his role, in the action as in the musical expression, continually divided. Lazaro sang this part.

In this opera, as in other works, my constant thought had been that of reproducing the words in music, not to comment on them, but to blend them. As I have said, to put words to be recited with orchestral commentary is *melologos*, not opera.

We need to be sincere. We Italians, who in life are ardent and sometimes brutal, cannot conceive of sentiment as a cerebral manifestation. Calculation is not for us. One must not substitute the design of melody for melody. One must not abolish true song; everything must be melody. The human voice, which is the most precious instrument of all, must not be suffocated; it must not recite the verse but sing it. I sometimes repeat a section of the verse out loud over and over, and gradually feel the melody being born by itself from the word. In this way one conserves the character of the text and its greatest expressive power.

Il piccolo Marat is strong, it has muscles of steel. Its strength is in its voice; it does not speak, it does not sing — it shouts! I wrote the opera with clenched fists, like my soul. Do not look for melody or learning — in *Marat* there is only blood! It is the hymn of my conscience.

BETWEEN TWO OPERAS
(1924-1932)

Giacomo Puccini and I were always friends, like two brothers, since our Conservatory days. When his opera *Le Villi* was rejected in the 1883 Sonzogno contest and as a result no one wanted to give it, I took up a kind of collection (begun by the painter Sala) with thirty lire and this was then continued by Boito and others.[75] And the opera was given on 31 May 1884.

The impression of that evening has always remained profoundly in my heart. It was not envy that I felt, but I saw my dear friend attain that goal which I had long dreamed of. I burned with the desire to do the same and did not see the possibility of doing so. I returned in this state of mind to the little room in my uncle's house, and inebriating visions again came to my imagination. Oh art! my beautiful art! So I could not attain the coveted glory which I dreamed of? From that day on I had no more peace. I found much comfort in walking all alone, through remote streets: I scanned my future which seemed so black to me and the saddest thoughts came to my mind. And when my uncertain and staggering steps led me again into a illuminated street full of people, then I hid myself, since I believed that everyone could read the sadness in my face, perceive the tears in my eyes. It took an enormous effort to face my friends again and have them believe I was happy. Six years later, after the first performance of *Cavalleria*, the first congratulatory telegram I received was from Puccini.

He was six years older than I; if he were alive today he would be eighty-six years old. When he died on 24 November 1924 I could not believe it. I could not conceive it. I did not know what to say. Puccini was dead! My mind was in a turmoil, completely filled with memories... and my soul was completely filled with sorrow... I wept... I wept for my friend, my colleague, my brother. I wept for the great composer, I wept for the man who was always good. Italy lost a son who had won glory in his own name and in that of his country.

---

75   See also *Personalia: Sala, Marco.*

I returned to Vienna in 1927, for the Beethoven centenary. I was designated by the government to represent Italy in the ceremonies. In Italy everything was done to frustrate this stubborn decision of Mussolini. There was a Foreign Secretary who at that time proposed to the Duce that a delegation be made up, headed by me. I refused. Mussolini became annoyed and still wished that I alone represent Italy, reasoning logically that Beethoven, a noted musician, should be honored by a musician.

I remember that I was supposed to give a lecture, to be translated into every language by the censor. I was advised that Mussolini himself wanted to see the lecture before I gave it. This irked me but I had to adapt myself and said so to the Under Secretary who presented me to Mussolini for the reading. The lecture was supposed to last only six minutes and Mussolini read it, re-read it and approved it. But he did not want to return the manuscript to me. I trembled because I did not have another copy, nevertheless I trusted my memory and rewrote the lecture almost exactly. It was reported to the Ambassador that my lecture was beautiful but several words should have been changed. I opposed this, naturally. I have never tolerated impositions.

In spite of this, I gave a fine lecture. One that I had given in 1901 on Verdi was finer but then I knew Verdi, I loved and felt him more. However, the Viennese lecture was successful and was very favorably commented on by official and popular criticism.

All the orators spoke in German. Only I had permission to speak in Italian, a homage to the musicality of our language. I am convinced that Italian is the language best adapted for music because of its triple possibility of accentuation; apocopated, plain and proparoxytonal. At bottom, the true character of music is vocal and the tunes, songs and melodies of the people are the most genuine manifestations of the spirit of music. An image: the earth gives you wheat, the composer makes flour from it, adds yeast, salt and if he does not mistake the proportion cooks it well and makes good bread from it.

In my trips I have collected folk music, songs from all over. I even searched among lost Indian tribes in America, having them sing and listening to them. In Hungary, where the sense of rhythm and the plastic art of music are so deeply rooted, one evening in the theater I sat down at the piano after a performance and drove them wild by having them sing their own songs. I am convinced that the most beautiful folk melodies are the Spanish, Italian and Hungarian. But who is it that seriously understands the beauty of *"Addio, mia bella, addio"*? A marvelous thing, but such simple and unadorned beauty is not for everyone. Illustrious critics are afflicted with this deafness, they will listen to such a song, but though it seems impossible, they will only hear the accompaniment and not the melody. They find an excuse, "Let us return to classicism!" But if you sing, you are always partaking of romanticism, no? Now let us understand one another about this classicism. Classicism means order, measure, perfect expression, completeness. Well, who are more classic that the great romantics? The trouble with these critical gentlemen is that they no longer know how to modulate, their musical speech is only a ruthless monotony. They fall in a hole and don't know how to get out of it. One should reform all musical teaching, especially harmony. The arithmetic part of harmony is slovenly. What does it matter that a man of genius like Guido d'Arezzo discovered the tetrachord (which has an incalculable value for the simplifications that the harmonic system derives from it) when no one takes note of it anyway? But Italy is a musical country, by the will of God, and it will have its music. Music set to words is written only in Italy.

And yet even in Italy a wind of madness has taken minds by storm. Today there is the snobism of glorifying foreign music. And the true Italian art, that which has drawn and still draws all to it, since the minds of artists beyond the Alps turn for inspiration to our country, is neglected, passed over, forgotten and I would almost say despised. It is a dream to hope that one can conquer this tendency — it is stronger than one believes. All, with an extraordinary thoughtlessness, are contributing to this state of things. Rossini put the libretto at the service of the music, Wagner put the music at the service of the libretto. What does that mean? That we are different; that in their public squares there are crows; in ours, doves.

When a man has attained a certain celebrity, it is the custom to celebrate his birthday every ten years. Thus it was that my seventieth birthday came to be celebrated when I reached just... 69 years.

I remember that on that occasion, at a banquet given me by my friends, I said among other things, "I thank you, moved by the lovely party which you have bestowed upon me... which, however, does not belong to me since I have not yet reached seventy." But the party was given just the same so as not to spoil the program and at the same time it served to demonstrate to me the immense goodness of friends and admirers who still remembered how much I have done for Italian art.

In 1932 I gave *Pinotta*. As I have already said, in 1881 I had written a work in two acts, very, very short, called *In filanda*; a little cantata with just enough words to make the music flow. Can it be imagined that at that time — sixty years ago — I would have a libretto? It was enough for me to imagine a love scene. A boy and girl who love one another, silently, and one fine day they tell one another so in a love duet which begins with timid words and ends with a promise, hand in hand.

From *In filanda* I kept four pieces from the first act and a small portion of the prelude. All the rest had already been scrapped in 1882-83 when I recomposed the cantata (for a Conservatory contest) and I gave it the name of *Pinotta*. *Pinotta*, as has been repeatedly and erroneously stated, was never left in pawn with any landlord. *Pinotta* had always remained with me, from 1883 until 1932, and for 17 years it lived closed up in my bookcase in Ardenza, in my study. It was the first in the long line of my operas, all of them written by my own hand. More than once I had taken it from my bookcase to see and hear it again; and once with my friend Vittorio Gianfranceschi, who was at Livorno, we had come to the point of deciding to have it performed; but then it was put back in its old bed to continue sleeping.

When in 1931 I received a box of things left in Milan with my landlord many years ago, in that box I found *In filanda*, which caused *Pinotta* to return to mind.

I went to Livorno and as soon as I arrived I telephoned my son Dino, who went to my study and brought out *Pinotta*, sending it to me at the Corallo. Dino himself brought it to me in ten minutes on his motorbike; and then (after hearing it again) I decided to have it performed. But until its premiere at San Remo on 23 March 1932, it had never been performed.

N*erone* was an act of faith: in God, in myself, in art and in the Italians. I took great satisfaction in this opera; with it I wanted to show how the strangest things can be represented in music. I wanted to write an opera in a certain new manner and believe I succeeded, in spite of those who considered me written-out at seventy. I wanted to write a theatrical work, not in the sense of spectacle, since this is an old, but outmoded, device to make an impression; but theatrical in the sense of virtually efficacious, adherent to the spirit and comprehension of the people. I wanted to give the people an interpretation of Nero a little less traditional, a little less the tyrant and the puppet; I wanted to depopulate history of its grim figures, to give these again, even with their defects and vices (since this is a heritage of every man and every epoch, a necessary ballast), a prestige, a halo, a significance worthy of ancient Roman grandeur. In short; to substitute living men for old statues carved in series down the centuries.

How did the idea of *Nerone* come to me? I had been in love with this subject since 1891. In that year I happened to read the play by Pietro Cossa, having already seen this drama acted by one of our greatest performers, someone like Salvini or Rossi. I thought I would do with it what I did with *Ratcliff*, compose my music to the original, without a libretto.

So I took this drama by Cossa and began to set all of his hendecasyllables to music. It was an extremely difficult undertaking, so much so that I was unable to manage it and decided to make an adaptation of this poem which fascinated me.

Meanwhile, Boito's *Nerone* was being talked about. In 1892, finding myself in Genoa, I played a few of my already composed pieces, and a journalist said, "But Boito?" I answered, "Do you believe Boito will write it?" "Why?" "Because I don't believe he will. Boito is one of the strangest musicians, one who does not even feel the necessity of writing an aria, a waltz or a polka: nothing, nothing. With *Mefistofele* written he has ceased to live." In fact he died without finishing *Nerone*. He barely began the last act and it has never been contemplated having others finish it. It is performed without the last act. The libretto exists but the music is lacking. There was a certain Maestro who wanted to poke his nose into it, to try and do something himself about completing the opera, but he ended up performing it as it is, incomplete.

So I said, "I'll let Boito have time; I won't do it now. I'll give Boito all the time he needs, unless he gives me the time."

Now comes the pleasant matter of Verdi, who became a great fiend of Boito's. Boito wrote Verdi's most beautiful libretti, *Otello* and *Falstaff*, hence the great friendship between the two men. One day Verdi wrote him a letter. This letter, which remained among Boito's papers, was later found by a famous bookworm, Alessandro Luzio.

Luzio wrote to me: "Dear Mascagni, I find myself in a difficult situation. Among Boito's papers I have discovered a letter by Verdi, which Boito certainly never showed to anyone. In this letter, Verdi exhorts Boito regarding *Nerone*: "Try to work, to go ahead; don't grow lazy; throw yourself rashly into this work. I tell you this in your own interests, because that prankster Mascagni is capable of beating you to it." This is Verdi's letter, Dear Mascagni, I must publish Verdi's letter. But if you tell me that you really don't like this phrase of Verdi's, I shall not publish it."

I replied: "Dear Luzio, I am grateful to you for this since to be called a prankster in this context, by a man like Verdi, pleases me very much." And in fact it was published. It wasn't the first time that Verdi had called me a jokester; the love Verdi had for me was something very moving.

I went to Rome and there met Rocco de Zerbi who had published his novel *La Vistilia*, a Roman tale of the times of Tiberius. I decided to set this work to music and had Targioni and Menasci fashion a libretto from the novel, but it ended up more a literary than a theatrical work. Then too the characters in *Vistilia* were not Romans; *Vistilia* herself was too fragile and frivolous to be a Roman lady.[76] And I longed to write a Roman opera.

I must confess that I had always dreamed of concluding my artistic life with a "Roman" opera. Rome, especially today, looms large in the world's thought; and on account of this I wanted my swan song to be dedicated to a work on a purely Roman subject. And so I thought again of *Nerone*. But before weighing anchor, one must look for safe moorings. Among Cossa's tempestuous scenes I saw three as indispensable: the tavern, the banquet, the death. Yet I didn't know how to give up the essential themes of the circus, of love, of the empire. Query: who

---

76   In fact, only sketches for the music were completed. See pp.187-88, above.

could concoct the logical plot of a libretto for me? Reply: I commissioned the libretto, still drawn from Cossa, from Targioni-Tozzetti.

In Cossa's ingenious and undeniably historical conception, Nero remains a character whom the Roman poet saw primarily as an artist in the last period of his life. For me too Nero is just such a figure, one very different from that which is generally conceived.

Different, for example, from that which Boito put on the stage. When I went to hear Boito's *Nerone* I was somewhat disillusioned. Above all it was his conception of Nero which left me cold. I do not look to see if Nero has a certificate for good conduct. It is a question of a human, affectionate, extremely interesting character. This important man died very young, at thirty-two, nineteen centuries ago,[77] yet everyone knows Nero, everyone talks about him. Even his most severe critics are forced to admit that he was a gifted man.

I believe that few musicians have gone about setting Nero to music because they have always considered him an emperor, a political man; instead he was neither.[78] His life was that of an artist, unsuccessful if we will, but an artist. Indeed, in this non-success, in his aspiration of wanting to be one and not attaining it, lies the interesting drama of his existence. One could repeat about him that which has already been said of other men, i.e., that he wanted to be great but contented himself with vanity.

This man, supreme commander of vast and glorious legions, who never led an army yet showed himself angrily invidious of his leaders, this man who had no personal dignity yet was placed on a throne whose power was never surpassed, was so very much smaller than what he could have been, but was also greater than that by which he was measured.

And on the other hand, could not this conflict, calmly considered, offer elements worthy of art? Nero was an artist; even the burning of Rome was a desire to clear the city of foul hovels; it was the vision of a Rome resplendent with palaces and marbles, and in the end, a dream of beauty. Historians may define this operation by a... city planner somewhat brutal, but history is the schoolmistress of life, and as a school mistress, given the years she has been teaching, she is necessarily some-

---

77 In 68 A.D.
78 It is important to keep in mind that Mascagni does not intend an historical portrait here but, with complete sincerity, he is explaining where his inspiration came from, and he is giving his reasoning as to how to put a personage on the stage.

what shrewish, and tedious, and pedantic. The reality is that Caligula surpassed Nero by a long way in cruelty. Of the five emperors who came from the Julian line Nero certainly was the least bad.

A matricide? But did not his mother wish to kill him in order to bestow the purple on Britannicus? A fratricide? But was not Britannicus his most dangerous enemy? And did not his brother plot to kill him by the sword or by poison? Nero was afraid. A coward, he became evil through cowardice, cruel so as to defend himself.

I studied my character in both the classic and modern writers, in the writings of his bitterest critics and most implacable enemies, and I became convinced that he was much less despicable than is generally believed. In the libretto of Monteverdi's *Incoronazione di Poppea*, written in 1640, Nero is good; Suetonius, calling him a born artist, claims to have "held in his hands the tablets on which he (Nero) wrote his poems," and as a poet proclaims him to be superior to Lucan. As a painter he was very bad, but as a sculptor he was on a level with Phidias and Praxiteles. He was a terrible singer, but he loved to sing for the love of singing. In short, he was an artist who tended to exaggerate, wishing to invade all fields of art.

And it is not true that Nero hated the Romans — the Romans adored him. For him the true greatness of Rome depended solely on the monumental beauty of the *urbs*. He never had a war, he never promulgated a law and when he was a child he was an angel. Nero may not have been that monster of cruelty which history desires; no historian will ever be able to prove that he made either good or bad laws, just as it can never be proved that he may have led the army. He was a megalomaniac, he busied himself with art, he lóved the East without ever having seen it, he was enamored of oriental display, he sang, he painted, he sculpted, he acted.

At any rate, I wanted to create a human Nero and believe I did not go astray. For this reason I used Cossa who presented a Nero made human, without trappings. Everything curious, fatuous, comic, quaint and bewitching which reverberated from this most interesting character was a reason for its attraction for me and was a musical color since it was a movement of spirit, passion, torment, illusion and delirium. And these are the colors of music.

That I set about giving a musical guise to such an important personage must not surprise anyone, neither my friends nor my enemies. Certainly, even these, because I am sure I have some enemies and am glad to have them; for as Bismarck was accustomed to say, the value of a man is measured by the number of his enemies. And then, in life, the real misfortune is not having any enemies. The greatest misfortune is not knowing how to distinguish which are friends and which are enemies...

Therefore, the character of Nero can stand very well in the gallery of my musical creatures, since in art I have never desired to have predilections for specific types of characters. Predilections are forms of slavery, and many times are a sign of impotence. I have chosen my characters wherever I found them, provided that they were capable of an emotion, a human expression and, in short, of living a life. I know that this is the old formula of romanticism, but in the end it is the most truthful, the most necessary and indispensable one in art. One can never do without romanticism if one wants to create art for the people (which, after all, is the true aim of art), and the musicians who think they can get along without it either deceive others or themselves. And then one must not forget that a character is never that which history gives us; history often presents us with a puppet. It is we who must give it eloquence, must soak it as one soaks a sponge in order to make it yield that which we want.

The death of Nero, for example, is a lyric page worthy of inspiring any artist. It may be ridiculous as an emperor's death, but as the death of a man, a dreamer, an artist, it is extremely interesting even in its cowardice. As a rule, poets do not have the obligation of being heroes — that is a function reserved for warriors. Did Nero die with a reproof to the centurion Icelo, a reproof which is that of a man, indeed, of an emperor, and which Suetonius has handed down in the celebrated words, *"Sero, haec est fides?"*, "Is this your fidelity?" (towards your emperor), or did he die disdainfully before those who wanted to seize his body to make public sport of it? Or was there not a ferocious and shrill irony in that scream of the dying man? I do not know. I know that in the drama of this death I had the drama of a thousand men, of a thousand abandoned or heroic men. But in reference to Nero himself, it intensifies the sad eloquence of life more than of death. Even this is a motive worthy of attracting an artist, perhaps even of deceiving him. Illusion is always more suggestive than reality.

One cannot put Nero on the stage and deny him his Roman-ness. Nero was very Roman and this opera needed to be Roman. By "Roman" one can mean many things, but one of these is fundamental when dealing with a musical work; I mean to say the Roman-ness of the musical language. For me the Roman musical language is a diatonic language, everything precise and unwavering intervals. For this reason the opera proceeds in blocks of diatonicism from beginning to end. The character of Egloge is the exception; she is Greek and a chromatic language suits her.

Melodic music, but not melody, not broad singing; in a word, no closed forms. I have always been a lover of sung recitative, fluid and full of music. I am an artist, I do not know about problems. I create if I have inspiration, otherwise I close the piano and go take a pleasant walk through Rome. The word, by definition, has importance in my opera neither more nor less than it has in Cossa's *Nerone,* in *Nerone* the prose drama.

At bottom, *Nerone* is this: an "Essay in musical expression of the word". I wanted to write these words under the title instead of the usual indication "opera in three acts". But it certainly was more prudent, as far as the public was concerned, to retain the customary formula and have them understand that one was dealing with an opera. But what is an opera? If the soul sings in a melody, it is in the recitative that the drama lives. For this reason the words are set syllable by syllable, accent by accent, and it is necessary for the music to give it its soul, that which the word possesses in itself in its won force, in its own substance, and not that which the musician capriciously lends it.

I began my journey on the harsh road of art with Targioni-Tozzeti: his artistic collaboration was always a good omen for me. As I wished, he did not depart from the essential lines of Cossa's work in so far as was possible. Nevertheless, we eliminated the first act of the play, thus reducing it to three acts and four scenes; we modified the figures of Atte and Egloge in certain respects, and omitted, in the tavern act, the character of Veronilla, the daughter of the slain Cassius Longinus.

When someone asked Cossa why in his drama he had not used dramatically the tremendous clash between worn-out paganism and rising Christianity, he replied that he did not want to do badly what Gazzoletti had done so well in his *San Paolo.* I, instead, wished that his titanic struggle might be made apparent, without dominating. An important scene, which Targioni-Tozzetti wrote only on the eve of his death, we added to the finale of our first act where they speak about the God of the Christians. But even here we only availed ourselves of a hint from Cossa, when he has the slave merchant say to a tavern client:

> *Già i miei schiavi*
> *Udii parlar di carità, e dritti*
> *Che loro accorda una novella legge*
> *Trovato da un guideo, che affisso in croce*

Morì sotto Tiberio.[79]

Into Nevio's mouth I put an invocation to Christ. Then the crowd of slaves takes up Nevio's song of freedom; it is the powerful voice of victory. I wanted this invocation to be made by the slaves, the rejected ones, because Christianity is charity and freedom, justice and love.

The music for this invocation came to me all at once, surging through my whole spirit. I even orchestrated this whole part of the first act which still had no words, hoping that Targioni could work and that he would be able to fit the words to that music which I absolutely could not change. But Targioni was seriously ill, and this work was done with great difficulty since I had to to go to his home in Livorno, where he was in bed in a deplorable condition and with a weak heart. I could only work with him about an hour a day, since he unexpectedly had fever daily, and then we would have to stop.

Targioni finished it just before his death; he who had once written the lines for an excellent hymn to the Madonna of Montenero concluded his life with this invocation to the blessed Christ. The day he died was a day of deep sorrow for me. No one will ever be able to imagine what a terrible blow his death was for me, just at the moment in which his great mind and his poetic vein wrote the final words for the libretto of *Nerone*, corrected, revised, made perfect in those last days of his unfortunate illness.

Poor Nanni! The fresh flower of your poetry awakened me with the classical libretto of *Cavalleria rusticana*; and that day you left me with your last song, with the libretto of *Nerone*, and you were unable to hear my words of admiration, of recognition, of emotion. What cruel destiny! But it was not important. This Nero was for me, as it was for you, a swan song. But your name will remain bound to mine from my first to last opera. No one shall ever be able to separate our names in art, as no one ever tried to break our friendship in life, a friendship always faithful and affectionate for more than sixty years. Your life is over. I fear for myself, for my art, but as long as God shall grant me a voice, I shall shout your name, oh my good Nanni, to indicate to Italian youth the symbol of faith, of friendship, of honesty; and to tell the world that my art ever had the need of a collaborator who was named Giovanni Targioni-Tozzetti.

---

79 "Already among my slaves/I have charity and rights spoken of/Which a new law grants them/Learned from a Hebrew who, nailed to a cross,/Died under Tiberius."

The premiere of *Nerone* was given at La Scala on 16 January 1935 with Pertile as the protagonist, coached in the action by Zacconi. The opera had a good success. At Livorno the work caused a furor and in certain cities the box-office was 82.000 lire each evening.

But naturally today's successes pale before those of fifty years ago. Then people understood art and took an ardent interest in it, making more fuss over a great tenor than they do over certain house painters today. I say that *Nerone* was a success and that it certainly was, but what do you want, compared with the success of *Ratcliff*, for example?

FIFTIETH ANNIVERSARY OF
CAVALLERIA RUSTICANA (1940)

Cavalleria remains the general background for my whole life. I say it with displeasure because many people believe that I've written nothing else, especially abroad. But there is something else. *Cavalleria* is so powerful that very often it even overwhelms the accomplishments of others. More than once it was my lot to read on posters, especially in the provinces, "*Cavalleria rusticana* and *Pagliacci* by Pietro Mascagni." But perhaps this mistake is explained by the fact that *Cavalleria* and *Pagliacci* are always performed together. And yet, what a strange fate!

The fiftieth anniversary of *Cavalleria* fell in 1940. Fiftieth anniversary! I confess that I did not feel much at home with those words, especially when they were applied to my first opera. It implied that I had become old, whereas I have never desired to become old.

For many years I have remembered a discussion with Verdi in Milan. I was very angry at the critics who had treated me somewhat badly, and Verdi consoled me by telling me that to be beloved by the critics one had to get old. "I myself," he said, "was badly mistreated by the Italian critics when I was young, even to the point that when I went to Paris for performances of my operas, I was followed by an Italian critic who came to France expressly to denigrate my artistic accomplishments. Milan was the focal point of these artistic adversaries, yet today in Milan I am loved and esteemed by all. Why? Because I am old."

"No," I said. "Guiseppe Verdi is adored and admired by all, in Milan, in Italy, in all the world, for his immortal genius which with its divine creations has given so much good and such emotion to humanity, thus receiving in return the purest and sweetest gratitude." "Now, yes, because I am old," retorted Verdi: and turning to Giulio Ricordi, who was present, he added, "This raw young man has the stalwart disposition of a fighter. I have read his lectures and know his proud character as a polemicist. That is dangerous... for him! Let us hope that one day Mascagni will be old, but I have the impression that he has little desire to be so." This discussion has always remained in my mind. Even today the words of Verdi resound in the depths of my soul.

But no, in spite of my stubborn ill will, everything forced me to realize that the fiftieth year of my *Cavalleria rusticana* was at hand. I tried to rebel against this event which established my age. I tried to distract myself with my usual good humor, which has been my only personal physician always in attendance. Yes, I could conceive of a golden wedding between two married people, I could admit to celebrating to my son's fiftieth birthday, but I could not conceive of the fiftieth anniversary of *Cavalleria*.

And yet I knew that it had arrived and that in spite of my every desire I was old. This fact saddened me even to feelings of self-reproach – it seemed to me I had broken a solemn oath. I felt depressed and disheartened. And desperately I fell back on my good humor. Patience! Very well. I shall be old, I said to myself, but I shall derive much comfort from everyone's esteem and affection and shall consider myself happy and consoled.

But no. I deceived myself. The relentless fury against my opera continued to prevail more evilly, more ferociously than ever before, and taking its cue from the announced fiftieth anniversary of *Cavalleria*, spat vituperation precisely about my *Cavalleria* music.

The Scalera cinematographic production firm was about to launch a film of Giovanni Verga's *Cavalleria rusticana*[80] and at any cost wanted me to consent to furnish the music from my opera in order to create a greater interest in Verga's prose. For my own personal and profoundly felt reasons, I thanked them for the honor tendered me, but refused in the most determined and absolute manner possible. The firm, however, did not stop with my first refusal and called personalities of the very highest rank to its aid in the hope of changing my negative attitude.

One afternoon I was at home with some friends. Alfieri, the Minister of Popular Culture, telephoned me: "Oh, Mascagni, please come here right away. I need to see you at the Ministry." I said to my friends, "Excuse me; the minister Alfieri is expecting me." I took a taxi (you could take one then) and went to the Ministry. I entered and saw the two Scalera brothers there. I made a wry face and greeted Alfieri. He said to me, "Do you know the Scalera gentlemen? So, these two want your *Cavalleria*." "I know it. I am sorry they were inconvenienced and also that they have inconvenienced you. They know my ideas and know I will not give them *Cavalleria*. It is the first time I have spoken with the Scalera brothers, but I have already let them know that I will not give them *Cavalleria* to film other than as a whole, as I wrote it, with a

---

80   Their production appeared in 1939. See *Personalia: Scalera Brothers.*

Mascagni, 50th anniversary of *Cavalleria rusticana*

Mascagni, 50th anniversary of *Cavalleria rusticana*

soprano, tenor, etc. Naturally the scenic problem must be revised, because in a film one can do what ones likes. When there is the procession, for example, the chorus can go behind the procession, run through all the streets of the little town and then return to the church. In a film one can do this very well." "Don't you worry about it, " said Scalera; "entrust your music to us." "No, because you do it in pieces; one piece here, one piece there..." (This is something completely mistaken. The idea has never dawned on these film producers to do an entire opera; they always go astray and will never do so, thus something serious will never be done.)

The Scalera brothers said to me, "But we do things seriously." "It doesn't seem so to me. If you want to do things seriously, listen to me and film the whole opera. If you do this, you will open a new path in cinematography which perhaps will be more beautiful and more lucrative than any other. I have many more operas and if *Cavalleria* pleases me I will also give you the others, but for me to entrust the opera to you because you want to use a piece of it here and there, with subjects that you do in your own way, no." "But you do understand that we can give *Cavalleria* to Mulè and he will write Sicilian music." "Do what you like, but it will not be my *Cavalleria* at all. Look where your mistake is; you begin with the principle that any other music will serve. Well then, you have no need of me." "After all, when one sees that a man like Mascagni turns down millions..." "I do not turn down millions, but neither do I run after millions. I have never been grasping. With me you could save several hundreds of thousands of lire on the two million you want to spend, but you must do what I want. Do you think I will entrust my *Cavalleria* to your directors who understand nothing? Today everyone is a director..." "Then we do not understand one another, dear Mascagni; so much the worse for you. Tomorrow we shall speak with Sonzogno in Milan." "Why go there? He doesn't enter into it." "But is he not the publisher?" "For giving the operas in the theater, for renting materials and for selling the scores, yes. But not for filming. I am the exclusive owner of the opera and I am not giving it up. I am not giving it to the films." It was a useless attempt: they could not ruffle me and I maintained my firm refusal.

I conceived the idea of refuting several evil words of our critics. But also this time I deceived myself. No one attacked my refusal of the film, but rather it was my *Cavalleria* which was attacked. On the release of the Scalera film, our leading critic, a member of the Italian Academy, was the first to publicly pontificate: "The highest praise goes to whoever prepared the plot and spectacle; it makes one forget immediately that a *Cavalleria* by Mascagni exists." (Thank you!) But first the stoning and then the bread. The critic continues: "Mascagni's *Cavalleria*, being a hundred times more famous and remembered than Verga's novella and rapid drama, would have been the most dangerous basis for a film." But then why not bestow on me "the highest praise for making one forget immediately that a *Cavalleria* by Mascagni exists"? Was it not I who, by my refusal, had "avoided the most dangerous basis for the film"? Rhetoric is an art, and its delivery is a virtue which enjoys a great appreciation in literature; but consistency is also worthy of being appreciated. In substance, the illustrious critic obtained three purposes; he destroyed the fable of the fox and bitter grapes, he established his renown as a critic and he rescued... the friendship of Pietro Mascagni.

There was one, however, who showed he possessed neither the art of rhetoric or the virtue of consistency. A Neapolitan newspaper, *Il Mattino*, still in regard to the film, printed that the production staff's greatest badge of honor was not to have used my music for *Cavalleria* which would have "contaminated" the beautiful film.

By God! What kind of spleen must the editors of the *Mattino* in Naples have if for fifty years they kept so much hate in their systems for my poor *Cavalleria* and chose to vent themselves precisely at that time in which some good and generous souls meant to commemorate a date which could arouse no antipathy in our people. If my *Cavalleria*, which had gone the round of Italy and the whole world for fifty years, could have the innate power to "contaminate" a film, who knows what disturbances it must have brought to humanity. Yet no one, neither the illustrious critic nor the editors of the *Mattino*, thought of praising me for preventing so many things and for saving so many men from such dangers!

But I still cannot reconcile myself to what the *Mattino* published, since I think that no Italian journalist should ever have dared to throw such a trivial outrage in the face of an old man, an artist who has nourished faith intact in his soul, who has felt love for his country even to giving a son to it,[81] an honest citizen who has always fulfilled his civic and political duties, a musician who for fifty years worked for the good of national art.

One would become maniacal if one did not have an optimistic temperament like mine. In difficult moments I call on my good humor for aid and this time my good humor advised me not to take it too much

---

81   Mascagni's son Edoardo had died in Africa in 1936.

to heart. At very bottom, one can only return to the past; the music of *Cavalleria* may be maltreated, but I shall not grow old. The prophecy of Guiseppe Verdi must triumph. And so I   became serene again, with the happy prospect of waiting a while before growing old. All the better if one can live in good health.

On the recommendation of Maestro Beppe Mulè, Director of the Conservatory of Santa Cecilia, a sort of small pamphlet, a little book, was published by the Syndicate of Musicians, wherein all the Italian musicians expressed their thoughts and opinions about me and *Cavalleria*. I said, "all," but should say "almost all" since several refrained from giving their real opinion and they did right. Rather than give unfelt praise, which doesn't come from the heart, it is better to be silent.

Of those who answered, several were very affectionate and full of enthusiasm, others exaggerated the dose somewhat, but one above all really amazed and moved me: Maestro Jachino, brother of an admiral, I believe. I've never had the occasion to visit with him since he is not a part of the group of my musician friends who come here to chat or play cards with me, yet he wrote a curious thing about me.

All spoke of Mascagni as the composer of *Cavalleria*, or *Iris*, of *Isabeau*, of *Ratcliff*; Maestro Jachino, instead, wrote: "To speak of Mascagni as a composer of operas is easy, since we musicians know his music well. It is simple to say of his operas, this is beautiful, this is powerfully dramatic, this is full of poetry and inspiration; but the difficulty is to know Mascagni not only as an artist, but to be able to say to the world what perhaps not everyone knows: how good a man he is." Of all the praise contained in that pamphlet, this gave me the most pleasure.

The Christian man, when he is overcome by the disturbance of tragic events which affect him, when he can no longer find the means of relief in his own soul, instinctively seeks refuge in the religion of Jesus Christ, in his House, in prayer.

Besides the torment of our country's state of war, the agonizing thought of our soldiers and the painful anxiety over the course of events, I had another sorrow, intimate and penetrating, which was breaking my heart. One of my grandchildren, the daughter of my poor son Edoardo (Silver Medal, three-time volunteer, killed in Africa), was struck by a pitiless illness, and I, trembling, saw this angelic creature wasting away little by little. I felt that I was unable to bear so much sorrow, but I had an inspiration: I made a request, for me and my wife, for an audience with the Pope,[82] placing all my hopes in this act of mine.

The audience was granted, and it is easy to imagine with what purity of faith I presented myself at the Vatican. I knew already that His Holiness was possessed of a divine goodness, crowned with a great mind and a great heart. But I would never have imagined to be received with such delicacy and such deference, which I have no reason to merit. It almost seemed as if His Holiness wished to descend to the level of my stature in order to speak freely with me.

And in fact he spoke with great simplicity to me of my art, remembering particularly the birth of *Cavalleria rusticana* when His Holiness was a boy, almost a child; and yet he said that he had never forgotten those days. He spoke to me about art with authentic competence. He also recalled the period in which I lived in Pesaro, directing the Liceo Musicale. He courteously asked my wife for news of our family, after which I described the sad case of our beloved granddaughter to the Shepherd of Humanity. With great benevolence His Holiness interested himself in the sick little girl, and gave her his best wishes.

We also spoke of other things, but I did not want to weary His Holiness and I rose to take my leave. The Pope, who was seated, all of a sudden rose, turned to me with raised arms, placed His hands on my

---

82   Piux XII (1876-1958). See *Personalia.*

shoulders, brought His face near mine and kissed me on the cheeks. I was moved and wept the sweetest tears of my life.

The Pope imparted the apostolic blessing on my wife and me, accompanying His gesture with the gift of a rosary for my wife and a beautiful silver medal, with His likeness, for me. Then He gave me another rosary, asking me to send it to our adored granddaughter along with His blessing.

The child was being treated for four months in the "Abetina" sanitarium at Sondalo (Sondino). I immediately sent the Pope's blessed gift. Soon there came for me, after only a few days, a letter from the mother of the sick girl (whom she had never left even for a minute) with these words: "The child is much better and strongly desires to return to Rome." I was amazed by this sudden news. I am not in the habit of ever denying anything to the creatures of my blood and of my heart. Nonetheless I hurried to ask the advice of the doctors in charge and who had visited her. And all were in agreement: "The child is growing worse daily and is extremely delicate, but given this sudden improvement, perhaps she may attempt the trip."

I lost no time. I give heartfelt thanks to His Excellency the Minister of Communications, Host Venturi, who immediately put a special coach from the State Railroads at my disposal. Not being able to go personally to Sondalo for reasons of health, I sent a very close relative, and the little girl made the long trip. For her arrival in Rome I arranged for an ambulance from the Red Cross to meet the train and transport the child to Dr. Marchielli's sanitarium "Maria Teresa" on Monte Mario. Everything went perfectly.

The train arrived in Rome at 7:40 in the morning. I thought that our little granddaughter would be tired by the journey, also because she was coming from a sanitarium where she had been in bed for four months. With an agitated heart I approached the coach, trembling. But I heard myself called by name and raised my head; it was my granddaughter at the window of the coach who called me and who immediately got down from the train completely dressed and threw her arms around my neck. I thought I was going crazy. But the child, caressing me, whispered in my ear, "Do you know what, grandfather? As soon as I received the rosary from the Pope, I felt better right away and every day I am getting better. Look, grandfather, I want to go to the Pope and kiss his hand." Dr. Morelli, who took her under his care, told me that the child's condition was very satisfactory.

Now all this, which savors of the exceptional, might seem to be a fairytale. But I who have absolute faith in the Divinity, think that that faith should create hope; and for this reason I hope. And that hope is based on the blessing of the Holy Father on the sick child and on the gift of the rosary He blessed. The Holy Father performed a miracle. And now with His prayers another miracle shall come about for all mankind: the end of the war and the coming of a civilized and just peace.

Mascagni with his granddaughter, c.1942

In the course of my life I have written fifteen operas. The fifteenth was the last, not because I lacked any more inspiration, but because I saw no reason to write any more. I am seventy-nine years old and shall make mistakes of all kinds, but never that one! And why? Let them give the fifteen already written. There's something in them for every taste. Of my fifteen operas only one, *Cavalleria rusticana*, enjoys world fame; the others are almost unknown to the public, though some of them may be as beautiful as *Cavalleria*.

Musical content is no longer desired. The general public looks for music which makes noise, music which they don't understand. It is a perversion! And they want me to write? For what purpose? With what satisfaction? Who would understand me? In the depths of my soul, which does not wish to grow old, many new ideas have sprung up, which I tell and repeat to myself in a low voice for fear of convincing myself that the whole world is going in the opposite direction.

The great majority of the public does not care about the opera; it has no interest for them because opera is a pleasure of the soul and today the general idea seems to be to hide the soul and avoid remembering as much as possible the existence of this little human weakness. People look for excitement and not artistic pleasure, they desire to amuse themselves in sensational ways which ruin the nerves and make a man incapable of doing serious work the next day, just as if tomorrow were the end of the world and such a prospect were an excuse to ruinously consume everything which may be obtained cheaply and indulge in all kinds of pleasures. The public asks new sensations from music. Ideas which essentially are the fruit of the intellect and not of intuition or feeling, ideas which do not touch the heart. The opera has had its day, many say. Today a new kind of music is needed, which in adapting itself to the changed conditions of life will be able to explain the ever-rising importance of techniques and the current of new ideas, new tendencies and new desires. Some composers even think that all this can be expressed in an opera.

The opera, however, is by its very nature elevated. The purpose of dramatic music has never been, nor ever shall be, meant to satisfy the grotesque desires of the audience; on the contrary, the purpose of opera is to touch what is most profound and best in human nature. Happiness, sorrow, passion, love and poetry are the motives of opera. It attempts to awaken all this in our hearts and this is the reason why the opera can never be replaced by jazz or any other form of music which is a derivation of the brain and not the heart.

I tend to believe that the decline of opera is due to a deficiency of publicity more than anything else. The publicity given to an opera is not at all equal to that given to light music and jazz. The young enthusiasts who used to sacrifice all their energies to its propaganda, the impresarios who in the past enthusiastically and successfully supported the opera and serious music throughout the entire world have become old or are dead. Their successors do not understand serious music, they are men of affairs whose purpose is only that of amassing a fortune as quickly as possible. From this point of view, light music and jazz (which aim at satisfying the most vulgar pleasures) are much more lucrative than opera.

It is clear that a composer of serious music cannot get ahead without good publicity, but the continuous battle with pub-lishers, impresarios and other people who are not looking for art and artistic creations but only money, is without inspiration for the composer and deprives him of every hope in the future.

But apart from this, I always think: what would be the purpose of giving performances and who would go to hear them? Could I have a theater full of really interested spectators? Perhaps so, if in the program it were announced that during the intermission Pietro Mascagni in person would have a boxing match with one of the spectators.

I am not an enemy of boxing or other sports — indeed, I tend to believe that they are useful and even necessary — but I prefer them in the form of physical education and not as a sensational exhibition of muscular force.

Automobiles, airplanes, technical marvels, all mechanical possibilities do not inspire me. The only modern thing which attracts me is the radio since it gives to the poor as well as to the rich the possibility of hearing concerts and operas which are transmitted over great distances and of enjoying that great treasure which humanity possesses: music.

But now jazz has taken over the radio. Shame! I shall never have peace until this barbarism is thrown out of Italy. Its terrible voice excites its listeners and kills that little love for serious music which may yet remain. Perhaps jazz will win and cut the opera out, but I hope that the public taste will heal quickly from this indisposition.

Today the films and varieties have submerged the theater. The theater still does much, and really it is a miracle what the theater is able to do. In fact, I would like to make films of my opera—people go to the films. As I have already said, *Cavalleria* was filmed, but not with my music. The one thing which I have been able to do has been to retain the operas as my exclusive property, so as not to give them to the films. The operas are mine, I am the owner of them. Sonzogno and I each have so much per cent: he until a certain date, I a little more.

But at bottom this is not right, a work of art should not have an owner. This has been the concept that I have always had of art. A work of art should be in the public domain: the public domain should be the owner. The artist composes an opera, paints a picture, writes a book, constructs a building—he is no longer the owner. Which means that the governments of civilized peoples must give artists a dignified way of living, of earning for a period of years, established by a special law. In short, the creative artist should have a serene life assured him by the State; there is no need to be rich to create art.

Art is a civilized people's greatest patrimony, it cannot and must not be the property of an individual. The individual creates, but he creates because of the need to create, because of that divine thrill which the Eternal Father put in his brain: to create is a need, it must not be a speculation.

All that an artist creates, if he is successful, is the work of Divine Providence. The musician is only the pen which the Eternal Father uses to write music. Before beginning work I have always said, "My God, aid me, if you believe..." In today's music you do not feel this petition to receive inspiration. No more faith, today, but rather "good faith" in a formula, which is why you feel the taste of the pharmacy, of the synthetic product. Composers think they are writing music but they are only writing intervals. Up and down, up and down, Russian mountains. Well, even that is enjoyment. At the end of it, however, you look around and wish for some solid ground. True music comes from the earth and sky, like all healthy and good products of the earth. What is music? It is lengthened, "held" speech, making what the composer wants to say heard better, speech which aims directly at the heart, but so much the worse for him if he mistakes in his aim, for who will save him from the wounded victim's reaction?

And now there are people who say, "The lyric theater is finished!" It's not true that it's finished. Enthusiasm is lacking, good faith is lacking, honesty is lacking, these are what is lacking!

During my time it was different, one had to sweat and be a serious artist. Not like now. They have made me a Vice President of the Italian Academy because they say that it's an honor. But what honor? — an empty honor! The sword, the cocked hat, the plumes... gorgeous stuff! But so much braying, my children! Are they asses? Well, not all, certainly, but it is better not even to compare those I'm talking about to asses: those useful and very humble beasts would be offended. Now a dictionary is being compiled and there is a commission formed expressly to Italianize foreign terms; I am only a musician, it is true, but at times I remain open mouthed in wonder.

But the lyric theater in Italy is not dead. There is still a lot to do. A pity that I'm old! But I am forced to recognize that it is not at my age that one may hope to change direction or do much that is new.

Oh yes, I'm already old, seventy-nine! However, with the exception of my legs which tremble a bit, I am still... on my feet. I have very acute hearing which allows me to distinguish the slightest nuance, and regarding my memory, the reader can easily see that it still serves me very well. I still don't consider myself a doddering old man!

But perhaps it is also because in my life I have never committed excesses; my eating is extremely frugal (perhaps too much so, but evidently in this hotel they are being careful that I don't die of indigestion). I am unable to give up only two things: my glass of Martini at the table and my cigar.

I go to bed at four or five o'clock in the morning; by now it's a habit. When there wasn't the war — this cursed and stupid war! — one could at least play *scopone*, but now with the dark, the streetcars cut back, and the sirens, few come to see me. So I content myself reading the paper.

Every once in a while I go to Livorno, but usually I live in this ugly old hotel. Yet what can I do? They treat me badly, but I've been here twenty years already!

Every Sunday the Pope has Mass said for me here in this room of the Plaza, because He knows that I can no longer go down the stairs. However, I confess that when I could get down them I did not always go to Mass. The Pope has helped me in every way; during the worst period, when it was not easy to find a bit of bread and meat, he sent me food. A great Pope, truly a holy man.

But now? Now I have been left to die of hunger! Around my operas a silence has gradually closed in. They are boycotted — this is the truth.

There is a theater, one of the largest Italian theaters,[83] which has as a general manager a Maestro who, so it would seem, is not content with my growing old, but rather wants me to die before giving an opera of mine in his theater. He may seem excessive in his wish, but a demonstration of the facts will show that I state the truth.

The theater managed by this Maestro has always performed operas by Italian and foreign composers—with the exception of three Tuscans who nevertheless have brought a certain activity to our theaters, large and small. These three composers are Catalani, Puccini and Mascagni. Shocked by the continued absence of operas by these composers on the announcements, I asked for an explanation from an intimate friend of this Maestro. And the explanation was simple. The guiding principle of this general manager is to perform operas by dead composers, accompanying them with the operas of those young composers who aspire to a positive success; and excluding operas of living and already established composers.

I must confess that, as a systematic principle of a theater director, it does not seem an outlandish point of view. In substance: with the operas of dead composers one has a theater of tradition; with the operas of young composers who are not yet established, we have an experimental theater; excluding the operas of living composers already established, one denies the people the enjoyment of music already known and certainly desired. But I haven't the energy to argue with someone who subjects a theater to such a system. However, I did object to the theater manager's friend that unfortunately Catalani and Puccini are not among the living; yet no opera of theirs up to now has figured in that theater's repertory.

I had to wait a bit for the reply to this objection of mine—one could see that my friend was somewhat uneasy. Finally in a timid voice he declared, "This year an opera of Puccini's will be given." I already knew that and I also knew that the admittance of Puccini to the repertory was due to the intervention of a High Lady. My friend then added, raising his voice, "And next year there will be one by Catalani." And he was silent... His silence was very eloquent and very clear: nothing by Mascagni because he finds himself on inferior terms—he is still alive. And then immediately afterwards, much affectionate flailing of arms and insinuating phrases to convince me that the general manager loved my operas very much, but... (he closed his mouth)... but he was incensed

83   Probably La Scala, but the reference is uncertain.

with me because I had not decided to die and give him the satisfaction of enjoying my music.

The general manager has certainly not thought that this state of things can continue for years and years; and perhaps I will be able to survive him, involuntarily giving him a painful death for not having heard my much-loved operas any more. Who knows what sorrow for the poor man! But who knows what joy for me...

"The sword, the cocked hat, the plumes... gorgeous stuff! But..." (p. 264)

After all this, it is easy to understand that the reason this general manager's theater did not commemorate the fiftieth anniversary of *Cavalleria* was so it would remain faithful to the directives of its Maestro.

Only the people, the good and generous people still remember old Mascagni, perhaps because my music has always known how to speak to their hearts. But this would be too lengthy a speech... and then today one cannot make speeches. However, I am at least still allowed to smoke my cigar. Yes really! Because Monopolio still makes cigars expressly for Maestro Mascagni. As a reward for him who has given so much glory to Italian music (and now the reader will really say I'm immodest), that's not bad at all!

Say what you like, even a candle gives light. When there is no sun, a candle is sufficient.

The Hotel Plaza, Rome — home of Lina and Pietro Mascagni
from 1927 until the composer's death in 1945

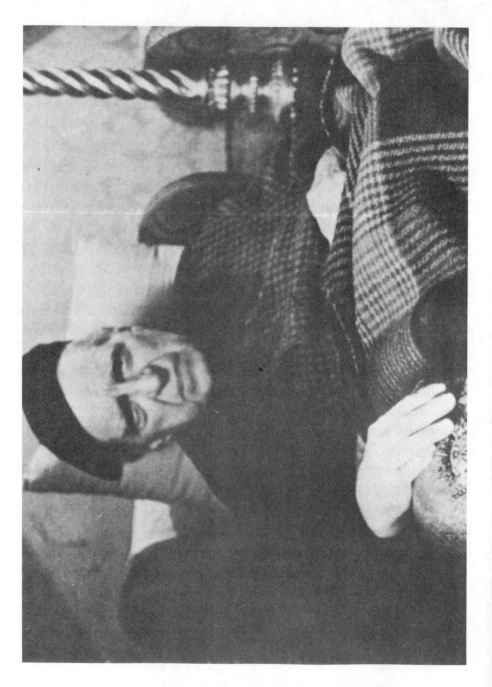

EDITOR'S EPILOGUE

The celebrations for the fiftieth anniversary of *Cavalleria rusticana* were the last great manifestations of public and critical acclaim that Mascagni was to experience. Verdi's prophecy that when Mascagni became an old man all would adore him and praise him to the skies did not come true. Mascagni's operas were now rarely performed, and to make a living he was forced to continue his career as a conductor. In 1943, at the age of eighty, he conducted a series of symphonic concerts at the Teatro Adriano in Rome. These concerts aroused enormous enthusiasm in the Roman public and moved the old man greatly. It was in July of this same year that he wrote his last piece of music, "O Roma felix", a hymn for voice and organ, which formed part of a volume presented in homage by a number of Italian artists and scholars to Pope Pius XII. The following December, invited by the German radio to comment on his eightieth birthday, Mascagni confessed that he had been most moved by the greetings sent him by the Pope.

In the last two years of his life he enjoyed playing *scopone* with his old friends, but with the war coming ever closer to Rome, their visits of necessity became fewer and be became almost totally isolated in his apartment in the Hotel Plaza on the Corso. Fortunately, his wife Lina remained with him and was able to attend to his needs. He became more and more afflicted with arteriosclerosis and finally his legs would no longer support him. He was forced to spend his time either in bed or in an armchair. Only three luxuries did he allow himself: his cigar, his glass of Martini after dinner and a small electric stove. In time his eyes became weaker and then his hearing. When the Allies entered Rome in June of 1944, the Hotel Plaza was sequestered for their use and all clients residing there asked to leave. Only Mascagni was exempted from this rule and he enjoyed visits from the men in uniform who brought him food and Havana cigars.

The end came on 2 August 1945, at 7:15 in the morning. Recent lung complications, combined with the arteriosclerosis, were too much for the old man's frail body to survive and he died with only Lina there in the room with him. The funeral took place two days later, 4 August, at the church of San Lorenzo in Lucina. Many notables had come to pay their last respects and on the day of the funeral the Corso was packed with crowds of people. As the cortege moved from the hotel to the church, a police band played Chopin's *Funeral March*. In the piazza before San Lorenzo the band played the Intermezzo from *Cavalleria*. He was buried in the Verano cemetery in Rome.

In 1951 the body was moved to its final resting place in Livorno. Though Italy did not recognize the 1945 obsequies, a representative of the government was now sent to pay the country's official respects. He lies in the Cimitero della Misericordia beside his father, mother and wife.

CHRONOLOGY

1863

7 December — Pietro Antonio Stefano Mascagni born, 6:30 a.m., in Livorno, son of Domenico Mascagni, a baker,and Emilia Reboa.

1872

Attends the Schola Cantorum, Congregazione S. Luigi Gonzaga.

1873

8 October — Death of mother. Pietro is sent to study at the Ginnasio Comunale di San Sebastiano run by the Barnabite Fathers.

1875

Alfredo Soffredini establishes an Istituto Musicale Livornese.

1876

7 June — Mascagni takes his first lessons with Soffredini.

1878-1880

Early compositions, including two symphonies (C minor, F major), performed at the Istituto.

1881

9 February — First performance of the cantata *In filanda* at the Casino San Marco (under the auspices of the Istituto) in Livorno. Soffredini conducts.

30 March — *In filanda* receives its second performance, this time at the Teatro degli Avvalorati (paid for by his Uncle Stefano) as a benefit for the earthquake victims at Casamicciola.

7 June — Mascagni writes about a visit to Ponchielli's Maggianico villa. He plays the recently composed

Alla gioia for his host. Ponchielli says "it seems to me that you should review all the rules of counterpoint," but is enthusiastic about the work in general.

10 October   Death of Uncle Stefano.

1882

27 March   First performance of *Alla gioia* at the Teatro degli Avvalorati, conducted by Soffredini.

April   In Milan, preparing for his entrance examinations to the Conservatory, he discovers Heine's *Guglielmo Ratcliff* in Maffei's translation.

July   Returning to Livorno for vacation, he sets a part of the *Ratcliff* love duet.

1883

March   Finishes the composition of the *Ratcliff* duet. Revises *In filanda*, retitling it *Pinotta*, for use in a contest among the Conservatory students. Since he does not submit the score in time, nothing comes of it.

November   Begins playing contrabass at the Teatro dal Verme in Milan.

1884

14 January   First performance of Verga's play, *Cavalleria rusticana*, in Turin.

12 October   First performance of *"Il Re a Napoli"*, sung by Mascagni's friend Dario Acconci at the Teatro Goldoni in Livorno. (This is a song for tenor and orchestra with words by Andrea Maffei, and not an operetta as is frequently stated.)

1885

March   Leaves the Conservatory to join the Forlì company as assistant conductor in Cremona, where he conducts his *"Il Re a Napoli"* at the Teatro Ricci. In April

	the company moves on to Piacenza, later to Reggio Emilia.
June	Parma. Mascagni conducts *Cuore e mano* (Lecocq). Bologna (Teatro Brunetti). Forlì disbands his company. Mascagni returns to Livorno.
Autumn	Invited to Naples by Forlì for a season at the Teatro del Fondo. When Forlì's company leaves the city, Mascagni remains, now as a conductor with the Scognamiglio company (Teatro del Fondo).
23 December	Scognamiglio's company is hired by Daniele Chiarella for 90 performances at the theater where he is the proprietor, the Politeama in Genoa.

1886

9 March	Last performance in Genoa. Mascagni goes on the road with Scognamiglio, travelling to Alessandria and Modena.
April	Ancona. Writes the Prelude to *Ratcliff*.
May	Ascoli Piceno. Scognamiglio disbands his company. Mascagni returns to Ancona and works on *Ratcliff*.
June	Goes at Acconci's suggestion to Naples to join the company of Duke Cirella.
Mid-July	When Cirella's company leaves Naples, Mascagni remains.
September or October	Mascagni joins Maresca's company. The *soubrette* is Argenide Marcellina Carbognani (Lina), Mascagni's future wife. When Maresca leaves the city, Mascagni remains with the company, travelling to Benevento and Foggia.
29 December	Arrival in Cerignola for the Carnival season.

1887

17 February	Mascagni abandons Maresca's company to remain in Cerignola with Lina who is six months pregnant.
22 May	Birth of Domenico ("Mimì"): the child dies a little more than four months later on 2 October.

1888

7 February	Marriage of Pietro Mascagni and Lina Carbognani in the Cerignola Cathedral.
April	First performance of the *Messa di Gloria* in the Church of S. Antonio in Cerignola.
July	In *Il Teatro Illustrato* for this month a contest for one act operas is announced by Casa Sonzogno.

1889

3 February	Birth of Domenico (also nicknamed "Mimì"), first child to survive. The next morning Mascagni begins the composition of *Cavalleria rusticana*.
5 May	Completion of the opera's composition. The orchestration and writing out of the full and vocal scores was finished on 26 May.
3 June	The opera is sent off to the Commission in Rome.

1890

22 February	A telegram arrives in Cerignola summoning Mascagni to Rome to play his opera for the contest Commission.
24 February	Arrives in Rome. Plays *Cavalleria* for the Commission on the 26th. Returns to Cerignola, arriving on 6 March.
8 March	Concert in Cerignola.
10 March	Leaves for Milan.

12 March	Arrives in Milan in the morning, lodges at the Albergo dell'Agnellino. He visits the Sonzogno office and works on the revisions of his opera (transpositions, cuts and additions). He sees Puccini, Orsini and Maresca. On Sunday the 16th he visits the Conservatory, visits the home of Saladino the following day and leaves for Livorno on the 18th, where he arrives on the 20th.
2 May	Arrival in Rome for rehearsals of *Cavalleria*.
17 May	First performance of *Cavalleria rusticana* at the Teatro Costanzi (now the Teatro dell'Opera) in Rome.

1891

3 January	Birth of second son Edoardo ("Dino").
4 February	Begins composition of *L'amico Fritz* in Cerignola with the first half of the "Cherry Duet". The last piece to be written is the Prelude (Florence, 6 October).
31 May	The *Messa di Gloria* is performed at Orvieto. Mascagni is asked to play the Intermezzo from *Cavalleria* during the Elevation.
31 October	First performance of *L'amico Fritz* at the Costanzi.

1892

21 August	Birth of a daughter Emilia ("Emi"). In this same month the difficulties with Verga begin.
September	Mascagni in Vienna.
2/3 September	D'Annunzio's attack on Mascagni, *"Il Capobanda"*, appears in the Neapolitan paper *Il Mattino*.
10 November	First performance of *I Rantzau* at the Teatro della Pergola in Florence.

1893

February   Berlin.

July   London. The Verga affair is concluded with a pay-
             ment to the author by Casa Sonzogno.

Mascagni at the time he was Director of the Liceo Rossini, Pesaro

1894

November   In Livorno Mascagni finishes the composition and revision of *Guglielmo Ratcliff*.

1895

16 February   First performance of *Guglielmo Ratcliff* at La Scala.

2 March   First performance of *Silvano* at La Scala.

26 October   Asked by the Liceo Rossini in Pesaro to become its Director.

1896

2 March   First performance of *Zanetto* (Pesaro).

1897

April   Illica reads the libretto of *Iris* to Mascagni at Castellarquato (Piacenza).

September   In Cerignola Mascagni writes the first piece in his new opera *Iris*: the chorus of laundresses in Act I. Osaka's *"Apri la tua finestra"* will follow, being completed on the 17th. Work on the opera will continue throughout 1897 and 1898 with the last piece (the reprise of the "Hymn of the Sun" which concludes the opera) being completed in Pesaro on 26 August 1898.

1898

12 April   Mascagni conducts the Italian premiere of Tchaikovsky's *Pathétique* Symphony at an orchestra concert at La Scala. During this same month Verdi meets Mascagni's wife and children.

29 June   Premiere of the musical poem *A Giacomo Leopardi* for orchestra (with soprano solo) at Recanati.

22 November   First performance of *Iris* at the Costanzi.

1899

23 March   *Iris* at the San Carlo in Naples. D'Annunzio and
            Mascagni are brought together and friendly rela-
            tions are initiated between the two men.

10 June   Death of Mascagni's father, Domenico, at Livorno,
            while Mascagni is in the midst of the composition of
            Le Maschere. Though he has given a series of success-
            ful concerts in Pesaro, the first rumblings of his
            difficulties with the Liceo over his absences begin.

October -   Mascagni conducts a series of concerts in Switzer-
November   land, Holland and Germany.

1900

January   Publication of the libretto "for the music of Pietro
            Mascagni" of *Vistilia* by G. Targioni-Tozzetti and G.
            Menasci (based on the eponymous novel by Rocco
            De Zerbi). Much of its music will later be used in
            Nerone.

March   Concerts in St. Petersburg and Warsaw.

9 August   Mascagni conducts a *Requiem Mass* (assembled by
            him from compositions by Arnerio, Victoria, Palestri-
            na, Renzi and Eugenio Terziani) for King Umberto I
            at the Pantheon in Rome.

1901

17 January First performance in six theaters of *Le Maschere.*

27 January Death of Verdi.

25 April   In the Vienna Musikverein Mascagni conducts a per-
            formance of the Verdi *Requiem.*

1902

April   Concerts in Bucharest.

May   Conducts three performances of *Don Giovanni* in
            Madrid.

August	Continued difficulties with the City Council in Pesaro.
4 October	Arrival in New York. Beginning of American tour. Cities scheduled to be visited are Philadelphia, Toronto, Montreal, Boston, St. Louis, Cincinnati, Chicago, San Francisco and Los Angeles.
8 October	Opening night of the tour at the Metropolitan with a double bill of *Zanetto* and *Cavalleria*, repeated on 9, 11 (matinee) and 17 October.
11 October	*Iris* is announced but not performed.
14 October	*Iris* in Philadelphia.
16 October	*Iris* in New York, as a replacement for *Ratcliff*, which had been announced.
6 November	In Boston the Mittenthals sever relations with Mascagni's company: Richard Heard assumes responsibility.
21 December	In Chicago the company is finally disbanded, with Mascagni deciding to conduct the local orchestras.

1903

11 January	First orchestral concert at the Chicago Auditorium.
7 February	Arrival in San Francisco.
2 April	Mascagni leaves New York for home, arriving in Florence on the 11th.
12 October	Mascagni assumes the direction of the Scuola Nazionale di Musica in Rome.

1904

June-November	Composition of *Amica*.

1905

January	Two concerts conducted by Mascagni in the Salle Lamoureux in Paris.
16 March	First performance of *Amica* in the Casino at Monte Carlo.
13 May	First Italian performance of *Amica* (Rome, Teatro Costanzi).
November	Publication of the pamphlet *"Per le opere dell'ingegno"* in which Mascagni polemicizes against his publishers Ricordi and Sonzogno.

1906

August	Final decision on the dispute with the Liceo Rossini: the Ancona Court of Appeals decides in Mascagni's favor.
17 November	Edoardo Sonzogno and Mascagni reconcile their differences through the efforts of Walter Mocchi.

1907

1 January	Mascagni's satirical novella, "How to Write an Opera", is published in *La Lettura*.
April	Concerts in Vienna, Chemnitz, Dresden, Jena and Berlin.

1908

14 September	Giulio Ricordi writes to Mascagni asking him for "a brother or a sister for the little Iris," but Mascagni is never to publish another opera with Ricordi.
October	Begins composition of *Isabeau*.

1909

February	A performance of *Vistilia* on the Palatine in Rome is proposed.

4 August	Mascagni assumes general directorship of the Teatro Costanzi.
10 December	He opens the season conducting *Tristan*. Other operas are *La Bohème* (Puccini), *Mefistofele, Maià* (Leoncavallo), *Don Carlo, Norma, Lohengrin, Iris* and a double bill of *Mese Mariano* (Giordano) and *Cavalleria rusticana*.

1910

31 May	Mascagni travels to Castellarquato where, as Illica's guest, he continues work on *Isabeau*. Returning to Milan in September he completes the composition of the opera.
29 October	Meeting in Rome of Puccini and Mascagni, at which the latter plays excerpts from *Isabeau* (the Intermezzo and "Song of the Falcon") for Puccini.
December	Orchestration of *Isabeau* completed.

1911

15 April	Mascagni departs from Genoa for his South American tour.
2 June	First performance of *Isabeau* at the Coliseo in Buenos Aires. Other cities visited are Rio de Janeiro, São Paolo, Santos, Montevideo, Valparaiso and Santiago.
31 October	Leaves on the *Tommaso di Savoia* to return to Italy.

1912

20 January	First performances of *Isabeau* in Italy: under the composer at La Fenice (Venice) and under Serafin at La Scala.
April	Mascagni receives the libretto of *Parisina*.
May	Mascagni (under the name of Armand Basevi) andhis daughter Emi settle in at the villa Castel Fleury in Bellevue (outside Paris) to work with D'Annunzio

on *Parisina*. The first piece to be composed, however ("*Or voi composto m'aversti*"), will be written on a visit to Rome in June.

1913

15 December   First performance of *Parisina* at La Scala.

18 December   At the second performance of *Parisina* small cuts are introduced in the first three acts and the entire fourth act is suppressed.

1914

March   Puccini becomes interested in Ouida's novel *Bebè, or The Two Little Wooden Shoes*. Mascagni has announced he will write an opera based on the same subject, but lets Puccini try to acquire the rights, knowing they have lapsed and the novel is in the public domain.

1915

22 March   Auction in Viareggio of the rights to Ouida's novel. The representative for Casa Ricordi declares that though the rights have lapsed, nonetheless Ricordi will offer 4000 lire for the book. But by September Puccini has lost interest in the project and Sonzogno acquires the rights from Ricordi for Mascagni.

1916

29 October   Mascagni begins the composition of *Lodoletta*, based on Ouida's novel. Forzano is the librettist.

1917

15 January   Completion of the composition of *Lodoletta*.

30 April   First performance of *Lodoletta* at the Teatro Costanzi.

1918

August   Begins composition of his operetta *Si*.

1919

2 May | Completes first piece composed of *Il piccolo Marat* (the scene between Mariella and the Carpenter in Act II). Works on the opera through the remainder of the year, finishing its composition (but not orchestration) on 30 December.

13 December | First performance of *Si* at the Teatro Quirino in Rome.

1920

6 September | Mascagni visits the workmen at the Orlando Wharf in Livorno. Newspapers proclaim his Communist sympathies as a result.

1921

2 May | First performance of *Il piccolo Marat* at the Teatro Costanzi. Enormous success.

1922

May | Mascagni undertakes to conduct a company on a second South American tour under the management of Walter Mocchi. Opening of the six month season is on 23 May, with *Il piccolo Marat* at the Teatro Colon. Other operas in the repertory are *Isabeau, Iris, La favorita, Rigoletto* and *Il barbiere di Siviglia*. At the same time Mocchi has engaged the Vienna Philharmonic, conducted by Felix Weingartner, along with a company of German singers. In mid-November the Italian company sails for Italy.

1923

Beginning of year | Mascagni's first interview with Mussolini. He narrates his bitter experiences during the South American tour, complaining of Mocchi's preferential treatment of the Germans.

14 March | Sudden death in Milan, while giving a lesson, of his old teacher Soffredini.

18 May   In the foyer of the Teatro Argentina (Rome), Mascag-
            ni delivers a tirade against Walter Mocchi at a con-
            vention called to investigate the causes of the crisis
            in the lyric theater.

July   Mascagni begins a sixteen month tour of Austria,
            Czechoslovakia, Germany, Poland, Belgium, Hun-
            gary and Serbia. Along with his *Cavalleria*, Mascagni
            conducts operas by Verdi, Donizetti, Bellini and
            Rossini.

1925

May-June   Berlin and Vienna. At the Viennese Burgertheater
            he conducts a revised version of *Si*.

November   Completion of tour.

1926

26 June   Mascagni writes a long letter to Mussolini outlining
            the reforms he feels to be necessary in order to alle-
            viate the problems affecting the Italian lyric theater.

1927

5 April   Mascagni's report as ambassador extraordinaire to
            the Beethoven Centennial in Vienna. Highly critical
            of the Strauss/Hoffmansthal *Ruins of Athens*, which
            he calls "a real profanation of Beethoven's art....
            Richard Strauss has taken the most famous themes
            from those symphonies which should be regarded
            as sacred things and has arranged them to his bar-
            barous taste, committing a real artistic crime."

1928

            Conducts performances of his *Ratcliff* in Pisa and
            Amica in Vicenza.

1929

18 October Inauguration in Rome of the Reale Accademia
            d'Italia ("founded on the model of the French one
            and in opposition to the Accademia dei Lincei
            which will be suppressed in 1939": Santini), which

Pietro Mascagni, *scopone* player

includes Mascagni, along with Giordano and Perosi, among its members.

1930

24 August — Commemorative performance of *La Bohème* at Torre del Iago conducted by Mascagni.

1931

June - November — In a series of letters to Mussolini, Mascagni begins "to attack those whom he considered responsible for the progressive decline of the lyric theater" (Goetz). Among other things, he accuses the officers of the Italian Society of Authors and Publishers (SIAE), of which Mascagni is the vice president, of corruption.

1932

23 March — First performance of *Pinotta* at the Teatro del Casino in San Remo.

1933

26 August — Completion of the composition of *Nerone*.

1934

30 May — Death of Giovanni Targioni-Tozzetti in Livorno.

June — Squabbles with the Mayor of Cremona over the festivities honoring the Centenary of Ponchielli's birth. At the last minute he is invited to attend but not to participate.

1935

16 January — First performance of *Nerone* at La Scala.

27 January — Writes a fulsome letter to Mussolini thanking him for his interest in *Nerone* and presents him with copies of the libretto and score: "They are modest things, but Your Excellency must remember that I have no publisher and I have had to do everything myself...."

1936

2 June   Telegram from Mussolini condoling with Mascagni on the death of his son, Edoardo, in Africa.

24 June   Mascagni writes to Mussolini requesting that his son's body be returned to Italy for burial. His request is refused.

1937-1939

Conducts operatic performances and orchestral concerts to enormous popular acclaim.

1940

5 March   Mascagni conducts *Zanetto* and *Cavalleria rusticana* at the Teatro Costanzi, the first of many celebrations honoring the fiftieth anniversary of *Cavalleria*. Mascagni records the opera for EMI.

1941

April   In honor of the fiftieth anniversary of *L'amico Fritz*, Mascagni conducts a series of performances at La Scala, later at the Florence May Festival and at Rome. He records the opera for Cetra.

1942

Spring   Mascagni requests and is granted a private audience with Pius XII, seeking help for his sick granddaughter.

1943

April   Mascagni conducts at La Scala for the last time: two performances of *L'amico Fritz* with Ferrucio Tagliavini and Jolanda Magnoni. During the 1943-1944 season at the Teatro dell'Opera (the Costanzi),he conducts the final performances of his career: *L'amico Fritz* and *Cavalleria rusticana*, the latter with Maria Caniglia.

1944

June   The Hotel Plaza, where Mascagni and his wife have lived in two rooms since 1927, is sequestered by the Allies when they enter Rome.

1945

July   Mascagni's arteriosclerosis is by now so serious that
            it prevents his leaving the hotel. "What a desperate
            old age is mine!" he laments one day to Luigi Ricci.
            During this month his mind begins to wander: at
            night he calls the switchboard asking for famous
            personages out of the historic and his own past:
            Emperor Franz Joseph, Queen Victoria, Nero.

2 August   At 7:15 in the morning, Mascagni dies peacefully.
            Only the French flag is lowered to half-mast. Atlee
            sends condolences from Great Britain and in Russia
            the daily broadcasts are interrupted to present
            selections from the composer's operas.

4 August   The funeral mass is celebrated at 10:30 a.m. in the
            Church of San Lorenzo in Lucina in Rome. Both in-
            side the church and outside in the piazza there is an
            enormous crowd. "And when," writes Corrado At-
            zeri, "at the Elevation the notes of the Intermezzo
            from *Cavalleria rusticana* resounded from a private
            phonograph, in that piazza in Rome, the crowd
            knelt reverently." Italy does not participate officially.

1946

11 March   Death of the composer's wife Lina.

1951

20 June   Mascagni is buried in Livorno.

Mascagni's final resting place, Livorno

"In art, as in science, there is no delight without the detail" notes Vladimir Nabokov, and the details which emerge from this *Personalia* only serve to enrich the picture of Mascagni's life, as well as explaining various *lacunae*. Indeed, it only mirrors the *Autobiography* itself with its "themes" which crop up in the most unexpected places: the Bellincioni umbrella which finds its antecedent in the summer of 1883 in Pisa and the all but hidden "Costa theme" beginning with *Cavalleria* which turns up behind the scenes of *Si* are only two examples among many. An attempt has been made to make this *Personalia* as complete as possible, giving birth and death dates where ascertainable. In many cases, however, those names which are easily identifiable from the context of the book have not been included, nor have personal friends of Mascagni who are only mentioned in passing. With well-known figures (such as Verdi, Puccini, etc.), it is their relations with Mascagni that are stressed.

ALBERTINI, see under **FRACCAROLI.**

ALFIERI, Dino (1886-1944). Italian Minister of Popular Culture under Mussolini, 1936-39. Named Ambassador to the Holy See in 1940, at the outbreak of the war he went to Berlin where he represented Italy until 1943. He was condemned to death in the Verona trials for defiance of Mussolini.

ALFONSO XIII (1886-1941). King of Spain, 1902-1931, when he went into exile. His acquiescence in the Primo de Rivera dictatorship was widely criticized. After the 1936-39 Civil War, Franco made it clear that Alfonso was not wanted in Spain; the ex-King never sought to regain his throne.

ALVAREZ (Albert-Raymond Gourron, called) (1861-1933). French tenor, made his Paris Opéra debut in 1892 as Faust. Appeared at the Metropolitan Opera 1901-03 in *Il Profeta, Carmen* and *Otello.*

ANCONA, Mario (1860-1931). Baritone, born in Livorno. A great favorite in London where he went for the first time in 1892, singing at Covent Garden (first appearing in 1893) for 17 consecutive seasons. He was the first David in *L'amico Fritz* at the Metropolitan Opera (10 January 1893) and also sang in Boston, Philadelphia, Chicago, St. Louis and San Francisco. In 1893 he sang the premiere of *The Veiled Prophet of Khorassan* by Stanford (*q.v.*).

ASCHERBERG, E. London music publisher. In 1906 the firm was combined with two others to form Ascherberg, Hopwood & Crew and is still in existence. *Cavalleria* is copyrighted by this firm in the United Kingdom.

BANCROFT, Sir Squire (1841-1926). English actor and manager who became famous for his new and original stagings of such dramas as Boucicault's *London Assurance*. With the help of his wife, who worked with him, he had a long career. Knighted in 1897.

BATTISTINI, Mattia (1857-1928). Italian baritone, famous for his elegant interpretations of the nineteenth century *bel canto* operas. He sang Gianni at the premiere of *I Rantzau*. Though the part would seem to be little adapted to his famous style, Amintore Galli, in reviewing his performance (*Il Secolo*, 13-14 November 1892) assures us otherwise: "Battistini was great, whether expressing hatred or love; one could not better imagine the way he sang, acted, and incarnated the figure of Gianni."

BAZZANI, Alessandro (1846-1911). Scenic designer. His fame began with a production of *Nerone* by Pietro Cossa (*q.v.*) in 1870 and becoming friendly with the poet, he designed many other plays by him. He was a representative of late nineteenth century historic-realistic theater design.

BAZZINI, Antonio (1818-1897). Italian violinist and composer. He was encouraged by Paganini to begin a career as a concert violinist and wrote numerous compositions for that instrument, the *Ronde des lutins* still being in the repertory. He was one of the first Italian composers to encourage the composition of symphonic music. Professor of composition at the Milan Conservatory (Catalani and Puccini were among his students), he became its director in 1882.

BELLATTI, Virgilio. The baritone on Mascagni's American tour, he sang Alfio and Kyoto. Later created the La Scala Tartaglia (*Le Maschere*) in 1901 under Toscanini. He also sang other Mascagni roles such as Douglas and David.

BELLINCIONI, Gemma (1864-1950). Italian soprano, wife of Roberto Stagno. She was the first Santuzza in Mascagni's *Cavalleria*. Verdi asked Boito's opinion of her as a possible Desdemona for the premiere of *Otello*, but Boito's response was on the whole negative. It was Edoardo Sonzogno who convinced Bellincioni and her husband to sing in the three operas which would win his 1888 contest. After her enormous success in *Cavalleria* she became known for her dramatic qualities, particularly in such operas as *La Traviata, Carmen* and *Fedora*. She wrote an autobiography, *Io e il palcoscenico* (Milan, 1920). Bellincioni later recalled the premiere of the opera which made her famous: "You cannot even vaguely have an idea of what went on at the Costanzi on that unforgettable evening. After the *Siciliana* the people applauded, after the Prayer they shouted enthusiastically, after the duet between Santuzza and Turiddu the spectators seemed literally to be crazed. They shouted, they waved handkerchiefs; in the corridors people embraced one another. *We have a composer! Long live the new Italian composer!* I still have in my ears those shouts repeated by a hundred throats. The poor, inexpert composer must have suffered a tremendous nervous shock in seeing himself carried in triumph like a new Caesar. No one expected such a success. He had been present at the orchestra and stage rehearsals, maintaining a modest, even humble attitude (after the first encounters), listening to every piece of advice from Maestro Mugnone with an extraordinary devotion, indeed, I would say with perfect compunction. I can even still see Mascagni with his umbrella under his arm, and with his floppy hat which badly held down his shock of hair."

BERTELLI, Luigi (1858-1920). Florentine journalist and educator who wrote under the name "Vamba". He founded the *Giornalino della domenica*.

BEVIGNANI, Enrico (1841-1903). Italian conductor. He was responsible for the first performances of *Cavalleria* in Russia (St. Petersburg, 3 January 1891) and the first London (23 May 1892) and New York (10 January 1893) performances of *L'amico Fritz*. Adelina Patti was so fond of his conducting that she made it a condition that he conduct all of her London performances. There are many references to him in the pages of Bernard Shaw's music criticism.

BIAGINI, Antonio. Mascagni's first piano teacher. According to Tartioni-Tozzetti, "he was a skillful organist and piano teacher until his very old age, and was justifiably proud of having had 'Pietrino' among his students" (*Ricordi*). Biagini taught at the Schola Cantorum in Livorno.

BIANCHI, Emilo (1824-1902). Baritone and voice teacher. He sang in the first performance of Mascagni's *Alla gioia*. He was director of the Schola Cantorum in Livorno.

BIANCHINI-CAPPELLI, Elena. Soprano on Mascagni's American tour. She sang Silvia and Santuzza on opening night at the Metropolitan (8 October 1902), the critic of the Tribune calling her Santuzza "a thrillingly pathetic impersonation which made one overlook her unfortunate figure and the distressful wobble in her voice." She also sang Amica (Livorno, 1905).

BOCK, Hugo (1848-1932). Berlin music publisher. He became proprietor of the firm of Bote und Bock (founded in 1838) in 1871. In addition to publishing the music of Mascagni (*Visione lirica*, 1923) he was the dedicatee of *Zanetto*.

BOITO, Arrigo (1842-1918). Composer, librettist and critic. He provided Verdi with the libretti for *Otello* and *Falstaff*, becoming very close to the great composer in his later years. Composer of *Mefistofele* (1866), the great operatic project of Boito's life was *Nerone*, an opera which he was never to finish. It received its first performance (La Scala, 1924) after his death. The "certain Maestro" who considered finishing the work is undoubtedly Arturo Toscanini (*q.v.*), who conducted its premiere. Boito's conception of *Nerone* dates from 1862 when he was still occupied with *Mefistofele*, and word of the opera had been in the air for a number of years before Mascagni made his unfortunate remarks to a journalist. These appeared in *Il Secolo XIX*, a Genoa newspaper, in August of 1892, while Verdi and Boito were working on *Falstaff*. An English translation of Verdi's letter regarding Mascagni's remarks may be found in Frank Walker's *The Man Verdi*, p. 501.

BONCI, Alessandro (1870-1940). Italian tenor. He made his debut as Fenton in 1896, soon becoming known for the refined and elegant style of his singing.

BOSSI, Marco Enrico (1861-1925). Italian composer and organist. He submitted an opera, *Leggenda umana o il Veggente*, to the same Sonzogno contest in which Mascagni entered *Cavalleria*. Though not among the three winners, *Il Veggente* was awarded a special mention by the judges and was later produced in Milan, at the Teatro dal Verme, in 1890. Primarily known as an organist, he was sporadically attracted by the theater. It was to him that Illica first offered the libretto that was to become *Isabeau*.

BRAMBILLA, Teresa (1845-1921). Italian soprano and wife of Ponchielli. It was as a result of her singing of the revised *Promessi sposi* (Milan, Teatro dal Verme, 1872) that she met and married Ponchielli two years later, becoming one of the foremost interpreters of his scores. She retired in 1889, three years after her husband's death. She shared Ponchielli's affection for both Puccini and Mascagni.

BUZZI-PECCIA, Arturo (1856-1943). Italian composer. Studied under Bazzini at the Milan Conservatory. He came to America in 1898, first to Chicago and then New York. Though he composed several operas (*Forza d'amore, Re Harfagar, Gloria*), it is as a composer of songs that he is remembered, perhaps the best known being *"Lolita"*.

CALVÉ, Emma (1858-1942). French Soprano, most famous for her interpretation of Carmen. She was the first Paris Santuzza (Opéra-Comique, 19 January 1892) and New York Suzel (Metropolian 10 January 1893). She wrote an autobiography, *Sous tous les ciels j'ai chanté* (Paris, 1940).

CAMPI, Annetta (1844-1924). Italian actress. A graceful figure and natural child-like quality in her pronunciation made her popular in ingenue roles. She joined the Pasta Company in 1882.

CAMPIONI, Guiseppe. Italian tenor, the first Flammen. He learned the part in a little more than a week and was not entirely successful with it, being a much better Folco. One critic wrote that Campioni "had to work very hard to manage the *mezzavoce* effects which the part is full of."

CANNONE, Giuseppe. Mayor of Cerignola when Mascagni first settled there, one of the composer's chief supporters and friends. The Maresca company arrived in Cerignola on 29 December 1886, the first time that an operetta company ever played the Teatro Mercadante since that theatre had opened in 1868. In this town of 30,000 inhabitants Mascagni quickly made friends during the two months of the company's stay. After Maresca and his troop left Cerignola for Sicily on 18 February 1887, Mascagni first lived in the Palazzo Pescatore, Via Francesco d'-

Assisi, later moving to 59 Corso Vittorio Emanuele and finally settling into the place where he was to write *Cavalleria*, Via Assunta 15. It was due to Cannone that Mascagni was nominated to create a Filarmonica in Cerignola. The city council's decree read in part: "After the vote, the result was seven against and fifteen for Signor Pietro Mascagni who is elected and nominated maestro of music and singing with the subsidy or stipend of 100 lire monthly, with the obligation, however, of organizing the members of the Filarmonica and the choral school, and for the admission of single students, without any recompense" (dated 25 March 1887). According to Cellamare (*q.v.*) the students numbered 6 in the choral school, 11 strings and 5 winds in the orchestra. For concerts other players (adults from Cerignola and nearby towns) were added to the students. Though Mascagni states in the *Autobiography* that he had to learn to play all the instruments in order to teach them, the fact remains that he had studied a number of them under Soffredini (*q.v.*) when still a student in Livorno and we know that he himself was proficient enough on the doublebass to play in a theater orchestra (see Chapter 2). In addition to teaching at the Filarmonica, Mascagni also gave private lessons in Cerignola and in the neighboring towns of Canosa and San Ferdinando. After the success of *Cavalleria*, it was Cannone who conferred an honorary citizenship in Cerignola on Mascagni, saying in the proclamation: "If Livorno justly exults for having given birth to Pietro Mascagni, Cerignola can certainly be proud of having received him among its favorite sons and for having first recognized his genius." Cannone remained a close friend of Mascagni, who dedicated *Silvano* to him.

CANORI, Guglielmo. Italian impresario, most famous for bringing the entire first production of *Otello* from Milan to Rome. A man of enormous resource and vitality, he lived by his wits, dying in poverty.

CAPON, Giacomo (1830-1909). Italian journalist in Paris who wrote under the pen names of "Caponi", "Jacopo" and "Folchetto". He appears numerous times, not always to his advantage, in Verdi's correspondence. He wrote about Parisian current events in *Ricordi di Folchetto*.

CARAMBA, see SAPELLI.

CATALANI, Alfredo (1854-1893). Italian composer. Born in Lucca, as was Puccini. From his earliest days Mascagni was an admirer of Catalani's music, writing to Soffredini in 1883 after hearing a performance in

Milan of *Dejanice*; "for me Catalani has individuality, genius, melody... there is always clarity. All is elegance, all is perfume. Then, too, the orchestral coloration is sublime."

CAVE, Guido (1862-1904). Born in Livorno, he was a close friend of Mascagni's, particularly during his student days in Milan. With Vittorio Gianfranceschi (*q.v.*) and Del Prà, he formed the *"Consiglio dei tre"*, who heard and passed on each of Mascagni's new compositions.

CELLAMARE, Daniele (b.1901). Born in Cerignola, he is a passionate defender of that city's claims on Mascagni. He has written two books on the composer and it is the first of these to which Mascagni refers in the *Autobiography*. In Cellamare's second book, which appeared in 1965, he quotes Mascagni's remark about his earlier volume, omitting, however, the composer's line that "much foolishness is said in that book" and confining himself to how much "the people of Cerignola loved Mascagni." Though Cellamare's books may err on the side of enthusiasm, they are a mine of information about Mascagni's friends and years spent in Cerignola.

CHECCHI, Eugenio (1838-1932). Italian journalist who wrote under the name "Tom". Born in Livorno, he was a passionate believer in Mascagni's talent. His famous prediction on the eve of the *Cavalleria* premiere is much quoted in the Mascagni literature. He was an author of several books on music (Rossini, Verdi, letters of Donizetti), librettist (Spinelli's *A basso porto*) and director of the *Fanfulla della Domenica*, the newspaper where Mascagni's reminiscences of his early career first appeared. Mascagni's satirical song, *"L'addio di Palmidone"*, is dedicated to him.

CHEVILLARD, Camille (1859-1923). French conductor and composer. In 1899 he became conductor of the Lamoureux orchestra, making a great reputation as an interpreter of the German classic masters, Beethoven, Schumann, Wagner and Liszt.

CHOUDENS, Paul (1850-1925). Head of the French publishing house of Choudens *fils*, founded by his father Antoine de Choudens in 1845. The company published most of the works of Berlioz, Gounod, Lalo and Offenbach in addition to many other composers' music. Paul Choudens wrote numerous libretti, often in collaboration with others, and nearly always under the pseudonym of "Paul Bérel". In addition to providing the libretto for Mascagni's *Amica* he also wrote texts for Erlanger, Février, Leoncavallo and Leroux, among others.

CILÈA, Francesco (1866-1950). Italian composer. His most famous opera is *Adriana Lecouvreur* (Milan, 1902). A member of the *"giovine sculoa"* of Italian composers, his contribution to Sonzogno's 1892 season at the Vienna Exposition was *La Tilda*, first performed at Florence that same year.

CIRELLA, Duke. Operetta company impresario. He hired Mascagni in June of 1886, on Dario Acconci's recommendation, to conduct Audran's *Il Gran Mogul* at the Teatro del Fondo in Naples. Mascagni put the work, which was new for Italy, together in twelve days, winning great success. He himself left Cirella's company in mid-July, remaining in Naples. He signed with Maresca (*q.v.*) in September or October of that same year.

CLARETIE, Jules (1840-1913). French playwright, librettist and journalist. He is primarily remembered for his volumes of dramatic criticism, published between 1895 and 1914. From 1885 until 1912 he was administrator of the Comédie Française.

COLONNELLO, Adolfo (?-1909). Italian actor. Member of a famous Italian acting family, he was particularly successful in youthful parts.

COQUELIN, Ernest (1848-1909). Member of a famous family of French actors, he was referred to as "Coquelin Cadet". He made his debut in 1867, becoming a member of the Comédie Française the following year. He was the first Frédéric in the play *L'ami Fritz* by Erckmann-Chatrian (*q.v.*). He was particularly famous as a monologist.

COSSA, Pietro (1830-1881). Italian dramatic author. Though his subject matter and handling of verse were traditional, he was modern in the manner of approaching his subject. Thus in the prologue to *Nerone* he claims to adhere "to that school which takes its laws from truth [*verismo*]." It was obviously this quality in Cossa's work which drew Mascagni to his "commedia" *Nerone* (1872) as the basis for his last opera.

COSTA, Mario Pasquale (1858-1933). Italian composer. Born in Naples, he was a prolific writer of songs. *"Carulì"* was one of the most popular, written in 1885 to a text by Salvatore di Giacomo. In October of 1919, only two months before Mascagni's operetta *Si* was first performed, Costa's operetta *Il Re di Chez Maxim*, to a libretto by Carlo Lombardo (*q.v.*), was produced in Milan with enormous success.

COTOGNI, Antonio (1831-1918). Italian baritone. Making his debut in *L'elisir d'amore* in 1852, he quickly established himself as one of Italy's leading singers. Invited by the conductor Mariani to sing Rodrigo in the Italian premiere of *Don Carlo* (Bologna, 1867), Cotogni earned praise from Verdi for his singing. Retiring in 1894, he became famous as a teacher at the Liceo musicale di Santa Cecilia in Rome. Among his students was Lauri-Volpi. He also gave lessons to Jean de Reszké and Mario Battistini.

DALLA RIZZA, Gilda (1892-1956). Italian soprano. A favorite singer of Puccini, she created the part of Magda in *La Rondine* (Monte Carlo, 1917). In addition to creating the role of Mariella, she was a noted Lodoletta.

D'ANNUNZIO, Gabriele (1864-1938). Italian poet, dramatist and novelist. Though a number of his plays were adapted for composers (*La figlia di Jorio* by Franchetti and Pizzetti, *La Nave* by Montemezzi, *Francesca da Rimini* by Zandonai, *Fedra* by Pizzetti), his only work designed to be set as an opera was *Parisina*. First offered to Puccini and Franchetti (whose name, it will be noted, contains ten letters), it was finally accepted by Mascagni. D'Annunzio's famous article *"Il Capobanda"* ("The Bandleader") had appeared in the Neapolitan paper *Il Mattino* on 2 September 1892. The passage referred to by Mascagni runs: "A friend, returning from Livorno a few weeks ago, told me of having seen, in the window of a hosier, certain shoes of a fiery red leather referred to on a card as 'shoes à la Mascagni,' and he assured me that the composer of *L'amico Fritz* enjoyed wandering among the delicate oleanders of his seaside villa dressed all in red, like a San Severo bandsman." The first attempt at a reconciliation between the two men took place in March of 1899 in Naples. Sometime later, it was announced that they would collaborate on an *Orlando innamorato*, which came to nothing. The "dinner among friends" referred to by Mascagni took place in Rome on 14 January 1908, after the successful premiere of d'Annunzio's drama *La Nave*. Once he had decided upon composing *Parisina*, Mascagni went to France incognito to avoid the publicity which he knew such a collaboration would excite. The newspapers, however, continued to publish stories about Mascagni's disappearance, at one time even declaring that the composer had "eloped with a vaudeville dancer and, along with his daughter, [had] taken her to either Paris or the south of France." The critical response to the opera after its premiere dealt primarily with its length, the first performance running from 8:30 to 1:15 the next morning. The opera was performed in Livorno, Rome and Buenos Aires in 1914 and not again until 1952 under Gavazzeni, this time with the fourth act restored.

DANOVARO, Fr. According to Targioni-Tozzetti, Fr. Camarda, and not Fr. Danovaro, was Mascagni's Greek teacher (in *Mascagni prima della "Cavalleria"*).

D'ARCAIS, Francesco (1830-1890). Italian composer, journalist and music critic. Studied composition in Turin. He was music critic for newspapers in Turin, Florence, Rome and Milan.

DASPURO, Nicola (1853-1941). Italian journalist, Neapolitan correspondent for the Milanese newspaper *Il Secolo*. He was Sonzogno's general representative for southern Italy and no doubt it was in this capacity that he first met Mascagni in Bari. Though he write libretti for Giordano (*Mala vita*, 1892; revised under the title *Il Voto*, 1897) and Luporini, he is primarily remembered as the author of Mascagni's *L'amico Fritz* libretto, which he published under the pseudonym of "P. Suardon". It was Daspuro who convinced Edoardo Sonzogno (*q.v.*) to hire the young Caruso for the Teatro Lirico (Milan), an occasion which launched the tenor on his career.

DE ANGELIS, Nazzareno (1881-1962). Italian bass. He made his La Scala debut in 1907 (in *La Gioconda*) after several years of singing in other Italian theaters. Noted for his dramatic abilities, he was also well known in the Wagnerian repertoire, his Wotan being especially admired.

DE LARA, Isidore (1858-1935). English singer and composer. He studied composition in Milan and Paris, later returning to England. His opera *The Light of Asia* (originally a cantata) was produced at Covent Garden in 1892, a work which was reviewed by Bernard Shaw. De Lara's songs are still heard occasionally.

DE LUCIA, Fernando (1860-1925). Italian tenor. Born in Naples, he made his debut at the San Carlo in *Faust* (1883). He soon became one of Italy's most admired singers. He created no less than four Mascagni tenor roles: Fritz, Giorgio Rantzau, Silvano and Osaka.

DENZA, Luigi (1846-1922). Italian composer of numerous songs in Italian, French and English, the most famous of which is *"Funiculì, Funiculà"*. He settled in London in 1879, becoming one of the directors of the London Academy of Music.

DEWEY. Admiral George (1837-1917). American Naval officer. Placed in command of the U.S. Asiatic squadron in 1898, he entirely destroyed the superior Spanish fleet at the battle for Manila during the Spanish-American War. The story of Mascagni's "Dewey March" is to be found in Salvatore Cortesi's *My Thirty Years of Friendships*. In 1898 Cortesi had been asked by a New York newspaper to persuade Mascagni to compose a triumphal march "for the return of the hero of the Hispano-American War." He went to Pesaro, convinced Mascagni to write the march and returned to New York where the announcement was made. As it turned out, Mascagni later asked $10,000 for the march, the paper decided that the price was prohibitive and the matter was dropped. The confusion in Spain in 1902 resulted from the Spanish Society of Authors not realizing that the march had never been composed. According to Cortesi, the march was taken from the music already composed for *Vistilia* and later became the *New World Processional March*, performed at the St. Louis exposition in 1904.

DE ZERBI, Rocco (1843-1894). Italian journalist, man of letters and politician who wrote a wide range of polemics and many parliamentary discourses. Also wrote novels, *Vistilia* (1877) and *L'avvelenatrice* (1884).

DOMINICETI, Cesare (1811-1888). Italian composer and teacher. Appointed professor of composition at the Milan Conservatory in 1880 after Ponchielli temporarily withdrew from that institution. He was one of the judges in the first (1883) Sonzogno contest, when Puccini unsuccessfully entered his first opera, *Le Villi*. He is principally remembered today as the composer for whom Boito wrote "his most mysterious libretto' (Nardi), *Iràm*. Whether Dominiceti set this to music or not has never been discovered, since only a single manuscript copy of the libretto, postmarked 1879, has survived.

DUSE, Eleonora (1858-1924). Famous Italian dramatic actress. After becoming a sensational success overnight at the age of 19, she was invited to join the company of Cesare Rossi. It was probably at her suggestion that Verga adapted his short story, *Cavalleria rusticana*, as a play. Her interpretation of Santuzza was a great personal triumph.

ELIZABETH, Queen of Rumania (1843-1916). Married in 1869 to Prince Carol (later Carol I) she became Queen in 1881. Under the name of Carmen Sylva wrote some 20 books.

EMANUEL, Giovanni (1884-1902). Italian actor. Noted for his interpretations of Shakespeare (he was considered the heir of Salvini and Rossi), Mascagni saw him perform in the Erckmann-Chatrian play *I Rantzau* in Livorno, July 1890. Noted for his realistic style of delivery, Mascagni later confessed that he attained the ability to hear the innate musicality of words "hearing Emanuel recite."

ERCKMANN-CHATRIAN. Joint pen name of Emile Erckmann (1822-1899) and Alexandre Chatrian (1826-1890) who collaborated from 1847 to 1889 in a series of short stories and novels which were immensely popular in their day. The six so-called "national novels" are still read, and one of them, *Histoire d'un conscrit de 1813* (1864) is considered their finest novel. Their plays, with one exception adapted from their own novels, enjoyed international success. Mascagni adapted two of them for operas: *L'ami Fritz* (novel, 1864; play, 1876) which became *L'amico Fritz*; and *Les deux frères* (novel, 1873; play, under the title *Les Rantzau*, 1882) which became *I Rantzau*. The sincerity and skillful characterization of Erckmann-Chatrian were peculiarly suited to Mascagni's needs after his success with *Cavalleria*.

FACCIO, Franco (1840-1891). Italian conductor and composer. Though his opera *Amleto* (1865), to a text by his friend Arrigo Boito, had been mildly successful, it was as a conductor that he obtained his greatest fame. In 1878 the orchestra of La Scala was invited by the Paris Exposition to take part in its concerts at the Trocadero Palace, along with other noted European orchestras. Faccio led the La Scala musicians in a series of concerts (which took place on 19, 22, 25, 29 June and 2 July) which included music by Beethoven, Berlioz, Boccherini, Cimarosa, Rossini, Donizetti, Verdi, Bazzini, Ponchielli and Catalani among others. The concerts were received with great enthusiasm by both press and public. The first performance of the Verdi *Requiem* was conducted by the composer (not Faccio as Mascagni states) on May 22, 1874 at the Church of San Marco in Milan. The second performance (at La Scala, 25 May) was also conducted by Verdi. Faccio conducted the third and fourth performances (26 and 27 May). The performance of the *Requiem* conducted by Faccio which was heard by Mascagni occurred on 22 May 1883, in honor of the tenth anniversary of the death of Manzoni.

FATTORI, Giovanni (1828-1908). Painter from Livorno, now recognized as one of the finest artists of his epoch. He is famous for his picture, *The Battle of Firenze*.

FERRARI, Rodolfo (1865-1919). Italian conductor. Graduated from the Liceo Musicale (Bologna) in 1882. He conducted all over the world: Buenos Aires, New York (Metropolitan), Paris, Berlin, Vienna, and the major Italian cities. He conducted the premiere of *L'amico Fritz* at the Costanzi in 1891.

FERRI, Enrico (1856-1929). Italian criminologist and politician. After studying at Bologna, Pisa and Paris, he worked under Lombroso (*q.v.*), later becoming a professor at Bologna. Since he was a follower of Lombroso's theories (that genius is a form of degeneracy) it is not surprising that Mascagni entertained little enthusiasm for Ferri's opinion of Verdi's genius.

FERRONI, Luigi (1884-1962). Italian bass. His career spanned 48 years, 1902-1950. He was the first Ogre in *Il piccolo Marat*.

FERRONI, Vincenzo (1858-1934). Italian composer. Studied composition with Massenet in Paris, in 1885 winning first place among 613 contestants with a *Hymne d'un pâtre lydien*. In 1888 he was nominated, again in a contest, successor to Ponchielli as a professor of composition at the Milan Conservatory. *Rudello*, to a libretto by M. Zucchetti, received only one performance at that time, on 28 May 1890, the last night of the season. The libretto is drawn from a situation dealt with by Petrarch and later Carducci. The action concerns troubadors, queens, knights, Christians, Turks, etc., and from all reports seems to have been a hopeless endeavor. Oddly enough, the opera was revived at the Carcano in Milan in 1892 and obtained a moderate success. In addition to operas, Ferroni wrote symphonic and chamber works.

FONTANA, Ferdinando (1850-1919). Italian librettist, poet and playwright. He wrote about forty libretti, among the most important being those for Puccini (*Le Villi, Edgar*) and Franchetti (*Il Signor di Pourceaugnac*). It is not surprising that Fontana asked Mascagni for money in advance for a libretto since the same thing occurred in Puccini's dealings with him in regard to *Le Villi*, but in that case it seems that Ponchielli was able to bring the arrangements to a satisfactory conclusion.

FORLÌ, Vittorio. Italian impresario, ran an operetta company in partnership with Giuseppe Castagnetta. *Il Re a Napoli* (a "song for tenor with orchestral accompaniment", not an operetta as is often stated) was first performed in Livorno on 12 October 1884 by Mascagni's friend Dario Acconci, who also performed it with the Forlì Company in Cremona on 14 March 1885 at the Teatro Ricci. Mascagni (who was hired as an assistant conductor) remained with Forlì until the company was disbanded in Bologna on 29 June 1885. The first time Mascagni conducted was on 13 June 1885 (Lecocq's *Cuore e mano*) due to the illness of the company's regular conductor, Diomede La Monaca. In the autumn of that year Mascagni rejoined Forlì (this time as a conductor) in Naples, where he joined the Scognamiglio (*q.v.*) Company after Forlì closed. The operetta *Satanello* (during a performance of which a seat cushion was hurled at Mascagni, who was conducting) is by Varney.

FORZANO, Giovacchino (1884-1970). Italian dramatist and librettist. Though a singer in his earlier years, he quickly turned to journalism, later to writing for the theater. His two libretti for Puccini (*Suor Angelica, Gianni Schicchi*) and those for Mascagni (*Lodoletta, Il piccolo Marat*) are among the finest written for any composer. He was also a stage director for both the lyric and prose theaters, later directing films. He wrote a volume of memoirs, *Come li ho conosciuti* (Turin, 1957) which contains a chapter on his work with Mascagni.

FRACCAROLI, Arnaldo (1883-1956). Italian journalist and author. In addition to writing numerous plays, he was the author of novels, short stories and travel books. He wrote two books on Puccini, *La vita di Giacomo Puccini* (Milan, 1925) and *Giacomo Puccini: Si Confida e racconta* (published posthumously by Ricordi in 1957). He was for a time a correspondent on the *Corriere della Sera* and the interviews Mascagni mentions in connection with Fraccaroli appeared in that paper in 1912 and 1913. The "Albertini" mentioned by Mascagni was Luigi Albertini, director of the *Corriere*.

FRANCHETTI, Alberto (1860-1942). Italian composer. After completing his musical studies in Italy, he studied in Germany with Rheinberger. Returning to Italy he produced his first opera, *Asrael* (1888), with a libretto by Fontana. Luigi Illica provided the text for his next work, *Cristoforo Colombo* (Genoa, 6 October 1892), which remains his best known opera. Attracted to d'Annunzio's poetry, he next set that poet's *Figlia di*

Jorio (La Scala, 1906) which had little success. It was Franchetti's experience with this d'Annunzio text which no doubt led to Mascagni's discussing *Parisina* with him. Franchetti's musical style, however, was completely different from Mascagni's (Franchetti began, wrote one critic, "by being the most Wagnerian of our composers"). It was this "German" quality in the older man's music which prompted Mascagni to describe it as "too sedate."

FRANKO, Nahan (1861-1930). American violinist and conductor. He studied violin in Berlin, 1864-69, returning to New York and making his debut there in 1869. From 1883 to 1907 he was concert master of the Metropolitan Opera orchestra. Beginning his career as a conductor in 1889, he was appointed "third conductor" at the Metropolitan in 1894. He was contracted by the Mittenthal Brothers (*q.v.*) on 3 October 1902 as follows: "We the undersigned, have given Nahan Franko the full power to engage an orchestra for our New York productions of six performances." When it was discovered that Mascagni was determined to use his Italian musicians, Franko filed suit for breach of contract. His attempt to have the Italian players deported later proved unsuccessful.

FRUGATTA, Giuseppe (1860-1933). Italian piano teacher and composer. He was a student of Bazzini at the Milan Conservatory and a member of Mascagni's circle of student friends.

FUAD I (1868-1936). King of Egypt, 1922-1936.

GALEFFI, Carlo (1882-1961). Italian baritone, created the role of Nicolò d'-Este in *Parisina*. He made his debut in 1907, soon singing such Mascagni operas as *Le Maschere* and *Amica*. He became famous in the great Italian and Wagnerian baritone roles, creating the part of Fanuèl in Boito's *Nerone*.

GALLI, Amintore (1845-1919). Italian composer, theoretician, musicologist and teacher. Between 1874 and 1904 he was an artistic director of Casa Sonzogno. Thus he was also one of the judges in Sonzogno's 1883 contest as well as in the following one (1888) which produced *Cavalleria*. He arranged the vocal scores for a number of Mascagni's operas: *L'amico Fritz, I Rantzau, Guglielmo Ratcliff, Silvano, Zanetto* and *Le Maschere*.

GALLIGNANI, Giuseppe (1851-1923). Italian composer. After completing his studies at the Milan Conservatory (1867-1871) he travelled throughout Europe as a conductor. He was director of the Parma Conservatory (1891-97) and later of the one in Milan. He composed a number of operas in addition to sacred music, piano works and songs. He became close to Verdi in the later years of the old man's life, providing the Gregorian texts when Verdi began to consider writing a *Te Deum*.

GANDOLIN, see **VASSALLO.**

GARIBALDI, Luisa. Italian mezzo-soprano, created the role of Stella dell'-Assassino in *Parisina*. Critics were unanimous in praising her performance of this taxing role, one remarking that it would be difficult to find competitors in the part.

GARULLI, Alfonso (1857-1915). Italian tenor. A specialist in the Massenet repertory, he created the role of Andrea Chénier at La Scala in 1896. He was one of the first Turiddus, singing the Verona performances of *Cavalleria* in 1890.

GASTALDON, Stanislao (1861-1939). Italian composer. Known today as the composer of the song *"Musica proibita"*, he also wrote a number of operas. *Mala Pasqua*, based on Verga's *Cavalleria rusticana*, was first performed at the Costanzi in Rome on 9 April 1890, only 38 days before Mascagni's opera. Though not particularly successful, it later had other performances in Perugia and Lisbon (under Luigi Mancinelli).

GAZZOLETTI, Antonio (1813-1886). Prolific Italian poet of a romantic nature who also was a journalist and a deputy in Parliament. He wrote novels in verse such as *L'ondina d'Adelsberga* (1853) and melodramas for the theater such as *Turanda*.

GHISLANZONI, Antonio (1824-1893). Italian librettist. He began his musical career as a baritone (1846-55), abandoning it to pursue journalism. He wrote about 85 libretti, the most important of which is *Aida*. He also assisted Verdi in the 1869 revision of *La forza del destino* and the 1884 Italian translation of *Don Carlo*. He provided Ponchielli with the libretto of *I lituani*. He also published novels, short stories and poetry. Mascagni set one of his poems as a song, *"Pena d'amore"* (1883).

GIANFRANCESCHI, Vittorio (1861-?). An engineer by profession, he was one of Mascagni's closest friends. They met while they were both students in Milan and it was "Vichi" who first suggested Heine's *Wilhelm*

Ratcliff as a possible opera libretto (p.17, above). Mascagni dedicated the score to him. Mascagni's letters to his friend after leaving the Milan Conservatory are an invaluable source of material regarding the pre-*Cavalleria* years.

GIANNINI BROTHERS. Music house in Bari. It was from this firm that Mascagni rented, in February of 1889, the piano on which he was to compose *Cavalleria* (contrary to his statement that he "didn't have one in Cerignola").

GIANTURCO, Emanuele (1857-1907). Italian jurist and politician who wrote books on government such as *Sistema del diritto civile Italiano*. He served as Minister of Justice, Public Works and was Vice President of the Camera.

GIOLITTI, Giovanni (1842-1928). Italian statesman. Five times prime minister of Italy, he was able to advise Mascagni on the Pesaro quarrel due to the fact that in 1902 he was not in office. He opposed Italy's entry into World War I. In 1894 Mascagni had written the words and music of a song, "*L'addio di Palmidone*", as a satire on Giolitti's public manner.

GIORDANO, Umberto (1867-1948). Italian composer. He was also one of the contestants in the Sonzogno 1888 contest with his opera *Marina*. Though praised by the Commission, Edoardo Sonzogno did not like the libretto and commissioned another opera, *Mala vita* (Rome, 1892, with Stagno and Bellincioni). This work, to a libretto by Daspuro (*q.v.*), was successful, particularly when it was later slightly revised and performed under the title *Il Voto*. Giordano's most famous opera remains *Andrea Chénier* (La Scala, 1896; libretto by Illica), though *Fedora* and *Madame Sans Gêne* are still heard. As in the case of Mascagni, Giordano visited Verdi at the Albergo Milano (see SPATZ, below) and it was the latter who suggested the subject of *Madame Sans Gêne* to Giordano. Mascagni and Giordano remained on friendly terms throughout their careers. In the *Autobiography* Mascagni states that Giordano's *Il Voto* was performed at the Vienna Exposition. The opera had not as yet been revised and was actually given then (27 September 1892) under its original title *Mala vita*.

GOMEZ, A. Carlos (1836-1896). Brazilian composer. In 1864, after having made a name in Brazil as a composer of some consequence, he went to Italy, studying at the Milan Conservatory. He was successful with *Il* *guarany* (La Scala; 19 March 1870), the opera by which he is still best known today. His music is essentially Italian, with only a few indications of his Brazilian heritage.

GUERRINI, Virginia (1871-1948). Italian mezzo-soprano. She made her debut in *Lohengrin* (Treviso, 1889), first appearing at La Scala in the 1891-92 season singing in *Norma* and *Falstaff* (she created the role of Meg). She retired in 1925.

HANSLICK, Eduard (1825-1904). Viennese music critic, famous for his quarrel with Wagner. He was enthusiastic over *Cavalleria* ("without doubt reveals a fresh, energetic and sincere talent"), slightly less over *L'amico Fritz* ("I could not say that with *Fritz* Mascagni's talent appears diminished; it seems, however, that he has here worked on material less congenial to his real inclinations") and considered *I Rantzau* the weakest of the three works whose Viennese premieres he reviewed ("we not only do not see [in *I Rantzau*] a great richness of invention, but there is not even a naturalness of expression and freedom of creation").

HARRIS, Sir Augustus (1852-1896). English impresario. He was general manager of Covent Garden, 1888-1896.

HEINE, Heinrich (1797-1856). German poet and prose writer. Though born a Jew, he was subjected in his early years to Roman Catholic and rationalistic French influences, thus producing the conflicting mixture of politics, culture and religion which was to characterize his life and work. He early became addicted to Byronian "*Weltschmerz*" and this is reflected in his *Wilhelm Ratcliff*, written in three days in January of 1822 (first published in 1823). This play had a number of operatic settings; Cui in 1869, Vavrinecz in 1895, Villafiorita in 1907, Pizzi (*q.v.*) in 1889, Leroux in 1906 and Mascagni in 1895. Critics have sometimes thought that Heine did not take the play seriously, rather intending it to be a satire on Byronism. That this is not the case is proved by Heine himself, who in later years referred to it as "a great act of confession."

HOST VENTURI, Giovanni (1892-1944?). Italian Minister of Communications from 1935 until the early '40s.

ILLICA, Luigi (1857-1919). Italian poet, dramatist, librettist and critic. His three libretti for Mascagni (*Iris*, *Le Maschere*, *Isabeau*) are the most poetic the composer ever set. Though it is a commonplace of Mascagni

criticism to compare Illica's libretti for that composer with
d'Annunzio's, in reality Illica was at the opposite pole: "The form of a
libretto is made by the music, only the music and nothing but the
music!" he wrote to Puccini in 1907. "What has true value in a libretto
is the word... Today, instead—Decadentism and Dannunzianism, in
corrupting the simplicity and naturalness of language, come to menace
(in the theater) truth and logic." In Illica's libretti for *Iris* and *Isabeau* the
action is condensed as much as possible, allowing Mascagni's music to
interpret his ideas and the emotions of his characters. In order to aid
the spectator, Illica writes elaborate prose pieces (not intended to be set
by the composer, but rather to be described by him in his music) into
the libretti, giving them the form of a "dramatic legend". In the libretto for *Le Maschere* these prose pieces are not nearly so elaborate, yet the
basic concept is the same. This opera, incidentally, is the only one of
Mascagni's works which was ever to undergo extensive revision. Mascagni discusses the first two versions (1901, 1905) made with Illica, but
makes no mention of the final and definitive one made in 1931. In this
he retained the 1905 cuts but restored the Prologue and original Act III
finale. In 1916 *Le Maschere* was adapted as an operetta (i.e., with spoken
dialogue). Illica opposed the idea of doing this, but it was finally carried out with the composer's sanction although he had no hand in the
actual revising. As an operetta, *Le Maschere* was performed throughout
Italy with great success by the Scognamiglio-Caramba-Caracciolo Company, which took the work on tour in 1917-18 to Spain, Portugal and
South America.

JACCHIA, Agide (1875-1932). Italian composer and conductor. Completed
his studies at the Pesaro Conservatory under Mascagni, 1891-98, later
working with Galli at the Milan Conservatory. He made his conducting debut in 1898 in Brescia and conducted the Venice premiere of *Le
Maschere* on the famous night of 17 January 1901. He lived for many
years in America, coming for the first time in 1902 with Mascagni on his
American tour. According to the New York *Times* (5 October 1902), it
was Jacchia who first said that "the imported musicians were not competent to render the Mascagni music according to his ideas. Mr. Franko
[*q.v.*], therefore, was called in." During the years 1918-26 Jacchia was
conductor of the Boston Pops concerts.

JACHINO, Carlo (1887-1971). Italian composer. Professor of composition
at the Parma and, in 1936, the Naples Conservatories. In 1938 he became
a professor at the Accademia di Santa Cecilia in Rome. He wrote an

opera, symphonic works and chamber music. In the 1940's he began writing music based on the twelve-note system.

JAHN, Wilhelm (1834-1900). Conductor and musical director of the Vienna Court Opera. He was succeeded at his retirement in 1897 by Gustav Mahler. Jahn conducted the Vienna premiere of *I Rantzau* on 7 January 1893.

LARDEREL, Count Florestano de (1848-1925). Count of Montecorboli and last descendant of Francesco (1790-1858), founder of the Tuscan borax industry. Count Florestano inherited his father Federico's virtues of gentleman and benefactor. He came to Mascagni's aid at the moment when the composer most needed it, not without first demanding proof of the young composer's ability. According to Soffredini (*q.v.*) it was he that first approached the Count for help. The Count answered Soffredini: "Let Mascagni give a yet greater and more complete proof [than *In filanda*] of his talent and of his studies if he is able, and then come to me." With renewed courage another work was chosen: the Schiller *Ode to Joy* ([*Alla gioia*). The performance of the work was successful and the Count guaranteed 150 lire monthly for Mascagni's education at the Milan Conservatory. The composer responded by dedicating *Alla gioia* to De Larderel. Mascagni's letters to Gianfranceschi (*q.v.*) after he left the Conservatory often mention his sorrow at disappointing the Count. Once he had achieved fame with *Cavalleria*, he acknowledged his debt to De Larderel by dedicating that opera to him.

LASSALE, Jean (1847-1909). French baritone. After singing in France and Belgium he made his debut at the Paris Opera in 1872. Seven years later he came to London, making his debut at Covent Garden as Nelusko in *L'Africaine*. He appeared there for many seasons, returning to Paris after the turn of the century. He sang Hans Sachs in London in 1889.

LAZARO, Hippolito (1889-1974). Spanish tenor. Making his debut in Spain, he later sang in Milan, Cairo and London. His singing of Folco (*Isabeau*) in the 1912-13 Genoa season began his specialization in Mascagni roles. He created the parts of Ugo (*Parisina*) and the Piccolo Marat.

LEONCAVALLO, Ruggiero (1858-1919). Italian composer. Mascagni's reference to Leoncavallo's "very solid success" in 1892 refers to *Pagliacci*, an opera which had a success at its first appearance almost comparable to Mascagni's own with *Cavalleria*. Contrary to some opinions,

Leoncavallo did not enter *Pagliacci* in the 1888 Sonzogno contest. The work was written in five months as a result of the enormous success of *Cavalleria* in 1890. Attracted to rather grandiose subjects, Leoncavallo even composed an opera (*Goffredo Mameli*) to inspire Italians to fervor in World War I (a war which he called "holy"). Mascagni, who was deeply troubled by this war, wrote of Leoncavallo's efforts: "those who write or set about writing works on patriotic subjects are making a mistake." Though often referring to Leoncavallo as "that double animal," when the composer of *Pagliacci* died, Mascagni attended the funeral.

LOMBARDO, Carlo (1869-1959). Italian librettist, operetta composer, impresario, publisher. After completing his musical studies at the Conservatory of San Pietro a Maiella (Naples) under Platania, he joined Maresca's company, first as conductor and later as chief comic. He later formed his own company. He became enormously popular, catering to the contemporary taste for apaches, cabarets in Montmartre, etc., in other words the very things Mascagni detested in Italian operetta. Why then should Mascagni choose to set a libretto by Lombardo? It was primarily due to the crafty librettist, since he had approached Mascagni with an operetta that he himself had fashioned from the composer's music (among other things was the women's chorus, *"Sulle balze erbose"*, in Act I of *Silvano* arranged as a comic duet in syncopated rhythm) and was seeking approval to perform it. Horrified, Mascagni agreed to write an original work, thus preventing Lombardo from proceeding with his plan. The result was *Sì*. When he announced the operetta, Lombardo also stated that another project was ready "for another celebrated composer." The press immediately presumed that this was to be Puccini, but the composer of *La Bohème* wrote an indignant letter to the newspapers protesting that he was in no way involved. It later turned out that the other "celebrated composer" was P.M. Costa (*q.v.*), the operetta being *Il Re di Chez Maxim*, a *pastiche* of Costa's dances and songs by the indefatigable Lombardo.

LOMBROSO, Cesare (1836-1909). Italian criminologist and founder of the science of criminology. He became widely known through his investigations of the abnormal human being, finding an analogy between the pathology of the madman and the physiology of the man of genius. His denial of Verdi's genius because the latter was too much a man of good sense, and was capable of handling his own business affairs, was publicly ridiculed by Mascagni on a number of occasions.

LUZIO, Alessandro (1857-1946). Italian musicologist. He is famous for his work on the letters of Verdi, editing the *Copialettere* for publication in 1913 and the four volumes of *Carteggi verdiani* in 1935 and, posthumously, 1947.

MAFFEI, Andrea (1798-1885). In addition to being a poet in his own right he made numerous translations into Italian of foreign literature, among the most noted being *Paradise Lost* (Milton), *Wilhelm Ratcliff* (Heine) and plays by Schiller and Shakespeare. It was his translation of the Schiller ode, *An die Freude*, that Mascagni set in 1882. Maffei was a friend of Verdi's, writing the libretto of *I Masnadieri* for him. In his will he named Verdi the executor of his estate. His translation of Heine's *Ratcliff* appeared in 1875. In his dedication to Torelli (*q.v.*), Maffei notes that this is "a youthful work of Heine, in which he wished to personify the struggle of man with destiny."

MAGGI, Andrea (?-1922). Italian actor. A handsome man, he played a wide variety of roles but was especially popular with the public as Hamlet and Othello. His greatest success was as Rostand's Cyrano. He was also the Giocadio (an acting role) in the Neapolitan premiere of *Le Maschere* on 19 January 1901.

MAGRONI, Jacopo. Born in Livorno, he was one of the board of directors at the Istituto Musicale Cherubini when Mascagni was a student there. He wrote the first book on the composer, *Del Maestro Cav. Pietro Mascagni — Memorie* (Livorno, 1890).

MAHLER, Gustav (1860-1911). Composer and conductor, director of the Vienne Court Opera 1897-1907. An admirer of Mascagni's early works, he conducted *Cavalleria* for the first time in Hungary on 27 December 1890, just nine days after the first performance of the opera outside of Italy (which occurred in Madrid on 17 December). He also conducted the Hamburg premiere of *L'amico Fritz* on 16 January 1893; the work was received with enthusiasm by the public. Mahler admired the work, writing to his sister Justine that he discovered many affinities between his own music and Mascagni's. Several months later he conducted *I Rantzau* in Hamburg, but it fared less well. On 29 April 1901, invited by Mahler, Mascagni conducted a performance of *Cavalleria* at the Vienna Hofoper.

MANCINELLI, Luigi (1848-1921). Italian cellist, conductor and composer. He made his impromptu debut as a conductor in 1874 at the Teatro Apollo in Rome, with *Aida*. He worked at the Teatro Colon in Buenos Aires from 1907 until 1911, the year when Mascagni conducted the premiere of *Isabeau* in that city. As a composer Mancinelli, like Mascagni, was attracted to the dramas of Pietro Cossa, composing intermezzi for that dramatisti's *Messalina* (1876) and *Cleopatra* (1877). He composed a number of operas, one (*Ero e Leandro*) to a libretto by Boito.

MANTELLI, Eugenia (1860-1926). Italian mezzo-soprano. She made her debut in 1883. At the turn of the century she appeared regularly at Covent Garden and was also a member of the Metropolitan, 1894-1900. The mezzo on Mascagni's American tour, she sang Zanetto and Lola. The critic of the N.Y. *Times* said of her performance on opening night that she "surprised her most accustomed hearers by the spirit and vigor of her acting."

MARCHETTI, Filippo (1831-1902). Italian composer. Though successful with his songs during his early career, operatic success came only with *Ruy Blas* (La Scala, 3 April 1869), a work which was soon performed outside of Italy. None of his later operas equalled the success of this work. He was appointed president of the Reale Accademia di Santa Cecilia in Rome in 1881, assuming the same position at the Liceo Musicale (Rome) in 1885, where he remained until his death.

MARCONI, Francesco (1885-1916). Italian tenor, generally called "Checcho". Roman by birth, he made his debut in the 1878-79 Madrid season in *Faust*. Returning immediately to Italy, he quickly made a name for himself and was much in demand in all the major opera houses. It is said that for size of voice, sweetness of quality and splendor of tone, he had no equal until the advent of Caruso.

MARESCA, Luigi (1858-1923). Italian comic actor and impresario. His operetta company was one of the hardiest and survived until the outbreak of World War I. Mascagni joined his company in Naples in September or October of 1886. The *soubrette* with Maresca's company was Argenide Carbognani (*q.v.*) who was later to become Mascagni's wife. Mascagni remained with Maresca until 17 February 1887, when he abandoned the company to remain in Cerignola with Lina, now six months pregnant. In a letter to the paper *La Lombardia* (18 February

1895), Maresca responded to Mascagni's by then famous story of the suitcase: "At Cerignola, after Mascagni had fled, I did not search for the manuscript of *Ratcliff*, the existence of which I was ignorant, but for the clothes and linen of the Mascagni couple in order to be sure that they had not hidden in the country, leaving their home ready to return to; and in fact Mascagni was hidden in the house of that delegate from the *questura* who, with an air of innocence, accompanied me in the search."

MARGHERITA, Queen of Italy (1851-1926). Wife of Umberto I (*q.v.*), she was enormously popular with her subjects. On the death of Umberto in 1900 she composed a prayer which greatly moved Verdi. He made a few musical sketches for it but the piece was never completed.

MARINELLI, Michele. Newspaper vendor in Cerignola who sold Mascagni the copy of the *Teatro Illustrato* announcing the 1888 Sonzogno contest.

MARINUZZI, Gino (1882-1945). Italian composer and conductor. Graduating from the Palermo Conservatory at 18, he was soon recognized to be one of Italy's finest conductors. He worked for many years in South America, giving the first performance (outside Bayreuth) of *Parsifal* in 1913.

MARTUCCI, Giuseppe (1856-1909). Italian pianist, conductor and composer. He gave his first piano recital at the age of 8, continuing this career for many years. He never wrote an opera, concentrating almost entirely on orchestral and chamber music. He was director of the Liceo Musicale B. Martini (Bologna) from 1886 to 1902 and it was in that city that he conducted the Italian premiere of *Tristan und Isolde* on 2 June 1888. In 1902 he became director of the Naples Conservatory, a post he retained until his death. He was a champion of symphonic music in Italy, particularly Schumann, Wagner and Brahms, and is still remembered in Italy as one of its great conductors.

MARTUCCI, Prisciano. Conductor of the Cerignola Banda Comunale from 1867 until 1891. That Martucci would be jealous of the interloper from Livorno is natural, especially in light of the fact that Martucci had conducted the performance of Mercadante's *La Vestale* which opened Cerignola's Teatro Mercadante on 6 November 1868. During Mascagni's lifetime it was frequently stated in newspaper articles that it was he who was the band leader in Cerignola rather than Martucci.

Mascagni never lost an opportunity to set the record straight, asserting that it was the Filarmonica (created especially for him) that he directed.

MASCAGNI, Domenico (1834-1899). Father of the composer. Originally from Florence, the Mascagni family settled in San Miniato al Tedesco, a small town 25 miles from Livorno, in the 18th century. Pietro's grandfather, Antonio Mascagni, had four sons: Stefano (*q.v.*), Giuseppe, Luigi, Domenico; and one daughter, Maria. Antonio came to Livorno around 1850 bringing with him two of his sons, Stefano and Domenico. Luigi and Maria remained in San Miniato, Giuseppe moved to a small town nearby. Domenico set himself up as a baker, marrying a girl from Livorno, Emilia Reboa (1839?-1873). They lived above the bakery on the Piazza dell'Erbe (today the Piazza Cavallotti) and here were born their five children: Francesco (*q.v.*), Pietro, Carlo (d. 1882), Maria (d. 1883) and Paolo. It was Soffredini (*q.v.*) who first said that Domenico wanted his son Pietro to be a baker, but as Targioni-Tozzetti pointed out, Pietro was to be a lawyer, since there were three other sons, one of whom could carry on the bakery. Much has been made in the Mascagni literature of Domenico's opposition to his son's career, but a letter of his, written when *L'amico Fritz* was first performed in Milan in 1892, proves that patriarchal pride was far from lacking. The initial performance was booed by "payed cowards" (Domenico's words) but the second and third were enthusiastically received. The proud father continues: "By now one knows that this both unexpected and triumphant apparition in the world of modern music has galled many people, and if they could they would knock him down using disloyal means; but by now it's too late." When Domenico died on 10 June 1899, it was a tremendous blow to Mascagni. He was then in the midst of composing *Le Maschere* and wrote to Illica: "He died without recognizing me; without knowing that I was there, at his bed, at his feet. What horror! He did not recognize me; he did not recognize his Pietro..."

MASCAGNI, Francesco (1862-1923). The composer's older brother, called "Cecco". In 1891 he met Amintore Galli; as a result he was hired to work for *Il Secolo*, the newspaper published by Casa Sonzogno (*q.v.*). When Renzo Sonzogno left the firm in 1910, Francesco remained with Riccardo.

MASCAGNI, Lina (1862-1946). Wife of the composer. Born Argenide Marcellina Carbognáni in Parma, she was an actress in Maresca's company, first meeting Mascagni in Naples when the composer joined that company in the autumn of 1886. She and Mascagni were married in the Cerignola Cathedral on 7 February 1888. In addition to Domenico (b. 22 May 1887, d. 4 mos. and 10 days later on 2 October), she presented Mascagni with three children: Domenico, called "Mimì" (b. 1889), Edoardo, called "Dino" (b. 1891, d. 1936 in Africa) and Emilia, called "Emi" (b. 1892, d. early 1970s). Lina died seven months after her husband, on 11 March 1946.

MASCAGNI, Stefano (?-1881). Uncle of the composer. Employed in Livorno by the Banco Tellini and being a bachelor, it is to his eternal credit that he saw fit to help Pietro become a musician. In his 1942-43 recollections (*Mascagni parla*), which are the main source for the material on his uncle, Mascagni said that it was a performance of *Alla gioia* that Stefano payed for. But since this work was not performed until 1882 (the first rehearsal was not until 5 November 1881) and Stefano died on 10 October 1881, it must have been *In filanda*. The first performance of this latter work occurred on 9 February 1881, in the Casino San Marco and the second, known to have taken place on 30 March at the Avvalorati as a benefit for the earthquake victims of Casamicciola, must have been the one that Stefano provided for. It was in the premiere of *Alla gioia*, however, that 110 performers took part.

MAURY, Eugenio (1858-1943). Italian government official, born in Cerignola. Mascagni referred to him as "the good Eugenio, a true brother to me." Maury was at the first performance of *Cavalleria* and, according to Mascagni, it was he who thought of sending telegrams to Mascagni's friends advising them of his triumph. In that same year, 1890, Maury had been elected a deputy from the province of Foggia; later he became a senator, a position which he held until his death.

MELBA, Dame Nellie (1859-1931). Australian soprano. She made her Covent Garden debut in 1888 and became the idol of the English opera and concert public. She was the first London Nedda (1893).

MENASCI, Guido (1867-1925). Italian writer and poet. He collaborated with Targioni-Tozzetti (*q.v.*) on four libretti for Mascagni: *Cavalleria rusticana, I Rantzau, Zanetto* and *Vistilia*, the latter published in 1900 and designated on the title page "for the music of Pietro Mascagni", though it was never completed by the composer. Menasci was an extremely cultivated man, being expert in English and French. He was responsible for the Italian translation, in collaboration with Targioni, of Massenet's

Werther (Sonzogno, 1893) and also an article on Puccini for the *English Magazine* in 1901. Menasci was called upon by Mascagni to doctor two scenes in the French text of *Amica* by Paul Choudens (*q.v.*) which were not to the composer's liking. Menasci also provided Mascagni with the texts of four songs: *"Ascoltiamo"*, *"Spes ultima"*, *"Stornelli"* (all 1906) and *"La luna"* (1913).

MENICHETTI, Giuseppe (1852-19??). Italian conductor and composer. Born in Pisa, he was director there of the orchestral and choral forces, organizing a performance in 1883 of Mascagni's youthful cantata *Alla gioia*. The composer attended the performance and was enthusiastic about Menichetti's work: "the members of the chorus are all very young. One must realize, however, that it is not a society, but rather a chorus school; and I believe that in a few years it will be one of the best choruses in Italy. At present it is made up of 320 members (and an umbrella). The conductor Menichetti is a very talented young man and full of spirit. He interpreted my work with great assurance..."

MICHETTI, Francesco Paolo (1851-1929). Considered to be Italy's leading painter of the 19th century. He first won fame for his paintings of children and animals and then with his painting *Corpus Domini*. The goyaesque features of his subjects and sparing use of color help to distinguish his work as well. A member of Mascagni's Cerignola circle, he was one of the composer's friends who brought about the reconciliation with d'Annunzio (*q.v.*). Michetti attended the premiere of *Parisina*, remarking afterwards: "I now understand the basic unity of art: here colors, sounds and words are nought but a single hymn."

MITTENTHAL BROTHERS. Aubrey and Harry E., managers of Mascagni's American tour. They had hired the Italian orchestra musicians who left Italy on 16 September 1902. Since this orchestra was 15 men short, they asked Nahan Franko (*q.v.*) to provide substitutes. When told by the Musical Mutual Protective Association (as the musician's union was called then) that this was impossible, the Mittenthals then asked Franko to hire a full local orchestra. Thus when Mascagni arrived at his first rehearsal at the Metropolitan at 2 p.m. on Sunday, 5 October 1902, he found two orchestras ready to rehearse. The local one was dismissed but assured they would be paid. The M.M.P.U. filed to have the Italian musicians deported under the Contract Labor law. Later, on 11 November, the Treasury Department ruled that the Italians could not be deported, being classified as artists. Thus Mascagni was able to use his Italian players for his entire tour. Mascagni's opening night at the Metropolitan on Wednesday, 8 October, with a double bill of *Zanetto* and *Cavalleria* was successful, but due to the mismanagement of the Mittenthals other performances were poorly attended. *Iris*, which was to have received its premiere in New York on October 11, was not performed until October 14 in Philadelphia, opening in New York on 16 October. The tour was managed by the Mittenthals in an atmosphere of sensationalism, a fact which the newspapers (hardly friendly to Mascagni) were not slow to mention. In an editorial in the *World* (26 October 1902), it was stated: "All the shortcomings of the local performances might have been remedied had the managers had the slightest knowledge of metropolitan exaction [i.e. standards demanded by New York audiences]. Their ignorance is the only explanation of the shabby and incomplete conditions under which Mascagni was forced to introduce himself to the public." On 6 November the Mittenthals announced that they were breaking with Mascagni because he refused to present *Ratcliff* in Boston the night before (Mascagni claimed it was not ready,) that Mascagni had grown careless and didn't care whether he gave a performance or not and that they, the Mittenthals, refused to accede to the Italian orchestra's "inordinate demands for advance salary." Mascagni was arrested on 8 November in Boston but released on $4,000 bail. The Mittenthals then agreed to continue the tour with Mascagni, but the composer sued them for $50,000 for false arrest. The tour was then managed by Richard Heard, the man "who spoke French correctly." Heard remained with Mascagni until December in Chicago. The company was finally disbanded and sent back to Italy on 21 December. That same day Mascagni had expressed his willingness to return to the Mittenthal management but his offer was refused. The San Francisco concerts given by Mascagni were an enormous personal and critical success for the composer. On 29 March 1903, the Mittenthals announced that they were dropping their two suits against Mascagni. In fairness to the two brothers, it must be admitted that a tour with Mascagni cannot have been all floral tributes and ovations. After they had severed relations with the composer, one of the Mittenthals said, "I still think Mascagni is one of the greatest conductors that ever lived, but I am sure he is also one of the greatest cranks. He would do nothing to help us, and if he did not get his own way he would sulk. It was the eccentricity of genius, perhaps, but it was trying in the extreme for any one who had to do business with him. One of his most troublesome idiosyncrasies was that of habitually coming late to the theater, so the performance could not start punctually. He also had a prejudice against getting up in the morning. We were scheduled to leave Montreal one day at 7 a.m., but he absolutely refused to rise so early. We had to charter a special car and put him to bed there the night before, so that it could be attached to the train in the morning without disturbing him. On another occasion he refused to ride in a car because it was not fitted with electric lights. But this was trivial compared with the way he stopped an express on which he was travelling. We were on our way to Buffalo, and were running at a rare clip, when Mascagni jumped up and pulled the bellcord. The train came to a stop with a jerk, and the trainman ran back to see what was the trouble. 'Going too fast,' said Mascagni. 'I want to die in Italy, not in America.' " (Quoted in *The Argonaut*, San Francisco, 16 February 1903.)

MOCCHI, Walter (1870-1955). Italian impresario, husband of the soprano Emma Carelli. Mocchi organized Mascagni's South American tour in 1911 and accompanied him there. He was director of the Costanzi from 1912 until 1926, overseeing all of Mascagni's Roman premieres in that theater. He was also the impresario for Mascagni's second South American tour in 1922. Mascagni felt that Mocchi favored a German company, which he managed there at the same time, at the expense of the Italian one. On their return to Italy the two men quarrelled bitterly in public, with Mascagni blaming Mocchi for the crisis occurring at the time in the lyric theater. Mocchi's second wife was Bidú Sayão.

MOLAJOLI, Lorenzo. Italian conductor. The first man to train a chorus for *Cavalleria*, he later conducted the first complete electrical recording of the opera.

MONALDI, Gino (1847-1932). Italian musicologist, critic, impresario and composer. Today remembered primarily for his books on Verdi, he also published others on a variety of subjects, among which one of the most valuable is *Cantanti celebri: 1829-1929*. As an impresario he ran into great financial difficulties, but continually returned to try his hand at it. When Ricordi refused to give the premiere of *Falstaff* in Rome (in spite of the agreement to that effect between Monaldi and the composer), Monaldi later mounted the work there, unfortunately without the hoped for success. Monaldi wrote one of the earliest books on Mascagni (1898) which is of no great value.

MONTEVERDE, Giulio (1837-1917). Italian sculptor, particularly noted for *Il Jenner* (1869), which is generally considered his masterpiece. He won many honors throughout his life and was nominated to the Senate in 1889.

MUGNONE, Leopoldo (1858-1941). Italian conductor and composer. Born in Naples, he attended the Conservatorio di San Pietro a Maiella in that city, producing his first work, a comic opera, at the age of twelve. His one act opera *Il birichino* (*The Scamp*) was first performed at the Teatro Malibran, Venice, on 11 August 1892, enjoying a moderate success. He began his conducting career at the age of sixteen, becoming one of Italy's most respected operatic and symphonic conductors. Edoardo Sonzogno engaged him for various undertakings and it was thus he became the first conductor of *Cavalleria*. He worked closely with Mascagni on the score of this opera, suggesting various cuts and transpositions which were accepted. Years later Mugnone was to make a cut at the end of *Isabeau* (unfortunately observed in the current edition), one which Mascagni most emphatically did not accept.

MULÈ, Giuseppe (1885-1951). Sicilian composer. He was appointed director of the R. Conservatorio di Santa Cecilia in Rome in 1925. The Fascist government later named him national secretary to the Fascist syndicate of musicians. He was an exponent of the use of Sicilian folksong and it was no doubt for this reason that the Scalera Brothers considered him for the composition of the *Cavalleria* film music when Mascagni turned down their offer. He wrote a number of operas, symphonic works, chamber music and incidental music for Greek plays.

MUSSOLINI, Benito (1883-1945). Italian premier and dictator. Emerging in 1919 as the head of the Fascist Party, Mussolini's influence on the arts was soon felt. After his famous March on Rome in October of 1922 it appeared to many that he was what the country, which earlier had been rocked by strikes, needed. In 1924 Puccini (*q.v.*) was named a *Senatore del Regno*, in 1929 Mascagni was elected to the Accademia d'Italia and there can be little doubt that both composers became, in Mosco Carner's words, "like so many others, honestly convinced of the need for [their] country to be ruled by a firm hand." Since Mascagni's relationship to Mussolini and Fascism is still a matter of controversy, it may be well to deal with it as straightforwardly as possible here. In recent years a certain amount of scholarship has been devoted to this subject (see Cantore, Goetz, Nicolodi and Sachs in the Bibliography) and it is only now that the extent of the relationship between the two men can be charted. It was after Mascagni returned from his South American tour in December of 1922 that he met Mussolini for the first time. Mascagni was dissatisfied with the state of opera in Italy and Mussolini needed "the collaboration of the intelligentsia to solidify his political position and further his personal standard" (Goetz). Thus the two men needed each other and as in all alliances where some form of power is being sought, the relationship was an uneasy one from the start. Naturally Mascagni desired as many performances for his operas as possible and with his usual flair for stating his own case he wrote to Mussolini on 26 June 1926 outlining in detail his ideas for reforming the current operatic situation, concluding with the proposal that the artistic director of the Costanzi "ought to be entrusted to a person who enjoys everybody's confidence." The following year Mussolini sent Mascagni as Italy's ambassador extraordinaire to the Beethoven Centennial celebration in Vienna; the composer later submitted a detailed report. In 1929 Mascagni was nominated "a member of the Reale Accademia d'Italia, newly founded as a Fascist organization opposing the venerated old Accademia dei Lincei" (Goetz). According to this same writer "the highpoint of the relationship between Mascagni and Mussolini had been reached." (Fifteen years later Mascagni was to ridicule the "empty honor" of being elected to the Italian Academy: see Chapter 34.) From this point on, the relationship between the two men gradually disintegrated, with Mascagni, feeling more and more that his operas were being boycotted, sending fulsome letters and telegrams assuring Mussolini of his devotion, at the same time writing privately to his friends deploring and ridiculing Mussolini and his Fascist government. The entire Mascagni/Mussolini correspondence, or as much of it as survives, can be found in Nicolodi (pp. 372-412). It makes very sad reading. Mascagni could not keep his sharp tongue silent in public and there are various letters of denunciation by informers reporting Mascagni's caustic remarks at the expense of the regime. The situation came to a head with *Nerone* which had been completed in August of 1933. Mascagni wished to give the premiere at the Costanzi, thus affirming the *romanità* of the work, but this fell through, as did another projected performance of the opera in the Coliseum in 1934. This naturally fueled Mascagni's suspicions of a boycott and it was at this time (12 June 1934) that he wrote the often quoted letter to Orsini which was intercepted, copied, and forwarded to the Duce: "And now there no longer exists the argument of the non-Fascist, since for two years I am also a Fascist, but earlier it was a spontaneous impulse, and all know how I, [as a] non-Fascist, had served the Regime with enthusiasm on account of the love I had for the Capo; today I feel humiliated, because I am ordered to show enthusiasm, which (I confess it with humiliation) no longer has the earlier perfume." Whether because of a favorable reaction to this letter by Mussolini, or for other now undiscoverable reasons, *Nerone* was accepted for performance at La Scala. An inordinate amount of publicity, including several radio speeches by the composer, attended the event. It was remarks such as the one in the 13 January 1935 broadcast (that he took up the composition of *Nerone* "when I had the joy of seeing in our Rome a man who was able to make live again, with his faith and his miraculous energy, the *virtù* of the Roman Empire") which gave rise to the myth that the opera was written specifically to glorify Mussolini and Fascism. The premiere on 16 January 1935 was a great personal success for the composer; he received thousands of congratulatory telegrams but one from Mussolini was not among them. Perhaps the Duce felt that he had repaid his debt to the composer (assuming he even thought in these terms by this point in their relationship) in seeing *Nerone* performed. Mascagni was also one of the recipients of grants from the government in the years 1933-1943. This list of 893 names (which also included such well-known literary figures as Sandro Penna, Vasco Pratolini and Giuseppe Ungaretti), came to light in January-February of 1986. It was a "complete list of people that the Fascist regime secretly paid in exchange for silence, for services rendered or promised, for requested help, for beneficence, and in the form of damages to the families of those who, fallen on the battlefield, had given themselves for the cause" (Cantore). Mascagni received the largest amount of any, 1.290.100 lire (approximately $774,000.00 in today's figures). Mascagni would also be eligible for a stipend under the "fallen on the battlefield" clause, since shortly before 2 June 1936 he received word that his son Edoardo had died in Abyssinia. The old composer's personal request to Mussolini that the body be returned to Italy for burial was refused. In 1938 Mascagni petititioned the Duce to find "the way to relieve a poor citizen, the work of whose long existence is unable to assure the slightest tranquillity to his old age." Whether a boycott against performances of Mascagni's operas and against his conducting did or did not exist (Goetz thinks it did, Nicolodi that it did not), Mascagni did do more conducting in the late thirties and his operas did appear more frequently, though not nearly often enough to satisfy the composer. Henceforward, his dealings with Mussolini consisted primarily of requests for audiences (usually denied) and good wishes (last recorded telegram, 5 April 1942). To sum up, in his dealing with Mussolini, Mascagni was, as always in his life, subject to his penchant for stirring up difficulties, not to say trouble, in any situation in which he found himself. As Harvey Sachs put it, he "couldn't help sowing trouble even when there was no personal benefit to be reaped." The almost grovelling letter which he wrote to Mussolini after the premiere of *Nerone* (a portion of which is quoted in the Introduction) was followed by a very arrogant and vulgar remark in public about the Duce having to accept the staging of the opera, referring to a part of Mussolini's anatomy which is normally not alluded to in polite society (see Nicolodi, documents nos. 33 and 34, pp. 404-405). In short, he could not leave well enough alone. And yet this quality in him was one of the factors in his enormous popularity with the public and contributed to the vitality of everything he touched, not the least of which is this *Autobiography*. It flattered him enormously to be on intimate terms with the famous and his dealings with Mussolini were no exception. Indeed, Nicolodi probably comes closest to the heart of the situation when she remarks that "concerning Mascagni's adhesion to Fascism... perhaps it will be more appropriate to speak of *mussolinismo*." Whereas the showy outer trappings of Fascism may have been attractive to the composer, it is doubtful that its more repugnant aspects had anything to say to him. It would seem, after all, it was the figure of Mussolini that he found attractive and was therefore determined to use for his own purposes.

NARDÒ, Domenico. Mascagni's medical doctor during the Cerignola years. It was also Nardò who, in 1897, discovered that the German governess of the Mascagni children, Anna Dietze, had died of typhoid and advised the composer to have his children moved out of the house. Mascagni discusses this incident in Chapter 16.

NAVARRINI, Francesco (1855-1923). Italian bass. A favorite singer of Mascagni's, he sang MacGregor in the Roman premiere of *Ratcliff*. He also accompanied the composer on his American tour, singing the Cieco in *Iris*. Possessed of an extraordinary vocal range, he was particularly noted for his elegant vocalism.

NEUMANN, Angelo (1838-1920). Viennese baritone and impresario. Forced to abandon a singing career because of an inflammation of the vocal cords, he became a co-director of the Leipzig Opera in 1876, later assuming full directorship of the Czech Opera in Prague.

NIGRA, Costantino (1828-1907). Italian diplomat, called by Cavour "the only person perhaps who knows all my thoughts, even the most secret."

First entering the diplomatic service after the war of 1848, he was later made ambassador to St. Petersburg (1876), to London (1882) and in 1885 to Vienna, where he presented Rossini's cane to Mascagni in 1901. Nigra had received the cane from Rossini's widow, and in presenting it to Mascagni wrote: "May you conserve this relic. It will remind you of the Master and be a testimony of my affectionate admiration for you" (letter dated 28 April 1901). Nigra was also a classical scholar, publishing Italian translations of Greek and Latin poems.

NOMELLINI, Plinio (1866-1947). Italian painter. Born in Livorno, one of his teachers was Giovanni Fattori. Nomellini favored a romantic rather than classical approach to his art, a trait clearly evidenced by his poster for the d'Annunzio-Mascagni *Parisina*. His paintings are housed in Italy's larger museums including the Museum of Modern Art in Rome. Mascagni acquired Nomellini's *Garibaldi* on 15 May 1907 at the Venice Exposition.

ORSINI, Giovanni (1886-1952). Italian writer and poet. Born in Livorno, he was a close friend and passionate admirer of Mascagni. In addition to poetry, drama and criticism (both musical and literary) he wrote a number of books on his friend: *Cavalleria, Maschere, Amica* (1912), *...di Pietro Mascagni* (1912), *Parisina! Parisina!* (1918), *Vangelo d'un mascagnano* (1926) and *Pietro Mascagni e il suo Nerone* (1935). For many years he was collecting material for a monumental biography which was left unfinished at the time of his death.

PACINI, Giuseppe (1862-1910). Italian baritone, he created the role of Douglas in *Ratcliff*. The critic of the *Perseveranza* declared after this performance that Pacini had "one of the most beautiful, healthy and spontaneous baritone voices heard for several years at the Scala." He was also to create the role of Renzo in *Silvano* that same year.

PAGLIARA, Rocco (1856-1914). Neapolitan journalist, contemporary of Scarfoglio (*q.v.*) He was an active music critic and one of the earliest Italian admirers of Wagner. One of Mascagni's songs, *"Rosa"* (1890), has a text by Pagliara.

PALLADINO, Vincenzo. Mascagni's barber in Cerignola. He also played the piccolo in the Filarmonica.

PANZACCHI, Enrico (1840-1904). Italian poet, best known for his book of collected poetry (1908). He also wrote narrative prose, biographical works and was known as a public speaker and teacher.

PANZINI, Angelo (1820-1886). Italian composer and pianist. From 1860 until his death he was professor of harmony, counterpoint and fugue at the Milan Conservatory, where he himself had been a student (1832-40). A prolific composer, he wrote over 200 works for piano, voice and various instruments.

PARISOTTI, Alessandro (1853-1913). Italian musicologist and composer. In 1880 he became secretary of the Accademia di Santa Cecilia (Rome); he was also conductor of a number of orchestral societies.

PASCARELLA, Cesare (1858-1940). Italian poet, editor and member of the Royal Academy. Noted for the local color and humor of his works, he was the author of *Il manichino* (1885) and *Le memorie di uno smemorato* (1910).

PASTA, Francesco (1839-1905). Italian actor. Making his debut in 1867, he soon established his name, particularly in plays by Scribe and Dumas. He was associated with the actress Annetta Campi from 1882 until 1887. Mascagni saw his company perform Verga's *Cavalleria rusticana* at the Teatro Manzoni in Milan during a run of performances which began on 11 February 1884. Pasta's company successfully toured America in 1897.

PATTI, Adelina (1843-1919). Spanish soprano. Born in Madrid, she made her English debut at the Royal Italian Opera in London in 1861. Her career lasted for fifty-six years, during which time she remained one of the most famous singers of her day, being a particular favorite in England. As far as is known, Mascagni never composed an "exclusive" song for her.

PAVONCELLI, Giuseppe (1836-1941). A very successful merchant from Cerignola who advocated the careful use of land when he served in the government. He was Minister of Public Works, 1897-98. An early friend and admirer of Mascagni, he was one of the committee which granted the composer honorary citizenship in Cerignola after the success of *Cavalleria* in 1890.

PEDROTTI, Carlo (1817-1893). Italian conductor and composer, today known only for his comic opera *Tutti in maschera* (Verona, 1856). He was director of the Liceo Musicale in Pesaro from 1882 until his suicide in October of 1893. Mascagni was named director in October of 1895, the two years between being overseen by a temporary director, Arturo Vambianchi.

PENNASILICO, Fr. According to Targiono-Tozzetti, Fr. Pennasilico was the Latin teacher (*Mascagni prima della "Cavalleria"*).

PEROSI, Lorenzo (1872-1956). Italian church musician and composer. He studied music at the Milan Conservatory in 1892-93, becoming a priest in 1896. Appointed musical director of the Sistine Chapel in 1898, it was in this year that he produced his most successful work, a trilogy of oratorios: *La Trasfigurazione, La resurrezione di Lazzaro* and *La Risurrezioni di Cristo.* His compositional style was a polyglot, being a mixture of Gregorian idioms, Palestrina, and modern orchestral textures. His most extended and elaborate work, *Il giudizio universale,* was first performed in 1904. In 1922 he was forced to enter a mental hospital after exhibiting symptoms of mental breakdown. In 1924 Mascagni gave a lecture on Perosi in which he declared: "The art of Perosi is genuine art because it is the fruit of creative genius... because the power of expression which Lorenzo Perosi demonstrates in his works is the sign of a divine gift...." Perosi conducted his own *Messa da Requiem* at the funeral services for Mascagni in Livorno (20 June 1951; Church of S. Maria del Soccorso).

PERTILE, Aureliano (1885-1952). Italian tenor. His successful career began in 1912 and from that time on he appeared in all the leading Italian opera houses. He made his La Scala debut in 1922 as Faust in *Mefistofele* under Toscanini. He was a favorite tenor of this conductor, who entrusted the premiere of Boito's *Nerone* to him (1924). Eleven years later he was to create another Nero, this time in Mascagni's last opera. Pertile retired in 1940.

PESCATORE, Nicola. Teacher and director of the newspaper *Scienza e Diletto* in Cerignola, one of Mascagni's supporters in the years before the *Cavalleria* success. In 1895 he invited Mascagni to contribute several articles to his newspaper: *"Libretti e Librettisti"* (30 June) and *"I Critici musicali"* (14 July). In the latter Mascagni wrote: "...I have always believed that music critics are nothing more than musicians gone stale, dead musicians."

PICCINNI, Niccolò (1728-1800). Italian composer. Born in Bari, his first opera was produced in 1754. But it was in Rome, in 1760, that his most enduring success had its premiere, *La buona figliuola*, a work which is still performed occasionally. In 1776 he went to Paris and the famous feud with Gluck soon began. Mascagni's lecture on Piccinni was delivered in Bari on 11 April 1900. A few sentences from it will show the tactics he used in proving Piccinni the victor in the battle with Gluck: "For today's cultured musicians, Piccinni has disappeared... and in the obligatory logic of their required culture (not their natural feeling) they demolish in the twinkling of an eye all the Rossinis, Bellinis and Donizettis of this world. And let us thank the Lord! At least Piccini finds himself in good company!... I am a sincere and convinced piccinnian because in Piccinni I find the genuine source of the Italian lyric theater."

PIERSON, Georg Henry (1852-1902). Berlin opera official, associated in the 1890s with the Königliche Schauspielhaus and the Court Opera. His wife, the soprano Bertha Pierson, sang in New York in 1888 (in Rubinstein's *Nero*) as a member of the ill-fated National Opera Company.

PIGNA, Alessandro (?-1928). Milanese music publisher. He encouraged young composers, printing in addition to Puccini's *Due Minuetti* for string quartet (c. 1892) the following songs by Mascagni: *"La tua stella"*, *"M'ama...non m'ama"*, *"Pena d'amore"*, *"Rosa"*, *"Alla luna"* and *"Risveglio"*. After rewriting *In filandia* in the winter of 1882-83 (changing its name to *Pinotta*) in the vain hope of it winning a Conservatory contest, Mascagni had given the manuscript to Pigna, with whom it remained a number of years. When, in 1890, Mascagni became the man of the moment, it was natural for Pigna to be interested in its possible publication. Mascagni withheld it, later rewriting it a second time. It was finally produced in 1932. In 1901-02 Pigna abandoned his publishing business, selling his entire catalogue to Ricordi.

PIUS XII (1876-1958). Born Giovanni Pacelli, he was Pope from 1939 until his death. During Mascagni's last years he helped the aged composer, sending the following message to the Mascagni family at the composer's death: "His Holiness is paternally present at the deep sorrow of this family and the world of art, to which the heart and genius of the illustrious Maestro revealed treasures of goodness and beauty. Praying for him who has abandoned his exile and for those who weep in sorrow, he sends the comfort of his Apostolic benediction." Mascagni had dedicated his last composition, *O Roma felix* (1943), to Pius XII.

PIZZI, Emilio (1861-1940). Italian composer. A student of the Milan Conservatory where he studied under Bazzini and Ponchielli, he had already won three contests in Milan, Florence and Bologna (*Guglielmo Ratcliff*, Teatro Comunale; 31 October 1899) before his meeting with Mascagni in Rome in February of 1890. *Viviana*, the opera he had submitted to the contest, was among the twelve chosen for a hearing before the Commission, but got no further. He later wrote a one-act opera for the exclusive use of Adelina Patti (*q.v.*), *Gabriella* (Boston, 1893), and was also to set a libretto by Luigi Illica, *La Rosalba* (Turin, 1899). He lived for a number of years in London.

PLATANIA, Pietro (1828-1907). Italian composer of sacred music, much respected throughout the musical Italy of his day as a master of counterpoint. He was director of the Naples and Palermo Conservatories.

POLI RANDACCIO, Ernestina (1885-1956). Italian soprano. She created the role of Parisina. In 1908, still in her early twenties, she had sung Amica in Florence, Bologna and Trieste. She sang the first Minnie at La Scala in December of 1912 and was to become a famous exponent of the part. In a 1920 interview Mascagni stated that he would use Poli Randaccio for the role of Mariella should *Il piccolo Marat* have its premiere at that time. In the event the part was created by Gilda Dalla Rizza (*q.v.*).

PONCHIELLI, Amilcare (1834-1886). Italian composer. Studied at the Milan Conservatory, 1843-54. The first version of *I promessi sposi* was performed in 1856 in Cremona, winning a local success for Ponchielli. It was not until 1872, when the revised version of the work appeared at the Teatro dal Verme (Milan), that his name became known to a wider public. His later operas include *I lituani* (1874), *La Gioconda* (1876), *Il figliuol prodigo* (1880) and *Marion Delorme* (1885). Though appointed professor of composition at the Milan Conservatory in 1880, it was not until the following year that he actually began teaching. Many of his students became known in Italy, but those who achieved international fame were two of his own favorites, Puccini and Mascagni. Ponchielli had first come into contact with Mascagni in February of 1881 in connection with *In filanda* and the Milan Musical Exposition. The latter constituted the great event in Milan for 1881, opening on 5 May, in the presence of Umberto I and Queen Martherita, and continued until November 1, almost six months. Thus the honorable mention which Mascagni received for his *Ave Maria* was no small honor. Mascagni's recollections of Ponchielli's opinion of *Alla gioia* come from the 1899 article by Soffredini (*q.v.*): "Six months of patience were necessary to put up with all the idiosyncrasies (he has always been eccentric) of the fiery musician in the gestation of this new composition.... The day before the dress rehearsal the dances were still not ready; ...in two hours he conceived and orchestrated those fifty stupendous pages of music which Ponchielli classified (letter to me sent 9 March 1883) as a masterpiece." Ponchielli was married to the famous soprano Brambilla (*q.v.*).

PRATESI, Luigi. One of Mascagni's first teachers when he was a boy in Livorno, Pratesi was a professor at the Schola Cantorum. This school was part of the Congregazlone S. Luigi Gonzaga, organized in 1872 by Don Francesco Cafferata. It was Pratesi who encouraged Mascagni, when still a young boy, to play the organ for services in the Cathedral. According to Targiono-Tozzetti (*Mascagni prima della "Cavalleria"*) a *Mass* by Mascagni was performed in 1880 in the Cathedral "under the direction of Maestro Giuseppe [sic] Pratesi, the *Sanctus* and *Agnus Dei* of which aroused great enthusiasm, so much so that the multitude of the faithful broke out in great applause." This *Mass*, however, was only partially by Mascagni (it was composed in collaboration with Silvio Barbini) and the performance was conducted by Soffredini.

PREVIATI, Gaetano (1852-1910). Italian painter preoccupied with naturalness of scenes and use of color. He felt that scientific awareness of life was vital to his painting. His most famous work is *Maternità*. He contributed four paintings (each descriptive of one of the acts) to the vocal score of *Parisina*.

PRIMO DE RIVERA, Miguel (1870-1930). Spanish soldier and statesman, known as the Marquis de Estrella. He was born at Jerez de la Frontera and studied at the Madrid Military Academy. He became dictator of Spain, 1923-30, taking control from Alfonso XIII.

PUCCINI, Giacomo (1858-1924). Mascagni's friendship with Puccini dates from 1882-83, Mascagni's first year at the Milan Conservatory, Puccini's last. For a time they roomed together in the Vicolo San Carlo, the Mascagni-Puccini literature containing numerous stories of their *vie de*

Bohème. After Mascagni left the Conservatory, he kept in touch with Puccini, even coming from Cerignola to Naples for the first performance there, on 15 January 1888, of *Le Villi.* Puccini expected a triumph for his first opera, but as it turned out it was a fiasco. He later told Arnaldo Fraccaroli: "I remember that Mascagni came especially from Cerignola in the hopes of being present at a success, and was discouraged" (*La vita di G. Puccini*). After the two men had become successful their friendship continued; on the few occasions they would meet it was renewed. But they watched each other's career and were conscious of always trying to cap one another's success. It was their adherents who were the main source of the discord; left to themselves their mutual respect would have won the day. With the establishment of Fascism, Puccini sympathized with the ideas of the young movement, even becoming an honorary member of the party. Mascagni, who lived to see its downfall, has had to pay for his own sympathy.

RANDEGGER, Alberto (1832-1911). Italian conductor, singing teacher and composer. Born in Trieste, he made a name for himself in Italy as a composer of church music, ballets and operas. He went to England in the 1850's and became known as a singing teacher, conductor and composer, producing a comic opera and choral music. He conducted Italian operas for Sir Augustus Harris at Covent Garden, 1887-98.

RAPISARDI, Mario (1844-1912). Italian poet, a friend and contemporary of Verga. In 1872 he married Giselda Fojanesi, having met her through his friend. In 1883 he discovered that for the past two years Verga and Giselda had been having an affair (Rapisardi being a very peculiar man the marriage was an extremely unhappy one), but oddly enough this did not ultimately sever the friendship of the two men. *Lucifero* (1877) contained an attack on the poet Carducci and a bitter quarrel between the two poets ensued in which all of literary Italy took sides.

RATTI, Federico Valerio (1877-19??). Italian dramatist and poet who won the Concorso Nazionale in 1911 for his drama *Il Solco quadrato* which dealt with the mythical founding of Rome. His greatest success was with his drama *Guida.*

REALE, Cesaro. Harpist of the Cerignola Filarmonica under Mascagni. It was he who mailed off the *Cavalleria* score to the commission on 3 June 1889.

RE RICCARDI, Adolfo. Author of *I segreti degli autori* (1928).

RICORDI, Giulio (1840-1912). Grandson of Giovanni Ricordi (1785-1853), the founder of Casa Ricordi, largest and most important Italian music publishers. Giulio inherited the directorship of the House on the death of his feather Tito in 1888. *Iris* was the only Mascagni opera to be published by Ricordi.

ROGERS, Della. See under **VIDAL**.

ROMANI, Felice (1788-1856). Italian librettist. Though he also wrote plays and poetry, it is as a librettist that he is primarily remembered today, notably for the texts he provided for Bellini and Donizetti. The correct title of his Columbus libretto is *Colombo*, not *Zilia* (the name of its heroine). It was written by Romani for Francesco Morlacchi and had its first performance on 21 June 1828 at the Teatro Carlo Felice in Genoa. Romani was an admirer of the Genoese navigator, having written a poem on him in his youth. In the preface to the libretto of *Colombo* Romani states: "An epic is necessary for the discovery of America. There is one who has meditated on it, but Fortune impedes him from finishing it." Romani was aware that his *Colombo* was anything but epic, declaring in the same preface that it is the fault of the kind of libretto demanded by the *melodramma* form rather than his own. The dramatic author, he continues, "had need of a way of bringing alive all the characters, and of a plot in which love, a passion to which music is more partial than any other, is set in relief." Mascagni's memory is correct as to the plot of Romani's libretto, but the book he found on "Columbus in music" gave him some wrong information when it stated that no composer wanted to set it. In addition to Morlacchi, it was used by Ricci (1829), Carnicer (1831), De Barbieri (1848, called *Columbus*), Mela (1857) and Casella (1865), the last two entitling their operas *Cristoforo Colombo*. Though Mascagni does not state what pages of *Ratcliff* used his *Zilia* (*Colombo*) sketches, the simplicity of the child Willie's prayer at the beginning of Act II is such that it could easily be the music of a thirteen year old. One of Mascagni's early compositions, a *Romanza* (1881), has words by Romani.

ROSSI, Ernesto (1827-1896). Italian actor, especially famous for his Shakespearean characterizations.

ROSSINI, Gioacchino (1792-1868). Called the "Swan of Pesaro", it was his *Ermione* (1819) which contained a prelude with a chorus sung behind the curtain. He first came to Paris in 1823, remaining there until his death. Due to his enormous European popularity, Rossini was welcomed enthusiastically by the Parisian public and a number of the critics, but also encountered some antagonism from others who resented a foreign intruder. This naturally soured Rossini and prompted his anti-French remarks. In his will, Rossini had specified: "As heir of the property I name the Comune of Pesaro, my homeland, to establish and endow a Liceo Musicale in that city after my wife's death. I forbid the magistracy or the representatives of the Comune of the said city to have any kind of control or intervention in my estate, wishing my wife to enjoy it in complete and absolute freedom...." After the death of Rossini's wife in 1878, the Comune put these terms of the Will into effect. Instead of erecting a new building, an unused convent was refurbished and Pedrotti (*q.v.*) was named director in 1892 (Bazzini had been approached but refused). In the same year the Conservatory was made an autonomous establishment under the jurisdiction of an Association named by the city council. Mascagni venerated Rossini, calling him "my eternal God" (letter to Orsini, 24 March 1919). Thus when he was asked to succeed Pedrotti he flung himself into the work with his characteristic energy. According to Giuseppe Radiciotti, author of the monumental biography of Rossini, Mascagni "carried the Liceo to the apogee of renown. Students swarmed in from everywhere; Italians and foreigners swarmed in to be present at the artistic revelations of the institute. And meanwhile, in spite of his marvelous activity, in spite of the triumphs of his converts and new operatic creations which exalted and enraptured the minds of his young disciples, the composer of *Cavalleria rusticana* did not lose sight of improving the school which had been entrusted to his care." Mascagni's troubles with the Association began in 1899 and were to become increasingly difficult until his departure from the Conservatory. The basic problem lay in Mascagni's wanting money to carry out what he felt were his obligations under the terms of Rossini's will and the Association feeling that his long absences from the Conservatory did not make him of any use as its director. As was usual with Mascagni's battles, this one was conducted in the newspapers with a great deal of acrimony on both sides. In January of 1903, as Mascagni was completing his American tour, the Association announced that he was being relieved of his position. The case was fought out in the courts and was finally decided in Mascagni's favor, but he resigned rather than return to the city where there was still so much bitterness. In 1905 Amilcare Zanella (*q.v.*) was named his successor as director. The years spent in the academic atmosphere were not without benefit to Mascagni, however. In the three operas composed during that time, *Zanetto*, *Iris* and *Le Maschere*, a new depth of poetry and refinement of technique are apparent, and in *Iris* particularly can be seen the results of his intensive work with an orchestra of his own and the studies necessary for his composition classes.

ROTHSCHILD, Alfred de (1842-1918). Member of the famous family of financiers. Alfred, the only one of the family never to marry, was a patron of the arts and a celebrated giver of lavish parties. He kept a symphony orchestra as a hobby, using an ivory baton with diamonds to conduct it. He managed Melba's financial affairs, discovered Mischa Elman and was even Director of the Bank of England. He was able to convince Patti to sing at a benefit (a practice which she refused ever to do), importing Alvarez from New York for the event.

ROVESCIALLI, Antonio (1864-1936). Italian scenic designer. After a number of years' experience in drama and operetta, he worked at La Scala, where, in collaboration with Caramba (*q.v.*), he established a solid nineteenth-century style of scenic design. His first Mascagni premiere was *Isabeau* which had originally been conceived by its creators to play in one set. When a second one was required, Rovescialli submitted a design; Mascagni, delighted asked for a third. Thus three separate settings for the opera were devised. Rovescialli also provided the scenic designs for *Si* and *Parisina*.

SALA, Marco (1842-1901). Italian journalist, critic, composer of dance music and amateur violinist. Mascagni refers to him as a painter, and though he well may have been an amateur one, there is no reference to him as such in the Mascagni-Puccini literature. After Puccini's *Le Villi* had been rejected by the 1883 Sonzogno contest commission (the judges were Dominiceti, Faccio, Galli, Platania and Ponchielli), primarily, it now appears, because of the difficulty in deciphering the composer's manuscript, Fontana (*q.v.*) interested Sala in the work. Puccini played selections from it on an evening in 1884 at Sala's home before Boito (who strangely enough had also been involved in judging the 1883 contest), Catalani and Giovannina Lucca (the publisher). The audition was successful and a collection was taken up in order to perform the work, an event which took place at the Teatro dal Verme in Milan on May 31,

1884. Mascagni's statement about his taking up "a kind of collection" is somewhat ambiguous (it is generally stated that the idea began with Fontana) and may or may not be true. He was at the time playing the doublebass in the Dal Verme orchestra (see letter to his father, Chapter 2) but on this occasion he was in the audience at Puccini's request. According to a number of Mascagni's biographers, at the conclusion of the extraordinarily successful performance Mascagni ran to the stage and embraced Puccini, who said: "Look, the first who runs to embrace me is precisely the one who can do more than I." Read in this context, Mascagni's remarks about walking disconsolately through the streets after this performance take on an added poignancy.

SALADINO, Michele (1835-1912). Italian composer and teacher of harmony, counterpoint and fugue at the Milan Conservatory beginning in 1870. He was considered one of the foremost contrapuntists in Italy and Mascagni was justifiably proud to have been his student.

SALASSA, Gaudenzio. Italian baritone, sang Alfio in the premiere of *Cavalleria*. The least successful member of the original cast, he was replaced by Pandolfini when the opera had a second run of performances at the Costanzi in November of 1890.

SALVESTRI, Giovanni (1841-1891). Italian actor, journalist and adaptor for the stage. A native of Livorno, it was he who supposedly obtained the permission from Verga (*q.v.*) for Mascagni to set *Cavalleria* as an opera.

SALVINI, Tommaso (1830-1915). Italian actor, most famous for his interpretation of Othello.

SAPELLI, Luigi (1865-1936). Known under the name of "Caramba". Famous Italian costume designer, particulary celebrated for his work at La Scala. He created the costumes for the premiere in the theater of *Parisina*. For many years he collaborated with the designer Rovescialli (*q.v.*).

SARDOU, Victorien (1831-1908). French dramatist. A number of his plays were adapted as operas, the most noted being Puccini's *Tosca* (1900), and Giordano's *Fedora* (1898) and *Madame Sans Gêne* (1915). In 1901 Mascagni was interested in adapting Sardou's *Théodora* (1884) as an opera (to a libretto by Giacosa) and later that same year went to visit Sardou in

Paris to discuss an adaptation of *La Haine* (1874). Neither project ever came to anything.

SCALERA BROTHERS. Italian film company organized in the 1930's by two brothers, Salvatore and Michele Scalera. They produced their first film, *L'Argine*, in 1938. They established themsevles at a time when the Fascist political monopoly caused the large American companies to withdraw their films from Italy. The Scalera *Cavalleria rusticana*, directed by A. Palermi, appeared in 1939.

SCARFOGLIO, Edoardo (1860-1917). Italian journalist, director of several Neapolitan newspapers, among them *Il Mattino*. Author of the *Libro di Don Chisciotte* (1883), a book which is not entirely forgotten today in Italy. He was married to the novelist Matilde Serao, from whom Puccini requested a libretto. Scarfoglio was one of the circle of friends that brought about Mascagni's reconciliation with d'Annunzio (*q.v.*), in spite of the fact that the poet's vitriolic *"Il Capobanda"* had first appeared in Scarfoglio's *Mattino*.

SCHIAVAZZI, Piero (1875-1949). Italian tenor. A student of the Pesaro Conservatory when it was directed by Mascagni, Schiavazzi sang Silvano there in 1899. He became known as an interpreter of Mascagni's operas, in 1901 singing Arlecchino in the Neapolitan premiere of *Le Maschere*. The tenor of Mascagni's American tour, he sang both Turiddu ("a very zealous, but untunable and exaggerative tenor," N. Y. *Times*) and Osaka ("he marred a good effort by constant forcing of the voice," N.Y. *World*). His passionate declamation caused wear on his somewhat small tenor and by 1911 it was already evident that he would not have a long career. A handsome man, he made a few films (in 1915 and 1916) and also left a volume of memoirs, *Piero Schiavazzi racconta!* (Cagliari, 1936).

SCHUSTER, Leo Francis (1852-1927). Wealthy London patron of the arts, he was a friend of Fauré and Elgar.

SCOGNAMIGLIO, Alfonso and Ciro. Managers of an operetta company who hired Mascagni as conductor in the autumn of 1885 in Naples after Forlì's company was disbanded. Mascagni remained with the Scognamiglio Company until May of 1886, when it, too, was disbanded in Ascoli Piceno. Mascagni then returned to Ancona, leaving there in June when he went to Naples at the invitation of his friend Dario Acconci, not the Duke Cirella as is stated in the *Autobiography*. Acconci was a member of the Cirella (*q.v.*) Company and it was he who introduced Mascagni to the Duke, who hired him as a conductor.

SEPPILLI, Armando (1860-1931). Italian composer, conductor and pianist. A student of Bazzini and Ponchielli at the Milan Conservatory, he was engaged immediately upon leaving it by Edoardo Sonzogno as a conductor in various theaters. *Andrea di Francia*, the opera Seppilli submitted to the contest, was one of the twelve chosen for a hearing before the Commission in Rome. In the event it received a special mention along with *Il Viaggente* by Bossi (*q.v.*). Seppilli later conducted in London (where he was Melba's accompanist), New York, Canada and Australia.

SGAMBATI, Giovanni (1841-1914). Italian pianist and composer. Roman by birth, after an early career travelling as a pianist, he settled in his native city in 1860. He was a strong defender of the classical in music and when Liszt arrived in Rome, Sgambati studied with him, soon conducting many concerts which included music by German composers, the first Roman performances of Beethoven's *Eroica* and E-flat piano concerto among them. He wrote no operas, confining his output to piano, chamber and church music, orchestral works, and songs. He taught at the Accademia di Santa Cecilia (Rome) beginning in 1869.

SINISCALCHI, Michele (1856-1900). Born in Cerignola, he became a friend of Mascagni when the composer settled there and was one of the first to recognize the young man's genius. Writing of an early (April 1888) performance of the Filarmonica under Mascagni, Siniscalchi reported: "The Filarmonica, made up largely of children, may be called a miracle; to play in an orchestra after a few months of school, to play as they played... is something which greatly surpassed the general expectations." Siniscalchi's letter to his friend Pagliara was not, as Mascagni states, for a *Cavalleria* libretto for Mascagni to set but for an "idyll, a fable or something similar" (letter quoted by Cellamare). After Pagliara's refusal, Siniscalchi, not knowing that by now Targioni had reminded Mascagni of *Cavalleria* and that subject had already been decided upon, asked another friend of his, Armando Perotti (1865-1924), for a libretto. Perotti responded with a sketch of a work to be called *Bivio* which Mascagni refused (letter dated 31 July 1889; quoted by Cellamare). The composer did, however, ask Perotti to help him with a *Vistilia* to be drawn from the novel by Rocco De Zerbi. This was ultimately written by Targioni and Menasci.

SOFFREDINI, Alfredo (1854-1923). Italian composer, critic and teacher. A student of the Milan Conservatory, he was for many years critic and correspondent for the *Gazzetta musicale* and also wrote a book on Verdi. In 1875 he founded, at his own expense, the Instituto Musicale Livornese which, in 1879, became known as the "Cherubini". On 7 June 1876, Soffredini gave the first lessons to Mascagni. Under Soffredini Mascagni studied organ, piano, violin, doublebass and several wind instruments in addition to harmony, counterpoint, fugue and music history. Practically all of Mascagni's compositions until he went to the Milan Conservatory in October of 1882 were written under Soffredini's guidance. An early *Kyrie* of Mascagni still survives in manuscript dated 14-16 April 1880 and not 1876 as Mascagni implies in the *Autobiography* (these could easily be two different pieces, however). Of these early compositions by his favorite pupil Soffredini was to write later in 1899: "I have a drawerful of his compositions; every one, I repeat, is a *promise*... of *Cavalleria*. A Symphony in F in four movements is a stupendous classical imitation; the song *"La tua stella"*, seasoned later in all kinds of sauces, is one of those melodies which characterize genius... all these quickly became popular, so that he was suddenly known to all of Livorno and Tuscany." When, in the winter of 1942-43, Mascagni came to recollect his early days in Livorno this article by Soffredini was not unforgotten. Mascagni's two largest choral works from this period. *In filanda* and *Alla gioia*, both received their first performances under Soffredini. It was also Soffredini who put the young composer in touch with Ponchielli, thus paving the way to the Milan Conservatory. Mascagni was always conscious of the debt he owed Soffredini and was quick to recognize it. Writing to this teacher from Milan in February, 1881 he confessed: "The great Verdi, arrived at the apex of glory in the divine art, exclaimed 'God created me, I made myself!' I who now begin to climb this difficult ladder, and who perhaps have arrived at the first rung, stop to rest and, looking backward, cry, 'God created me, my teacher made me!'" After he left the Conservatory in 1885 Mascagni continued to wrote to Soffredini, still depending on him for counsel and aid during the difficult years in operetta companies and in Cerignola. When the success of *Cavalleria* occurred, Soffredini's name was unfortunately all too seldom mentioned in the attendant publicity, Mascagni's conservatory teachers receiving the credit. Thus relations between teacher and former student became somewhat strained. Mascagni was able to regain the old relations between them, however, and Soffredini's 1899 article (see Bibliography) demonstrates nothing but pride in the by then famous composer.

SONZOGNO, CASA. Important Milanese publishing house founded in 1818 by Giambattista Sonzogno. In 1861 **EDOARDO** (1836-1920) inherited the business from his father Lorenzo, who was the son of the original founder. In 1866 Edoardo first published the newspaper *Il Secolo* (the old *Gazzetta di Milano*), later adding *Il teatro illustrato* to his list. Edoardo, a man of refinement particularly attracted to French culture, added music publishing to the firm's interest in 1874, the following year importing French operas and operettas in Italian translation. Amintore Galli (*q.v.*) was placed in charge of the musical branch of the business. Because he was criticized for his French propensities, in 1883 Edoardo announced the first of a series of contests for Italian composers. It was to this contest that Puccini submitted *Le Villi*, which did not even receive an honorable mention (for the probable reason for this see SALA, above). Mascagni won the second contest, announced in 1888, with his *Cavalleria*. Further contests were held in 1892, 1902 (the "solemnly international" one mentioned by Mascagni), 1904 (for a libretto only), and the final one in 1907 which commemorated the Centenary of the Milan Conservatory. After Casa Ricordi, the Sonzogno house was the most powerful music publisher in Italy and for a time seriously rivalled the older firm. Among the composers which Sonzogno published were Giordano, Leoncavallo and Cilèa, in addition to Mascagni. In 1894 Edoardo opened the Teatro Lirico (the old Canobbiana) in Milan, but unfortunately he was to lose a great deal of money on the venture. Deciding to retire, Edoardo in 1907 put his two nephews in charge of the firm: **RICCARDO** (?-1915) and **RENZO** (1877-1920). Riccardo handled the books, Renzo the music. But the two cousins quarreled in 1910 and Renzo left to form his own firm, dedicated primarily to operettas and music for films. His company did, however, publish Puccini's *La Rondine*, Pizetti's *Fedra* and Mascagni's *Si* and *Parisina*. At the death of Riccardo, the two firms were united (November 1915), Renzo assuming the presidency and general direction. With the exception of *Iris*, Casa Sonzogno published all of Mascagni's operas from *Cavalleria* to *Marat*. *Pinotta* and *Nerone* were published at the composer's own expense. Mascagni had a great regard for Edoardo (though there was a period of estrangement), naming his second son after him and dedicating *L'amico Fritz* to him.

SPATZ, Giuseppe. Owner of a chain of hotels in Switzerland and Italy, among them the Grand Hotel de Milan where Verdi maintained a suite of rooms in his later years. Spatz' daughter Olga married Giordano.

SPINELLI, Nicola (1865-1906). Italian pianist, conductor and composer. Among his teachers were Mancinelli and Sgambati. *Labilia,* his first opera, was produced at the Costanzi on 7 May 1890, ten days before Mascagni's *Cavalleria.* It was performed four times that season. The libretto was by V. Valle. The opera takes place in Corsica and concerns Labilia, bride of Volello. When she hears that he has been killed in battle, she prepares to remarry. Volello, who contrary to report was only wounded, returns and throws the traitress and himself into a river gorge. Spinelli's most famous opera is *A basso porto,* to a libretto by Eugenio Checchi (*q.v.*) based on a play by Goffredo Cognetti. It received its first performance in Cologne (in German) on 18 April 1894, the first Italian performance taking place at the Costanzi on 11 March 1895. It is written in the then fashionable *verismo* style.

SPONTINI, Gaspare (1774-1851). Italian composer who lived in Paris 1803-1820 where he produced his best known operas, *La Vestale* (1807) and *Fernand Cortez* (1809). His passion for pure drinking water was well known.

STAGNO, Roberto (1836-1897). Italian tenor, husband of Gemma Bellincioni (*q.v.*). He sang in both London and New York. Creating the part of Turiddu at the age of 54 (Bellincioni was 26), Stagno had had an illustrious career in the theater, singing in such disparate operas as *Barbiere di Siviglia* and *Carmen.* After his enormous success in the new "veristic" *Cavalleria,* he created the leading tenor roles in two of the many operas written in similar style which followed: Vito in *Mala vita* (Giordano) and Cicillo in *A Santa Lucia* (Tasca).

STANFORD, Sir Charles (1852-1924). Irish composer, conductor and teacher. He was known for his orchestral works, operas and church music. Professor of Music at Trinity College (Cambridge) from 1887 until his death.

STORCHIO, Rosina (1876-1945). Italian soprano. She studied at the Milan Conservatory, making her debut at the Dal Verme in 1892. She became famous as Mignon, Manon (in the Massenet opera) and Mimì, and was probably the Italian singer who best expressed the intimate vein of Massenet and Puccini. It was this quality which no doubt caused Mascagni to ask her to create the part of Lodoletta, a role in which she obtained great success.

ŠUBERT, F. Adolf (1849-1915). Director of the Czech National Theater in Prague when Mascagni was at the 1892 Vienna Exposition. An enthusiast of the *verismo* school of Italian opera, Subert gave the premieres of Mascagni's first three operas in Prague: *Cavalleria* (4 January 1891), *L'amico Fritz* (18 April 1892) and *I Rantzau* (2 May 1893).

SYLVA, Eloi (1847-1922). Belgian dramatic tenor. He sang in *Le Prophète* and *Rienzi* during the 1885-86 Metropolitan season.

TARGIONI-TOZZETTI, Giovanni (1863-1934). Italian poet, librettist, critic and journalist. Born in Livorno the same year as Mascagni, they were intimate schoolmates and friends from earliest childhood. In collaboration with Menasci (*q.v.*) or alone he was responsible for six Mascagni libretti; *Cavalleria, I Rantzau, Silvano, Zanetto, Pinotta* and *Nerone*. He also provided the Italian translation of *Amica* and a number of verses for *L'amico Fritz* and *Il piccolo Marat*. Together with Menasci he wrote the libretto for Giordano's *Regina Diaz* (1894) in addition to the *Werther* translation. Though Mascagni had seen the *Cavalleria* play in 1884, it was actually Targioni who, when asked for a libretto in 1888, suggested the subject. Mascagni replied from Cerignola: "It was unnecessary for you to write me, since I am completely in your hands. Do what you wish... *Cavalleria rusticana* has been among my projects since I saw it performed for the first time by the Pasta (*q.v.*) Company. Indeed, Giannino Salvestri (*q.v.*) urged me to set it to music then" (letters of 14 December 1888). Seldom mentioned is the fact that the Sonzogno contest also awarded a prize for the best libretto. This was won in the 1888 contest by Targioni and Menasci. Mascagni was not unaware of what he owed his librettists for their work. After it had been announced that he had won first prize, he wrote them from Cerignola (10 March 1890): "Oh! how can I ever repay you for the success, for the triumph which you have caused me to have? Since without doubt the greatest part of the merit is due to you.... Do you want to work together?" Their answer was yes, and their suggestion was *I Rantzau*. Mascagni later dedicated this score to his two collaborators. Targioni proved to be Mascagni's most faithful librettist. The composer became accustomed to turn to his friend for help because he knew "Nanni" could always be counted on to provide exactly what he asked for. In 1932 Targioni wrote the words for a hymn *Invocazione alla Madonna*, which Mascagni composed for the Feast of the Madonna of Montenero.

TCHAIKOVSKY, Peter Ilyich (1840-1873). Russian composer. His setting of Schiller's *An die Freude* (Russian translation by K. S. Aksakov) was his "leaving exercise" at the St. Petersburg Conservatory in 1865. Written in six movements, it is for solo quartet, chorus and orchestra. Using the same forces, Mascagni divided his setting into three parts. When Mascagni was at the Vienna Exposition in 1892 he discovered that Tchaikovsky was also there, lodging in the same hotel. The two composers were unable to meet, due to the crowds of people which always surrounded Mascagni. The Russian was only able to send his card. Tchaikovsky's sixth symphony (*Pathétique*) was composed the following year, in 1893, and though its first performance on 28 October of the same year in St. Petersburg (the only time the composer conducted it) met with a tepid reception, repeated hearings after the composer's death (on 6 November) made a deep impression. The *Pathétique* was a favorite work of Mascagni's. He conducted its Italian premiere (La Scala, 12 April 1898) and continued to perform it throughout his long career as a conductor.

TEBALDINI, Giovanni (1864-1952). Italian composer and musicologist. He studied at the Milan Conservatory (1883-85) under Bazzini and Ponchielli. After further study in Germany he returned to Italy where he became known for his work in church music. In addition to his orchestral and sacred works, he prepared modern editions of Cavalieri's *La Rappresentazione di anima e corpo* and Peri's *Euridice*. In an article published in 1950, Tebaldini stated that he was not at the 1890 Sant'-Agata reading of *Cavalleria* for the simple reason that he did not come into personal contact with Verdi until 1896 when Verdi wrote him asking to examine a *Te Deum* by Vallotti. In the same article Tebaldini gives Verdi's own words, supposedly spoken during a walk the two men took in the summer of 1898, about the first contact Verdi had with Mascagni's opera: "Having heard the sudden noise and great success related over *Cavalleria*, I immediately wanted to see the new opera and began to read it in company with Boito. Prelude: beautiful, fresh, mercurial, the idea of Turiddu's serenata a happy discovery. The first chorus similarly happy, also for the popular character which animates it from top to bottom. Then comes the carter's song. And what is this? Coming to the chorus, *'Inneggiamo al Signore risorto'*, which pretended to be a *concertato*, I almost felt angry. And I said to Boito, 'Enough, put it down.' But during the night I was unable to sleep. Something had impressed me which I was unable to drive away. And I rose early the next morning. I took up *Cavalleria* again and came here into the garden to read it. Coming to the '*Addio all madre*' I exclaimed, 'By God, this boy understands (*sente*) the theater!'"

TORELLI, Achille (1841-1922). Neapolitan dramatist. His most famous play is a comedy, *I Mariti*, first performed in 1867. Maffei's translation of *Guglielmo Ratcliff* is dedicated to Torelli, the man who was responsible for its first Italian performance (Milan, Teatro Manzoni, 1875).

TOSCANINI, Arturo (1867-1957). Italian conductor. Studying in Parma and Milan, he began his musical career as a cellist, conducting his first opera (*Aida*) in Rio de Janeiro. He quickly became known in his new capacity and is now generally considered the greatest of Italian conductors. He was engaged as chief conductor of La Scala in 1898, assuming the same position at the Metropolitan in 1907. When La Scala reopened in 1922, he became its director. Toscanini was not Mascagni's idea of an ideal conductor, the composer writing in 1897, "Toscanini is a good conductor, scrupulously precise, but somewhat hard and angular, and his orchestra never has that elasticity which for me is essential in every kind of music." Relations between the two men had been cordial until the end of 1892, when Toscanini was to conduct the Roman premiere of *I Rantzau*. The orchestra of the Costanzi sent a congratulatory telegram to Mascagni on the occasion of the world premiere in Florence and Mascagni, interpreting it in his own way, responded that he would be happy to lead them in the Roman performance. Offended, Toscanini resigned from the whole enterprise. When in 1899 *Iris* was given its premiere at La Scala under Toscanini and was unsuccessful, Mascagni blamed the failure on the conductor. Nevertheless, Toscanini must have retained some affection for the work since in later years he conducted it not only at La Scala but also at the Metropolitan. It was Toscanini who led the Milan premiere of *Le Maschere*.

TOSTI, Paolo (1846-1916). Italian composer. He became popular in Italy as a composer of songs, and was appointed by Princess Margherita (later Queen of Italy) as her singing teacher After a series of visits to London beginning in 1875, Tosti settled there in 1880 upon his appointment as singing teacher to the English royal family. He was knighted in 1908. His many songs were extremely popular and a number of them are still sung today.

TOZZI, Luigi. The Cerignola cashier who did not believe Mascagni had the signature of a borrower.

UMBERTO I (1844-1900). King of Italy, 1878-1900. He married his cousin, Princess Margherita of Savoy (*q.v.*) in 1868. A believer in colonial expansion and of firmness toward the Vatican, he was greatly respected by the Italian people, who called him "Humbert the Good." He was assassinated on 29 July 1900 at Monza by an anarchist. The *Requiem Mass* which Mascagni assembled for the funeral (9 August 1900) consisted of the following pieces: *Requiem* and *Kyrie* (Anerio), *Dies Irae* (Victoria), *Offertorio, Sanctus* and *Agnus Dei* (Palestrina), *Benedictus* (Renzi) and *Libera Me* (Terziani).

VAMBA, see **BERTELLI.**

VAN WESTERHOUT, Nicola (1857-1898). Italian composer, member of a family of musicians of Dutch origin. Though he wrote a number of operas, it was for his vocal and piano compositions that he was primarily known. In his 1900 lecture on Piccinni, Mascagni eulogized Van Westerhout as "brutally stolen from art and country in the full vigor of his mind and heart."

VASSALLO, Luigi Arnaldo (1852-1906). Italian journalist and writer, best known under his pseudonym "Gandolin". He was the founder of the Roman journal *Don Chisciotte* and author of a number of plays, but it is as a writer of monologues that his name is remembered today. He himself sometimes recited them, but most often entrusted them to well known actors.

VENTURINI, DITTA. Florentine music publishers (*ditta* = firm). Mascagni's first publisher, it was they who printed the *"Ave Maria"* which had won an honorable mention in the 1881 Milan Music Exposition.

VERDI, Giuseppe (1813-1901). At the time of the success of *Cavalleria* much was made of the idea that Mascagni was Verdi's heir. There is no proof that Mascagni ever considered himself as such, since his feeling for the older composer amounted to veneration. On Verdi's side, rumors abounded that he disliked the opera or that he praised it. It now seems that the account by Tebaldini (*q.v.*) is as close as we shall ever come to knowing the truth. Verdi's reaction to Mascagni's second opera, *L'amico Fritz*, is known, however, from a letter to Giulio Ricordi (dated 6 November 1891): "Thank you for the score of *Fritz* which you have sent me. In my life I have read a great number of bad libretti, but I have never read a libretto as silly [*scemo*] as this one. As for the music, I have read on a bit, but I soon tired of so many dissonances, of so many false relations when modulating, of all those suspended cadences, of those deceits, and more... than a number of tempo changes in almost every bar. All very piquant things, but ones which offend the rhythmic sense and sense of hearing. The setting of the words in general is very good; yet he never molds [*scolpisce*] the situation to the truth." This last statement is a quintessentially Verdian one, and one which the older composer had spent a lifetime in hammering out for himself, not, it may be noted, by theorizing but by writing opera after opera. It is bound up in his ideas on "inventing the truth," the *parola-scenica* and the *dramma scenico-musicale*, concepts which Verdi himself had hardly arrived at when he was 28, Mascagni's age when he wrote *L'amico Fritz*. And yet all the things in *Fritz* that Verdi complains of were precisely the very features that Mascagni was beginning to experiment with and which would later (culminating in *Parisina*) become some of the active ingredients in his own musico-dramatico esthetics. When Verdi and Mascagni first met, the old man had all but retired from the world. Yet he was not unaware of the younger composers. Giulio Ricordi kept him abreast of Puccini, he met Giordano through Spatz (*q.v.*) and we know from his correspondece that the names of Franchetti, Bossi, Cilèa, Catalani, Leoncavallo, Perosi and Smareglia were not unknown to him. During the winter months he lived at the Albergo Milano and it was here, while Mascagni was preparing the Scala premiere of *Ratcliff*, that it seems the two men first met. It was not until three years later, in April of 1898, that Verdi met Mascagni's wife and children.

VERGA, Giovanni (1840-1922). Sicilian author. His literary name rests on four books: two volumes of short stories, *Vita dei Campi* (1880), *Novelle rusticane* (1883); and two novels: *I Malavoglia* (1881), *Mastro-Don Gesualdo* (1889). He is generally conceded to be the originator of literary *verismo*, though Verga himself disclaimed any part in literary classifications, claiming that it was the critics who invented the category. The same is true of Mascagni in the field of opera. Verga'a aim was story-telling in his own manner: the reader must be unaware of the author, and the language used must both suit and set forth the characters. "*Cavalleria rusticana*", Verga's short story which was written in accord with these principles, was first published in a literary weekly, *Il Fanfulla della Domenica*, on 14 March 1880. It was later collected into the volume of short stories, *Vita dei Campi*. Verga himself adapted it as a play, the first performance taking place in Turin on 14 January 1884 with Duse (Santuzza), Flavio

Andò (Turiddu) and Tebaldo Checchi (Alfio). In spite of Verga's fears
that the play would fail, it was a success. Being a one-act play, it was
preceded by a short farce, *Tredici a tavola*, adapted from the Spanish by
Giovanni Salvestri (*q.v.*). It was doubtless as a result of this that Salvestri
was able to assure Mascagni that he was a "good friend" of Verga's.
Contrary to Mascagni's statement, he did not receive permission at the
time of the Pasta (*q.v.*) performance in Milan from Verga (through Salvestri) to set the work as an opera. According to Salvestri's second letter to Verga (when the opera had already been submitted to the contest), in 1886 or 1887 Salvestri had written for permission for another
friend of his, also a composer to set *Cavalleria*. In this letter, dated 15
February 1890, he now asks for permission for Mascagni to use Verga's
play. (Could the '86 or '87 permission have been for Bartocci Fontana,
the librettist of Gastaldon's *Mala Pasqua*? That agreement is dated 3 June
1888). Shortly after Verga received Salvestri's second letter, he read that
Mascagni's *Cavalleria* was one of the twelve selected to be heard in Rome
by the Commission. Mascagni did not write to Verga requesting his permission until 9 March 1890, after he had been declared the winner. A
provisional agreement was drawn up, which they both signed at the
beginning of April, assuring Verga whatever profits the copyright law
granted him. Verga was in the audience on the opening night of
Mascagni's opera and witnessed its triumph. Hearing nothing from
either Mascagni or Sonzogno throughout the summer of 1890, Verga
finally wrote the latter inquiring about his royalties. Sonzogno at first
offered 500 lire, then 1000, then 1500. Verga, who was in severe financial straits, refused and submitted the problem to the Society of Authors
in September. The Society stated that Verga was entitled to what he had
coming under the law: equal profits. This was ignored by Sonzogno
and the case was taken to court by Verga on January of 1891. The court
decided in Verga's favor, but the decision was appealed by Sonzogno
and Mascagni. When the appeal was heard on 16 June, Verga again
won, being granted one quarter of the profits. This was appealed a
second time, and Sonzogno, knowing of Verga's debts, offered him a
lump sum of 20,000 lire. Verga refused, convinced he was entitled to
more. When the court heard the second appeal on 15 February 1892, the
case was yet again decided in Verga's favor. But Sonzogno was able to
continue delaying and finally Verga accepted 143,000 lire as full and
final compensation on 2 January 1893.

VIDAL, Renée. Mezzo-soprano noted for her dramatic qualities. Ill for the
premiere of *Guglielmo Ratcliff*, she sang the role of Margherita for the

first time at the operas's second performance on 20 February 1895. The critic Nappi, in *La Perseveranza*, wrote of her performance: "The first part of the fourth act, which had to be omitted on Saturday, is made up of a narrative for Margherita, a gloomy melody which is developed from the themes of the lullaby and first act prelude, and ends with a scream of terror at the entrance of Ratcliff. It was here that Vidal's interpretation aroused general admiration: her art as a singer is united in the best manner to a very distinct mimic art." Contrary to the *Autobiography*, Della Rogers, a mezzo-soprano, appears to have *sung* the first performance, omitting only the long and difficult fourth act narrative.

VITTORIO EMANUELE III (1864-1948) King of Italy after his father's assassination in 1900 (see UMBERTO I).

WILHELM II (1859-1941). German Kaiser, ruled 1888-1918. A firm believer in the divine right of kings, it is no wonder Mascagni was unable to convince him of Heine's genius.

ZACCONI, Ermete (1857-1948). One of the most famous Italian actors of his time, Zacconi was known for the extraordinary tension which he was able to impart to a performance. It was no doubt this quality which Mascagni sought to impart to Pertile when he asked Zacconi to coach the tenor in the role of Nero. It was a performance of Cossa's *Nerone* in September 1920 by Zacconi that finally decided Mascagni to compose the opera.

ZANDONAI, Riccardo (1883-1944). Italian composer. He was a pupil of Mascagni's at the Pesaro Conservatory. In 1939 he himself was appointed director of that institution, a post he retained until his death. In addition to operas, the most famous of which are *Conchita* (1911), *Francesca da Rimini* (1914), *Giulietta e Romeo* (1922) and *I cavalieri di Ekebù* (1925), he composed orchestral and church music.

ZANELLA, Amilcare (1873-1949). Italian pianist, conductor and composer. When Mascagni left the directorship of the Pesaro Conservatory in 1902, he was temporarily succeeded by Antonio Cicognani. In 1905 Zanella was named director.

ZICHY, Count Géza (1849-1924). Hungarian composer, pianist and theater director. A student of Liszt, he lost his right arm in a hunting accident in 1863 and thereafter dedicated himself to concertizing as a left-handed pianist. From 1891 to 1894 he was Intendant of the Royal Hungarian Opera in Budapest, part of which time Mahler was engaged there as a conductor.

CATALOGUE OF WORKS

1. OPERAS

Cavalleria rusticana
> LIBRETTO: Giovanni Targioni-Tozzetti and Guido Menasci (from
> Giovanni Verga's short story and play)
> FIRST PERFORMANCE: Rome, Teatro Costanzi; 17 May 1890

L'amico Fritz
> LIBRETTO: "P. Suardon", pseud. of Nicola Daspuro (from Emile
> Erckmann and Alexandre Chatrian novel and play)
> FIRST PERFORMANCE: Rome, Teatro Costanzi; 31 October 1891

I Rantzau
> LIBRETTO: Targioni-Tozzetti and Menasci (from Erckmann-
> Chatrian's novel *Les deux frères* and play *Les Rantzau*)
> FIRST PERFORMANCE: Florence, Teatro Pergola; 10 November 1892

Guglielmo Ratcliff
> LIBRETTO: Heinrich Heine, It. transl. by Andrea Maffei
> FIRST PERFORMANCE: Milan, Teatro alla Scala; 16 February 1895

Silvano[84]
> LIBRETTO: Targioni-Tozzetti
> FIRST PERFORMANCE: Milan, Teatro alla Scala; 25 March 1895

Zanetto
> LIBRETTO: Targioni-Tozzetti and Menasci (from François
> Coppée's *Le passant*)
> FIRST PERFORMANCE: Pesaro, Liceo Musicale Rossini; 2 March 1896

Iris
> LIBRETTO: Luigi Illica

---

[84] The original title of this opera was to be *Romano d'Ehedat*, based on a novel by
Alphonse Karr, but at the last moment the author withdrew permission and the
libretto had to be entirely recast.

FIRST PERFORMANCE: Rome, Teatro Costanzi; 22 November 1898

Le Maschere
  LIBRETTO: Illica
  FIRST PERFORMANCE: Genoa, Teatro Carlo Felice; Milan, Teatro
    alla Scala; Rome, Teatro Costanzi; Turin, Teatro Regio; Venice,

Isabeau: Italo Cristalli as the first Italian "Folco"
Venice, La Fenice — 20 January 1912 — cond. Mascagni

Teatro la Fenice; Verona, Teatro Filarmonico—all 17 January 1901; Naples, Teatro San Carlo—19 January 1901 (delayed owing to indisposition of the tenor)
First revision: Rome, Teatro Adriano; 28 November 1905
Second revision: Milan, Teatro alla Scala; 8 March 1931

Amica
LIBRETTO: "P. Bérel", pseud. of Paul (Bérel de) Choudens (in French)
FIRST PERFORMANCE: Monte Carlo, Casino; 16 March 1905

Isabeau
LIBRETTO: Illica
FIRST PERFORMANCE: Buenos Aires, Coliseo; 2 June 1911

Parisina
LIBRETTO: Gabriele d'Annunzio
FIRST PERFORMANCE: Milan, Teatro alla Scala; 15 December 1913

Lodoletta
LIBRETTO: Giovacchino Forzano (from Ouida's *Two Little Wooden Shoes*)
FIRST PERFORMANCE: Rome, Teatro Costanzi; 30 April 1917

Il piccolo Marat
LIBRETTO: Forzano ((with minor contributions by Targioni-Tozzetti)
FIRST PERFORMANCE: Rome, Teatro Costanzi; 2 May 1921

Pinotta[85]
LIBRETTO: Targioni-Tozzetti
FIRST PERFORMANCE: San Remo, Casino; 23 March 1932

Nerone
LIBRETTO: Targioni-Tozzetti (from Pietro Cossa's drama)
FIRST PERFORMANCE: Milan, Teatro alla Scala; 16 January 1935

---

85   See also cantata *In finlanda* (Choral Music, below).

2. OPERETTAS

Le Maschere
> LIBRETTO: Simoni (from Illica's libretto but without his consent)
> FIRST PERFORMANCE: Rome, Teatro Quirino; 12 February 1916

Si

> LIBRETTO: Carlo Lombardo and A. Franci (from Granichstädten's
> *Majestät Mimì*)
> FIRST PERFORMANCE: Rome, Teatro Quirino; 13 December 1919

3. INCIDENTAL MUSIC

The Eternal City
> LIBRETTO: Hall Caine
> FIRST PERFORMANCE: London; 2 October 1902 (Mascagni contri-
> buted 4 interludes and a vocal serenade)

Dante
> LIBRETTO: Maso Salvini
> FIRST PERFORMANCE: 1917 (Mascagni contributed *La ballata di
> maggio*)

Fiori del Branbante
> LIBRETTO: Forzano
> FIRST PERFORMANCE: Turin, Teatro Regio; 10 February 1930
> (Mascagni contributed the *Danza dei Gianduiotti e Giacomette*)

4. CHURCH MUSIC

Kyrie, for male voices and organ (1880)
Christe, for tenor, baritone and organ (1880)
Mass, for tenor, baritone, bass and orchestra (in collaboration with
  Silvio Barbini) (1880)
Kryie Larghetto in F major, for male voices, organ and orchestra
  (1880)
Salve Regina, for soprano, tenor and baritone (1881)
In Nativitate Domini (Gradual—First Mass) (1881)
In Epiphania Domini (Gradual), for voice and organ (1882)

Motet in the Dorian mode, for voice and organ (1882)
Introibo, Alleluja and *Sanctus* for a Mass (1883)
Requiem (1887)
Messa di Gloria in F major (1888)
O Roma felix, for voice and organ (1943)
Undated early compositions: *Kryie; Pater Noster* in E flat, for voice,
   2 violins, viola and doublebass; *Ave Maria* in F major; *Sanctus*, for
   boy's voices, tenors, basses, organ and orchestra

5. CHORAL MUSIC

In filanda (Alfredo Soffredini), cantata for soil, chorus and orchestra
(1881)
   [Revised in 1883, under the title *Pinotta*, for a contest at the Milan
   Conservatory; final revision as *Pinotta* performed in 1932 (see
   under OPERAS).]
Strofe a coro (1881)
La pensosa (1882)
Alla gioia (Friedrich von Schiller, It. trans. by Maffei), ode for soli, chorus
   and orchestra (1882)
Coro nuziale, for two-voiced chorus with solo (1882)
Canzonetta (1883)
Hymn for the Palermo Exposition, for seven-voiced chorus and
   orchestra (1890)
Savoia, hymn (1891)
Inno ad Adelaide Cairoli (1899)
Corda fratres (Pascoli), Goliardic Hymn (1900)
Il coro dei fanti (1915?)
Il canto del lavoro (Bovio and Rossoni), for chorus and orchestra
   (1928)
Invocazione alla Madonna (Targioni-Tozzetti) (1923)
Undated early compositions: *Pater Noster* in E flat; *Coretto*

6. ORCHESTRAL WORKS

Symphony in c minor (1879)
Symphony in F (Adagio-Allegro, Larghetto, Minuetto, Allegro
   molto) (1880) [This symphony exists only in a piano 4-hand
   transcription. It is doubtful that it was ever orchestrated.]
Symphony in F major (Allegro, Adagio, Minuetto, Finale) (1881)

Elegy on the death of Richard Wagner (1883)
Leggenda (for piano?) (1883)
Sinfonia religiosa (for piano?) (1883)
Military March (1889)
Danza boema (1889)
Danza esotica (1891)
A Giocomo Leopardi, poem for orchestra with soprano solo (1898)
Gavotta delle bambole (1900)
New World Processional, Triumphal March (1904)
Rapsodia satanica, symphonic poem (1915)
Visione lirica, Contemplating Bernini's Saint Teresa in the Church
    of S. Maria della Vittoria in Rome (1923)

7. CHAMBER MUSIC

Melodia, for voilin (1880)
Minuet in C, for string quintet (later inserted in the 1880 *Symphony*
    in F) (1880)
Canzone militare, Canzone popolare, Canzone amorosa — for flute, violin,
    violoncello and piano (1882)
Melodia, for violoncello (1882)
Waltz, for string quartet (1887)

8. PIANO

Novellina (1881)
Il canto dell'agricoltore (1882)
Sulle rive di Chiaia (1883)
Motivo di danza popolare (1885)
Polka di Titania (1888)
Pifferata di Natale (1890)
Tema di Andante (1899)
Pastorale (1905?)
La prima bagnante (1908)

9. SONGS

With piano accompaniment unless otherwise indicated.

"*Duolo eterno!*" (1878) [Mascagni's first known composition, dedicated to his father.]

"*Elegia*", for soprano, violin and piano (1879)

"*Ave Maria*" (Capellina) (1880)

"*Pater Noster*" (Capellina), for soprano and string quintet (1880)

"*Leggenda*", for tenor (1880)

"*Romanza*" (Romani), for tenor, violin, harmonium and piano (1881)

"*La tua stella*" (Fiorentino) (1882) [Later used in *Pinotta*.]

"*La Stella di Garibaldi*" (Cappelli) (1882)

"*Alla luna*" (Cipollini) (1882)

"*Pena d'amore*" (Ghislanzoni) (1883)

"*Serenata*" (Cappelli) (1883)

"*Sulla riva*" (1883)

"*M'ama...non m'ama*" (1884)

"*Ballata*", for voice with orchestral accompaniment (1884)

"*Il Re a Napoli*" (Maffei), for tenor and orchestra (1884)

"*Romanzina francese*" (1886) [Later used in Act IV of *Ratcliff*.]

"*Sol le gioia d'amor*" (1886)

"*Va' mio povero sospir*" (1886)

"*Una croce in camposanto*" (1886)

"*Sorriso di fanciulla*" (1889)

"*Messaggio d'amore*" (Petri) (1890)

"*Rosa*" (Pagliara) (1890)

"*Risveglio*" (Ducati) (1890)

"*Scherzo*" (1890)

"*Allora ed ora*" (1891)

"*Sintomi d'amore*" (Ferruzzi) (1891)

"*L'addio di Palmidone*" (1894)

"*Serenata*" (Stecchetti) (1894)

"*Sera d'ottobre*" (Pascoli) (1894)

"*Ascoltiamo*" (Menasci) (1906)

"*Spes ultima*" (Menasci) (1906)

"*Stornelli marini*" (Menasci) (1906)

"*La luna*" (Menasci) (1913)

Undated early compositions: "*Mattinata*", for voice and mandolin; "*È morta*" (Scempri), for soprano, violin and piano

BIBLIOGRAPHY

1. SOURCES

--------"Come Pietro Mascagni ha visto il suo 'Nerone' e come lo vede il pubblico della 'Scala'". In *La Tribuna*, 13 January 1935. (Ch. 31)

--------"La 'Lodoletta' di Mascagni". In *Corriere della Sera*, 24 April 1917. (Ch. 28)

--------"La Ripresa di 'Maschere'". In *La Perserveranza*, 15 September 1907. (Ch. 20)

--------"Mascagni e la musica straniera". In *Corriere della Sera*, 27 February 1909. (Ch. 24, 30, 34)

--------"Parlando con Mascagni e con Illica: la 'Vistilia' al Palatino". In *Corriere della Sera*, 15 February 1909. (Ch. 24)

ANTONGINI, T. "D'Annunzio e Mascagni a Parigi". In *L'Illustrazione Italiana*, 19 May 1912. (Ch. 27) Antongini was d'Annunzio's private secretary for many years.

BELLI, A. "Pietro Mascagni parla del 'Piccolo Marat'". In *Corriere d'Italia*, 22 June 1920. (Ch. 28, 29)

BERNARDINI-MARZOLLA, U. "Carteggi inediti mascagnani". In *Liburni Civitas*, 1940. (Ch. 6) An expanded version of this article appears in the volume by various editors (Livorno, 1963).

CAVICCHIOLI, G. "Colloqui con Mascagni". In *L'Illustrazione Italiana*, September 1955. (Ch. 30, 34)

CELLAMARE, D. *Pietro Mascagni* (Rome, 1965). (Ch. 7, 8) An expanded version of the author's 1941 volume, there are nevertheless scraps of information in the earlier one not found here.

CENZATO, G., ed. *Nascita e gloria di un capolavoro italiano* (Milan, 1940). (Ch. 1, 7, 30) Contains Mascagni's letters to his librettists during the composition and first performance of *Cavalleria*.

CHECCHI, E. "Pietro Mascagni e la nuova opera 'Iris'". In *Nuova Antologia*, 1898. (Ch. 14, 17)

COGO, G. *Il nostro Mascagni* (Vicenza, 1931). (Ch. 20)

DE CARLO, S. *Mascagni parla* (Milan-Rome, 1945). (Ch. 1-28, 30-32, 34)

FRACCAROLI, A. "Mascagni e la sua 'Isabeau'". In *Corriere della Sera*, 19 October 1910. (Ch. 25)

--------"Mascagni e 'Parisina', i tagli e la soppressione del quarto atto". In *Corriere della Sera*, 18 December 1913. (Ch. 27)

--------*Mascagni si sfoga e presenta 'Parisina'"*. In *Corriere della Sera*, 13 November 1913. (Ch. 27)

--------*"Mascagni vicino con 'Parisina' all'orizzonte"*. In *Corriere della Sera*, 23 April 1913. (Ch. 27)

GASCA, A. *"Come fu creata 'Parisina'"*. In *La Tribuna*, 21 December 1912. (Ch. 27)

INCAGLIATI, M. *"A Colloquio con Mascagni"*. In *Il Giornale d'Italia*, 13 October 1919. (Ch. 28, 29)

--------*"Un colloquio con Mascagni"*. In *L'Orfeo*, 15 March 1913. (Ch. 27)

MASCAGNI, P. *"Amilcare Ponchielli"*. In *La Lettura*, 1934. (Ch. 3) Reprinted in Morini, vol. 2.

------*"Come è nata 'Parisina'"*. In *La Lettura*, January 1914. (Ch. 27)

------*"Come nacque 'Cavalleria'"*. In *La Domenica del Corriere*, 17-23 March 1940. (Ch. 2, 6-8) Reprinted in Morini, vol. 2.

------*"Il cinquantenario della 'Cavalleria rusticana in musica'"*. In *Nuova Antologia*, January 1940. (Ch. 8, 9, 32, 34) Reprinted in Morini, vol. 2.

------*"Il testamento musicale del secolo XIX"*. In *La Cronaca Musicale*, 15 March 1900. (Ch. 5) Reprinted in an abridged form in Morini, vol. 2. An English translation of the complete essay was published in *The International Library of Music*, vol. 2 (N.Y., 1925).

------*"L'opera ha fatto il suo tempo?"* In*Le Opere e i Giorni*, 1 August, 1929. (Ch. 30, 34) Reprinted in Morini, vol. 2.

------*"Nel quarantesimo della morte di Giuseppe Verdi"*. In *Giuseppe Verdi, nuovi contributi*, ed. by Franco Abbiati (Milan, 1951). (Ch. 15, 21, 22) Reprinted in an abridged form in Morini, vol. 2.

------*"Pastor Angelicus*. In *L'avvenire d'Italia*, 2 June 1942. (Ch. 33) Reprinted in Morini, vol. 2.

------*"Perchè ho scritto il 'Nerone'"*. In *La Lettura*, 1933. (Ch. 31) Reprinted in Morini, vol. 2.

------*"Per le Opere dell'Ingegno"* (Rome, 1905). (Ch. 10, 24) A polemic against Ricordi and Sonzogno.

------*"Prima di 'Cavalleria'"*. In *Il Fanfulla della Domenica*, 4 December 1892. (Ch. 1, 4, 5, 8, 9) This article has been widely reprinted and translated, nearly always repeating the faulty dates which it contains. Most of it was reprinted in Pompei and Morini, vol. 2, though the wording is not always the same.

------*"Verdi (ricordi personali)"*. In *La Lettura*, January 1931. (Ch. 15, 21)

------*"Verso le fonti della melodia"*. In *Mondo* (Sonzogno), 7 November 1915. (Ch. 28). An essay on the tragedy of war. A complete

English translation may be found in Stivender, *Mascagni's 'Lodoletta'*.

"MEMOR" *"Ricordi di Mascagni"*. In *L'Osservatore Romano*, 12 August 1945. (Ch. 1, 31)

MORINI, M. *"'Il piccolo Marat' di Mascagni"*. In recording of the opera, Fonit-Cetra #1268. (Ch. 28, 34)

MORINI, M., ed. *Pietro Mascagni*. 2 vols. (Milan, 1964). (Ch. 11, 20, 25, 27, 31, 34) Contains the best work yet done on Mascagni and is the basis of any serious study of the composer.

ORSINI, G. *Vangelo d'un mascagnano* (Milan, 1926). (Ch. 27, 29). A collection of essays on Mascagni's operas, including Orsini's essay on *Parisina* and quotes from several letters to him from the composer.

PALADINI, C. *Giacomo Puccini* (Florence, 1961). (Ch. 28) The author was a personal friend of both Puccini and Mascagni. The volume includes letters from the two composers to him.

POMPEI, E. *Pietro Mascagni nella Vita e nell'Arte* (Rome, 1912). (Ch. 2, 4-8, 11-13, 15, 17-26) The most valuable of the early books on Mascagni, it contains numerous letters and quotations by the composer.

TARGIONI-TOZZETTI, G. *"Ricordi e rettificazioni mascagnane"*. In *Liburni Civitas*, 1932. (Ch. 1, 30) Contains much valuable information on the composer's early years in Livorno.

VARIOUS EDITORS. *Pietro Mascagni* (Livorno, 1963). (Ch. 6, 24, 27, 28, 30, 31) A necessary volume for any serious study of the composer.

2. ADDITIONAL WORKS CITED AND CONSULTED

ABBIATI, F. *Giuseppe Verdi* (Milan, 1959).

ALEXANDER, A. *Giovanni Verga* (London, 1972). A large part of the book is devoted to Mascagni, exhaustively treating the various Verga-Mascagni-Sonzogno quarrels.

ATZERI, C. *"Mascagni italiano"*. In *Rassegna musicale Curci*, anno XXIX, nr. 3, December 1976.

BONAVENTURA, A. *"Pietro Mascagni"*. In *Liburni Civitas*, 1928.

CANTORE, R. *"Sul borderò del Duce"*. In *Panorama*, 22 February 1987.

CARNER, M. *Puccini: A Critical Biography* (New York, 1959).

CELLAMARE D. *Mascagni e la "Cavalleria" visti da Cerignola* (Rome, 1941).

CORTESI, S. *My Thirty Years of Friendships* (New York, 1927).

FRACCAROLI, A. *La vita di Giacomo Puccini* (Milan, 1925).

GARA, E., ed. *Carteggi pucciniani* (Milan, 1958).

GOETZ, H. *"Die Beziehungen zwischen Pietro Mascagni und Benito Mussolini"*. In *Analecta Musicologica*, vol. 17, 1976.

MASCAGNI, P. *"Come si scrive un'opera"*. In *La Lettura*, January, 1907. A satiric novella. Reprinted in an abridged form in Morini, vol. 2.

------*"Il centenario della 'Norma'"*. In *La Lettura*, 1932. Reprinted in Morini, vol. 2.

------*"Il melodramma dell'avvenire"*. In *Corriere della Sera*, 23 November 1903. Reprinted in an abridged form in Morini, vol. 2.

------*"Niccolò Piccinni"*. In *La Cronaca Musicale*, 15 June 1900. Reprinted complete in *Bari a Niccolò Piccinni* (Bari, 1964) and in an abridged form in Morini, vol. 2.

MORINI, M. *"Mascagni umorista"*. In *La Scala*, August, 1955.

NARDI, P. *Vita di Arrigo Boito* (Verona, 1942).

NICOLODI, F. *Musica e musicisti nel ventennio fascista* (Fiesole, 1984).

ORSINI, G. *...di Pietro Mascagni. Cronologia artistica* (Milan, 1912). A valuable chronology of the years of 1863-1912, though Orsini accepts Mascagni's faulty dates for the operetta and Cerignola years.

RADICIOTI, G. *Gioacchino Rossini* (Tivoli, 1927-1929).

RICCI, L. *34 Anni con Pietro Mascagni* (Milan, 1976).

RINALDI, M. *Felice Romani* (Rome, 1965).

SACHS, H. *"Music in Fascist Italy: Puccini, Mascagni and the Duce"*. In *Opus*, February 1988. An excerpt from his book *Music in Fascist Italy* (New York, 1988).

SANTINI, A. *Mascagni. Viva e abbasso* (Livorno, 1985).

SOFFREDINI, A. *"L'adolescenza di Mascagni"*. In *Natura ed Arte*, 15 July 1899. Much of this article is reprinted in Pompei.

STIVENDER, D. *The Genesis of a Masterpiece. Notes on "Guglielmo Ratcliff"* (New York, n.d.).

--------*Illica, Mascagni and the Writing of "Isabeau"* (New York, 1973).

--------*Mascagni and "Iris"* (New York, n.d.).

--------*Mascagni's "Lodoletta"* (New York, 1974).

--------*A Note on "Le Maschere"* (New York, n.d.).

--------*Notes on "Zanetto", "Nerone", "Silvano" and "Amica"* (New York, 1972). These six essays were included in private recordings of the various operas.

TARGIONI-TOZZETTI, G. *"Mascagni prima della 'Cavalleria'"*. In *La Lettura*, 1 March 1932.
WALKER, F. *The Man Verdi* (New York, 1962).

INDEX

Italicized numerals indicate placement of illustrations